Angela Goode raises cattle and grows lucerne seed with her husband on their farm near Naracoorte, South Australia. She has spent her writing life bringing the images and issues of rural Australia to a wider audience through books, in her popular newspaper columns and on radio.

Her many editions of *Great Working Dog Stories* and *Great Working Horse Stories*, plus *For Love of the Land*, *Through the Farm Gate* and *Top Dogs* celebrate lives beyond the cities where animals and humans still work together closely.

In 2008, Angela was inducted by Rural Media South Australia as a Rural Media Icon for her work in bridging the city–country gap.

Angela's love of horses took her buffalo mustering in the Northern Territory, trail riding on old bullock tracks in the Adelaide Hills, jumping logs in farm paddocks, bringing mobs of cattle into the yards, and enjoying learning the skills of dressage. These days, there are ponies in the paddocks for grandchildren.

Also by Angela Goode

Great Working Dog Stories
More Great Working Dog Stories
Working Dogs—Stories from All Round Australia
The Complete Book of Great Working Dog Stories
Great Australian Working Dog Stories
Great Working Horse Stories
For Love of the Land

GREAT AUSTRALIAN WORKING HORSE STORIES

ANGELA GOODE

ABC Books

To Charlie, your love of horses began in Guyana
and inspired our four daughters

 The ABC 'Wave' device is a trademark of the
Australian Broadcasting Corporation and is used
under licence by HarperCollins*Publishers* Australia.

First published in Australia in 1995
This edition published in 2018
by HarperCollins*Publishers* Australia Pty Limited
ABN 36 009 913 517
harpercollins.com.au

Copyright © Angela Goode 2018

The right of Angela Goode to be identified as the author of this work has been asserted by her in accordance with the *Copyright Amendment (Moral Rights) Act 2000*.

This work is copyright. Apart from any use as permitted under the *Copyright Act 1968*, no part may be reproduced, copied, scanned, stored in a retrieval system, recorded, or transmitted, in any form or by any means, without the prior written permission of the publisher.

HarperCollins*Publishers*
Level 13, 201 Elizabeth Street, Sydney NSW 2000, Australia
Unit D1, 63 Apollo Drive, Rosedale, Auckland 0632, New Zealand
A 53, Sector 57, Noida, UP, India
1 London Bridge Street, London, SE1 9GF, United Kingdom
2 Bloor Street East, 20th floor, Toronto, Ontario M4W 1A8, Canada
195 Broadway, New York NY 10007, USA

A catalogue record for this book is available
from the National Library of Australia

Cover design by Hazel Lam, HarperCollins Design Studio
Cover image by State Library of New South Wales (Digital order no: hood_02637)
Typeset in ITC Bookman by Kirby Jones

Contents

	Foreword	1
	Acknowledgements	3
	Introduction	5
ONE	Horsepower: the original variety	11
TWO	Stock horse: champion of the outback	41
THREE	Long distances: tough people and horses	83
FOUR	Horse sense	121
FIVE	Team work	144
SIX	Life's great lessons	166
SEVEN	Horsing around	185
EIGHT	Street work	227
NINE	The job comes first	249
TEN	Talented performers	266
ELEVEN	Horses in uniform	291
TWELVE	Tales of misadventure	317
THIRTEEN	Farewelling the big horses: the Clydesdales depart	330
FOURTEEN	The new golden era	350
FIFTEEN	Horse people	369
	Glossary	419
	List of contributors and characters	422

Note: Both imperial and metric measurements appear in this book, to remain faithful to each author's voice.

Foreword

Time is running out. The men and women of the horse and buggy days are going out with the tide—and soon there will be no-one who remembers.

These stories are from those who lived in another era, a time when the horse was what the motor is today: heavy horse for hauling, harness horse for transport, saddle horse for anyone who lived in those times. Horses were the subject of conversation everywhere that men gathered; blacksmith shops were in every town, much as petrol stations are today. The horse was king.

Everybody had a horse story to tell, for horses were living things with differing temperaments—every one another person. Every day someone had some fresh experience to relate of living with this emotional animal. They were very much a part of our lives.

I have read these stories with deep interest. They tell of experiences that did, or could have, happened to me, and I feel pleased that Angela has put together this excellent book.

R M Williams, December 1994

Acknowledgements

The first edition of *Great Working Horse Stories* was launched in August 1995, and what a day it was! If there was ever any doubt that horses had been overlooked or unappreciated in their role of hauling this nation to its feet, that day at Adelaide Showgrounds proved they still enjoyed immense love, gratitude and admiration. A baker's delivery horse and a brewery Clydesdale team recreated the days when suburban streets rang with the clip clop of hooves and when the pace was more gentle.

We all agreed that day our debt to the working horse must never be forgotten. Spurred on by the spirit of urgency, family archives had been raided and elderly friends encouraged to spread the word that their everyday horse stories were needed. In the avalanche of stories that reached me, there was almost a sigh of relief that someone wanted to share them.

This edition, updated twice since that first triumphant collection, holds stories of contemporary workers, as well as medal winners and entertainers.

My gratitude to the vast number of people who got behind this quest endures, even though so many have now died.

They are: R M Williams who wrote a moving foreword, author Max Fatchen who launched the original book, Denis Adams, Geoffrey Blight, Wendy Treloar, Margaret Muller, Addye Rockliff, Jim Gough, Jim Green, Mike Keogh, Dolly Van Zaane, Dale Meyer, Anna Leake, Barry Francis, Jack Cawley, Dick Hobley, Hugh Jones, Colin Cox, Tony and Pam Davis, Rosalie and Franco Vaccari, Edna and Bill Chandler, Senior Sergeant Greg

Williams, Senior Constable Liz Matheson, Peter and Kirsten Biven, Leesa Kemp, Sandy and Steve Jefferys, Christine Rippon, Hannah Ruwaard, Bill and Julia Jeffery, Paul Mabarrack, Harry Martin, Virginia Love, Di and Wendy Schaeffer, Gill Rolton, Lindy Young, Roy Griffiths, Sue Haydon, Jane and Paul Stone, Wayne Roycroft, Liz Murphy, Steve Brady, Brett Parbery, Guy McLean, Colleen O'Brien, Richard and Lucy Barrack, Anne Lindh, Andrew Graham, Deborah Brennan, Leanne Bruce-Clarke, Sandi Simons, Toby Gorringe, David Campbell, Marketa Mensikova, Jade Kudrenko, Peter Dempster, Pauline and Robert Leitch, Joy Motter, Rob Goldsworthy, Chris and Peter Hopton. Organisations that gave support were *The Weekly Times*, The Adelaide Showgrounds, Price's Bakery, Coopers' Brewery, the CWA, Fremantle Arts Centre Press, Charles Darwin University and Equitana. All in one way or another generously helped with research, a place to stay, stories and photographs.

Major accolades of course go to Brigitta Doyle and her team at ABC Books for continuing to recognise our working horse heritage with this bright new edition.

Introduction

Contemporary horse people owe a mighty debt to the old timers of the horse era. With knowledge accumulated through their reliance on four-legged horsepower, the horse people of the past left a heritage of good solid wisdom for modern equestrians. Sadly, much of their old-fashioned horse sense has been lost in the dust of the saddle-room, in the cobwebs festooning rotting wagons. This book, while not setting out specifically to teach these old skills, certainly contains the pearls of wisdom that underpinned normal horse practices in days past. The bush skills of our great horse pioneers and outback riders provide us with a rich heritage of riding and horse management to draw upon. Bush riders tackled distance and inhospitable terrain as a matter of course, and left us a legacy of genetically agile, robust horses.

These stories from the horse era, past and present, bring to life the sounds of creaking harness and galloping hooves, the blisters, sweat, terrors and laughter that all who work with horses know so well. Many writers were aged in their eighties and nineties and one was over one hundred. Some contributors died even before publication of the original book, underlining rather too well the urgency behind putting down their stories of everyday occurrences like broken harness and jibbing horses, of mercy dashes to save lives, of fun and of their special bond with their horses. Our predecessors could do little without a sound and willing horse. They could not send letters, visit friends, draw water from wells, make roads, dig dams, shop, go to school or to a doctor. No crops could be produced without leather-creaking muscle power. A wise horse, however, was sometimes a useful ally when it came to love and life.

Geoffrey Blight of Western Australia writes: 'I was conceived in a moving cart, after the ball was over, in the dark, on a bumpy road ... It was the same horse and cart that became my pram, my playpen, my school bus and my first money-earner. It was the couch on which I seduced my beloved.' And so the wheels keep turning.

Many readers will be shocked at the apparent cruelty inflicted on animals that wouldn't pull their weight. They may also be jolted by how hard horses worked in those days. Horses often put in eight to ten hour days, frequently without a drink even in hot weather. Milk and bread delivery horses used to cover about 25 miles, 40 kilometres, on their daily runs. These days this couldn't happen as misguided sentiment leads an ignorant public to intervene in the name of cruelty, as happens regularly in present-day tourist ventures. Indeed, horses today lead a hallowed existence by comparison with those in the past. Most work far less than their physique, energy and enthusiasm would allow. Cruelty, ironically, is more often inflicted through inactivity and over-feeding by a new wave of first-generation leisure horse owners who have few links with the complex knowledge and long-established traditions of the working horse era.

The hardest working horses are found on cattle stations. Police horses, bred mentally and physically tough for street work and crowd control, also put in solid hours each day. Sporting horses, trained to the pinnacle of their talents and fitness, lead lives of daring and sometimes glamour. Theirs is an existence far removed from the toiling drudgery of history. True working horses are now almost museum exhibits.

When affordable engines displaced horses from many of their everyday jobs in the 1930s and 1940s, vast numbers of well-bred Clydesdales and light-draughts were sent to slaughter, an end made even more inevitable by the devastating drought of

Introduction

1941 which depleted fodder stocks. Lost from the city landscape were the haymarkets which now exist in name only, and oat paddocks surrounding each city were broken up into housing blocks. The last commercial delivery horses departed from the streets in the mid-1960s and all that remains to remind us of the enormous contribution of working horses in developing our nation and turning the wheels of commerce are the occasional hitching post, water trough, mounting block, mews, coach house and stable block.

The Clydesdale had become the premier heavy horse in Australia, reaching its genetic pinnacle in the 1930s with supreme muscle bulk, strong bone and quiet temperament. Top breeding horses had been imported from Scotland at great expense and the Clydesdale, numerically, was unassailable. It took just a few decades after the proliferation of the piston engine for the Clydesdale to teeter on extinction. An enthusiastic band of supporters now has ensured the Clydesdale's future in Australia for the time being. Breeders enjoy steady demand for their horses from people working small farms, who want to show them, compete in ploughing competitions or harness them into wagons for tourists. It would be a sad day if the breed that did so much to haul this nation to its feet disappeared altogether, remembered only through photographs and the occasional sculpture. Even a fine bronze like the one in the main street of Angaston in South Australia's Barossa Valley cannot compensate for the real thing in all its muscle-bulging splendour.

The evocative language of the horse era is perhaps one of its most colourful and lasting legacies. The origins of many horse terms are probably forgotten, but let's look at a few. 'Offsider' was the term given to the horse taking up the right-hand position on a team, its most indispensable member, the leader which followed the line of the machine's previous sweep around the paddock, keeping the rest of the team straight to do a clean ploughing, sowing or reaping job. Being named as someone's offsider translates literally to being a 'right-hand man', a high order human compliment, of course applied to women too. The offsider was also the horse which 'walked the straight and narrow', another term still used today to indicate a good work ethic and high morals.

The similar-sounding term 'offside' also had its origins in the horse era. Since mounting and most handling of horses is done on the near or left side, someone who is offside is on the wrong side, even though technically it is on the right!

The derogatory term 'thin-skinned' to describe someone who can't take a ribbing or hard knocks comes from horses who developed sores under their collars and therefore were useless for work, being 'work-shy'.

Common terms like 'blinkered vision', 'getting back into harness', 'handing over the reins' and 'kicking the traces' are self- explanatory. Do people still talk of 'putting on their nosebags' in reference to having lunch? What about the term 'slacker'? This is also pure horse talk but now mainly applied to humans. A slacker was a lazy horse that allowed its traces or chains to hang in loops while the rest of its team-mates kept theirs taut by 'pulling their weight', another horse term.

I overheard an elderly woman in the hairdresser's say that her grandson 'was feeling his oats'. Then she laughed apologetically: 'Oh, you wouldn't understand that term,' she said to her young attendant. 'It's from the horse days. When we put our horses on to oats, they got a lot more energy and were sometimes hard to handle.'

This nostalgic tribute to the working horse era celebrates not just the past, but the world of the horse today. At their height in the early twentieth century, it is estimated there were around 2.4 million horses in Australia. Today, we still have about 1.2 million and it is estimated that at least 75 per cent of them are sport and leisure horses. This would explain why Melbourne's Equitana, a biennial festival celebrating everything to do with the horse, is so crowded!

Introduction

Clearly, many people are having a lot of fun on horseback or carts—and even more are still making a living out of working with horses. When equine influenza hit Australia in August 2007, economic losses were put at almost $4 million a day when the national horse lock-down went into effect. Horse transporters lost their jobs, farriers could not work, mares missed out on being mated, trainers and instructors had no clients, saddlers and fodder merchants lost sales, strappers were put off, horse shows were cancelled and equestrian clubs stopped meeting.

The total annual contribution of equine-related industry was estimated in 2001 by the Rural Industries Research and Development Corporation as $6.3 billion, around $17 million a day.

There is much to suggest that the horse, still more affordable in this country than in most others, is enjoying a resurgence of popularity. Horses are indeed good for the soul. What better way to escape the pressures of our foolish world and its overdose in recent years of greed and over consumption?

Past our farm recently, fifty horses, riders and wagon drivers followed the still visible tracks of the horse-drawn mail run of eighty years ago. In a small town west of Geelong, a mother drops her children to school by horse and cart. Near Ballarat, an old man whose eyesight is crook drives a jinker to the news- agent for the daily paper. Groups of riders camp out on the Bicentennial National Trail which follows the Great Dividing Range from Victoria to Queensland. Others tackle the newly opened Kidman Trail of 255 kilometres through the Adelaide Hills of South Australia. Polocrosse and campdrafting, Australia's own inventions, enjoy increasing popularity.

With stories from past to the present, this book is not just for horse-lovers. It also connects all of us to our shared heritage of four-legged horsepower.

Angela Goode, 2017

One
Horsepower: the original variety

Tractors can't think, nor do they give you a big clumsy rub with their heads at the end of a day's work. In little pockets of this nation, Clydesdales still lean into their collars and tramp over the soil as majestically as a century ago. It's not that their handlers are anti-tractor, they simply like using horses to do particular jobs on their farms. Many are young people who want to keep the old skills alive. You'll find them, as well as crusty old timers, gathering each September at the heavy horse ring at Melbourne Show, 'mecca' for working horse people. Just as they have done for years, they'll compare horses, harness, vehicles and driving techniques.

In northern Victoria, not far from Echuca, Bill Chandler has bred and worked Clydesdales nearly all his life. Horses are integrated into his farm's normal routine as naturally as the wind blows through the redgums along its bordering creeks.

Further south, Clydesdales routinely plodded the asparagus patches pulling wagons through the clagging soils. Now just one grower continues this long-standing tradition.

These two stalwarts of the era maintain it will be many years before they hang up their hames. They no doubt agree with the sentiments of Max Fatchen.

Mates
Max Fatchen

    I loved our old farm horses,
    White blazes down each nose.
    Along the paddocks' courses
    They made the furrowed rows.

    The red earth softly turning,
    The sky with cloudy veins,
    Autumnal breezes stirring
    (Both hands upon the reins).

    The big hoofs' steady plodding,
    The sound of harness clink.
    The pause for lunch and nosebags,
    At troughs, the grateful drink.

    At night the stables' comfort,
    The rolling in the sand.
    Such was the life of horses
    That tilled the farming land.

    But though a world mechanical
    With electronic brain,
    And vast, unfeeling juggernauts
    Now cultivate the grain.

    These memories assail me
    Nostalgia and remorse,
    Of mates who'd never fail me
    God bless the working horse.

Bill's Clydesdales stop the traffic

Bill Chandler can't for the life of him understand why cars scream to a halt, ejecting camera-toting occupants falling over themselves to take photos. All he is doing is running the harrows over the paddock or cutting and binding hay. Bill uses real horsepower—five flowing-fetlocked, head-tossing, snorting Clydesdales. 'When I give the horses a blow on the headlands, there's always someone bobbing up to take photos,' he says, quietly incredulous that anyone should find a bloke simply doing his job all that fascinating. 'It's just what we've always done,' Bill says in his low-key way, looking as though I, too, was batty even to be asking why he persisted with teams.

Compact and quiet moving, Bill, 77, hat perched on top, walks through the stable yard among his team, giving a rub here, a word there. Alongside their powerful, imposing bodies, Bill looks frail and small, yet they all stand to attention like soldiers.

Bill and wife, Edna, 71, were born with horses vibrating in their genes. When Bill was a boy way back in Gippsland his parents were market gardeners who used horses for all their work. Tall, direct, hardworking Edna came from a dairy, also in Gippsland, where working and riding horses were integral to her life too. Bill and Edna met at the 1950 Melbourne Show when their parents were showing draught horses. Married in 1952, with no cash to spare but with a team of horses, they bought a bush block near Warrigal. Their only other possessions were a breaking cart and a few tools. With a swing saw they cut posts and firewood. The horses hauled out logs and they used a pony and cart to get into town until they bought a second- hand car in 1954. A few years later they moved to 250 acres at Werribee and when suburban housing started to squeeze them out in 1974, they settled on their present farm, a big stretch of fertile river flat country at Barmah on the Murray River in northern Victoria. It has expanded now to 2000 acres.

Always the horses accompanied them, plus wagons, harness and a wide variety of horse-drawn implements.

'We never sell horses. We get married to them,' says Edna wryly.

The sheds bulge with rows of collars, chains and winkers. There are breaking carts and jinkers, binders and seeders. Bill buys horse machinery at clearing sales to keep a supply of spare parts, lamenting, however, that it's getting more difficult to find what he wants when something on his two working binders breaks. But this is no museum farm; it is a highly successful debt-free enterprise, turning off Hereford cattle, lambs and top-quality oaten hay for chaff. The Clydesdales on the place, about eighteen of them all up, are integral to keeping costs down, as is the philosophy of rarely buying anything new, making do and repairing. The horses cost little to run, rarely need a vet, and new foals replace retirees. A new horse, after handling and mouthing, gets trained by his team-mates hitched to the harrows. 'After a mile in heavy ground with two strong horses by his side, he soon gets the idea what he's there for,' says Bill. 'By the time they get to the end of the first row, they are different horses. Might have a kick and a bound, might pull back, but they soon come right.' Bill talks about how he gets the best out of his teams by linking their heads in his own special way, and how he deals with a horse that's not pulling its weight.

Bill uses one horse-drawn binder and two tractors with binders to harvest his hay. He points out matter-of-factly that the horses are far more efficient, because they need only one driver. The tractors need a driver each, plus someone working each binder—and they can't go any faster than the horses because the machines can only go so fast. Sons Greg, 39, and Tige, 48, are just as committed to the horses and even think Bill should have two teams on the go.

By delicious and ironic contrast, the day I visited Bill and Edna a disabled tractor in the shed was occupying the expensive

Horsepower: the original variety

and protracted attention of a mechanic brought in from a nearby town.

A farm like Bill and Edna's, which despite tough times in the past decade has managed to go forward, calls into question high-input, high-cost farming methods that need high yields to be profitable. Instead, Bill and Edna have built attractive, old-style stables out of redgum slabs, and use hollowed out half logs as horse-feed troughs and burnt-out trunks filled with straw as dog kennels. The horses save fuel by carting the thousands of tons of oaten sheaves they cut annually on a huge old brightly painted wooden hay wagon with steel-rimmed wheels. Bill bought it at a clearing sale for 30 pounds in 1948. Those sheaves are then laboriously and skilfully built into haystacks in the English tradition, all cosily round and cottagey like loaves of bread. The Chandlers are some of the last remaining stack builders around and consequently, like the horses, the stacks get their share of visiting admirers too.

Each sheaf has to be laced into the fabric of the stack so the middle stays springy, rain runs off the shingled straw top and the internal hay stays sweet for years. Until recently, they used a horse-driven elevator to lift the sheaves up to Tige, the stack builder. Bill started learning the art as a boy but when they moved to Werribee, the major hay production area for Melbourne's horse population, Hugh Barrie, one of the great stack builders, gave him extra tips. The elevator now has a motor because the horse gearing has worn out and can't be replaced. Up on top of those stacks until not so long ago, it was Edna doing the pitching of sheaves to Tige. 'I gave up milking the cow at 50 and pitching hay at 60,' says Edna, adding that she couldn't find anything to give up at 70—only because this powerhouse of a woman is so indispensable. When the family cuts chaff using an ancient wood-fired steam engine, another clearing sale buy, Edna's in charge of the fire and hand sews the chaff bags. Their genuine steam-cut, high quality chaff is sought after by local horse people.

In the sheds are long rows of horse collars and winkers that Bill oils with horse tallow, which he buys in 44-gallon drums. 'It's just as good as the fancy stuff,' he says. 'But it is very cheap.'

Edna is still actively involved in the local pony club as an instructor, has a Shetland wandering around the garden for her grandchildren, and laments people's general loss of horsemanship these days. 'They don't know any better,' she says, worrying about how their ignorance often leads them into danger.

Bill, with a lifetime of horse-work behind him and a head full of knowledge of the old ways, says he too finds it hard to pass on what he knows.

Neighbouring Echuca each year celebrates its history with a ten-horse team pulling a wagon-load of wool, but Bill stands silently watching from the sidelines. 'Young people, new to horses, think they know it all,' he says sadly. 'They don't want me to tell them anything.'

Now there's only one

In asparagus country, it was once common to see a draught horse pulling a strange offset wagon along the rows while its handler walked along picking up bundles of freshly cut spears. In Australia's major asparagus growing region, Kooweerup, southern Victoria, where the soils are rich and dark and the rain falls plentifully, horses were part of the workforce, because they coped with the sticky conditions and did not compact the soils between the rows. The best of them would plod along at an even pace and helpfully stop the wagon beside each waiting bunch. Then a special tractor was developed which would drive itself slowly along the rows just like a horse and didn't need someone sitting at the controls. Slowly the horses were pensioned off— and now there's only one. He's called George and I'm told he won't be hanging up his horseshoes for another ten years, so long as his best mate, Hayden Giles, 47, doesn't do anything stupid like expanding his asparagus patch beyond its present horse-friendly size of 20 acres and so long as Hayden stays fit enough to walk the daily 16 kilometres behind him, picking up the bundles and putting them into the crates on the wagon. If Hayden doesn't work with George, there won't be anyone else. It's not that George would go on strike with another at the helm. There simply are no more people around who have the skills to handle a Clydesdale in an asparagus patch.

Hayden: 'When you rely on seasonal workers as you do with asparagus, you find they don't have horsemanship skills. They have no confidence to manage an animal if it starts doing something unexpected. It will put its rump into the wind which blows across these paddocks quite a lot, or it will increase its speed to escape the wind, or it will refuse to stop. If you grow up with them, you don't get wild and angry and pick up clods of dirt and throw them at the horse. But that's what inexperienced people do, and it doesn't do a lot of good. The horse will refuse to work for them at all after that.'

Hayden said a neighbour once had a horse bolt because of the inexperience of its handler. The cart was smashed, the harness broken and the horse would never work properly again, as it had become too spooked by the incident.

George would be out of a job if the current patch gets any bigger simply because one of those dreaded tractors would have to be bought. Since it can handle about twice the area a horse can cover, it would be goodbye George. Plus it's set up so the workers can sit on its tray while they pick up—much more appealing than walking through sticky mud between 5.30 am and midday every day. No wonder the workers shake their heads when they are given the option of using a horse.

'But how can you retire your best mate?' asks Hayden, appalled at the thought of putting George out to pasture. 'He's only 14 and in his prime. It takes a while to turn a young horse into a good horse, eight to ten years, and he's still got plenty of years left in him. What would I say to him—"Sorry, mate, you're finished"?

'I like my horse. I know he can do the job. Plus I have already got all the equipment I need. Setting myself up with a tractor would cost me $16,000.'

Besides, horse language has permeated Hayden's brain completely, he'd probably be swearing at the chugging machine like he sometimes does to poor old George. Hayden's dad, who is 80, finds his son speaks horse language even to him. He helps out by driving crates of asparagus in his ute to the packing shed but finds he gets told to 'giddup' and 'whoa'. 'I'm not a bloody horse, son,' the old man snaps.

Claiming that his wife, Judy, doesn't see anything strange about his relationship with George, Hayden talks about the horse with the fondness a bloke usually reserves for a drinking mate, the sort of bloke you'd do anything for. 'It's a male thing,' says Hayden. 'We're two men working closely together, as a team. It's real mateship. We understand each other.' Plodding the rows together, mostly in silence, there might be the odd cross word when George is in one of his silly moods, or when he is too busy watching traffic on nearby Manks Road and forgets to stop at the bunches, making Hayden puff after him. 'He knows I'm swearing at him—I see his ears twitch and go back. He's probably swearing back at me.'

Hayden has been around draught horses—and asparagus for that matter—all his life. The Giles family has been in market gardening for three generations, and like all the other farm kids in the district, Hayden was sitting in carts being pulled between rows of carrots, onions, potatoes and asparagus, holding the reins and thinking he was in charge—when of course the horse knew better than to take any notice of a silly little four year old.

Horsepower: the original variety

Every morning during asparagus season, which goes from August to mid-December, Hayden is at the shed at ten past five, his pockets carrying the usual treats of pieces of carrot and apple. George nickers a greeting, gets his morning feed and half an apple when he is harnessed and half when he is between the shafts. It's a routine that has continued for ten years and Hayden laughs at how enthusiastic George is to get ready for work, swinging his head around for his reward as soon as the straps are fastened. He's a sociable horse, this George. As dawn breaks and he makes the first pass down a row, he stops to nod at and get a rub from the pickers, some of whom have been on the job as long as he has. He's even got one girl organised to bring him toast and raspberry jam every morning. George certainly is making the most of being the last 'sparry' horse left.

Staying with tradition

Don Black has never quite left the working horse era behind. Sure, his sons think he is slightly crazy and the neighbours sometimes laugh. Don, however, says he is no eccentric, and that his team of horses are an integral, contributing part of his productive 900-acre farm at Branxholme in Victoria.

'I've had a lot of mud slung at me,' he says in his quiet, unassuming way.

But then again, every now and again, his critics are silenced. While he uses a tractor for his initial ploughing, he finishes off with the horses. They cope with boggy ground better than the tractor. He also finds he can continue seeding for an extra three weeks or so using his horse team in the district's usually wet seasons.

'In wet winters, I can take the horse in boggy ground with a four-wheeled rubber tyre trailer and feed out 30 bales of hay without getting bogged,' he says. 'And one really wet winter twenty-odd years ago, the biggest topic of conversation among the men was how to feed out their hay. But I had a win that year—I really let them have my threepence worth!'

And when, one year, he bogged the tractor, he used one of his horses to pull it out—and no doubt let all those tractor buffs know about it.

Don, 68, started working horses at 15, and had always wanted to be a teamster from a very young age. It delights him that there has been a resurgence in interest in Clydesdales in recent years among hobby farmers and people interested in embarking on tourist ventures.

'There are as many members in the Clydesdale Society now as when the horse was at its peak,' he says.

'The tractor is the greatest slave-driver. You only have to look around—there are plenty of contractors working half the night.' He points out that in his many years of sowing and reaping crops, they were usually limited to an eight-hour day, because the horses got tired, and needed to be home before dark to be

cooled down, dried and fed.

'While they were long days, we had to work calmly and gently. You can't rush with horses and there just wasn't the pressure. 'People who worked horses were terribly fit, and many live

well into their eighties and nineties.'

When I dropped in to visit Don, he was cleaning out the stalls belonging to his team. Standing between the shafts of the old Melbourne City Council tipper dray was Prince, head drooping and eyes closed. Each full load of manure was backed very neatly into wife Merle's garden—nothing got squashed, and then we all hitched a ride back to the stable with its thick redgum posts, troughs of hardwood and collars hanging at each stall. There's no better way to do the job, Don insists. A front-end loader, even if he had one, would be noisy, unable to manoeuvre into such tight spaces and would cause great damage in the garden. What's more, it would use fuel and smell horrible.

Horsepower: the original variety

Among Don's extensive collection of horse-drawn farm implements and vehicles is a Bennett wagon, originally made near Sydney and considered the Rolls Royce of wagons. They were usually drawn by seventeen-horse teams to carry wool, a task Don re-enacted for the bicentenary celebrations in 1988. Merle and Don are planning sometime soon to hitch up a few less than that, put a bowed canvas top on it and go off for a holiday around Victoria.

But what really put a smile on Don's face was the celebrations for his 61st birthday. He and Merle contacted their horse friends and invited them over to yoke up a team of twenty—just like in the old days when teamsters carting wool and wheat through the Riverina's boggy plains had to have such numbers. For teams that size, a teamster would have had a couple of heeler dogs to keep his horses working. They did a few rounds of the paddock—Don contributed thirteen of the team—and all had a great time.

This man, with a love of the old ways, who tries to continue the authentic style of the teamsters of the past with the right sort of everyday working harness and plain, honest horses, worries that when he dies, his collection of gear won't be valued, and that it will just be burnt as a pile of old rubbish.

A great life for horse-lovers
Bill Carberry

In the days of real horsepower—before tractors—when the Clydesdale horse was the backbone of agriculture, people seemed to accept long hours as part of a normal day's work. The following is a very brief outline of a twelve-month cycle of work on a farm at Horsham as I experienced it up until the time I enlisted for the war in 1940 at the age of 23. I had started working teams at the age of 15.

Working horses were looked after with the great care and attention they deserved. They very seldom ran in paddocks but were kept in what were known as 'stable yards'. The stable itself was a long, low shed, usually of slab walls with a straw roof. These stables were very warm in winter and very cool in summer. Each horse had its own stall and feeder. It was not uncommon for these feeders to be made of hollow logs cut in two, or into whatever size would make a suitable container for half a bag of chaff.

On an average farm 80 to 100 tons of chaff would be needed each year for the teams, so sufficient land had to be sown to oats in late autumn to ensure that enough hay could be cut. This usually took place in late November, using a reaper/binder drawn by three horses. Sheaves were dropped from the carrier, usually about five at a time, at the same places each round. This was very heavy work for the horses so they usually only worked shifts of two to three hours, after which time they were changed for a fresh team.

When sufficient hay had been cut, stooking was begun. This consisted of standing or leaning the sheaves together in conical stooks of twenty to 30, their butts on the ground. They remained like this for two to three weeks to ensure that the hay was thoroughly dried before carting, because, of course, horses must never be given musty feed. The hay was carted to the stacks on a wagon that carried 3 to 5 tons and was drawn by three to five horses; two or three men did the loading and stacking with the aid of pitchforks. Great skill was required to build haystacks that would neither tip over or let in the rain. The hay was then taken from the stacks as needed, for cutting into chaff.

While this sounds a lot of work, I wonder if any other fuel for horsepower could have been produced for less expense, and without polluting the environment.

Early starts were uncommon during stripping—or reaping, as it is known in South Australia—so there was time to groom the horses thoroughly in the morning while they ate, and to put on their collars and hames before breakfast. They had to be as fit as race horses for harvest, as they seldom knocked off before sundown. Varying numbers of horses were required for the stripping, depending on the size of the machine and whether it was a harvester or header. For a header with an 8-foot comb, for example, eight horses were required. After they had knocked off, a good teamster would spend an hour or so thoroughly rubbing them down with a bag or piece of hessian, to dry off all the sweat so they would not get chilled at night as it dried.

When the crop had all been stripped and most of the bags sewn, then came the wheat carting. The wheat was carted to the nearest siding on wagons carrying about 100 bags (a little over 8 tons) and drawn by eight to eleven horses. Wherever possible, the horses were yoked abreast, as it was considered that nine abreast, being nearer the load, would do the same work as ten yoked in tandem.

The bags were loaded onto the wagon with the aid of a horse-operated loader. Two horses, known as 'shafters', were then harnessed to the wagon shafts. The ones in front of them were harnessed in threes. The shafters played a very important role: since the weighbridge was only a little longer than the wagon, great care had to be exercised by the shafters in stopping the wagon in exactly the right spot. Because there were no quick-acting brakes on wagons, they did this by leaning back into their breechings, the leather bands that go round the rump of a harness horse and are attached to the shafts.

On one farm where I worked, the siding was 11 miles away. I would rise at 2 am, feed and groom the horses, have something to eat and leave at 3 am, often meeting up with other wagons and teams to form a convoy. We'd often congregate on the leading wagon and play cards or just talk. The teams would all follow along behind, each horse doing its fair share. Their honesty was extraordinary.

When the wagon had been unloaded, and the bags of wheat put in place on the stack by the wheat lumpers, I would unyoke the horses, give them a drink from the water trough in the middle of the town, then a feed of oats and chaff. While they were eating I would go to the hotel, where my boss would have organised for me to have breakfast. After I had eaten I would yoke up the horses again and head off the 11 miles home, going straight down to the paddock, where I would put on another load, ready for the next morning. Back at the stable, the horses were then unyoked and allowed to have a roll while I put out their feed. I would then brush them down. By then it was usually time for the evening meal, after which the horses were given enough feed to keep them going until morning.

It is easy to imagine how leg-weary the horses became, travelling such long distances after having worked so hard. This was the one time of the year when they were given a rest for three or four weeks and allowed to run in the oat or barley stubble. After that the cycle began again. The ground which had been ploughed and left fallow the previous winter would be worked again, usually with a scarifier, in late April or May when the first rains came. Early in May the horses would have the hair clipped from the lower parts of their bodies to reduce sweating, and allow them to spend the nights without wet coats.

At seeding time it was necessary to rise at about 4 am, so as to be in the paddock with the team by first light. Sometimes on frosty mornings it was necessary to put your hands under the collar of one of the horses in order to get enough feeling back into the hands to handle the bags of seed and Super. About 20 acres a day, or 100 acres per week with a sixteen- row combine, was considered good going. Some considered it silly, me being in the paddock waiting for daylight, but an early start enabled me to knock off before dark and give the horses a rub down so they would not be standing overnight with wet coats. Seeding was carried out in two shifts: dawn till about 11.30 am, when the horses were returned to the stable for a drink and a feed, before returning to the paddock at 1 pm for the afternoon shift.

As soon as the crop was in, it was time to start ploughing ready for next year's crop. This was a slow, tedious job, as the five or six furrow ploughs only cut about three or four feet. In every team there was a 'furrow horse', which walked in the furrow while ploughing, or on the mark when using other implements. People often wondered how we could plough so straight, but it was easy, so long as you had one very intelligent horse. After the ploughing came the harrowing, then the scarifying to control the weeds.

By the time the fallowing was completed, it was usually about time to begin the hay-cutting again, thus completing a cycle which may sound boring, but for anyone who loved horses it was very interesting work. A good teamster became very attached to his horses and I feel sure this attachment was not all one way, because on a Sunday—and incidentally no team ever worked on Sunday—you could walk out into the stable yard and the horses would walk up to you, each expecting a pat and a few kind words.

Vignettes of the past
Denis Adams

I can still see Grandfather Queale's team at work, settling their harness in place, bracing themselves like a tug-of-war team preparing for the tussle. Then the great heave, the scrabble for foothold, the steady bite of hooves, driving like blunt mattocks into the rich brown loam of Rosella Farm as they kept the iron wheels rolling. Leaning into their collars, manes, tails, forelocks and fetlocks aflutter, great muscles flowing smoothly, plough-chains tight, the mouldboards gliding, gliding, folding the damp, dark soil into neat contours. The flat ground of Greens Plains West enabled teams of up to twenty to be used sometimes.

My clearest memory of a horse-drawn mower at work was of one near Angaston in the 1950s. The farmer had just started his mowing and the horses were spirited, to say the least. They probably hadn't done anything for a while and the 'clickety click' of the mower blades so close to their hocks really had them doing some high stepping. They were working at a racing pace, on a very steep hillside, fairly flying downhill, yet the old gent holding the reins appeared unruffled. Obviously he'd seen it all before.

I remember seeing meadow hay raked into windrows with a dump rake drawn by one horse back in those war years at Torrens Vale. As I neared school one morning I heard the familiar sound of a rake and, looking up, saw an old chap I knew, just cresting the hill. He was looking as relaxed as though going for a Sunday drive, his pipe clamped in his mouth, a wisp of smoke trailing behind him. In spite of his casual air, he was steering the horse so that not a blade of hay was missed. As he tripped the lever, the rake tynes bounded over the curl of the hay with the grace of a kangaroo.

Grandpa Adams was presented with a beautifully ornamented buggy whip after delivering the first trolley-load of wheat to Saints siding near Balaklava. I must have delivered one of the last loads of bagged wheat to Saints in our ex-army truck. Dad said one aspect of the horse days he'd enjoyed was delivering wheat to Saints. It was a leisurely trip both ways, with a stop at the Whitwharta store to buy some little luxury to enjoy on the way home—a tin of sardines, usually.

I remember going into my cousin's stable with him to feed his team. The building was warmed by the body heat of a score of hard-worked Clydesdales. There was a draught stallion, but he was kept locked away in a yard made of railway sleepers. The only sound in the stable was that of breathing, feeding and the odd scuffle of a hoof. From the stallion's yard you'd often hear a kick or a frustrated squeal.

The stable smells were unforgettable—so warm and friendly. A heady mix of chaff and meal, sweat, urine and hot, fresh dung, soon ground into the floor by the shuffling hooves. Nothing smells better than fresh horse sweat and chaff. Nothing smells worse than horse urine in a confined space!

Morning routine
Gloria Godlonton

We had a team of magnificent Clydesdales for the farm work when I was a child. In the early hours of the morning I would hear my father getting wood from the box to light the stove for an early morning cup of tea, and to have a good fire roaring ready for my mother to cook a hearty country breakfast. My bedroom was opposite the kitchen off a large open verandah, so I always woke early.

Dad would go up to the stables calling out, 'Chirp, chirp', and the draught horses would come trotting in for their morning feed, which was placed in long wooden troughs with a rail dividing each horse.

While Dad organised the day's work, I would slide the slip rails in behind the horses, who were munching contentedly on their feed. Then I would drag a collar over to the feed trough, rest it on the edge and as the big horses put their heads down to feed, I would do the two straps up on top of the collar. These gentle horses were so patient with me, which was just as well, as I was only a small girl of seven. Not once did I ever get hurt or trodden on. I also managed to put winkers on the very quietest ones, leaving their bits out of their mouths until their feed was finished. Dad and I really enjoyed our hot breakfast after those early mornings.

All so different then

The Marriott name is one that crops up repeatedly when working horses are mentioned. The family has been inextricably linked to Clydesdales for generations and there are still over 90 horses spread between Alan Marriott, 84, and his two sons Max, 54, and Ross, 47, and grandson Andrew, 26. They are all show horses these days, but this highly regarded family of horsemen has its roots in market gardening, and relied on its horses to cart vegetables to Melbourne's Victoria Market, plough their paddocks and cart manure.

It was all so different then. I can't imagine lads of today doing what Alan Marriott as a 14 year old used to do. Three days a week, he was responsible for getting a lorry laden with 5 tons of vegetables into the market by 2 am. He would leave the family's 100-acre farm in East Brighton at 11 pm for the 10-mile drive that took him along St Kilda Road and through the heart of the sleeping city. After rugging his horses and giving them each a nosebag, he would spend the rest of the pre-dawn morning selling the load off the back of the lorry. His was stall 120, the first stall in Queen Street, a site he occupied for 43 years. 'I was the fellow at the bottom of "C" shed with the white shirt,' he said, remembering those wonderful, noisy mornings surrounded by sparkling, dewy, brightly coloured vegetables and the noisy banter of spruikers. All year round Alan sold carrots and parsnips; as well, there were cauliflowers and cabbages in winter, and potatoes and onions in summer.

Vendors' horses lined the cobbled alleyways, side by side, backed into their usual positions. They stood quietly between their shafts, munching away in their nosebags until it was time to return home, perhaps with a back-load of hay.

As the city stirred, the streets filled with hansom cabs, four-wheel cabs and jinkers.

'Melbourne was all horses then,' Alan says. 'When I first

started going to market over 70 years ago, there were no trucks. It was wonderful. Horses were everywhere. Vaughan's, the big delivery and carting contractors, had between 4000 and 5000 horses working in Melbourne. At one stable alone, which was opposite the North Melbourne football ground, 1200 horses were tied up in stalls under the care of Jack Brasher.'

It was from this stable that Alan would cart out about 5 tons of manure a week, to be spread on the family's 90 acres of vegetable crops. In all, those 1200 horses generated between 50 and 60 tons of manure every week, all of which was taken away by market gardeners.

The streets clattered with the sound of horseshoes and iron-rimmed wheels. There were the flour millers, Kimpton's and Brunton's, with three-horse teams; the Murphy's, who carted sugar; and to feed the huge horse population, hay was delivered daily to the Haymarket, just near the Royal Melbourne Hospital. After auction, it was hauled out to be turned into even more manure. The Victoria Market delivery routine lasted until 1926 when Alan was 17 and his father bought a solid-tyred truck. Because it could carry an extra ton of vegetables, Alan said the family had to work even harder to make a pay-load. 'We didn't know anything but work and sleep,' he said. 'In fact, the only leisure I ever had was when I started playing cricket at 18.' His day in the vegetable paddocks started at 7 am and went until 6 pm, for which he was paid three pounds a week. 'But everybody was happy,' he said.

After the war, in 1946, Alan was to discover another sort of leisure that to this day still has him hooked—showing horses. It started out innocently enough with gymkhanas to raise money for the comfort fund for soldiers. The Marriotts, like their friends and neighbours, showed some of their working Clydesdales, and between one and two thousand pounds would be raised at each show. From there, Alan graduated to the Royal Melbourne Show.

'Jock Gray, a Scotsman, drove a team at the show the first few years I was delivering vegetables,' Alan recalls. 'He asked me to bring a pair of our Clydesdales. They were just working horses and we didn't win anything while we had that type of horse.'

Alan had been bitten by the showing bug, however, and bought a few showy yearlings, grew them out and then, with that fresh, young, newly broken team, won for the next three or four years. Kimpton's and Brunton's, and many of the other commercial drivers of the time, also competed. Alan remembers the great fun of those days, which are kept alive by an increasingly enthusiastic band of competitors at Royal Melbourne Show—the 'mecca' for those interested in the great traditions of working harness horses.

Alan has judged at Melbourne and Sydney Royals and in New Zealand. In 1993 Alan Marriott carried off for the 22nd consecutive year the four-horse-team event which, in the 49 years since he first started competing, he has won 35 times. The beautifully painted lorry pulled by those four stylish horses is the very same one he had in 1923 to transport vegetables to market.

By the light of the silvery moon
Jim Kelly

My youth coincided with petrol rationing, and during the early part, when dedication to the war effort was paramount, we filled in applications for petrol honestly. Our ration was about enough to go to the bowser to pick it up and get home—so travelling to the Literary Society was a real horsepower job. Pepper was the favourite family pony. He spent the entire petrol rationing period of at least eight years doing for nothing what any old utility or light truck does today.

After the Society's summer recess, a special meeting was held to arrange our programme for the rest of the year. Because I was a committee man, I had to go to this meeting by myself, so on this particular evening, a moonlit night in March 1941, I rode Pepper rather than put him in the sulky.

After drawing up our programme of a concert and a debate and five other meetings, the chairman brought out the calendar to decide when they would be held. There was none of this first Tuesday or fourth Wednesday stuff in those days. The meetings had to coincide with the phases of the moon. A week before or two days after full moon was the limit for safe, pleasant horse travel, and it was understood that if the weather was bad or heavily overcast the meeting would be cancelled. The people who print calendars still continue to add the phases of the moon, but users of this advice must be fairly thin on the ground these days.

Ride-and-tie
Joyce Shiner

A common way of covering big distances when I was young, when there was only one horse between two people, was to take turns along the way. Dad called it 'ride-and-tie'. The first rider would tie the horse to a tree, then walk on. When the second rider found the horse waiting, he would ride a distance past the walker, tie the horse and walk on. They kept on in that way, sometimes covering a distance of 20 miles, doing 10 miles each on foot, and 10 miles each on horseback, while resting the horse at pre-arranged intervals.

Loading the wagon
Elsie Dunn

In 1918 we had around twenty horses working daily at different tasks, and being an outdoor type of girl, I had plenty of opportunities to see first-hand the strength, loyalty and gentleness of those huge Clydesdales as they plodded through a day's work. At 16 I was as strong as any man, and knew all the ways to make difficult tasks easier. I lumped bags of wheat with my brother and Dad, not because I had to, but because I wanted to, and to be out in the fields with them.

We had a bag-lifter fastened on the side of the wagon and we three in turn would get hold of a bag of wheat by the ears, turn it onto our backs, carry it a short distance and tip it onto the lifter. It had an iron frame into which a bag fitted, and on our word of 'yes', the old Clydesdale, fastened by a long pull chain to the bottom of the lifter, would walk forward. The bag would flop onto the wagon and the horse would immediately step backwards until the lifter was again in position to take the next bag. The horse did this without any leading or guiding from us. This could keep going half a morning until the wagon was fully loaded.

Farm horses—another view
Bruce Rodgers

I have been mixed up with horses for all 84 years of my life. I did not start school until I was nearly seven, as first I had to be able to ride, unsaddle and tie up a pony so I could get to the school. I did the seven grades in six years and did one year at high school before finishing my education due to financial difficulties on the farm. I spent my 14th birthday driving four horses in a stripper, helping my father reap a lousy crop of wheat. That is where my real education began.

Horses were the only means of power on our farm. There was not a tractor in the district and only one motor car, and it was always regarded as a miracle if it did a trip of 20 miles to the town with no trouble. So a smart-looking buggy and pair of ponies was considered more reliable and better value.

The main type of draught horse used at that time was the Shire, which seemed to be more popular in our district than the Clydesdale. Much could be written about the qualities of both breeds.

Horses were cheap power while they were actually working, but in the long term, not quite as cheap as was often claimed. Land had to be used to grow hay for horse feed and the crop had to be cut and tied into sheaves with a binder. The sheaves had to be stooked and later carted and stacked. During the year, they had to be put through a chaff-cutter whenever horse feed was needed. Some farmers used a stationary engine to turn the chaff-cutter but other farmers used the horse as a means of power. When horses were used it also was necessary to employ more labour for handling hay and chaff-cutting, and if more than one team was used, there needed to be a driver.

At certain times of the year a horse team does not need to be kept in a stable, because in the spring and summer and after harvest they can be grazed in the paddocks.

The day usually began by getting out of bed at 5 or 5.30 in the morning. The routine was as follows. First light the fire in the kitchen stove and then go to the stable and feed the horses—they needed almost an hour to eat their first feed for the day. Attend to a few usual odd jobs, such as making sure all harness is in good order, also filling the nosebags, which have to be taken to the paddock for the midday feed. Have breakfast and secure a cut lunch for midday. Drive the horses into the smaller yard and put winkers on each horse, then couple them side by side using a leather coupling with a strong spring or snap hook which is fastened to each end. Move the horses as near as possible to the harness shed and get the horse-brush and curry comb and groom them, which means dislodging all dry sweat and dirt that has accumulated during the previous day. Special attention must be paid to the shoulders where the collars have been in contact, as any hard matter left there can cause a sore shoulder. Should a suspicious-looking lump or abrasion appear on the shoulder the collar should be examined for any unusual shape and, if possible, rectified. In the case of a bad lump or abrasion, that horse should not be worked and should be replaced by another horse.

When the collars and hames have been placed on the horses, the nosebags can be hung on top of the hames, which extend about 6 inches above the collars. Put the reins on and drive the team to the paddock, which could be one or more miles away.

Such an early start as this usually took place at seeding time, which is generally when the daylight hours are short, and the usual aim was to be in the paddock ready to start at sunrise. The reason was that horses should not be working on heavy work after sundown and should be unhooked from the implement and heading for home so that the sweat has a chance to dry off before the cold night air sets in. Any experienced horseman knows that any horse that has been worked after sundown looks fairly dejected the next morning.

After arriving home and removing the harness, it may be necessary to saddle up a hack and drove the team to the dam or well for water—and of course that was also necessary before starting work in the morning. Many years ago when farms and districts were being developed, water was a problem and people had to use dams, which, of course, had to rely on the rain always being sufficient. The horse team had to have its last feed for the day before the driver went to bed, so no exact time can be stated for that job.

Stabbed in action
Denis Adams

I recall, just after the war, helping cart loose meadow hay on a tip-dray drawn by an enormous Clydesdale mare. The farmer's son—still in his khakis, having just been de-mobbed—was stacking it with a pitchfork. His father was gently teasing him, saying his 'Pacific Island holiday' had spoilt him for work. Actually, the young fellow was flat out trying to keep up with three of us pitching the hay to him, his fork flashing this way and that. Then one of the prongs accidentally stabbed into the broad rump of the half-dozing mare.

Though it didn't pierce the skin, it did gain her attention. Her head shot up and I'm sure all four hooves were airborne at once. The resulting jolt to the dray almost tipped the young bloke off. 'Sorry, old girl,' he said. 'Didn't mean to bayonet you!'

Horses seem to understand when it's an accident, so the mare didn't bear a grudge. This is not to say she didn't give us hurt, disappointed looks for the rest of the day.

By horse, of course
Frank Condon

I pulled out my very oldest photos and was surprised at how often horses appeared. Then memories from my childhood came trickling slowly back.

On our dairy farm at Tyagarah near Byron Bay during the 1940s, we were without electricity, telephone or motor vehicles. All transport, power and communication was supplied by—the horse, of course. Dad's pony, Timmy, enabled him to court Mum, who lived up in the hills at Coorabel—where Dad's pushbike couldn't go. So I reckon I owe my very existence to—the horse, of course.

Doctor was the little brown horse that pulled the sulky through the heath and sand dunes on shopping trips to Byron Bay. On the return trip I would be placed in the boot beneath the sulky seat to sleep. Mum used to sing an old nursery rhyme as we gently jogged along: 'Tick tack, strike jack, blow the bellows old man, shoe the horse, shoe the mare, and let the little foal go bare, bare, bare.' When I awoke, we were always home, thanks to—the horse, of course.

Star was the temperamental cart horse and saddle pony who always played hard to catch. Her main duties were to pull the light cart that took our produce to market—cans of cream to the Norco Butter depot, cases of bananas to the railway—and to bring home our mail, groceries, meat and bread. Star was also the transport that enabled moonlight fishing trips to the beach, resulting in bags of whiting, bream and flathead. She was the horse that shied at a snake and threw Dad. He was hospitalised for two weeks for his first ever 'holiday', courtesy of—the horse, of course.

We had a strange little brown conveyance named Possum that hated to leave her home paddock, but as soon as her head was turned for home, would be off like a shot, usually dumping her rider smartly to the ground. When town kids visited and began to act superior by treating us like country bumpkins, we persuaded them to have a ride on our 'friendly' little Possum. They were usually brought back to earth with a thud by—the horse, of course.

Horses also kept us in touch with life and death. Urgent news was always conveyed by a horseman from one of the nearby farms that were connected to the telephone lines. Usually the sight of a lone horseman approaching across the distant paddocks meant the death of a loved one. We came to dread the sight so much that when it turned out to be only the 'tick dodger' or the dairy inspector, we were almost glad. They, like everyone, came—by horse, of course.

Horsepower
Margaret Glendenning

White frost rimes the branches, a diamond crystal flame
Catches fire as sunrise tips the trees.
The brown earth falls in furrows behind the jolting plough
Old Mac walks the mornings again on days like these.

Stable straw spun golden in the lantern's swinging circle,
Sleepy swallows somewhere sound alarm.
Soft greeting from the night stalls, noses searching feed bins,
Nugget's warm breath misting across an outstretched palm.

A dreaming into distance, muzzles dripping water,
Seeing things our human eyes cannot.
Playful nipping, squealing, heads together flirting,
Princess sidling coyly, teasing big black Lancelot.

Dust and damp sweat breaking, staining hides and harness,
Over Bess, Up Baldy, old friends of days long gone.
Your loyalty, your courage, your strength and pride
   and beauty,
Helped to build our nation, the memories will live on.

Memories from the wheat country
Wendy Treloar

Richie Kloeden is a wonderful old identity who lived in our area. He knows what life's all about after his days with the horse teams, out seeding, winnowing and bagging grain. 'Yes, times were hard,' he told me. 'But we didn't think they were, because we didn't know any different. We certainly worked hard physically, but life was good too.'

Richie says he always enjoyed watching a harnessed team putting their backs into moving a wagon-load of bagged wheat. After the whistle, the horses would push and strain with their back legs and, with muscles heaving in a mighty display of unified power, would get the wagon rolling.

'It was a beautiful sight. But of course there would be times when I'd whistle them up and they wouldn't go anywhere!

'We didn't have any money to buy horses, so other farmers in the district would give us their leftovers. This was in about 1944 and I was about 23 years old. We had all the unbroken, outlaw horses for miles around. We'd break them, and some were marvellous team horses.

'During droughts the horses were often weak from lack of good feed, so we could plough only 3 to 6 acres a day. The country was too rough to cut hay, so we fed them "cocky chaff" mixed with a few oats, if we had them, and molasses—a bit of a lick for us and some for the horses.

'We would always be harnessed up before dawn, take the horses out then, on their return, we'd feed and water them. It was good when we got the wireless, because we could listen to that until the last 10 pm feed for the night. Some days, the horses didn't have a drink all day, but they always had a nosebag. When we left for the paddock in the mornings we'd drag a little three wheeler thing behind the wagon, which contained spare nosebags, and tucker and a bottle of tea for us.'

Protecting the crops
Elsie Dunn

Summer was always a frightening time on the farm because of the threat of fires through the crops. Dad kept two sturdy horses in the stable yard all summer, grain-fed for strength, and, in the shed, two sets of well-oiled harness and a square red tank full of water. At the first sign of that dark curling ring of smoke heralding a bushfire, Dad, my brother and a workman would harness the horses to the trolley with the water tank and dash off to help. They would cut any fences in their path. It did not matter if the crop to be saved was Dad's or a neighbour's, all helped each other.

Keep it brief
Denis Adams

One thing the names of working horses had in common was their brevity. Geldings had names like Bob, Bill or Ben, perhaps something macho like Captain or Soldier, or Dandy. Mares had names like Meg, Peg or Dolly. Some names were descriptive. I remember hearing of a mighty gelding named Chunk.

One of the interesting features of nineteenth century newspapers were the pages of advertisements for stallions, mostly immense draught horses with their tails hitched up ludicrously and tied with ribbons, and names like Grand Inquisitor of Seville.

One horse's name I don't believe I have ever come across is Dobbin. Did anyone ever really own a Dobbin?

In an awful bind
Hurtle Baldock

One thing a lot of horses didn't like was the binder which we used for cutting hay, as it was a heavy dead pull and noisy, right close behind them. Since the mechanism was driven from the ground wheel, it took a good steady pull to get it moving. It was with a binder team that I made a bad error of judgement in picking my team of horses.

I had just started farming on my own after the war. The hay was ready to cut, but I had no horses who had worked previously in a binder. So, keeping in mind the heavy pull needed to start the machine, I picked three horses that had plenty of strength. As soon as they had got the machine moving, the noisy clatter right on their heels was too much for them to bear. Two of them bolted and the faster they went, the louder the noise became. After a while, the horse on the nearside, who was taking things more placidly, decided that a gallop was no pace at which to work a binder. He began hanging back, which helped me to bring the team around in a circle until we eventually stopped.

It took a day or so of repairs and picking up the parts that had been put into orbit—and all the tools that had been thrown out of the tool box. I had been very lucky too to have been able to stay aboard the binder, as I had been standing up well clear of the seat with my feet planted wide, hauling on the reins.

Stitching hair from the spell
Elsie Dunn

At the end of harvest and after the wool and wheat had been carted, all the horses were turned out into the back paddock to rest over winter. When they returned after three or four months, my sister and I would sit up on the rails and just drink in the beauty of their shining coats and long flowing tails and manes.

Dad and my brother would catch each horse, cut their forelock short enough so we could see their eyes, trim the manes and pull the tails. Dad had a sharp pocket knife and would pull a certain amount of tail hair through, thinning it out to hock length and tapering it off.

I learnt to sew my doll's clothes with these long threads of hair, which Dad put in bundles up in the rafters of the stable.

Two
Stock horse: champion of the outback

A well-bred stock horse has more mustering sense than a human and can go where vehicles cannot. A good horse is
 poetry in motion, a lot quieter and less smelly than a motorbike, and picks its own path through rocks and ruts, leaving the rider free to watch the stock.

Despite those attributes, stock horses took a beating in northern Australia from the late 1970s until very recently. Their dominance was undermined by government subsidies for helicopter mustering during the intense BTEC programme which required all cattle and buffalo—feral, cleanskin and branded—to be eradicated or tested for blue-tongue, brucellosis and tuberculosis so export livestock markets could expand. The urgency and scale of the mustering of the north meant the horse, in many areas, literally couldn't keep up. Jackaroos on some stations no longer needed to know how to ride. Horses languished in paddocks as rocky ridges, creek beds and thick bush were scoured from the air. Many were sold off for pet food, and some were exported.

In 1978, during the BTEC period, I spent three months in the saddle on a buffalo quarantine station at Adelaide River where animals were tested and quietened prior to export to New Guinea and Indonesia. I found myself teamed up with a tall chestnut and our job in the cool early morning hours was to bring in mobs of buffalo cows and calves from distant paddocks to the yards.

As we weaved through gum saplings, in and out of dappled shade, on the tail of buffalo determined to escape, it soon became obvious that the horse under me knew more about Northern Territory mustering than I did. My expertise was on southern horses trained to take orders. A few wrong decisions by me about where to place ourselves on the mob of cranky buffalo and Legs, a Territory-bred horse, persistently ignored all further commands. It didn't matter what I suggested—stop, wheel right, left—Legs had other ideas. 'You pig-headed old fool,' I shouted occasionally when I reckoned he was way off beam. But we did turn the mob and get them yarded despite their best efforts to return to their swamp.

Buffalo hate being moved in the heat of the day, so a team of us had started work at 3 am to bring in a mob for another round of blue-tongue and tuberculosis testing.

Where I was, our horses were our most useful tools. They kept the stock quiet, but they could take off into a flat gallop with the click of the tongue and flick of a heel, to head off escapees. They would shoulder bolting animals to turn them. They would stand bravely still in the face of a charging buffalo female. My mount's calmness and good sense won my trust, so much so that when a grumpy cow hit his side, and her two sharply pointed horns poked chestnut skin at elbow and flank, between which hung my defenceless right leg, I felt no panic. The horse did what no motorbike ever could by snorting and facing the cranky cow, which walked off psychologically defeated.

The other aspect of my job was to handle twenty newly broken stock-horse fillies booked to sail to the Sepik Valley, New Guinea, on the underdeck of a rough, flat-bottomed barge with a consignment of buffalo. Of famous Victoria River Downs blood, they were reputed to have been sired by classy French and English thoroughbreds. Part of the ethos of landowners in the early days was to have fine horses, win country races and be the envy of the neighbours. The clean long necks, intelligent heads and athletic bodies of my charges certainly indicated good breeding. However, these stylish young horses had been broken in the rough way and freaked out badly when even a friendly hand was put on them. They didn't even know they had an offside. All work and contact had obviously been only from the left, or near, side. I set to work using techniques based on the Jeffery method to win their trust and allow them to be handled all over. Within a short time they ceased cowering in the far corner of the yard when I approached and gradually stood to be caught. The wild look in their eyes disappeared and they looked more like horses that could be walked onto a boat and penned in cramped quarters without going berserk.

I saw them just before the barge loosed its ropes for what was to be a horrendously rough passage across Torres Strait. I was proud that they were unfazed by the unfamiliar noisy, dark underdeck atmosphere. They arrived without incident in the Sepik Valley where they were to start work as stock horses and be involved in a breeding programme. I was devastated to learn later that my calm and pretty mares were speared and eaten by hungry tribespeople from surrounding regions.

Revival: the stock horse returns to restore calm to the north

Cycles turn, times change, and so it happens that once again famous old Victoria River Downs is among prominent Northern Territory stations which are re-embracing the stock horse.

The big, tough, bruising ways of the BTEC days have passed and, in their place, gentleness and calm are coming to station country. Australia's disease-free livestock now needs to be stress- free and unbruised. Bruising caused by rough handling or because animals are nervous and hurl themselves into yard railings can destroy large sections of carcase. Stress causes the meat to be tough and unpalatable.

One station owner who has embraced the gentleness revolution and put stock horses back on a pedestal is Heytesbury Beef's principal, Janet Holmes à Court. With eight stations in the Northern Territory and Queensland, one of which is Victoria River Downs, not only has Mrs Holmes à Court directed that more horses be used, but she has instigated Australia's biggest breeding programme of registered Australian Stock Horses. This breed is renowned for its stock sense, ability to work long hours in the heat without water, comfortable paces, intelligence and coolness.

Out of deference to those little Victoria River Downs mares that had met such a grisly fate, and fascinated by what the powerful and forward-thinking Mrs Holmes à Court was doing, I travelled 530 kilometres south-west of Katherine to arrive at the brightly lit doorstep of Mount Sanford Station one balmy night in September.

Jane and Paul Stone manage the 2748 square kilometre station with its 25 staff. They run 26,000 Brahman cattle, mostly bound for the live export market. Jane, 38, a keen polocrosse player and horserider all her life, oversees the station's horse breeding and training programme. The Stones' passion for the Australian Stock Horse breed has established Mount Sanford as the breeding and training depot for the thousand or so stock horses now at work across Heytesbury's 33,000 square kilometres of holdings, stretching across the Kimberley, Victoria River Downs and Barkly regions. A total of around 200,000 head of cattle graze land which ranges from harsh and stony to wet and fertile, depending on seasons and locations.

Gonged out of bed by the cook at 6.30 for breakfast, to the added sounds of neighing horses, screeching peacocks and squawking parrots, we were soon in the homestead's horse yards where Jane's polocrosse team and Paul's campdrafters enjoyed lucerne hay, chaff and grain. Injured workhorses had their wounds dressed, injections were given and they got a friendly pat.

Stock horse: champion of the outback

At the main yards half a kilometre away, already, at 7.30, the first of the day's pupils were in the two round yards cooled and shaded by high brush roofs and beautiful flame, mahogany and rain trees. Immediately, I recognised the same clean lines and intelligent heads that my Adelaide River fillies had. Jane readily confirmed that many of the mares in the Mount Sanford programme indeed had come from Victoria River Downs and would have been related to those I had handled almost 25 years before. I was chuffed.

Unlike the methods used when my little horses were broken, the whole philosophy at Mount Sanford is based on gentleness. Even the most difficult student is treated with respect, voices are kept low and movements smooth. Martin Oakes, chief horse breaker, and assistant, Tom Curtain, spend about a week getting the 'fright' out of every horse by carefully bagging them all over, by flapping plastic on the end of poles over their bodies and by rattling tin cans. Martin also gets the horses used to carrying a fearsome home-made scarecrow and 40 kilogram sandbags on their backs before he finally rides them and despatches them to their allotted station and new rider.

'It is time consuming and a lot of effort but if it is going to save someone getting kicked, it's worth it,' Martin, a breaker for nine years, says. Because the character of every horse is so different, Martin says he likes to think through what methods suit each animal. Quiet, intense, tall and lanky, he was brought up on a dairy farm and always loved horses. He spent a year in the United States working with trainers of cutting horses and then spent four years at Stanbroke Pastoral Company, the biggest landholder in Australia, which has about 3000 workhorses. He continues lunging a chestnut gelding, turning it with the flick of the rope, working calmly and silently, giving respect and earning it. Ears flick attentively, the neck arches and the gleaming body relaxes. Using classic Jeffery techniques of advance and retreat, challenge and reward, as well as methods learnt from old timers around campfires and cattleyards, Martin says he never tires of turning a raw, frightened animal into an effective and quiet worker.

In another round yard, its slab timber sides padded with rubber from old conveyor belts to protect hide and limb, Tom Curtain, 22, works on just the eighth horse in his breaking career, which began two months before when his horsemanship skills had attracted attention in the station's stock camp.

A flashy bay with four white socks and a big blaze is being introduced to the joys of a mop. Tom is attempting to touch the horse all over with the terrifying object and getting a series of snorts and frantic leaps for his trouble. When the mop head manages to make contact with the horse's rump, Tom retreats and lets the horse think about the experience. 'He'll realise it didn't hurt him,' says Tom, who takes off his hat and leans against a railing to have a yarn. His pupil stands still, looking at him intently, its ears moving quizzically and tail swishing gently. Tom, unhurried and at ease, talks of his love for the animals which he's been round all his life since growing up in Kingaroy, Queensland. 'The biggest thrill is getting a horse from this stage,' he says, nodding towards the horse which until a few minutes before had been whirling around the yard away from the mop, 'to seeing someone else riding him. It makes all the time in the yard trying to get into his mind worthwhile.'

Tom resumes the mop treatment and soon there are white legs lashing out ferociously and a muscled body propelling itself into vigorous bucks and rears. The docile horse that had watched Tom with fascination while he yarned now gives an impression of wanting to kill him. 'There's no real safe zone,' Tom says as he keeps the mop head questing for contact with the rich red flank. Little by little he makes progress. Before long, the flashy colt branded on its rump with Heytesbury's distinctive bull's head and its ASH registration number, stands for a pat and a rub while the dreaded mop, which it has grown to tolerate, lies

Stock horse: champion of the outback

benignly on the sandy floor. 'He'll be a good quiet horse,' says Tom, going on to explain that horses going into stock camps after their two weeks of training needed to be unruffled and calm, even if flying plastic bags wrapped themselves around their legs or a helicopter suddenly landed beside them.

'They have to realise that there's nothing to fear except fear itself,' Tom says with a smile, 'and that anything that happens is quite normal.'

Later, in the golden glow of evening, I watched as the six horses that had graduated from the round yards just two days before were brought in from the paddock. Their new 'owners', selected from the ten young stock workers living at Mount Sanford, fussed over them, grooming them and picking up their feet. Saddles were girthed up, bridles adjusted and boots gently put in stirrups. The horses were ridden out into the still hot evening, slashed with the long shadows of Mount Sanford's numerous trees. It was Saturday night and almost seven o'clock by the time they were rubbed down and turned out. Lawrence, 19, who had started to ride just a year ago, scratched his new mate, Maverick, between the eyes. A special sort of bond had formed already. His friend Sam, also 19, was murmuring sweet nothings to newly named Mambo. Such is the glorious isolation of station life that two handsome, charming young men can be found unself-consciously schmoozing to their horses in the moonlight in the yards instead of downing beers in a pub. The dinner gong interrupted the scene and the horses ambled off to their lucerne hay.

Everywhere you look at Mount Sanford, the resurgence of working horses is apparent. A big mob of registered mares and foals run with resident $14,000 stallion Ocean Demise, bred in New South Wales and carrying the illustrious genes of Cadet Abbey and revered sire Warrenbri Romeo. Jane checks each mob several times a week, driving around vast paddocks looking for individual mares who might be foaling or injured.

She hugs the gleaming stallion whose docile nature, solid build and intelligence are already a part of a crop of handsome foals and yearlings. The country where the horses run is tough and stony, but after three good seasons the native Mitchell and Flinders grasses, Queensland blue grass, spinifex, cane grass and bachelor button cover the black basalt soil with a thick thatch. Eucalypts such as snappy gum, whitebark, blue gum, bloodwood, cabbage gum and silver box soften the rich, rolling country and shade numerous water-filled creeks.

Mount Sanford has 90 brood mares, of which 45 are registered. All have been successful working horses, selected for temperament, hardiness and stock sense. The stock horse breed was recognised as such in 1972 by a group of enthusiasts who recognised that the blend of Timor Pony, Clydesdale, Thoroughbred, Arab and Waler had produced something pretty special. Jane's father, Jim Ramage, was one of the breed's original classifiers. It is little wonder that Jane carries that same family passion for the breed, a passion that urged her six years ago to convince Heytesbury to centralise the reviving horse breeding programme under her supervision. Jane now classifies the beef group's mares and buys in stallions, organises weaning, breaking, feeding and budgets. She has a feed bill of over $27,000 because she insists on weanlings and workhorses having hay from New South Wales and a grain mix from Victoria. Freight costs are equal to the cost of feed.

Each year, some 45 two year olds are sold for $1500 to Heytesbury stations—Victoria River Downs, Moolooloo, Pigeon Hole, Flora Valley, Birrindidu, all in the Victoria River Downs region, and Eva Downs and Anthony Lagoon on the Barkly Tableland. Elite mares are then bought back at the age of eight to be mated and continue their lives as brood mares.

Work for the newly broken young horses generally involves plenty of walking and tailing stock to build up their strength, fitness and confidence slowly.

Stock horse: champion of the outback

In the four years since the first of the horses bred by Jane were sent to work, stock riders have been full of praise. According to Jane, they are appreciating the difference in having well-bred and trained horses. All stockmen have three horses each.

Another small mob of mares runs with a $3000 grey stallion named Yarranoo Tarmac, whose dam Tara is the dam of leading New South Wales sires Silver Minstrel and Yarranoo Stroller. Jane says although Tarmac seems to be sexually rather coy, never having been seen mating in daylight, he manages to be a prolific breeder. She proved the point by using an ultrasound testing kit to confirm the pregnancies of several mares brought to Tarmac by outside owners to produce cool-headed, highly athletic polocrosse and campdraft horses.

Nearby, 45 stylish two year olds enjoy their morning rations. They are next in line for the round yards and will find themselves in stock camps within months.

Some of these smart-looking youngsters are by the station's third stallion, Toganbah Wheels, which was bought for $10,000.

All 26,000 cattle at Mount Sanford are mustered twice a year—for sale, or for weaning, cutting, branding and dehorning—into any of three huge yard complexes, the furthest of which is 100 kilometres from the homestead.

Heytesbury Beef concentrates on Brahmans, all of which are selected for calm temperament to suit the live shipping trade to the Middle East and Asia. Accordingly, instead of needing quietening prior to shipping, Heytesbury cattle are loaded straight on board and are renowned for settling down and eating without any fuss.

'During BTEC, they didn't use a lot of horses because of the government subsidy for choppers to test disease quickly,' Paul Stone, 38, explains. 'A lot of people got rid of horses to the meatworks or shot them. A lot of good breeding went.'

A generation of young people also missed out knowing how to ride. Instead of virtually growing up in the saddle as in days past, they are now schooled by qualified instructors, encouraged to get involved in horse sports and learn how to work closely with their horses to get maximum results.

'You need the horses to keep the cattle nice and quiet,' says Paul, who when he is not at work is an A-grade campdraft competitor.

Helicopters handle the major part of the muster, but then the horses come in to mop up. A lot of cows and calves are left behind because they can't keep up, and cunning old mickey bulls and cleanskins also know how to hide from the choppers. Paul and his workers on horseback use 'coachers', quiet mobs, to collect them and bring them into the yards. It is skilled work, and well-trained, unflappable horses make the job much easier.

'It's bred into the horses to watch cattle,' said Paul. 'And when you start getting good horses, and start feeding them, you don't need so many. We reckon one good horse is worth two average horses. We also like them to be absolutely quiet. Janet pushes this for safety. She doesn't like to see her people hurt.

'We also find that horses bred on these places are a lot better for chasing cattle. They have grown up as foals on the rocks, in rough terrain, so it's just part of what they know. Outside horses don't handle the rocks, the black soil, the holes, as well as the home-bred horses.'

Paul, born in Winton, Queensland, grew up with horses. After schooling at Charters Towers he returned to station life as a ringer and eventually got a job at Mount Sanford in 1989 when Peter Sherwin owned it. He and Jane, who was from nearby Ivanhoe station, met at a polocrosse match.

To boost profitability, the best of the horses bred at Mount Sanford are sold to promote the breeding programme. An outstanding four-year-old polocrosse mare had recently been sold for $5000. Others have brought $3000 and $2000 after being seen in Jane's polocrosse team or Paul's campdraft team.

On the lush lawns surrounding the newly built, well-designed corrugated iron homestead, with double doors opening to its wide surrounding verandah, there is a monument to the former tough and rough days of station life. It is an old bronco rail, saved from an outstation to remind everyone of the days when bronco horses held calves for branding and castrating. In the gentle warmth of evening, with the birds settling into the trees along the creek, those cruel days for man and beast seem appropriately far behind. I ran my hands over the worn timbers of the sturdy structure against which many thousands of struggling calves had been pressed after being roped and dragged, plunging and bellowing, by a heavily built clumper horse. Things have certainly moved on from those tough and bruising days.

A B 'Banjo' Paterson
'The Man from Snowy River' [Excerpt]

He was hard and tough and wiry—just the sort that won't say die—
There was courage in his quick impatient tread;
And he bore the badge of gameness in his bright and fiery eye,
And the proud and lofty carriage of his head.

Where the stock horse is still king
Carolyn McConnel

I always say the only good thing about living in this southern part of Queensland is that the country is too rough to be able to use anything but horses for mustering, so this must be one of the few parts of the country where the stock horse is still king.

We were talking to a noted breeder of stock horses not so long ago and he asked where we sourced our horses, as we have over 30 working horses and kids' ponies on the place. He was horrified to hear that I got them from anywhere: failed pony clubbers, failed endurance horses, you name it, it's here in the horse paddock—even an old dressage horse, although I confess he isn't a lot of use, except for droving a mob along. If someone has a sad story about how they don't want to 'dog' a horse but it's no use for what they want, it usually ends up here. Most horses enjoy stock work, and so long as they will try, I will too, and as that same breeder of stock horses said, 'It's amazing how quiet your cattle get when you only have just-so horses.' He's quite right, as you don't look for trouble or try to teach your cattle a lesson if you are not sure your horse is up to the task.

We run 2000 head of mostly Droughtmaster cattle on rough country with our just-so horses. In fact, my newest one is a failed pony clubber, an ugly palomino gelding who is taking to cattle work like a duck to water. If I can just find the brakes, he will be great, as he's certainly enthusiastic. It's just that he hates stopping, but oh well, we'll get there.

We bought a new paddock a few years ago—high country on both sides of a big valley. The tops are timbered and full of lantana-covered gullies and there is a lot of broken ground on the sides of the hills. Until a year ago, the bullocks had been pretty good; a few short each muster, but we'd drive out afterwards and so long as we could see them, it was okay—they were there, that was the main thing. At the end of the selling season, we'd try for a clean muster, as it's a growing paddock, and we'd move the two-year-old bullocks into the fattening paddocks then, and put the yearling steers in to grow.

Well, the clean muster last year was still a few short—and come to think of it, the last muster the year before was too. So that meant there were upwards of twenty head of three and four year olds in there. We mustered the paddocks and saw the ferals, as we had come to know them, take off for the hilltops.

Stock horse: champion of the outback

We moved all the cattle we could muster easily, and decided that tomorrow it was on for young and old.

We had three good horses that could really handle this rough country and they were spelled and ready to go. Vick is a brown mare. We'd poddied her after her gallant mother broke a foreleg. She goes back to the old Glenhaughton bloodlines and is not much bigger than a galloway, but clean-legged and will go all day and still be ready to gallop at the end as we yard a mob. The station hand rides her.

John's mare is Princess, a tall clean-legged but heavy-bodied mare with a baldy blaze. She'll get along with her head up all day and be up and down the hills with never a care and never a foot put wrong. She probably has a dash of Arab, going by the head and the way she holds herself. We bought her not far away up near Kilcoy, so she is used to the hills.

My mare is Mad Moll. She is a scruffy, hairy-hocked, Queensland itch-ridden bay with a blaze and three socks. She is no beauty, with her mad white-ringed eye on her offside, and a temper to match that of any other horse—she is the queen of the mob, and no-one dares forget it. From near Kilcoy, too, she is bred in the purple, a pedigree that reeks of top show ponies that goes years back, with brothers and sisters sitting snugly in show stables in many parts of the state. Poor old Moll, she was born with the mad eye, and the itch attacked in the first summer of life, so the breeders were glad to sell her very cheaply as a stock pony—anything to get her off the place, I think. She and I have been together for a good few years now, as she was only just over two when I bought her. We had some battles royal in those years, but now she is as reliable and as loyal as any horse, so long as it's me on board. The little devil won't take kindly to anyone else, and although we have tried other riders at times, she will take off and leap around like a maniac until they are only too happy to get off her. With me, she is lively, but works on words rather than reins. With a rough muster coming up, there is no other horse I would rather be astride.

The big day comes and we wait until about 10 to try to get the cattle off the hills and down around the waters. Then we ride as quietly as possible into the paddock, with a mob of quiet bullocks as coachers. The mob is down on the camp on the flat, but a big Droughtmaster bullock soon sees us and is on his feet. The next moment, the mob is galloping towards the hills. You just lean forward and try not to think of the rough ground you are flying over and the lantana that is scratching your arms as you get beside the leaders. They swing away for a moment but soon turn uphill again, and although they are tonguing badly, they don't seem to want to stop at all. Moll is a lather of sweat, but still galloping and pulling like a steam train whenever I try to steady her. She won't listen to my cries of 'Steady! Steady!', which usually slow her down. My arms are like jelly, anyway—and I have no idea just where we are anymore as we wheel the big bullock again. This time he stops, and a few more catch up and stand watching me with tongues lolling and sides heaving, while I try and see where we are and where the men are.

John has a quieter mob on the flat and is pushing them into the mob of coachers, so I try to get mine to start down to them. Soon we are galloping again. I think we are slowly heading down, but we are still high on the ridges and going backwards and forwards across them—but I am determined not to let them get any higher. Finally the big bullock falls over a log, and when he gets up, it's as though he suddenly sees the light, for they turn, and with him limping in the lead, they take one of the many pads down the slope towards where the other mob is now standing.

Moll is still alert and watching them as we follow, ever ready to spring into a gallop if they try to turn back. The fight has gone out of them, though, and they are happy to merge with the other mob. Vick has obviously been galloping too, as she is sweaty and scratched by the lantana, and all the horses have skin off their lower legs. Princess has over-reached and is bleeding quite badly, but is still up on her toes and ready for anything those cattle might throw at us.

I would like to check Moll, but John says we must yard the cattle now before they get a second wind. So we move them off towards the yards, and as they jog along, we keep an eye on the wings. Only one bullock has a half-hearted go at heading off and all three mares immediately break into a canter, ready for anything. Noting they are so keen, he soon decides the mob is a safer place to be and gets right into the centre of it, and stays there until we have the gates shut on them. Only then can we dismount. Legs are like strands of spaghetti and our arms are a mess, with bleeding scratches. My hat went somewhere in the hills and I don't even remember it being torn off, although I have a good scratch down my cheek, so it must have gone then.

We unsaddle and check the mares over. Plenty of skin off and a few deeper cuts on their legs, but other than Princess's over-reach, we have come out of it pretty well. Once they are trucked home and the cuts that need it are treated and sprayed, they are let go.

I am constantly amazed at how after a long hard afternoon like that, they still have the energy to canter down the paddock, neighing to their mates about how they finally yarded the feral bullocks that all the others had missed.

We had yarded all but three of the feral bullocks—and we finally got them a week later. They stayed in the yards at the homestead on a grain ration for 100 days. Despite their very uncertain temperaments and all sorts of conformation faults, they all graded Jap Ox at the meatworks, so we were pleased to see them go. The mares suffered no ill effects from such a mad gallop and were not even noticeably stiff the next day—although the same could not be said for their riders!

A wagon on the track
Ron Kerr

I cannot be sure when I was first put on a horse but I could ride at any pace on horseback before my first trip in a motor car at the age of six years. At the age of eight, I could handle four-in-hand in a wagonette. My biggest problem was putting the collars on the wagon horses, and I carried a square four gallon kero tin on the nearside of the wagon, which I would use to stand on to get myself high enough to do up the straps on the collars and put the hames over the collars, onto which the trace chains were hooked.

Most times two horses were used to pull the wagon where the country was flat or there were no steep creeks or hills. There were a lot of times where there wasn't a road or a track and no regular creek crossing and it was these sorts of places, or steep hills, four horses were yoked to the wagonette.

The brakes of the wagonette were applied by pressing a lever forward with your foot, and this worked two wooden blocks against the two near wheels. Also there was a single pole running up between the two horses closest to the wagon. On the front of this pole, two straps were attached, one attached to each pole horse's collar. These pole straps are used for turning the wagon, and also when going downhill. The pole horses can be held back by the reins, which in turn let the pole horses hold back on the collar straps from the end of the pole, giving added braking to the wagon. In my case, only being eight years old, I never could put a lot of weight on the brake lever and, most of the time, the two pole horses would do more than their share of holding the wagon back. Dad had rigged the brake pedal so that I could stand up and apply the brake with a rope attached to it, which I could use to tie the brake down hard.

One time, I had to get down a long, steep hill without much road to follow. I waited until Dad came along with the cattle.

He rode around the top of the hill until he found a suitable log, one that had an end that was spiky with roots. Driving the wagon alongside, we chained the small end to the rear axle of the wagon. This worked quite well as an anchor on steep hills, as the horses were up in their collars most of the time. Other times, going down into creeks that were steep, both rear wheels would be chained, and the horses would pull with the rear wheels skidding.

When we came to set up camp, the horse tailer would tend to the horses' needs before going off with one of the wagon horses to drag back wood for the camp. Complete dead trees could be snigged to the camp site and would last all night.

What I liked about droving in my early days was meeting other drovers. Some would be heading out to pick up a mob. Others would have just finished, but whenever two camps came together, you knew there would be campfire yarns that night. Most times there would be small talk about the weather or the feed ahead and behind, as well as good watering places. But always the talk turned to horses, and this is what interested me.

One would only have to listen to this campfire talk to learn about horses. I often wondered why my father had so many different types of horses in the plant, and the many campfire yarns soon made it clear that every breed of horse had its purpose in the camp.

The night horses, on night watch, were lightly built, of racing breed, and most were grey, blue, baldy-faced or piebald. They were smart on their feet and quick off the mark. I learnt that their light or broken colour was so they could be seen at night by cattle, so they didn't bob up out of the dark and start cattle off their camp. For the same reason, the night watchman would sing while riding around cattle at night. These night horses would only be used for night work.

In the wagon days, half of the plant horses would be quarter-draught horses or hairy-legged clumpers, also referred to as utility horses. They could be used in the wagon or as saddle horses. Sometimes they were called good mud horses, bronco horses or long distance horses, meaning their trotting ability could get you over a long distance in a day by trot and walk, the most natural pace of a horse.

If a horse got sore shoulders from the collars, it could be used as a saddle horse while its shoulders healed, and if it had a sore from the saddle, it could be worked in the wagon. These became very useful horses, and nothing looked better than a well-matched pair of wagon horses.

One time, I was driving the wagon and cooking. I was ahead of the cattle, waiting for them to come to dinner camp, where the cattle would spend the hot part of the day on a waterhole before moving on to night camp that evening. There was a railway line running parallel with the stock route and along the line was very good feed. As I had plenty of time to put in before the cattle came, I hobbled both wagon horses—and they didn't take long to find green feed.

When the cattle were safely camping and the rest of the plant horses were at the waterhole, Dad told the horse tailer to go down the line and bring back the two hobbled horses, so they could be watered before being reyoked to the wagon. The horse tailer came back half an hour later carrying the hobbles. He told us both horses were dead. Dad rode down to see the horses and reported they had been poisoned. We found out a few days later that the grass had been sprayed with arsenic. It was a bitter lesson in man-made hazards.

Beauty and the beast
Hod Cay

Tucked away in the mountains of the north-west slopes and plains of New South Wales, Arizona was a wild, rugged, beautiful

Stock horse: champion of the outback

property of 4000 acres. Precipitous mountains formed the eastern and western boundaries, protecting a hidden valley that ran the length of the property. The slopes were densely covered by cypress pine, but the floor was wide and less heavily timbered, with semi-permanent waterholes scattered along Maules Creek. When we purchased Arizona in 1956, the previous owner told me that mobs of sheep, unshorn and wild, ran freely about the precipitous ranges. There was even supposed to be a brumby stallion haunting the run. I dismissed the story of the stallion as fanciful.

The first few months of ownership were spent in the saddle, getting the hang of the place. It was not a property you could run from a deckchair on the verandah. I noticed sheep tracks in the hills and occasionally caught sight of long-woolled sheep on the cliff tops, but thankfully no long-tailed, yellow-toothed stallion.

The horse I chose to ride one winter morning almost 40 years ago was Beauty. And just as well, too, or I wouldn't be writing this yarn in the sunny backyard of my Coonabarabran home. The peaceful autumn scene surrounding me here couldn't be more different from the explosive events that happened unexpectedly that day long ago.

Every stockman at one time in his life rides a horse that stands out in his memory as the best he has ever ridden, or for that matter, that anyone else has ever ridden. Beauty was that horse, a brown gelding of 15 hands. Bred in the high hills of the Upper Hunter, he really was a crackerjack. He came from a famous line of campdrafters and polo ponies, well known from the Royal to the campfires of the outback. Well mannered as befitted his breeding, he could, at a touch, change from a smooth canter to a blurring gallop that on a cold morning brought tears to the eyes. He could change direction and spin so fast on his power-packed hindquarters that it brought the best out of his rider to stay with him.

I had set out as usual for a day's mustering, lunch in my saddlebag, quart pot buckled to the dees, a pipe in my mouth, and not a care in the world. It would have been about 6 miles from the house, down near the sawmill paddock, when Beauty snorted, and stopped—neck arched, ears pricked, muscles tense. I touched him lightly with my heels, but his only response was a quivering of bunched muscles.

I must have been woolgathering, probably thinking about some sheep coming up for sale. All that changed in a split second. I looked above Beauty's pricked ears just in time to see a long-maned, yellow-toothed half-clumper stallion burst out of the scrub 30 yards away. Ears flat, neck outstretched, hooves the size of dinner plates. He was moving like a tornado, straight for us.

No doubt my mouth dropped open, but fortunately experience clamped my legs hard against Beauty's sides. Just as well, or I'd have been left sitting in the air. Beauty spun of his own accord and was away like a flash. I heard snapping teeth and the stallion's screech just where I'd been a moment ago. I risked a glance and ducked as iron-hard hooves slashed through the air like pile drivers. Stallions hate geldings and will kill them if given the chance. On top of that, I think that stallion had it in for me as well.

Beauty headed up the creek as if a fiend out of hell was after him, as indeed it was. To be caught was to die. We headed through shiny bush and cypress pine, seeking the more open country along the creek. The noise behind us would have frightened braver hearts than mine. It really was a case of ride as I had never ridden before. Beauty was magnificent, sure-footed as a cat and quick as a possum; he dodged in and out of that scrub with always a yard or two to spare.

The creek loomed in front of us and I dropped the reins on his neck. His muscles bunched and we were in the air. I had a brief glimpse of rocks lining the creek bed, and then he landed sure as a cat on the other side. After that, the stallion had no chance. Beauty would have left Phar Lap behind that day.

I never saw the stallion again, which was just as well for him. From then on, I carried an old army 303 with me whenever I was working that end, and would have used it without hesitation. Nevertheless, I was not sorry that he had cleared out. In his own way he was grand, though dangerous, and I had the feeling, like a lot of ex-servicemen, that to live and let live wasn't a bad idea. Beauty and I were together for many years after that. Arizona was eventually sold and I went back to managing The Braes at Manilla. One shearing time at smoko, a friend of mine rode up with the sad news that Beauty had died of snake bite. I'd lost

the best horse that I'd ever known.

Bush justice
Patty Cahill

We were on a cattle muster in the station country of Western Australia, north-west of Kalgoorlie. Along with four stockmen, I'd been sent out to find some wild maverick cattle and bring them back to the main yards at the homestead. Some of these cattle had roamed the station for years without ever seeing a human being before. So our task was a formidable one.

Pilot wasn't my usual mount, but I ended up with him through luck of the draw. Terry, his larrikin owner from a neighbouring station, had brought the stylish-looking brown gelding with its four white socks and blaze along as a spare horse. Terry enjoyed taking the mickey out of me and I noted the sly grin on his face as I rode off. No-one told me then about Pilot's unconventional mustering style.

As we rode along the rock-crested hills and later across the expansive lake country, a mob of seven renegade cows was spotted hiding in the midday tree shadows. We broke into a gallop and surrounded them. The cows were fiercely wild and charged at our horses and then tried to break away into the safety of the tangled scrub. We blocked their escape efforts and slowly hazed them in the direction of the yards.

Sometimes they grew stroppy and renewed their efforts to break free of us. With lowered heads, these lean brindled cows would lunge at our horses and try to gore them with their sharp, pointed horns. One horse was lifted off the ground by a cow that ran under his belly. Pilot, however, gave me no concerns, and I forgot Terry's strange grin.

After we'd travelled a few erratic miles through the prickly bush, one old red cow with long horns decided she wanted to quit the mob.

She flicked her white-blazed head, snorted a warning and then galloped off into the heavy undergrowth of bush and stunted trees. While one rider held up the other six cows, the rest of us went after the red one. She galloped for a long time before we bailed her up in a small clearing. Her blood was hot from the chase and she snorted and pawed the ground in fury, and violently charged anything that moved. After a while she grew cunning and stood facing us belligerently, refusing to move off in any direction.

To divert her back towards the other cattle, one by one the men began to run in towards the cow's head at a flat gallop. As they rode in close, the cow charged. The riders then wheeled their horses around at the last moment and galloped off in the desired direction. The cow would angrily chase after them for a short distance. In this spasmodic way, they led her closer and closer to the other cattle. The entire performance resembled a bullfight as the jackeroos rushed in like mounted matadors and then spun their agile horses around in a swirl of dust. Each time, the cow's horns narrowly missed grazing the horses' flashing legs and swirling bodies.

Stock horse: champion of the outback

I decided that I should take a turn as matador and pushed Pilot forward. He responded eagerly and ran directly at the cow, who stood with a menacing glare near a mulga tree. As we neared her head, I pulled Pilot to the right in an effort to swerve away. There was no response. He continued to gallop flat tack towards the cow. The more I sawed on the reins, the harder he pulled.

Just when I thought we'd collide with the cow, Pilot suddenly applied the brakes. What happened next was beyond my comprehension at the time. Suddenly Pilot's head and neck disappeared and his body swung violently around. Later I was told that he'd pulled up short and ducked his head low between his forelegs. Then he whipped his hindquarters around and tried to kick the cow square in the forehead with both hind legs. Unfortunately, he missed. The cow bellowed with rage and lunged at the horse. Pilot jerked his head upright and spun away from the crazy cow. He plunged through the scrub, dodging the low-branched trees and belly-high bushes. The cow was right on his tail.

Meanwhile, I had been thrown halfway out of the saddle when Pilot had unexpectedly spun around and kicked. In my panic, I screamed and grabbed hold of his neck. As he galloped haphazardly through the bush, my grip loosened and I slowly slipped further down on his left shoulder. I'd lost my right stirrup, and tried to hook my right leg around the cantle of the saddle. My efforts failed and I continued my slide towards the ground. My head was jarred by the thrusting motion of Pilot's fast-moving legs. The bushes and sky swept by my line of vision at a dizzying pace. Yet I was still aware that the cow remained in hot pursuit and I was too frightened to loosen my tenacious hold. Finally a big mulga tree loomed in front of us. I saw my chance to bail out. As Pilot surged past it, I released my hold on him and leaped towards the trunk of the tree, hoping it might offer protection if the cow charged.

Fortunately the other riders had managed to gallop in and distract the cow. Somehow they manoeuvred her away from my prone body under the tree. Pilot galloped off into the distance, as did the cow. Shakily I stood up and dusted myself off.

'What the blazes happened?' I asked the others who had gathered round to see if I was injured.

Terry chuckled to himself, then explained Pilot's habit of kicking cows. 'I reckon I forgot to tell you about it beforehand.'

'I reckon you did,' I replied with sarcasm, and the other riders laughed while I shook my head in disgust.

When my horse had been retrieved, we tracked the red cow and headed her back to the original mob. After her wild chase, she was more docile this time and it wasn't long before we met up with the other cattle and drove them the short distance to the main yards.

On the way, Terry, who was taking it easy and not paying attention to where he was going, got knocked out of his saddle by a low-lying tree limb. As I laughed heartily, I realised fair justice had been exacted.

A B 'Banjo' Paterson
'The Man from Snowy River' [excerpt]

For the bushmen love hard riding where the wild bush horses are,
And the stock-horse snuffs the battle with delight.

Whopper
Gregory Mitchell

I can see the bay horse now as I saw him in the Gulf country all those years ago. He was over 16 hands with a blaze on his face and three white stockings. Most of his breeding was thoroughbred, but somewhere there was a splash of draught, as his massive build and hairy fetlocks showed.

I had arrived at the mustering camp unexpectedly and none of my regular horses was there, so the boss picked me out a team from the spare ones. I was horrified when he selected the big bay for me. He looked clumsy and was one of a draft of badly broken horses sent up from the company's other property.

I protested, and the boss was sympathetic to a degree. He too had his doubts. 'Just get him quiet enough to throw ropes off and we'll use him as a bronco horse,' he told me.

Bronco horses were heavy animals used to drag cattle up for branding. Speed was not important, but they had to be strong. Someone christened him Whopper, and the name had stuck. In fact, the rest of the camp was having a great laugh at my expense. I think they were relieved that they had not copped him.

There were no yards at this camp and it was a case of saddle him up and mount in the open. As I hit the saddle, Whopper started bucking. He was one of the roughest buckjumpers I have ever been on. I don't think I found the offside iron, and soon lost the nearside one. Dazed and shaken, I was on the pommel when the horse stopped bucking. I was lucky to still be there at all and did not kid myself that riding skill had saved me.

There was no more bad behaviour that day, although the horse was terribly green and one-sided in the mouth. He took to stock work immediately and, to my surprise, was remarkably agile. He had brains, and used them, even if I was not overworking mine. I still had reservations, though, and lived for the day when I could hand him back.

Whopper was an affectionate horse and, much to everyone's hilarity, would mooch about me like a big dog. Even while I was trying to dislike him, he won me over.

He only ever bucked twice with me. On the second occasion, we were poking along half asleep behind some cattle. Something frightened him and the volcano erupted again. Before the fright subsided, he had thrown me up and caught me twice, and again both stirrups were gone when he stopped. If he had been really trying, I would never have lasted the distance with him. He was right out of my class, but fortunately lacked the killer instinct.

Despite this, he had plenty of talent and seemed to have a knack of sizing up the situation. I was riding him one day when I threw a scrubber, intending to tie it down with my belt. However, the belt became stuck in the loops of my pants and I could not get it while struggling with my captive. Then I spotted the neck strap on Whopper where the hobbles were carried. I called to him and, step by step, he advanced to me. It is hard to get a horse close to a fallen animal, especially if it is struggling, but he seemed to sense the urgency. Hesitantly, he came forward, until I was able to reach up and get the strap off him. The penny finally dropped and I started to realise what a good horse I had.

Working with wild cattle, you do a lot of throwing, and when a beast is let up it will often charge anyone in sight. The first time Whopper was charged, he nearly gave me heart failure. He side-stepped the horns, spun like lightning, hit the surprised bullock with his shoulder and knocked him flying. A stock horse that takes to knocking over cattle has to know what it is doing. Many a man has been killed when a horse has hit the beast too far back and knocked it under its own hooves. But Whopper knew instinctively where to hit them.

When throwing wild cattle, it is safest to work in pairs, with one man staying mounted to protect the thrower, in case things go wrong. Scrubbers can be vicious and are not like the cattle you see in the more settled areas. Consequently Whopper was soon in great demand. When a thrower fell, or lost his grip on the tail of the beast, or when the beast was being let up, Whopper and I would be there to knock down the enraged animal if it tried to attack the man before he remounted.

Stock horse: champion of the outback

It is not surprising that my horse was soon considered to be very good life insurance. At some time or another, every man in the camp had reason to bless him. This big horse with his bravery and honest ways was slowly but surely working his way into everyone's heart. We would be driving a mob of cattle and the word would be passed along that Whopper was needed. Frequently the cause of the trouble would be a scrub bull that was attacking all and sundry. He would be thrown, marked, ear-marked and de-horned. Then in a raging fury he would be let up.

I would ride Whopper in so that we would be the first ones charged. Cattle are quicker off the mark than horses, but they are not as agile. The charging animals never missed us by much, but they always missed. There would be a thump as Whopper swung onto them and hit them solidly with his shoulder. The angry beast would go down and think twice about charging again. Some showed more fight than others, but the majority soon learned that they were safer in among the quiet cattle, and were happy to go there and behave.

Feed was scarce, work was hard and injuries common, but the big bay held his condition as well as any horse in the mustering plant. He fell in for more than his share of work because he was so fit. Because I was his rider I copped it too, but I didn't mind—working with Whopper was always good.

Poor fellow, I can remember him stumbling along at the end of a very hard day, but if a beast broke from the mob, he would summon up some hidden reserve of strength. With no urging from me, he would catch and wheel back the runaway. No whip or spur was ever needed. He would work till he dropped, if necessary.

The boys gave me no mercy about my early complaints. With innocent looks on their whiskered faces, they would ask me how the horse was going with the rope. Others would observe that he would not make a bronco horse if I did not start roping off him soon.

The bond between us grew. I well remember one day when we were mustering along the river and I decided to take a short cut across a boggy creek that ran at right angles to the main stream. It was a bad place for crocodiles, but we always reckoned that if you moved quickly and made plenty of noise there was not much danger.

This time we were halfway across when Whopper struck a soft patch and went down in the mud. I jumped off and, as he struggled, I could only think that the sound of a trapped animal would bring crocodiles, even if it were only to investigate. The bank was just a few metres away, but I would not leave him while he was helpless. Fortunately he struggled out and not a single croc was sighted, but I told myself that no horse was worth getting killed for and probably would have bolted if we had been attacked; but I'm glad I stayed with him that day.

In his own way, but in less serious circumstances, Whopper was to return the favour a short time later. The station Aboriginals were in town for the races and some of their dogs had been chasing calves. The boss sent me down to bring the dogs back to the main homestead, where they could be tied up until their owners returned. Because they didn't know me, the dogs were wary and would not follow me, so I dismounted and played with them for a while. Gradually they came around and a couple of pups started to jump on me. Next minute, Whopper was in the middle of the dogs lashing out with his hooves and snapping at them with his teeth. He thought I was being attacked.

Finally, the work was over for the year and the wet season was coming. For the last time I unsaddled my mate, rubbed his back and said goodbye. I fully intended to return again next year, but circumstances prevented that, and I never saw that great horse again.

Will Ogilvie
'White in the Eye', Saddle for a Throne

You check up the length of your leathers,
You pull up the slack in his girth,
And you wish for a yard full of feathers
Instead of this hard-trodden earth.

The breaking of a stock horse
Bill Clissold

With the handling and bagging over,
The mouthing and driving done,
The time has come to ride him
Out there 'neath the western sun.

The saddle girth is fastened,
The surcingle's good and tight,
His stirrup lengths are tested
And the crupper's adjusted right.

The colt, he stands and chews the bit,
As if about to spring.
He stands with feet both wide apart,
Like a fighter, in the ring.

With nostrils flared a livid pink
And muscles hard and tight,
His ears laid back against his head
And his eyes are rolling white.

The breaker tightens the nearside rein,
And a handful of mane he took.

*His toe finds the stirrup iron,
As around the monkey, his fingers hook.*

*The horseman swings up off the ground,
The horse beside him to straddle.
Swift and lightly does he move
To the seat of his knee-pad saddle.*

*Then 'Come on boy—get up you brute,
What are you made of,' he goaded.
Then with a touch of his heels (that's all it took)
And the whole damned world exploded.*

*The creamy dropped his head and spun,
He bucked, he squealed and twisted.
He threw himself onto the ground.
They rose, both bruised and blistered.*

*Around the yard the young 'un bucked,
Oh, still so full of fight.
But the rider there aboard him
Was still there good and tight.*

*Yes, the rider there upon his back,
T'was like he was painted on.
Like the well known brand of paint,
He just kept on keeping on.*

*Then with its pent up fury spent
And his strength now almost dead,
The pony mustered one final lunge
Then stopped, and hung its head.*

His breath came short and winded,
But his blood, it still ran hot.
For he would make a stock horse,
And a bond with man, his lot.

The breaker from his stool stepped down,
Every bone was sore and jarred.
A pat of respect, he gave the steed
As he led it from the yard.

His time with the colt was over,
His job with him now done.
He walked across to the stockyard
To catch another one.

Riding the outlaw
Hod Cay

It was one of those blue-sky days of long ago, when the glorious autumn weather of western Queensland warmed the hearts and souls of all those lucky enough to experience it. Mitchell grass rippled in the breeze, clumps of grey-green gidyea trees merged with the horizon, and silence covered the land.

Apart from an odd crow and two men seated on the top rail of a round yard, there was nothing to break the silence, for in all that vast area that made up the Wild Horse Run nothing else moved or spoke.

My mate and I sat in companionable silence, our attention focused on a bay mare standing disconsolately in the powdered dust of the horseyard.

'Doesn't look as if she'd go crackers,' my bow-legged friend, master horseman and fellow overseer remarked.

I didn't bother answering. He often spoke his thoughts aloud. 'Still ...' His voice trailed away and he resumed his scrutiny of the mare. Having been born on a Queensland cattle run, my mate's life had hinged around stock since he was a nipper. He probably learnt to ride before he could walk and only a stint in an independent unit during the war years had separated him from his beloved horses.

He rolled another cigarette before continuing in an aggrieved voice—'Can't see what Tom's problem was.' Tom was an experienced boundary rider then languishing in Longreach Base Hospital with a broken leg. The mare in the yard had tossed him, neck and cropper. We both remembered his parting remarks as he was loaded into the station ute en route to hospital: 'Don't let her kid you. Looks as if butter wouldn't melt in her mouth. Take it from me she can turn herself inside out at the drop of a hat.' 'Talking about hats ...' My mate removed his battered old Stetson. Skilfully using the wind, he floated it across the yard to land at the mare's feet. I tensed, waiting for the reaction. Nothing happened. I could hardly believe it. I'd seen many a rider go for leather when a so-called mate shied a hat in front of his horse just to take the mickey out of him. Even more extraordinarily, the horse sniffed the hat as though it might contain a handful of oats.

'I dunno,' my friend repeated thoughtfully before sliding off the rails into the yard. 'Well there's only one way to find out,' he remarked philosophically.

With practised ease he caught and saddled the mare, paying her the compliment of leading her around the yard before finally tightening the girth. Shortening his reins, he grasped her ear firmly, turning her head towards him. His foot quietly found the stirrup and he pivoted on his knee, smoothly sliding into the saddle so gently he would not have crushed an eggshell.

I held my breath, waiting for the explosion. That was the trouble, the mare didn't react. She could have been any old broken-down hack in a North Shore riding school for all the notice she took.

Repeating himself once for luck, my mate said, 'I dunno, I just don't know.' With that, he drove both heels into the mare's flanks and slapped her down the neck with his battered old hat. The peaceful countryside erupted into a cloud of dust. Above the dust, the mare was a silhouette against the bright blue sky. She was arched like a bow, head between her back legs, and spinning too. Lord, she could buck. And couldn't my mate ride. I've seen good contests both before and since, but nothing ever matched that exhibition for sheer bloody-mindedness on the part of both horse and rider. The mare was possessed but, twist and turn as she might, heels slammed into her shoulders and flanks, driving her into new frenzies. She was grunting and squealing with rage, while high above all that noise and thudding hoofs, the rider's 'Yippees' were enough to awaken the dead.

The mare was tiring and close to being beaten when she stumbled into the fence, stunning the rider. With a desperate surge to her feet, she was free, and a second later the gate smashed to pieces as she headed for the horizon. Taking note of the direction, I turned my attention to the rider, who was climbing groggily to his feet.

He shook me off angrily and between spitting out dust he increased my knowledge of the vernacular by at least 80 per cent. 'What the so and so do you think you're doing,' he yelled. 'Get after her, man,' so I took off, hearing his mutterings about shark bait.

I found her at the boundary fence, head down, panting and dripping with sweat. She made no objection as I rubbed her down, changed saddles and mounted. I arrived back at the yards later that afternoon riding the outlaw and leading my own horse. I've ridden rocking horses that gave me more trouble.

My mate limped towards me, eyes glinting angrily when he saw I was riding the mare. 'Well,' he demanded pugnaciously.

I smiled disdainfully—'She's right, old son. Only needed a decent rider.'

For a moment I thought he was going to clobber me, then he grinned and said—'You're a lying bastard, Cay.'

We both knew he'd ridden every buck out of her.

Unconvinced by the mechanical age
Ron Kerr

In the 1950s, I was about 16 and working my own droving plant, taking cattle down the Coopers Creek. The plant consisted of a modernised droving plant, with all stores and gear for a job that could last five or six months carted on a three to four ton truck. The truck replaced the wagonette, which was limited in the size load it could carry.

The truck was to bring in the new era of overlanding long distance without running out of supplies; after all, there was up to 40 horsepower in a little motor under the bonnet. This innovation would enable me to cut the number of horses needed to complete a droving job, as only night horses and riding horses were required. This made a marked improvement to droving—as long as there was a road available on which to drive a truck.

In the early days, however, trucks were of little use getting along the stock route down the Cooper, south of Windorah, as the route went out across the Channel Country, over ground so rough the cattle could out-walk any motor vehicle across this bumpy surface and survive punishment for days on end. I never had complete faith that motor vehicles could stand up to this punishment and be expected to complete a job some hundreds of miles from towns if there was a major breakdown.

To guard against this, I always had extra horses and packsaddles, so a camp could be carried along with the cattle. The cook would then be sent around the outside of the Channel

Stock horse: champion of the outback

Country with the truck to wait our arrival with the cattle and packhorses. This could be a wait of up to a week. But at all times, we would be mobile.

To my mind, the introduction of the motor truck to the droving industry only increased the worry of being in the isolation of the Channel Country of south-west Queensland, no matter how much horsepower was under the bonnet. As far as I was concerned, the four-legged kind would always be the master over motor power. The mobility of the packhorses was a comforting safeguard against the possibility of being stranded with many thousands of dollars' worth of cattle that had to get to water each day. To be caught flat-footed because of a vehicle breakdown with 1500 head of cattle and no water is to be reminded of the true value of the working horse.

The endurance of the working horse and the mileage covered in a lifetime by a single horse is evidence of what these animals can do. A horse ridden behind a mob of cattle in a drive of eight to ten miles per day would mean the legwork of the horse would be a minimum of 20 to 25 miles per day, plus another five to six miles getting a feed or a drink at night.

On a droving trip of, say, 1000 miles at a minimum of 25 miles per day, the legwork of the horse covering the 1000-mile trip in 100 days is 2500 miles for the droving trip—and then its job is only half finished. It'll make the return trip at the rate of 25 miles per day over 40 days, and that doesn't count the walking at night to get itself a feed of grass. After a few weeks' spell, the horse is likely to be saddled up for another droving trip, and its working life could go on for ten to twelve years.

The heap of metal that has replaced the working horse will, within five years, need a partial rebuild. If worked as hard as the working horse over ten to twelve years, it would end up on a scrap heap, beyond repair. As it doesn't eat grass, it also costs money just standing still. It is only now when we daily work the replacement of the working horse that we truly appreciate what we always took for granted. The working horse has been a tool for mankind for thousands of years. Yet it never relied on man to survive, being able to live on what nature produced, and reproduce itself at no cost. The only cost to the human race is when the horse is confined and needs maintaining. Relatively speaking the upkeep of a working horse in relation to the mechanical one is almost nil.

Pizz-Whizz
Bob Batchelor

You hear talk of the mountain riders—
Well! We were just boys from the plains.
Back o' Wentworth we'd muster brumbies
In the scrub where it seldom rains.

Lennie Farrands, Dick Palmer, George Risbey,
As wild as their pony mounts—
And the best of those was Pizz-Whizz,
Full of fire and spirit and bounce.

With arched neck and dancing footsteps
Always ready and willing to run,
From the bit to your hands, ten inches of rein,
He'd go like a shot from a gun.

As fast as a streak of greased lightning,
He could turn on a threepenny bit.
As strong at the end as the start of the day,
Still pulling and still full of grit.

Hang onto the reins, jam your feet in the irons,
Lean forward and give him his head.

They talk of The Man From The Snowy's horse,
Well Pizz-Whizz would leave him for dead.

Over logs and flat out through the bushes,
Watching and ducking and weaving.
If a leader broke he gathered him in,
And stopped any others from leaving.

It's a wonderful feeling to ride a fine horse
Full of spirit and willing to run.
There was never one better than Pizz-Whizz
To go chasing those brumbies, for fun.

Solid worker
Patty Cahill

Cochise was built solid like a front-end loader. He was a tall liver-chestnut quarter horse gelding, with the type of bulging muscles that would make Arnold Schwarzenegger envious. But for all of his mammoth proportions and rough gaits, Cochise was surprisingly lithe and agile when it came to working cattle. With an inborn cow sense, he could second-guess a cow's next move and block her up with amazing swiftness. His rider always needed a deep seat in the saddle and a bit of nerve to stay with him.

We were working half-wild station cattle on our bush block up at Mullewa. The cattle were cunning and refused to leave the scrub. After much manoeuvring with the utes, motorbikes and Cochise, we finally managed to yard the indignant beasts. However, when we drove out at dusk to check on them in the yards, two mad cows had escaped. My husband, Kym, saddled up Cochise and swung around the two wary cows grazing nearby. That's when the real show began. The cows immediately split up and dodged, darted and spooked in all directions. Kym swung the stockwhip high in the air and cracked it with authority, but the cows weren't impressed. After shouldering them with his massive body, Cochise got the two cows back together. He matched them spin for spin, stop for stop, in an unrehearsed dance of cadenced movements. With his head lowered, front legs poised, and swinging around on his hindquarters, Cochise blocked the cows at every turn. When he finally got them into the funnel-shaped wing that led to the yards, Cochise was in a lathered sweat. Kym's face was grim, but he had never moved in the saddle. Only later did I learn that one of his stirrup leathers had broken off and a stirrup had dropped in the dirt earlier.

Next morning we were awakened by a loud crash. We ran out of the old unused farmhouse where we had camped for the night and found Cochise standing on the verandah. He had knocked down the paddock gate and backed himself up against an opened window. There he was, with his enormous rump, innocently scratching it on the wooden frame. Shattered glass from the broken window lay scattered all around his enormous hooves. When the mighty Cochise had an itch, nothing stood in his way.

Dave's explosion
Des Coombes

Packhorses were extremely valuable assets for cattle drovers in the days before trucks took over their work. A good, strong, reliable packhorse was a real treasure, and hard to come by. Dave was one of those treasures. Grumpy and disagreeable, he objected to being a human conveyance, but was quite happy to be loaded up with full packs, blankets, oilskins and billycans. There was no need to lead Dave; he looked after himself, following along behind the mob and stopping to graze where he felt like it. He didn't like to lose sight of the cattle, though, and would come trotting and whinnying along the road to catch up and join us. Bends in the road created real nuisances for him, cutting down his grazing time.

Due to Dave's intense dislike for saddle occupants and his nasty habit of bucking violently whenever anyone tried to ride him, his former owner, Dave McIver, on the Upper Macleay, was only too pleased to let someone take the cranky chestnut gelding off his hands. Thus, he became Dave the packhorse, for the Johnston cattle mobs. My brother Jack had worked out how to handle Dave and the two got along very well on the droving trips between McKenzie's Creek on the Upper Macleay and Clybucca on the Lower Macleay.

I happened to be on a trip with my brother, droving down from McKenzie's Creek, when Dave blotted his copybook and put on one of the best rodeo acts I have ever witnessed from a packhorse. We had camped out overnight at a travelling stock reserve, resting the slow-moving mob. After an early breakfast the horses were caught and saddled. Dave was neatly packed up with all our camp gear and we set out to round up the mob and get them on the road for the trip to Clybucca. Dave did his usual thing, jogging along with billies jangling and following us as we rounded up the bullocks.

As we threaded our way through the sapling scrub in the reserve, Dave was suddenly galvanised into frantic uncontrollable action when the billycans caught on a small sapling and rattled loudly. Spooked by this unusual clamour, Dave took off as if some weird monsters were descending upon him. Bucking, twisting and thrashing wildly about, the whites of his eyes showing out more than usual, he tore through the saplings at an ever- increasing pace.

We could only listen and bemoan our bad luck as Dave rampaged through the trees, kicking and snorting like some rodeo rogue determined to shake off the tormentors on his back.

Following the trail of destruction, we eventually caught up with a wild-eyed, terrified, panting animal, now dressed only in his halter. Dave had shed himself of his torment. He had managed to strip off the billycans, blankets, oilskins, cooking utensils, packs and packsaddle. Not a scrap of his load remained intact. Seeing was believing—what he had achieved in a few minutes was amazing. Houdini would have been proud of him.

Putting everything together and back on Dave—using an extraordinary amount of wire we removed from a fence—took most of the morning. When he calmed down, he looked almost sorry for the trouble he had caused. Dave's stocks had dropped very low, he gained many new names and we even talked about turning him into dog meat. However, he soon went back to his normal self and the morning he went berserk became no more than a good conversation piece. But my brother still recalls Dave's rampage as one of the most exciting events in all his droving years.

One hundred miles in twelve hours
Denis White

During my time as a jackeroo in the mid-1930s, I worked on a property named Mount Enniskillen in central Queensland. It had several outstations and covered one million acres. I lived on one of these outstations, Castlevale, which was 100 miles from the head station and 50 miles from the neighbouring outstation, Kelpum. Rations were brought to Castlevale about once a month by car or truck over a very rough road that crossed a mountain range.

For some reason or other, at one stage the vehicle did not arrive with our rations and we were running very short. We badly needed more coarse salt, which was used to cure and preserve the beef we killed. The overseer at Castlevale decided to send me to the neighbouring outstation to get some salt, so at least we could kill a beast and have some meat to eat. I was given a beautiful dark brown gelding of over 16 hands which had not long been run in after a spell.

I left Castlevale at 7 am, knowing I had 100 miles to do on a very soft horse. I had not ridden him before, but found him very comfortable. He was an ambler, so I decided to amble for what I estimated to be a mile, then trot for a mile and canter for a mile. I kept this up all the way there and, after a one hour rest at Kelpum, put a 75 pound bag of salt across the back of the saddle and returned to Castlevale, again alternating the paces. I arrived at 7 pm, having ridden 100 miles on the same horse in twelve hours.

He was a nice free horse who never faltered and was going just as well when he arrived back at Castlevale as he was in the morning. Unfortunately, having not been in work for long, he had been rather sore around the girth and under the saddle before we even departed on our trip—a fact I had mentioned, without result, to the overseer before leaving. This only serves to further underline the capabilities of a good Australian Stock Horse.

Mollycoddled
Colin Wade

Thinking back to my time in the Murchison district of Western Australia in the 1930s, it's worth comparing those days with today's ballyhoo about horses and long distance trials—and how they are mollycoddled. My average week consisted of a minimum of five days' riding, with the horses mostly living off the land. When possible, I had a change of horse after seven days.

I would leave camp at about six in the morning and, if mustering sheep, finished just before sunset—about twelve hours in all, minus a short break for lunch. Travelling a minimum of 5 kilometres an hour, I did about 60 kilometres a day, or 300 to 400 kilometres a week. Plus we didn't have the service of vets, just horse sense. Until the horses were too old, or suffered an accident, attrition was almost nil—in fact, they always appeared healthy and to enjoy their work. I rode something like 9000 kilometres a year, and never had a horse 'knock up', apart from the odd girth gall or sore back.

More often than not, I was much more weary than the horse, because I didn't get turned out into the paddock after a week or fortnight's work, and sometimes expended an enormous amount of energy just trying to stay in the saddle of a station horse brought fresh from the paddock and with a few bucks and pig-roots to get rid of.

Three
Long distances: tough people and horses

The hours of work in the past were long; the dangers were many. People and animals were often tested to their limits.

That tradition of pushing the boundaries and testing the limits, in partnership with a horse, continues today. Endurance riders, in particular, keep alive the spirit of the mercy dash, the mail run and the long distance trek.

An extraordinary bloke, Ken Hobday, has the endurance-riding bug badly. Long retired and of senior years, he shames every slothful couch hugger with his passion to cover the demanding 160-kilometre Tom Quilty ride as often as possible. He makes me wonder if old age is more endurable with a horse. Or does riding just keep the body young?

Joy Poole is another who doesn't like taking the easy path. She was an organiser and part of the team that rode from Broome to Sydney in 2000, setting a record for the longest relay ride in the world. Her passions are our nation's own breed of horse, the Australian Stock Horse, and the sport that is a purely Australian invention, polocrosse.

Ken Hobday's enduring passion: with a horse he makes the distance

Ken Hobday was sustained through a long career as a marine engineer by the scent of a horse. Anyone who has ever brushed against a grass-kissed velvet muzzle will know the seductive sweetness that lingers there. Like rain on dry grass, it's a heady scent evocative of long childhood days riding bareback in the sun, of innocence and simple pleasures. Ken was first pulled into loving horses and the freedom they offered as a boy of four from the outer reaches of Melbourne, more than 70 years ago. His family lived next door to a racing stable and, with the son of one of the stablemen, he would be put up on top of one of the more sensible racers. He remembers the silky feel of warmth on his legs and the sensation of lurching power as they were led around the yard. 'And that beautiful smell of horses, I love it,' says Ken, who is 78 but has no respect for the supposed limitations of age.

When he was finished with marine engineering, which had him consulting on tug boats and supervising the building of a couple of passenger ships for the West Australian government, all Ken wanted to do was get back on a horse and spend the rest of his days riding.

A couple of times he had escaped from his Port Hedland office as manager of Adelaide Steamships to get on a horse at nearby stations, but until he retired in 1986 and went to Perth it had been more than 40 years since he had done any serious riding. On horses with his friends, he had explored the country around Melbourne, much of which is now covered with houses. In 1945, at the age of 21, he went away to sea for the last year of the war, spent time in the tropics and, for his efforts, collected some souvenir diseases and disabilities, none of which he pays much attention to.

Ken has more than made up for time lost out of the saddle. He didn't just start quietly hacking around, which most people in their sixties would do. He decided to get right into horse sports, the toughest, the most demanding. At the age of 71, he took up endurance riding and did his first 160-kilometre Tom Quilty ride a year later in 1995 at Toodyay. Just to complete this gruelling event is a feat in itself and all who do so are rewarded with a silver buckle. From 58 middleweight entrants, Ken Hobday finished 33rd, he and the horse still fit. 'I am still grinning from that one,' says Ken, a wiry, lean man who has won teams of admirers for his gutsy determination and passion for riding.

The Tom Quilty Endurance Ride, which carries a gold cup perpetual trophy for the winner, began in 1966 after a campfire chat between Kimberley cattleman Tom Quilty and R M Williams. Quilty put up $1000 to prove the spirit of the pioneers lived on, that people still had the toughness and the horses to ride 100 miles like they used to, just to post a letter. He thought Australia shouldn't be outdone by America which was already staging a ride of a similar distance. The 24-hour event began at Richmond in New South Wales but is now held in a different state each year. Tightly scrutinised by vets, the Quilty sorts out ill-prepared horses or any with lameness or injury. Forget completing, just lining up to start, especially at any Quilty held outside your home state, would be enough to stop most people, especially if you're from Western Australia.

Hooked on the camaraderie of long distance riders and the pioneer spirit they embody, in 1996 Ken loaded up his mate Blue, a tough station-bred horse—a mix of Arab, Percheron and Thoroughbred—from south of Broome, and drove four days to Myrtleford in Victoria. He earned himself another hand-crafted buckle. In 1997 he took Blue to Watagan Mountain in New South Wales, but this time Blue was vetted out during the ride with a sore back. Undeterred, Ken went to Mount Pleasant in South Australia the next year, but an asthma attack split him from his group. Colour blindness then made pink arrows look orange in his torchlight, so Ken and Blue got lost. This old bloke who doesn't give up and who says he is known for attacking everything with gusto was not beaten. In 1999, at the age of 75, he and Blue went to Deloraine in Tasmania. Over steep and muddy country in the freezing dawn after a midnight start, he again earned himself a Quilty buckle. Queensland was next, earning him a fourth Quilty buckle at Boonah with a ride of just over eighteen hours, not bad for a 76 year old a very long way from home. Perversely, with the 2001 Quilty held practically in his backyard, at Tumbulgum Farm, Mundijong, Western Australia, Blue, at 15, was vetted out lame for the first time ever.

In between the Quilty rides, Ken and Blue did a few extra trips 'over east' to fit in the gruelling Shahzada, described as the ultimate in endurance tests. Equestrian masochists ride 400 kilometres in five days. Ken and Blue have contested four times and won themselves four buckles for their efforts, averaging around 8 kilometres an hour for the distance in a time of some 46 hours all up. Named after an Arab stallion of note, the Shahzada is held in the last week of August at St Albans in the Hawkesbury Valley, New South Wales. 'Talk about rugged country,' says Ken, gasping slightly. 'You've no idea ... creek beds, steep hills, steps of rock to climb up and down. The first time I went there, I couldn't believe it. One slip and you are hurtling down into nothing. On my first Shahzada, I actually did slip on sheet rock. I looked down and it was as high as a table to the next step. Blue had all four feet on a piece of rock the size of a chair, but you know what he did then ... he reached out and bit a piece of green bush as casual as anything.' Ken loves that bloke Blue, the grey horse that he initially thought was built too heavily to make an endurance horse. But he liked his stretch of neck and magnificent presence, so he coughed up $900 and they've been inseparable ever since. They've built up immense trust in each other, obvious from Ken's description of negotiating huge, almost vertical rock steps in the 2000 Shahzada. 'Blue leans back as he is going down, he is sort of gripping, using his own weight to hold his back feet, and wedge himself safely. Then he gradually slides his front feet down to the next level. He's never been a bit fazed.'

In this sport it is unusual for riders to compete with the same horse year after year, but Blue and Ken have done seven Quiltys and four Shahzadas and along the way have become special identities, with Ken enjoying a bit of special fussing over simply because he is by far the oldest competitor most places he goes. He's had to take a bit of a break recently though, because he thought it was about time to get surgery on his crook shoulder with its torn tendons.

'Riding is the secret to good health,' he says. 'It shakes up the liver. Actually I didn't know at this age I would be so entertained too, and have such an active interest. And it's great to be with younger people. And I think the contact with horses gives me energy.'

To get Blue in training for endurance work, Ken says he took things quietly. 'When you first get a horse that's not done endurance riding, you do six days a week, about an hour a day then build up to two hours. We never went faster than a trot for the first 100 kilometres. If you build up muscle too quickly, you strain tendons. You have to be tuned into your horse and listen to them.' A lot of what he knows came from listening to the old timers talking about horses when he was a child. When the horse is conditioned, he walks and trots up the steep hills around his place at Bindoon, 90 kilometres north of Perth. 'To build up their wind, you let them race up hills if they want to, but you stop at the top and let them recover. It is important to do no harm.'

Ken says he doesn't do much more than two hours of faster training four times a week when a horse is fit. When he was doing an 80-kilometre competition ride every fortnight, Blue needed just a couple of workouts of about two hours in between events to keep him in at his peak.

After just four years of endurance riding, twelve years after 'retiring', Ken showed what a dominant force he and Blue had become. At the 1998 Western Australia endurance club awards night, he carried off nine separate trophies, including the top annual distance for a middleweight rider, top distance horse and the National Top Distance rider with a total of 1700 kilometres covered in the year. He says it was all because he and Blue enjoyed what they were doing, even those long float trips eastwards when he stopped every four hours to let Blue out for a rest, a stretch and a piddle.

'But you have to go through the pain barrier,' says this bloke who chops wood for a hobby. 'And that's why a lot of people don't do things. I see too many people in their forties and fifties who are immobile.'

Ken Hobday, in just seven years of competition, has covered almost 8000 kilometres in every state of Australia in endurance trials. He can't see any reason why he won't still be endurance riding at ninety.

Joy Poole keeps the legends alive

In the central Hunter Valley, not far from Singleton, in rolling hill country, Joy Poole is saddling up the first of three horses she'll ride that day. It is 6.30 and the landscape is still camouflaged in mist and semi-darkness. The pines in the gully below the stable block are a dark smudge; the lights shine from the windows of her house down the hill; a fence, running over the landscape like a startled rabbit, disappears into the gloom. Walking among the six horses in the yard, Joy is a woman of strong presence. Her erect posture is a legacy of years of active sport. She chats to the horses as their feeds are put out, giving a pat here and a rub of a neck there. The horses, all of a type, strong boned and athletic, kind of eye and glossy coated, drop their heads respectfully. Tied up to a rail is a striking chestnut with blaze and stockings. This is Kookaburra, the horse that became so famous during the epic Heritage Horse Ride from Broome in Western Australia to Sydney prior to the 2000 Olympics that remote Northern Territory communities of Aboriginal children would mob him and school children in Queensland towns would call out his name.

When the idea of riding horses from one side of Australia to the other was first made public, the sceptics shook their heads. Strict deadlines and numerous public appearances were to be a feature of the 120-day trek, and horses and riders, far from the comforts of home, had no choice but to keep sound and fit. The plan seemed not only idealistic, but foolish and naive. Anyone who knew the terrain and climate and understood the sheer distance involved doubted it could be done. Hadn't these people heard of the spectacular failures of Burke and Wills and other parties of explorers where the horses were eaten and riders perished?

The doubters did not reckon on Joy Poole, OAM, former school principal, international polocrosse coach, tireless promoter of Australian Stock Horses and Singleton's Citizen of the Year 2001. Her powerful presence inspires an attitude that anything's possible. With fellow organiser, Neville Holz, the Spring Valley Heritage Horse Ride was pushed and shoved into not only achieving its goal of reaching Sydney on time, but Australia's home-bred workhorse won worldwide recognition.

Joy is not ashamed to say she has been obsessed with horses all her life. She owned her first 50 years ago and now, silver-haired and 60, shows no sign of letting up. Until she retired in 1995 as principal at Singleton school after fifteen years in the position, she had always risen at 5.30 am to work her horses before work. She says horses are used for all mustering on the 150-acre house block and another 600 acres nearby. 'We are so old-fashioned here, I'll ride a horse to turn off the pump. We haven't got a motorbike.'

She enthusiastically talks of the success she's had breeding Australian Stock Horses since 1963, way before the breed was officially established in 1972. The grand names of the breed, such as Cadet and Rosebrook Abou, bob up in the pedigrees of many of her horses. 'We are probably the most unusual stud ever,' Joy says, giving Kookaburra another rub over his bright honey-coloured coat. Almost reverently, and with quiet pride, she continued, 'The first horse we ever bred turned out to be a champion—J-Star Impact. Most people try for years to get a good horse. But Impact was my first ever foal and he went on to be a champion polo pony. He played from 1970 to 1978 and is listed among all the great playing horses of all time.' Her J-Star horses, bred for quiet temperament as well as talent, toughness and sense, are always in hot demand.

Joy's great eye for a good horse extends too to being able to pick up champions at horse auctions, always a danger zone for the unwary. Once at a horse sale she found a chestnut mare that turned out to be a 'very special athlete' and went on to produce many champion foals.

The Heritage Horse Ride left Broome with two groups of riders travelling in separate directions on 14 April 2000. The plan was to meet up again in Sydney on 13 August and provide a spectacular equine curtain raiser to the Games by crossing Sydney Harbour Bridge to hand over to Sydney's Lord Mayor the flags and messages of support which the two groups had carried along their respective 8000 kilometres of country roads and through each mainland capital city. At that stage, no-one except those who were directly involved knew just how hugely horses would feature at Sydney's Olympic opening ceremony and how they would triumph so emphatically at the Three Day Event. The Heritage Horse Ride turned out to be a tantalising foretaste of what was to come, nicely linking past with present.

Internet technology let people all over Australia follow the hoof beats of this pioneering ride. The fifteen people and horses on the northern route and twenty-eight on the southern route became mini celebrities in many of the towns they visited on the world-record-breaking relay.

The logistics of organising an event to celebrate the contribution of horses to Australia's heritage are mind-boggling. Credit for tying up the ends and ensuring everything ran smoothly goes also to Claudia York, Joy's partner since 1973 and also a former teacher. Claudia decided to retire a year before the Heritage Horse Ride to work full time on the huge task of letter-writing to all towns along the route to seek support, drawing up the timetable, answering queries from riders from all around Australia who were interested in joining the ride, and organising those willing to spend three months on the road. Ironically, this celebration of the horse's contribution to opening up the nation's vast distances was heavily dependent on the very mode of transport that eventually edged horses aside. A small armada of floats and horse-trucks, driven by a task-force of supporters, accompanied the ride. Before it got underway the complete route, north and south, was driven by Neville Holz and his wife, Lynette, to map out overnight camps, water points and feed collection points, and to determine which schools and town councils they would be able to include in their public appearance programme.

The ride, which Joy says changed participants' lives, taught them new skills and built new confidence, is best described as a relay in stages of various lengths, depending on weather, terrain and the number of horses available each day.

From the solitude of the Kimberleys to the mayhem of the more populated areas, Joy says it was an unmitigated success. The sponsors were delighted, the riders loved it, and the act of circling the continent with a string of horses was a symbolic way of unifying us all.

'We were trying to make people proud of being Australian as we moved towards the Olympic Games,' Joy said. 'But not long after we left Broome, we started to notice just how proud people already were. Not one vehicle didn't stop, wave or slow down. People would call out to us. They seemed really moved by what we were doing.' Joy pauses: 'I remember one woman on an outback road with tears running down her face as she patted the horses. The ride seemed to touch a chord right from the start,' and Joy allows herself a little, proud smile. 'A tangible feeling of pride kept building the further the ride went. The Aboriginal communities in particular got behind what we were doing. Some of them have their own radio stations and they asked us in to do interviews with them. It was really good fun. A lot of them had been following our progress on the Net and as we came into their towns they'd know the horses' names, especially Kookaburra,' and again Joy's hazel eyes dance. 'Aboriginal stockmen joined in with the ride around Halls Creek and the communities there put on a rodeo specially for us. It was really wonderful.'

This event, which set out to promote Australian Stock Horses but went on to be much more, was also, in terms of media mentions, the biggest in 2000 apart from the Olympic Games and Torch Relay.

Joy estimates that main sponsor, Spring Valley, as well as putting cash of $120,000 towards the event, probably contributed about $1 million all up, through providing water trucks, uniforms and Drizabones, bags and personnel to accompany the ride on both routes.

Between long stretches of loneliness, many were the adventures for horses and riders. Between Laidley and Ipswich in Queensland, the horses were loaded into open carriages pulled by a steam train. While riders hung out of windows fussing and worrying that swirling smoke and soot from the puffing engine might unsettle the horses, the well-travelled mounts were totally unconcerned and seemed to enjoy the passing scenery interspersed with pitch black, echoing tunnels. On the Gold Coast, celebrating their crossing of the continent, bands

Long distances: tough people and horses

played on the beach while a sand modeller made an enormous horseshoe. Pony clubs joined them, and even several Light Horse regiments. Mayors of towns large and small greeted them with speeches, banners and letters of support. And throughout, the horses, the stars of the show, took it all in their stride.

Joy embraced the experience as a way of reliving the past, of getting a small taste of pioneer life, albeit with mobile phones, laptop computers, truckloads of water supplied by Spring Valley and horse feed from Cool Fuel Copra. The ride was criticised by some for being too soft, for only pretending to emulate the heroic feats of the past, and some said it was little more than a comfortable relay where horses and riders could get away with covering just 8 kilometres a day.

Joy bristles at these charges and says such criticisms were 'sour grapes' by people who probably wanted to be involved but who couldn't spare the time and expense. 'Sometimes we would be on those horses for six to seven hours at a time,' she says. 'On one of the legs, we covered 160 kilometres in a day. You didn't have time to relax and look at the birds. We were too busy trotting and cantering to make our overnight stop.' She is looking every bit the former principal, with chin jutting ever so slightly and strong nose lifted defiantly.

'The schedules were tough. We met schools at set times. You couldn't only do your ride, you also had to fit in trucking horses to these appointments. Someone also would go ahead each day and put out markers every 8 to 12 kilometres to indicate changeover points for riders. Anyone who thinks it wasn't hard on horses ... forget that. It was a wonderful tribute to horses as well as being the biggest test of temperament of any horse I have seen.' By this, Joy is referring not only to the ultimate test of crossing Sydney Harbour Bridge in peak hour traffic, but also the road trains which swept past them at horrifying speeds, producing lashing winds which sometimes wound the Australian flag carried by the lead rider around a horse's head.

Horses stood among bobbing fishing boats at Yeppoon, marched with brass bands and had small children patting them in strange places and walking under their bellies. 'Stock horses have had good temperament bred into them, but that really was a super test.'

As a mark of respect to old drovers, the Heritage riders moved 100 head of cattle near Camooweal, an activity which neatly meshed with Joy's philosophy of linking past and present.

The phone interrupts our kitchen table discussion. It is a request by Simon Knight of Sherwood for Joy to open his stock horse sale up at Condamine and give a talk about 27-year-old Warrenbri Romeo, one of the most influential stallions of the breed, sire of 400 foals, 120 of which are registered stallions. 'I would be very proud and pleased to be there,' she tells the caller without a moment's hesitation.

Returning to the conversation, she continues: 'I love horses. They are a passion. I cannot remember a time when I wasn't totally engrossed in them. And I can't foresee a day when I wouldn't have a horse to walk outside to feed.' All around the walls of the house are photographs of horses competing in a variety of sports.

'The Australian Stock Horse is dear to my heart. I will do anything to promote the breed and I am always first in the queue to help. For too long the Australian Stock Horse was a secret. And that's what was so great about the ride. It was the first time the breed has had a brand name.'

Joy played polocrosse at a top level for twenty years. She last represented New South Wales as a player in 1986 but is still its state coach. A purely Australian invention, polocrosse came into being in 1939 at Ingleburn, New South Wales. It was first exported in 1949 to South Africa and Rhodesia, and since then to sixteen other countries including Papua New Guinea and New Zealand. Joy introduced the sport in 1984 to Indonesia. She has coached in the United States three times. In 1987, she helped put in place a Level 1 coaching scheme in Zimbabwe.

'Horses have been my life,' says Joy, looking through photograph albums stacked with memories. 'Where they have taken me is unbelievable.'

Joy grew up in nearby Maitland and remembers riding her first horse to school, but only when it needed shoeing. She would drop it off at the blacksmith in the morning so he could put on another set of shoes, costing then just five shillings.

She says she was lucky knowing great horsemen such as Bill Hedges, an Aboriginal and a former jockey, buck jumper and campdraft rider who taught her to be in touch with a horse's mind and spirit and to have 'incredible patience'. 'He was a great mentor and a great hero. He had a wonderful affinity with animals.' Joy says she has come to the conclusion after a lifetime of working with horses that you train them by getting into their minds. 'We break them in by asking, not telling them. They have to understand what it is we are trying to get them to do.'

Because of the generous hours put into her development by Bill and many others, Joy is similarly big-hearted when it comes to passing on her knowledge. Her farm often hosts overseas students who help out in return for training, and she travels widely throughout Australia giving polocrosse and riding clinics. She is pleased the Stock Horse Society now has a team of coaches who have been appointed to pass on the bush skills and horsemanship that present-day riders have lost.

Realist though she most certainly is, Joy is no doubt more disturbed than she lets on by one observation from the Heritage ride. Not only in towns and cities, but in country areas too, many children shyly approached the horses saying they had never previously touched a horse. Would it be all right to touch one, they asked, because they didn't know what they were like. Joy is pensive, but there's a hint of outrage: 'It saddens me to think that this animal that opened up Australia is now so foreign.'

A B 'Banjo' Paterson
'In the Droving Days' [excerpt]

Over the flats and across the plain,
With my head bent down on his waving mane,
Through the boughs above and the stumps below,
On the darkest night I could let him go
At a racing speed; he would choose his course,
And my life was safe with the old grey horse.

Mercy dash shame
Peggy Hodgson

In 1915, out past Jibberding, in Western Australia, further inland than the rabbit-proof fence, where agricultural land becomes station country, a young man had set up his camp with his wife. Their tent was far from any established farms and no-one in the settlements of Wubin or Dalwallinu knew that they were there—let alone that she was heavily pregnant. It is possible that they were sandalwood-cutting in the area.

This story was told to me in 1979 by an elderly woman who was involved in the drama that unfolded. For reasons that have no meaning today—largely because of our changed relationship to horses—she had kept the story a secret for 64 years.

The young wife went into labour, but soon it was obvious she was in dire trouble. Leaving his wife ill and alone in their tent, the father-to-be mounted his horse and rode the long distance, some 40 to 50 kilometres, into Wubin for help.

Once there, he asked one of the local grandmothers to help, but she knew she was too old and frail to make the journey, so the young man remounted and rode a further 24 kilometres to Dalwallinu, to the south, for assistance. There a trained nurse and a pioneering lady who had put herself through a midwifery course expressly so she could help at births in the young district bundled themselves and their medical kits into a sulky. With the young man as guide, they made their way out to the suffering girl alone in the bush.

It took them a whole day to get there. When they entered the tent and examined her, it was clear to the two women that they could not help the desperately ill girl. They decided to stay with her while her husband saddled up again to ride back to Wubin, to try to get the doctor from Goomalling, 145 kilometres away to the south.

The railway line through Wubin was only a year old, but it was not the scheduled 'train day', so no train travel for help was possible. Since it was 1915, mid-World War I, very few young men were available for mercy dashes. So it fell to the lot of the Wubin teamster's 14-year-old son, a good horserider, to ride the distance for help. Taking a good, strong horse from his father's stables, he set off on his marathon ride, keeping the horse travelling as fast as it could go, hoping all the time that the doctor was actually in Goomalling and not far away on another errand of mercy. The lad was riding at night through land which is now highly productive farm land, but in those days it was sparsely developed and the tracks in wintertime, the time of the ride, were treacherous.

Every so often there were native *gnamma* holes and wells where he could quickly water his horse and himself. Before he reached halfway, he knew that the sturdy horse beneath him was close to collapse. He managed to make it to a nearby farm, where his horse died, and another was provided for him to ride on to Goomalling.

At 14 years of age, tired and hungry, he took off again into the night to complete the last 50 kilometres of his ride. At last, exhausted, with the second horse knocking up beneath him, he croaked out his story and a plea for the doctor's assistance. Fortunately, the doctor was in town. The borrowed horse, however, was so distressed by its fast journey that it too fell down and either died or had to be put down.

Fortune then started to smile on proceedings. It happened to be 'train day' in Goomalling, so the doctor and the lad were soon aboard and on their way back to Wubin. There they got hold of a horse and sulky, which took them out to the young man's camp, where his wife had been suffering for three days and must have been near death. It is not remembered by those who were involved how long the doctor stayed with the young woman, but she did recover. However, the baby was born dead.

The elderly lady who told me the story was a member of the teamster's family. Although the family was overjoyed that the young mother had been saved, and that another of the tragedies that were so common in those pioneering times had been averted, they were dreadfully ashamed to think that one of their own family members had caused the deaths of two horses. The teamster prided himself on his horses and had a much envied reputation throughout the district for his skill and care in the management of his animals. They were always carefully prepared for their work, for it was on his horses that the community relied to bring in their supplies and take out produce.

The woman who initially told me the story, in confidence, has now agreed that it can be published. However, she still wants no identifying names used. The extraordinary shame they felt about the deaths of those horses illustrates perhaps better than any tales of heroism the high esteem in which good horses were held.

Working hard to have some fun
Shirley Low

Through sheer necessity, during the years of petrol rationing in the 1940s, horses made something of a comeback. Sulkies and jinkers that had long been languishing in sheds were resurrected; harness was polished and made ready to use.

Our black pony's previous owner operated a milk run, so Darkie was always exceptionally quick off the mark. As a result, we had to become very nimble at climbing aboard the sulky before he took off at a smart trot. This posed few difficulties for everyday outings, but it wasn't so easy or much fun if you were off to a formal ball, wearing a very full evening dress and high heels. With the skirt bunched up around your knees, you would hope madly that you, and the dress, would land on the seat in one piece. Pounding along at a spanking pace before you were even settled, Darkie would have the sulky bouncing and the lantern hanging on the back swinging wildly.

Such was our determination to get some entertainment that we endured five miles of Darkie trotting along a hilly country road, then we stabled him, taking the next stage in a buckboard, before finally boarding a car to arrive in style at the ball. We would reverse the process to arrive home eventually at around 4 or 5 am, unharness the pony and creep into bed.

Cutting a living from the bush
Thomas Rush Hall

My father was a cripple because of a fall from a high load of hay, so he was able to do very little work. He employed men to cut and cart firewood to feed the boilers of the Bendigo Mines. The invalid pension then was two shillings and sixpence a week, so caring for a family of five sons and a wife was not easy.

My working life started when I was nine years of age, in 1914, and I became a firewood cutter and carted railway sleepers with two horses and drays. My work with horses continued on until 1948 when motor vehicles took over.

For the next 40 years of using trucks, I savoured the memories of my horses hauling their loads fifteen hours a day, six days a week, 12 to 15 miles into the bush. They carted firewood, sleepers, poles and all sorts of bush timber. What a wonderful life to look back on, from boyhood to manhood. I had, at most times, two or three horses and drays, all following one another. I could drive them mostly by word of mouth. Although these hard-working horses had to be replaced after about six or eight years on the job, it was always a sad day when we parted. Most times they were sold to finish their lives doing a bit of casual farm work, but I will never forget the help they gave me in earning a living for my wife and seven children.

Now, at 89, I am the only one left of the old timber-cutters in our area to tell of those days.

Logging the scrub
Bruce Rodgers

Horse teams were responsible for the development of farm land in the early days of Australia. The only other power was bullocks and donkeys, but they were never as versatile as horses. Scrub-rolling and logging was done with horses, and it was rough work for them. I have seen them staked in the body with broken sticks and the jarring of the load played havoc with their shoulders, as does ploughing new land for the first time.

The type of log used for scrub-rolling was usually about 25 feet long and approximately 12 to 15 inches in diameter. A heavy chain approximately eight or ten feet long was attached to each end and a two-horse swing or spreader-bar fixed to the chain. A four-horse team in pairs and in tandem was harnessed at each end of the log.

One team would work in the scrub and the other team on the newly logged scrub. Two drivers were needed, and the driver rode on the nearside horse of the back pair. The drivers found it necessary to wear a good pair of leather leggings to avoid their legs being bruised by the chains, which were often under immense strain.

The first 1100 acres of our present farm was logged with horse teams, and eventually, the next 1100 was done with a tractor. I always was the driver of the team in the scrub. We usually selected two fairly intelligent horses as leaders and used branch reins in order to steer them through the scrub a bit better. It was a rough job for horses and riders, but I only had one mishap, when an overhanging branch of a tree wiped me off over the rump of the horse. As I went off, I hung onto the reins and yelled out to the team to stop, and fortunately they did.

The type of scrub being logged was mallee, fairly thick and about 10 to 15 feet high, with a dense covering of undergrowth from two to five feet high. The horses soon seemed to become accustomed to pushing through the scrub. I always attempted to steer them through a gap big enough for their two heads to go through and they then crashed the rest of their bodies through. After one day's logging the scrub down, we logged the same area in the opposite direction, in order to break off all the scrub which was leaning away from the log the previous day. This meant a clearer burn later.

A rare breed today
Don Willcox

I grew up on a small farm just north of the Western Tiers mountain, about 13 miles west of Deloraine in Tasmania. One of my neighbours was Vin Walters. He was 82 years old and had some kind of heart complaint.

Vin had a cattle run back in the mountains, as well as his farm. His cattle run consisted of two plains beside the Mersey

River. The first plain, where the huts were, was called the Mash Plain; the second was called the Horse Plain. His run was not fenced—it only had natural boundaries, the Mersey River on one side and a mountain range on the other—so he was not allowed to breed cattle back there. He just used to take young cattle there, let them grow out and become prime, then they would be mustered, brought out and sold at the Mole Creek cattle sale.

Vin, being old and his health not good, had let his son and the man who married one of his granddaughters manage his cattle run back in the mountain. However, these young men did not have the skill of Vin at mustering and had let one steer become a rogue. Each time they mustered the cattle, it would hide in the mountain range so it could stay there. Vin knew if it was not mustered, brought out and sold, it would eventually cause a lot of trouble.

Vin asked me if I would go back there with him and one of his employees and muster a mob of prime cattle, that steer included. I had never mustered cattle in the mountains, but I could ride and use a stock whip well. I was only 19 years old, and this was to be a great adventure for me, so I gladly accepted.

Vin had a mob of young cattle he wanted to take back and put on his run. Some were a bit weak, so the first day we drove them steadily to his holding paddock at Liena, where we stayed that night. Next morning we had breakfast and left at 4.30 am so that we could get up the north face of the mountain before the day became hot; otherwise some of the weak cattle would go down and we would lose them. We reached the table top of the mountain while it was still cool, with all the cattle still in good shape. We kept going until 4.30 pm. When we reached a small creek, Vin said, 'We can let them rest here while we boil the billy. We can reach the run easily this evening now.' This was the first time we had eaten since breakfast.

When we reached the ford where we had to cross the river, Vin pointed out a rock that was showing in the middle of the river. He told me that if the rock is not out of the water, it is too dangerous to ride across the ford.

The next morning Vin showed me how to set snares in the scrub around the hut to catch small grey kangaroos or wallabies, as these were to be our main food for the fortnight Vin intended to spend up there. The only other food we had was the flour, tea, sugar, salt, potatoes and onions we carried tied to our saddles and on our backs.

The animals I caught in the snares, Vin would skin and dress. He was an excellent bush cook. The skins of the kangaroos or wallabies he would peg out in the other hut used by the snarers in the winter to dry the skins they got. When the skins were dry, Vin would tan them with kerosene and make them into rugs for the bunks we slept in. There were no blankets, only skin rugs. We were to muster the Mash Plain first, but before we went out, Vin gave us strict instructions that we were not to speak or make any noise when we found the cattle. He would know at a glance if the rogue steer was with them. If it was not, we were to ride quickly around the mob to look for tracks in the soft dirt where the rogue steer had run off.

When we found the mob, Vin said, 'He is not here. Quick, look.'

There were no tracks, though, so Vin said he would be on the Horse Plain. He wasn't with that mob, but we did find tracks where several cattle had run off into a gully going into the mountain range.

Vin rode a young black pacing mare. He put the spurs to her sides and rode into that gully like the man from Snowy River. Our ex-Light Horse horses were good stock horses, but much slower than Vin's, so we were soon left far behind. Then we heard him yelling and his stockwhip cracking. He had found them, so we got to where the noise was coming from as quickly as we could and helped him put the runaways back in the mob. Then we put them all in the holding paddock to be drafted out.

The night before we left the run to come home with a mob of prime cattle—which included the rogue steer—a thunderstorm struck which brought the river up, making it unsafe to ride across the ford. A big tree had been dropped across a narrow part of the river upstream a bit so people could get across when the river was too high to ride a horse across the ford.

Vin sent his employee over on the log first so he could catch the horses when we sent them across. I helped Vin put the cattle over the ford. Then we tied the stirrups and reins securely before sending our horses across, and then walked over the fallen trunk ourselves, very mindful of that swirling, murky water beneath us.

We did not take the mob of cattle far that day—just down the track a little, where we put them in a safe holding paddock. Without the cattle to slow us up, we were able to ride our horses all the way home that day. And that was really the last time I saw Vin, because I left Tasmania soon after.

Brumby reinforcements
Hurtle Baldock

Some people couldn't work brumbies, but I always found them to be mostly good workers, as well as faithful friends. They did have a different temperament to the farm-bred horse, but if handled quietly and firmly, most turned out to be quite good horses, and certainly very hardy.

About the time I left school in the early thirties, agriculture was expanding rapidly on Eyre Peninsula. The supply of draught horses couldn't meet the demand, so Sir Sidney Kidman used to bring 1000 brumbies from Central Australia and sell them at Kapunda, about 70 kilometres north of Adelaide, each September. My uncle on the neighbouring property used to buy about ten of these horses, put together a mob with other buyers from Eyre Peninsula and drive them about 300 kilometres around the top of Spencer Gulf past Port Augusta. In 1933 there were 250 horses in the mob.

During harvest we would handle Uncle's horses and break them in—then would keep the best and sell the rest. Both Dad and Uncle Stan were very good horsemen, so it was an education working with them.

These tough little brumbies not only worked on the farms, but the lighter ones made good hacks and stock horses. Our buggy pair usually contained at least one brumby, so we often had some thrilling rides. For instance, if we had been to a dance, the horses were keen to get going after being tied up for a few hours. Being the eldest, it was my job to help harness the horses and hold their heads while the rest of the family got settled. Then I had to grab the back of the buggy as they flew past.

On one occasion Dad set out to bring home a mob of unbroken horses from about 30 kilometres away, but they knew their way around through the scrub better than we did and kept finishing up back where they started from. By the third attempt, we had worked out which was the ring leader, so Dad caught her, handled her for half an hour, then without mouthing or further education, put her in the buggy with the old mare and set sail for home. The other horses were driven along behind the buggy, following their leader. Next time Dad saw the local police officer, he was informed that he really should have been arrested for speeding.

A bit of restraint
Eva Martin

My aunt, with two young women aboard, both of them sadly handicapped by polio, or infantile paralysis as it was called in those days, had driven from her farm below the range up the Toll Bar to the city of Toowoomba, perched right at the top of a 2000-feet climb of the Great Dividing Range.

On arrival, the horse was unharnessed from the vehicle and the bit lowered from her mouth so that she could pick the grass of my uncle's yard while they were shopping. When the time came to go back home, the horse was harnessed up—but Uncle forgot to replace the bit in the horse's mouth. Though the horse didn't need much guidance going home, it was, of course, a very steep gradient for some miles, and she needed to be restrained somewhat. With Aunt unable to do this, the vehicle travelled so fast that it was likely to overturn and all be injured. Aunt, realising that she must do something, crawled out over the dashboard and over the horse's back, and putting her fingers in the mare's mouth, managed to avert disaster to them all. This happened about 65 years ago, but to this day, the steep climb and equally steep descent are still formidable to modern traffic. Scarcely a month goes by without some truck 'bolting' on the downward journey.

I well remember travelling with my grandmother and aunt on a shopping trip—and our horse would beat the cars to the top, as often they had to stop when the engines boiled, then be cooled down, sometimes with the addition of water from the gully below. It was a heavy drag for horses too and no doubt there were many accidents. Before I was even born my grandparents, taking a pair of horses hitched to a cream wagon, had the misfortune to have it overturn somehow. One can imagine the confusion with broken harness, spilt passengers and cream and kicking horses.

A B 'Banjo' Paterson
'Conroy's Gap' [excerpt]

He rode all night, and he steered his course
By the shining stars with a bushman's skill,
And every time that he pressed his horse
The Swagman answered him gamely still.

190 miles and still keen to travel
GEOFF HAMILTON

I can't imagine there'd be too many horses around these days that could work like Shakespeare did and still be in good shape. Shakespeare, a bay thoroughbred type, was one of many stock horses my father, Wally Hamilton, owned back in the 1920s. We lived on a big property called Ewingar on the western side of the upper reaches of the Clarence River. My grandfather still lived and worked there, too.

Not only did we do all stock work on horses, but since there were no telephones in country areas, all communication with people in surrounding towns involved long trips by horseback. We spent days in the saddle as a matter of course, but the stamina and endurance feats of Shakespeare were exceptional.

Dad told me of the time they had spent many hectic days mustering and drafting cattle that were to be sent to market in Sydney by train. To be loaded onto the train, they first had to travel 50 miles, a two-day journey, from Ewingar into Tenterfield through bush and over mountain ranges. Because there were so many cattle, two trains had been ordered. When Dad, riding Shakespeare, and the two stockmen arrived in Tenterfield with the first mob of cattle in the evening of the second day, the cattle were rested briefly before the men commenced loading them into the cattle trucks. It was about then that the station master informed my father that the second train would be arriving in two days.

The next mob of cattle needed to get moving almost immediately so they would get to Tenterfield on time to meet the train. Loading did not finish until around midnight, at which time Dad got back on Shakespeare and rode the 50 miles to Ewingar in the dark to get the other mob on the track. The trip took him between three and four hours. He rubbed down the horse, gave him a good feed of grain and chaff, and went to bed.

Just on daybreak, Grandfather came out to the stables and saddled the first horse he could see—which just happened to be Shakespeare, who was still wet with sweat, and just finishing his feed. Grandfather cantered off for Grafton, 70 miles away, to sign some documents, and after a short rest and a meal, returned the same day.

Most people can't believe that a horse is capable of covering such distances in the one day, but we were in the habit of doing these sorts of trips quite frequently. What made this one exceptional was that the horse had mustered and driven cattle solidly all week, then after the 50 miles through the bush and over the mountains from Tenterfield carrying my father, had only a short rest and a feed before travelling the 140 miles with my grandfather. And although Shakespeare had covered 190 miles in no more than 20 hours, Grandfather said he was still keen to travel, was on the bit the whole way and moving with a smooth and easy gait that was not tiring for the rider.

125 kilometres to the rescue
Vyvian Mengler

This story comes from about 100 years ago. My late father and his parents lived in the small town of Nebo, Queensland, and their home became known as a place to go for medical help. Dad and his parents were not qualified, but they had taught themselves a lot from the doctors they came in contact with. They could set fractures and do many other things, which was very necessary in those days, since the nearest doctor was at Mackay, roughly 100 kilometres away.

On one occasion Dad was summoned by a stockman—who had been sent from an outlying station—to help a seriously ill woman. The message said if Dad could not help, would he please get them a doctor from Mackay. Dad and his parents realised the woman's symptoms were too severe for semi-trained help, so the doctor was promptly contacted.

The doctor got his sulky driver to harness his pair of well-bred horses and they set out on the first leg of their journey, which would have taken them at least ten hours. They arrived in Nebo at about 2 am and met Dad, who had a pair of good horses ready. The doctor and his driver were given a meal, then at 3 am Dad took over the reins of the sulky, as the doctor's driver did not know the way to the station, which was about 25 kilometres away.

On arrival at the station the doctor hurried to his patient and, fortunately, was able to save her life. Dad attended to his horses, fed and watered them, and made sure they were rested. The doctor spent four or five hours with the woman, so he and Dad were able to have a good rest and a decent meal. They then made the two and a half hour journey back to Nebo.

The doctor and his original driver spent that night in Nebo, then left at daybreak for Mackay with their now well-fed and rested original pair of horses. Our early settlers in remote regions certainly owed a great debt to the speed and stamina of horses, as well as to doctors willing to make such long, tiring trips.

Horses underground

Few working horse environments would have been more dangerous or less hospitable than a coal mine. Deep in the dripping, seeping blackness of gaseous tunnels, many hundreds of horses sweated through eight-hour shifts hauling coal skips back and forth from coalfaces. Clanging metal, explosions, drills, dust and mud added to the hostility.

One of the greatest users of pit ponies in Australia was the Wonthaggi State Coal Mine in Victoria, operating between 1910 and 1968. With seven above-ground stables during its peak production period from 1929 to 1931, more than 300 ponies toiled through its erratic, fractured tunnels, made all the more dangerous because of the jagged seams of coal that twisted through the earth and the ever-present threat of rockfalls. It was because of the nature of Wonthaggi's coal seams that pit ponies continued to be used for so long. The tunnels' steepness and unpredictable turns meant that more modern extraction methods were impractical. For insights into the life of pit ponies in Australia, I am indebted to Joseph and Lynette Chambers of Wonthaggi for use of their book *Come Here! Gee Off!—Wonthaggi's State Coal Mine Pit Ponies*, written with the help of the Friends of the State Coal Mine for the nation's bicentenary.

Chunky, powerful and docile, and mostly around 14 hands high, pit ponies were guided by six voice commands only: Get up, Come on (come forward), Gee off (turn right), Come here (turn left), Whoa and Whoa back (reverse), as well as perhaps a few more colourful phrases, depending on circumstances. Only the dim light of the wheeler's helmet lamp assisted them through the pitch blackness. After just a few days on the job, most could readily thread their way through the maze of tunnels and crossroads from coalface to dump with very little assistance.

The wheeler took full coal wagons, or skips, from the coalface, emptied them and returned the empty wagons to the miners. The ponies not only pulled but also had to push and hold heavy loads, turning and twisting in cramped quarters. Accidents were frequent. In one month alone in 1910, it is recorded that seven ponies were killed. In the 59 years of mining at Wonthaggi, 442 horses died in accidents, often rockfalls, but frequently because of poorly braked and heavily laden skips crushing horses on steep declines. The leather, reinforced skull caps each horse wore only gave protection from stray falling rocks or from grazes to their heads from the jagged rocky ceiling.

One miner, Fred Brown, recalls: 'I can remember seven or eight horses being killed while I was in the mine. One time a wheeler, new to the job, missed all four sprags (wheel pins used for braking) and the horse bolted down towards the flat. As it happened, there were skips on both rails and there was no room at Eight Side. The horse jumped up onto the skips, hit his head on the roof timber and killed himself.

'Another little mare, Una, wasn't hooked up to the skips when they got away. She raced ahead of them, but at a road junction the figure-of-eight on the tail chain got caught up short and the skips hit her and broke her back.'

Allan Birt tells of a rockfall: 'When we got in there, all you could see was a great heap of stone. The first skip was covered, and if Red had been on the front buffer (normal position for the wheeler), he would have been under the stone, too. I could hear the horse breathing loudly and I started throwing lumps of stone out. It was a hazardous job—you never knew when more of the roof would come down. I reached the horse's head and found a lump of timber jammed across his throat. I got that out and he breathed a bit easier. Sammy Nelson, the boss pumper, came along and the two of us managed to clear the stone off the horse.

'By then Nobby Smith (the stableman and vet) had arrived. The horse could hardly raise his head and Nobby said, "I think I'll have to shoot him."

'"Like bloody hell you will," shouts Sammy. "Do you think I've done all this bloody work for nothing?"

'After a lot of trouble we got the horse onto his feet. He looked as if he was drunk, but Sammy and I held him upright and Nobby led him out. After a hose-down and disinfectant on his cuts and bruises, he looked a bit better and within a few weeks he was right again.'

Bonds between most wheelers and their horses understandably became very strong in the water-drip eerie silences—shattered only by sudden explosions and the metallic racket, and isolated from the sights, sounds and smells of the safer world above.

Miners reported it was not uncommon to see a man with his arms around his horse's neck giving it a cuddle. Many shared their lunch with their horses and chatted to them like old friends. In return, a horse's instinct saved many a miner.

Harry Sainsbury reports: 'We were working a road with an air-door across it (for ventilation). Usually I would go ahead and open the door and call, "Come on, Nipper." Then as he came through, I would jump on the front skip and ride. This particular day he wouldn't budge a foot when I called him. Finally I moved back to him, shouting, "I'll shift you, my boy." He made a sudden bolt through the doorway and the roof fell in and filled the front skips with tons of stone. I would have been under the fall, if it hadn't been for Nipper.'

Fred Brown tells a similar story about one of his favourite horses: 'About halfway into the bords [coalface], Doodle stopped short and his ears pricked up—a sure sign that he had heard something. Suddenly he bolted forward and, at the same time, the whole roof fell in, covering the empties on which I would have been riding if not warned by Doodle. Doodle survived the fall and, I can tell you, I always paid attention to what his ears were saying.'

Not all horses, however, were noble, stoic and co-operative.

One, Porky, was notorious for laziness and insurrection.

Fred Brown tells how one day he and a mate took a short cut through a narrow, unused roadway: 'We came on a horse and skip standing in front of an air-door. The skip carried rails, timber and roadman's tools, and the horse was Porky. He was leaning over to one side of the roadway and when we got close we could see that he had Ralph Ladner jammed against the side of the tunnel. Ralph was a small light chap and there was no way that he would shift Porky's weight. He had been there for three-quarters of an hour.'

And not all dangers came from recalcitrant horses or mine misadventure. There was indeed the dreadful problem of too much lush green feed during weekends off in the mine's paddocks.

Allan Birt takes up the story: 'Jimmy was wheeling with Old Girlie to the horizontal wheel at the end of a jig in West Dip in West Area. There was a very steep slant and about halfway up, a low beam in the roof. Girlie had to arch her back to get under it. Jimmy used to hang on to her tail to help himself up the slant.

'One Monday morning, on his first trip, they reached the beam and prepared to squeeze through. After a weekend out on the lush green grass in the paddock, the strain of getting under the beam was just too much for Old Girlie. She let go and Jimmy got the lot right in his face.'

When the seams of Wonthaggi were exhausted in 1968, the last 22 working pit ponies in Australia were put out to pasture or sold—never again to queue for the cage to go below or to rush back for a washdown at the end of their shift. A colourful side of our mining history had ended.

Henry Lawson
'The Roaring Days' [excerpt]

Oft when the camps were dreaming,
And fires began to pale,
Through rugged ranges gleaming
Swept on the Royal Mail.
Behind six foaming horses,
And lit by flashing lamps,
Old Cobb and Co., in royal state,
Went dashing past the camps.

Don't spare the horses— the mail must go through
Research: Angela Goode and Alan Jones

The South Australian experience in developing mail routes is as colourful as any, and no run was more treacherous than between Adelaide and Mount Gambier. Vast tracts of the country were covered in water, and habitation was sparse. Until 1849 mounted police troopers and packhorses were deployed to ensure the mail got through. The highly unpopular 450-kilometre task (340 miles approximately) took about eleven days, during which time the men had to camp out and fend for themselves. Because they had to carry so much camping gear, their horses frequently developed sore backs. When contractors took over the routes, use of vehicles or packhorses was optional, but by 1862, vehicles were compulsory.

For a vivid description of what such a journey was like, I hand over to a correspondent whose account was published in the *Adelaide Observer* on 9th June 1866.

THE OVERLAND JOURNEY
On a dull drizzling morning, Monday, May 23, a little before 5 o'clock, I ascended, at the door of Roger's Inn, Naracoorte, the somewhat non- descript conveyance provided by Mr Rounsevell for the conveyance of H.M. mails from the South-East to Adelaide. The appearance of the turn-out in the grey morning was anything but promising. The vehicle, a square box on wheels, looked very clumsy and suggestive of aching bones, and the couple of horses provided by the contractor were poor, raw-boned, hungry-looking brutes, who seemed to have very little go in them. The living occupants of the vehicle were the driver, a smart young fellow of considerable humour and good nature; the mail guard, not a bad fellow to travel with; and myself. Another mail left at the same hour for Border Town, and the time

we spent outside the Post Office was pleasantly employed by the two drivers chaffing each other about the merits of their respective horses. Each advised the other to take care his team did not bolt, which was, of course, a piece of delicate irony, there being no more chance of such animals bolting than of a donkey being entered for a steeplechase. The mails being all aboard, we started on a journey such as I have no ambition to travel again. I learnt, in the course of the few days I was on the road, the three grand qualifications necessary for a successful mail driver on the overland route—first, a powerful voice; secondly, a strong arm; and thirdly, an unlimited supply of whipcord.

Our nearside horse had an unfortunate tendency to pull himself away from the other, which did not add either to the straightness or the celerity of our journey. After proceeding a few miles, during which the driver had shouted and bellowed at the pitch of his voice, almost exhausting all the endearing and all the objurgatory adjectives in the English language, he pulled up, and changed the position of the horses. This did not improve matters much, and when I suggested that perhaps the refractory animal had a sore neck, 'Of course he has,' was the reply; 'but he need not make such a row as that.' It appears that to have a sore neck is the normal condition of the poor unfortunate beasts that work the South-Eastern mail. My subsequent observation showed me this. After this little colloquy the driver brought down his whip on the poor brutes, and that failing to produce much effort he tried to 'talk them along'. 'Now darlings—get up, ye cripples— confound you, you crawling sweeps,' all in one sentence sounded funny enough. For twenty or thirty yards a faint gallop would be got out of the wretches, and they then sunk back into their usual walk, or a weak trot that was hardly better than a walk. At length our Jehu was in danger of losing his temper, and as he got excited the aspiration of his vowels became most emphatic. 'You haggravatin hanimals, cannot you get along!' and then came in a pitiable and almost hopeless tone, gradually decreasing, 'Well, well, well!' But by dint of flogging, coaxing, vociferating, and strong adjectiving, a stage of about 17 miles was got out of the poor overworked and ill-fed animals. The next stage, we had three horses, which in hungry looks, prominent bones and general unwillingness to work were pretty well matched. The mailman and guard beguiled the way and endeavoured to keep me in spirits by the promise of the greatly improved team which would be picked up at the next stables for the third and concluding stage that day, one of 28 miles. When I saw them, however, my hopes were not very much raised, and yet they managed to get us along by the forcible motives already referred to, and at 7 o'clock in the evening, a great portion of the journey having been done in the teeth of a heavy rain storm, we pulled up at the Inn at Lacepede Bay, where a good fire and a comfortable tea almost led me to forget the hardships and annoyances of the journey.

At Kingston we changed vehicles and drivers. On Tuesday morning before 5 o'clock we left Kingston for the longest stage this side of Naracoorte. We had about 90 miles to do before reaching Magrath's Flat, our resting place for the night, and George, the new driver, a thoroughly genial nice fellow, was anxious to get off as soon as possible. I may say, in passing, that Mr Rounsevell generally manages to select capital 'whips' for his conveyance. However ill-horsed they may be, they are as a rule well manned. George had a pair of good horses out of Kingston, and we did the first stage of 17 miles in two hours, which was not bad travelling. Our second team had rather a wild and rough look, and their performances did not belie their looks. The leader was a mischievous brute answering to the name of The Baker. Our first attempt at a start was a dead failure. The Baker, having 'got his head' did not seem to know what to do with it. He stood up straight on his hind legs for a moment, and then made a rush forward and broke the swingle-tree in two pieces. This was promising. The damaged article was hastily repaired, and The Baker having behaved so ill as leader was changed into a 'poler', and a raw-boned brute who seemed to be decidedly weak in his intellect took his place. With this change a start was effected, but our new leader showed a strong inclination to run us against trees, and the greatest objection to go on the proper road. More than once we owed our escape from an awkward collision to the skill of the driver, who at length began to look gloomy at the prospect. He was bound to make his eight miles an hour over a road which he knew too well, and he had a very unpromising start. George quickly got out, and tried the effect of a good thrashing on the refractory leader, who showed how much he profited by the painful lesson by again rushing us within an inch or two of a tree, and then turned round to see how we liked it. Our driver had one resource left. He took off the winkers, hoping that the horse would be impelled to do from fear what he would not do from punishment. This last move was successful, and we at length, got underway, when we went along at a pretty good pace. We kept by the side of the Coorong, sometimes crossing and recrossing it, over hills of sand and long flats of moist pipeclay, as adhesive as glue, through large sheets of water, which were always taken at a smart gallop to the infinite discomfort of the poor passenger, who was bespattered from head to foot with mud.

After pursuing our journey in this manner, stopping once or twice by the way for such moderate refreshment as the limited resources of the country afforded, about 7 o'clock we approached Magrath's Flat, cold, weary, and aching. The road was very trying, and the wonder to me was how the poor-looking horses managed to get over stages of upwards of 20 miles in the time they did. A better class of horses would have done it quicker; but the contractor seems to put all his screws on that road. I heard that recently the manager of the route selected all the best horses and sent them to Adelaide, leaving only the worst behind. This is very different from the way in which Cobb & Co. manage the mail service on the other side. There the best cattle are selected, well-fed, and well-groomed; and though I was assured the roads were quite as bad as ours, a speed of ten miles per hour is maintained.

On Wednesday morning, at the usual hour, a little before 5, we started for the last uncomfortable stage in the journey. We should reach Strathalbyn that evening, when the comforts of civilization would again be accessible. As far as the roads were concerned, this was the worst day's journey we had. Through the wretched desert of sand, through the muddy swamp at Lake Albert, the weary horses urged their way. More stamping, shouting, whipping, with 'cursory' remarks not a few; more trials of patience, more shaking and bumping, till at length we reached Wellington where we began to breathe more freely. We felt the worst of our journey was over; the overland route was nearly accomplished.

When we left Wellington we went along at a spanking pace. We had got into a region where the horses were stable-fed, and not poor, weedy wretches living on the miserable pasture of the bush. At the next stage we found the horses were shod, and punctual to our time we entered Strathalbyn, where I found, as I had done before, a comfortable temporary home at the Victoria Hotel. Here my troubles ceased. Next morning by 10 o'clock I was in

Long distances: tough people and horses

Adelaide, I hope both wiser and better for my journey to the South-East.

As if the journey wasn't bad enough and despite frequent broken axles, overturnings and boggings, the South Australian government decreed that from January 1867 the five-day daylight journey for the mail between Mount Gambier and Adelaide should be reduced to a 48-hour non-stop trip! It was a pragmatic political decision; mail took only two days between Mount Gambier and Melbourne, so business was increasingly starting to flow to the east—rather than to Adelaide.

Because much of the south-east trip was through sand and swamp, the horrors of not only trying to find the tracks in the dark but also of making good time resulted in increased numbers of accidents and graphic newspaper reports from correspondents of the time.

Border Watch, 3 April 1867
We are informed that the Mount Gambier mail capsized ... near Coolatoo when coming to Adelaide, owing to the driver running into a telegraph-post. All the passengers ... were thrown out. The guard fell under the front wheels, which passed over him, and then the conveyance fell upon him, inflicting some severe bruises, but no other injuries.

Border Watch, 14 March 1868
As the Adelaide mail was driving into Mount Gambier on Thursday ... one of the horses fell and was dragged a considerable distance before the others could be pulled up. It was frightfully injured, the skin being literally torn off one of its sides.

Mount Gambier Standard, 16 December 1870
On Sunday, December 4, the mail driver, on his journey

to Naracoorte, was going at top speed on a dry part of the track to make up time in the prospect of travelling over probably the worst road in the colony. When about a quarter of a mile from Kingston, the horses took fright at a bullock lying in the way and shied. This movement of the team sent the coach right over, the wheels in the air. Cuttings run on each side of the line, and into one of these a traveller was pitched, without, however, being seriously hurt. The inside passengers were much cut and scratched; but fortunately escaped without breaking any bones.

But while the stage-coach drivers were flogging their horses to get the mail through on time, drivers on feeder lines that connected with the main mail routes also had their troubles. Pity the luckless Mr John Sinclair, who in July 1868 was driving the 55 miles between Bordertown and Naracoorte at night. He strayed off the indistinct track and found himself entangled in the clothes-line of a nearby household.

Mr Sinclair was unseated from his trap, his face was severely cut and several of his teeth were torn out.

On a moonlit night a year later, Mr Sinclair, at almost the same place on his seven to eight hour trip, hit a stump with his trap. The pole broke and the two horses bolted. Mr Sinclair, clearly aware that the mail must go through, no matter what, clung on to the reins, and was dragged about 50 yards along the ground before the horses stopped. When he attempted to raise himself from the ground by leaning on his left hand, he found that it was broken. Undeterred, Mr Sinclair lashed the buggy together again, yoked up the horses (using his right hand and what teeth of his remained) and drove on to Naracoorte to deliver his mail, presumably still managing to make his connection.

FOUR
Horse sense

Stories of animals going beyond the call of duty or demonstrating unexpected talent always make good

reading. They beg the question of whether animals, and horses in particular, have powers of reasoning.

The tale of Shrimp, an equine saint if ever there was one, illustrates just how well a horse can bury its flight reflexes for a good cause. After twenty years of helping severely disabled children without ever an impatient stamp of her hoof, she deserves a medal.

Gordon Phillips, a retired dairy farmer from Gippsland, exhibits a human sort of horse sense which almost defies reason. Gordon has been blind all his life. He has never seen a horse, yet he has earned a living working with horses and he breeds and shows them.

Equally as astounding are the following stories from other writers. Their lives, which were so closely entwined with their working horses, brought common understanding and, in some cases, a life-saving relationship. I still find Hilda Cherry's account of being saved from quicksand by her horse, Biscuit, particularly amazing. She retold it when I visited her during her annual break from droving. Without the horse's help, since no-one else was around, Hilda would most certainly have perished. She told me the reason the bridle didn't break was because she had made it herself, good and tough as always.

Saintly Shrimp

It takes a special sort of horse to keep walking calmly while a rider struggles with apparent terror. It's more than training that allows an animal to be calm when all around is chaos, noise and a child in panic. It has to have wisdom and a sense of duty, as well as realising that no matter what happens it must not react, throw a wobbly or try to flee. This is what is required of the horses used by the Riding for the Disabled Association to give profoundly disabled children some improved quality of life. Very few horses make the grade.

At the Riding for the Disabled base at Hamilton College in western Victoria, you'll find a pony that has served the area's disabled children since the founding of the branch in 1981. Every Wednesday at the school's huge rubber arena is Riding for the Disabled day for four rostered horses and eight helpers, and Shrimp, at the age of 26, is still the front-line pony for a child's first ride.

Shrimp has heard the screams as a child feels warm horse flesh for the first time or reacts with alarm or joy at the sight of a muzzle, eyes and ears. She has felt the spasms of children with cerebral palsy, felt the grip of tense legs around her body. She has heard the involuntary shrieks of nervous, uncomprehending riders who have never seen a horse before or been so far above the ground. Many have never known what it is like to have their bodies moving freely and independently of wheelchairs.

Comforted and held secure in the saddle, fearful riders eventually cease grabbing out and trying to escape. They relax and become silent. The rocking rhythm of life, a pony walking on evenly and purposefully, and the child's primal memories are stimulated. Suddenly a smile will break out, the atmosphere lightens, and a mother feels joy in her chest. Few are the ways of lifting the misery of a child with a closed-in, powerless life. The little dark brown pony with big white blaze and four white feet has a knowing look. Shrimp, 13.2 hands, is unflappable, wise and gentle. She has given many hundreds of blind, deaf, autistic, Down's syndrome and brain-damaged children their first experience on the back of a horse, helped them to feel secure and enjoy gentle muscle-stretching therapy and a sense of freedom. This great little trooper spends two hours every week doing the sort of work that most horses find discomforting. Shrimp copes with clumsy hugs and kisses aimed at her head, gets dressed in antlers, Christmas tinsel and bells, or carries 'jockeys' wearing silks on Melbourne Cup day.

'It is her warmth and apparent understanding of these children that is so special,' says Lindy Young, long-time Riding for the Disabled volunteer and owner of the former show pony, which she bought as an unbroken two year old 'because she was so cute'. Lindy, well known in showjumping, dressage and eventing circles, said Shrimp's outstandingly benign temperament was apparent from a very early age.

Lindy had no need for a pony in 1977 when for some unknown reason she decided to buy the pony with the friendly face and look-at-me presence. She already had her hands full with several other horses, which she was showing on the weekend that she collected Shrimp from her breeder, Kym Peglar, at Mount Gambier. The little half-Arab registered pony with the name, coincidentally, of Warilla Lindy, was pushed into the float and spent the weekend at the showgrounds learning to be tied up and to cope with the fluttering flags, loudspeakers and boisterous activity of a country show. It seemed to do the trick. Shrimp was soon being ridden and shown successfully herself.

Lindy lent Shrimp to friends and their children, and in 1981 when she married and moved to Cavendish, near Hamilton, she contacted the founder of the newly formed Riding for the Disabled branch, Judith Riffkin, and offered Shrimp's services. There are believed to be few longer serving ponies. Shrimp deserves a medal.

'The ponies have to be long suffering to cope with tense bodies that grip tightly with their heels,' says Lindy. Normally pressure from the heels indicates to a horse that it should go faster. 'But she just puts up with it all. Some ponies can't bear it. Some children just yell all the time they're in the saddle. You are not always sure if it is fear or joy, but Shrimp is the one that we always use for those children.' All Riding for the Disabled ponies are led, and children have someone walking beside them to ensure they don't slip sideways. Walking pace is generally quite fast to generate a backwards and forwards momentum and prevent the passenger wobbling sideways.

Lindy says many of the children, aged from six to 18, have no ability to cope with changes in their environment and some are not aware of their surroundings. To be sat on a horse challenges them greatly, but their parents say they always sleep best after riding days. Just being able to get out for the afternoon is good for them. Their minds are stimulated by different sights and sounds, as well as the feel and smell of a horse. Their taut muscles and tendons get gently stretched and strengthened. Games help the children's balance and co-ordination. Most of the children learn to get onto the horses themselves from the specially constructed mounting block, which accommodates wheelchairs and unsteady walkers.

Lindy, 49, says that although she was overwhelmed by the disabilities of the children when she had her first contact with Riding for the Disabled at the age of 17, she gets an enormous buzz from their enjoyment of the horses.

Shrimp, having taught Lindy's two now grown-up children to ride, plus countless others, continues on between Riding for the Disabled duties as a live-in mount at Hamilton College, in the junior riders' horsemanship course. This extraordinary little horse has no plans for putting up her hooves just yet.

Consummate horseman, yet never seen a horse

Gordon Phillips is the sort of blind bloke who can make sighted people feel useless, especially around horses. He's never seen a horse in his life, but he can tell a good one from a bad one with no trouble at all, has worked with them since he was eight years old and still shows and breeds them.

Long ago, he ignored his parents' advice to have nothing to do with horses. They're dreadful, untrustworthy, kicking creatures, he was told. 'You'll come a nasty cropper with them,' his parents warned him. 'They can be very nasty animals and let a kick go quick and lively.'

Born in 1926, he grew up in Parkdale on Port Phillip Bay where, during the Depression, his father got a job managing a dairy. In those days, milk was delivered in cans and bottles from a milk cart pulled by a horse. Without refrigeration, deliveries had to be made between 3 am and 7 am. Young Gordon, keen to be involved with his dad, would be out of bed to help harness the horse, then they'd set off on the regular round, where the horse would reliably stop in the same spot outside each house, which Gordon duly memorised. 'Going the same way every day was good training. I got to know the sound, smell and feel of every place and it stood me in good stead later.' His job was to carry in the one pint and half pint bottles to front verandahs or hiding spots in hedges. Then he would go off to school for the rest of the day!

At 13, he went to the Blind Institute in Melbourne to learn maths and Braille. When he finished there at 16, he found work at a poultry farm, got a pound a week, gave his mum 15 shillings and kept five shillings for himself. He put that towards buying a cow, then bought a few more so he could sell their progeny and put a bit more cash away.

The milk-round experience with his father had given him the confidence to have a go at almost anything. He was determined to be independent, so at 17 decided that having his own horse and cart was the way to go. From then on he took on jobs which could reasonably be considered outlandish for a blind bloke. He was a bottle-o, had a rubbish run for a while, then got a tipping dray and sold sand all round Parkdale and even a bit beyond.

'He was a very kind horse. It was an act of God that I got that horse,' says Gordon about Dan, the draught horse he bought in 1943 at the Dandenong horse sale during a terrible drought. One hundred and twenty skinny and unwanted horses were sent in for sale from outlying farm areas, which also were starting to welcome the arrival of tractors. Gordon got Dan for two pounds, a good price even then. 'It was definitely a gift, a message from above, because I never knew anything then about what makes a good horse,' he said. So straight away, Dan went into a spring cart and Gordon, who had learnt how to harness up as a child under his father's tutelage, set out collecting the empty bottles of Parkdale, along the streets that he had got to know so well as a child. He initially took a friend to guide them both, but Dan was sensible about following the gutters of each street. 'If there was something in his way, he would just stop.' Gordon walked along calling out the familiar bottle-o's cry, leading Dan. With his and Dan's other enterprises, Gordon was able to buy 320 acres at Heath Hill, in Gippsland, where he and his wife, Rita, still live and which he developed from a heavily timbered wild block, using contractors. In 1955, on honeymoon, he bought nine dairy cows to graze on his new pastures, and built a dairy that he designed himself. Over the years, he and Rita built up to 137 cows. Someone told me how he had dropped round to see Gordon a few years ago to buy a horse. For some reason they had to go into the dairy. Gordon forgot to turn the lights on for his sighted visitor, who then proceeded to knock his head on every low beam in the place, while six-foot-tall Gordon neatly ducked every time.

Gordon started breeding Clydesdales in 1952 and showed them at Melbourne Royal in harness as lorry horses and in the led section. He gave up in 1955 because he couldn't be sure he'd 'dress' his horses correctly. It was one thing this extraordinary man had to admit was beyond him. Showing resumed for him in led classes in Melbourne in 1975, and when he got someone to plait manes and tails for him, he started winning ribbons. He gets others to lead his horses in Melbourne, but at nearby Warrigal Show he manages the job himself. The notion of leading half a ton of horse and not being able to check where its dinner plates of feet are putting themselves is scary, certainly for me, but Gordon says he has only had a couple of bad experiences with horses. 'I don't run risks,' he says, insisting it's all to do with handling a horse correctly. He always puts his hand on a horse's wither 'so I know where the two vicious bits are, the end that bites and the end that kicks.'

That trick of always going first to the wither has another motive. It's the wither that he says determines the quality of much of the rest of the conformation. He likes a good, well-proportioned wither with enough substance to support a nice, arched neck, well- set head with deep jaw and plenty of space under it for gullet and windpipe. He describes every aspect of his ideal horse as he runs his hands over its spring of rib checking for lung capacity, down front and back legs feeling for strength of bone and setting of joints and then listens intently as they are trotted and cantered for correctness of gait and soundness of wind.

Gordon has fifteen mares in his Myrtle Park Stud and sells progeny to a waiting list of clients ranging from people using Clydesdales for traditional farm work to those in tourism, showing or breeding. He handles all the foals early, again with his focus on their wither for protection. He used to break in all his horses, at one time having 25 breeding horses and five in work, mainly pulling heavy sections of railway line over his newly developed land to break it up and level it. He would co-opt Rita or a friend for that sort of work, but when feeding out of hay needs to be done, Gordon and a horse and trolley still do that, with him walking along in front and the horse following, just as they did in his early days.

Skipping the drinks
Doug Harkin

We worked long hours, only stopping when we could no longer see, and then we'd travel home in the dark. The horses would be tired. Once they were unharnessed they would often have to trudge about a quarter mile from the stable to get a drink, especially in summer when the creek was drying up. Off they would plod, around the sheds and out of our view, while we put out their chaff in the stable by the light of a hurricane lamp.

We only became suspicious that something was amiss once they started returning without muddy feet. So next time they set off, we sneaked around the corner of the shed—and there they all were, just standing there. We watched as they waited a decent interval—and then appeared again in the stable out of the gloom. Once they realised we had become wise to their trick, they went off for their drink as they were supposed to in the first place.

I always wondered how they worked out how long to wait, and how did they all agree to forgo their nightly drink?

Biscuit saviour
Hilda Cherry

In 1969 we were droving a mob of 7000 weaner sheep on the Breeza Plain. It was very hot and dry and the Murki River was very low. It had fallen well back and was boggy. The sheep were very small and weak and had been transported from the

Riverina district, the owner hoping for a sale for them in the north. We would spend hours dragging them from the muddy banks.

One day while riding the river to check for damsels in distress, I found one which had ventured out further than the rest and was in trouble. I climbed off my chestnut stock horse, Biscuit, took the reins over his head and dropped them, then waded into the mud. With a lot of difficulty I lifted the sheep up. They were full wool and the water and mud made it quite a burden. I then went to step out and climb up the bank to Biscuit, only to find I was stuck and being slowly pulled down. Panic, it was quicksand. What to do? No-one was about—too far away to hear my calls.

Then I remembered I had left the reins dangling, so I started calling Biscuit. Each time I spoke he moved slowly closer to the edge, until the reins dropped over the bank. I still couldn't reach. I just kept calling and asking him to help me. He seemed to realise I was stressed out and began to neigh and shake his head up and down, causing the reins to flick towards me. They'd shoot forward, then fall short.

After what seemed like an eternity, I grabbed them. Now I had to get him to back away—it was the only way I would get out. So I began pleading with him to 'Back Up'.

Slowly he got the message and started moving backward. I hung on and prayed the bridle wouldn't break. It didn't take forever—but for me it seemed like a lifetime before I was on solid ground again. Biscuit had probably saved my life.

Shining eggsample
Nancy Hyde

Over 60 years ago on the farm at Coomunga, our Clydesdale stallion, Peter, reigned supreme. He was intelligent, a bit arrogant, but a wonderful worker.

In the corner of his yard was his stable, and against one wall was the wooden manger. This was a favourite nesting place for the fowls and several habitually laid their eggs in Peter's hay, which he then regarded as part of his rations. My mother-in-law, being a true Scot, liked to gather *all* the eggs produced by the hens, but Peter refused to relinquish them. Every time she attempted to get them, Peter would stand guard with a look which said—'These are mine'. He ate every egg the fowls provided and his coat was so shiny you could almost see your face in it. Gran only got her full quota when Peter was in the paddock working.

Intelligence almost human
Margaret Glendenning

'Jess, what on earth …?' Grandad leapt to his feet as the big bay mare thrust her head over the half-door of the kitchen. The small girl blinking owlishly in the lantern light slid thankfully from the horse's back into his arms. Quickly the story tumbled out … a broken gig wheel … a load of groceries and goods on board from Bendigo … Grandma alone out in the cold, dark bush almost 10 miles away.

Grandma had stripped the mare of most of her harness, lifted the little four-year-old rider (my mother's sister) aboard and instructed the mare: 'Go home, Jess.' Grandma was duly rescued—and so another tale about Jess, the magnificent, was added to the family archives.

Many of the tales credited Jess with an intelligence almost human. On that night, she had bypassed the stable where she usually pulled in, carrying the child right to the house. It was a departure from her normal routine, whereby she eagerly tried to get her head into the feed bin at the earliest opportunity.

Jess was a tall Cleveland Bay, and one of those totally versatile do-anything horses. She was good to ride, pulled the dray, gig or anything else necessary in the course of a working day at my grandfather's eucalyptus factory at Whirrakee, out in the Whipstick north-east of Bendigo. She worked driverless between the factory and where the boys were cutting wood to fire the boilers. A brief 'Go home, Jess' and the laden dray was hauled in.

Once unloaded, a terse command from Grandad of 'Back to the boys, Jess' sent her back-tracking to the axemen. The same procedure saw her bringing in the high loads of silver mallee leaf to be steamed. She contributed to every process of eucalyptus oil production, delivering the final products to the Raywood railway station.

Everybody is quite sure that among Jess's long list of talents was included that of counting. Apparently she knew that when the used leaves were removed there would be four 'sections' waiting. Willingly, she backed under the crane for four cart-loads of waste, taking them to the spot Grandad had selected to dump them for drying out. Later on they were used to fire the boilers. After the fourth trip, she returned unbidden to the shed where the 'section cart' was stored, backed it in, and waited to be unhitched.

This remarkable mare lived to the grand old age of 27, spending her last days on a neighbouring farm doing occasional light work. My mother thinks she had foaled once before Grandad purchased her, but she surprised everyone by producing a fit and healthy foal when she was in her mid-twenties.

Doctor returns
Leta Padman

Alick Hiscock, whose father had a Clydesdale stud at Narrung, told how they once sent several horses to a special sale at Tailem Bend. All were sold, except for one called Doctor, who was left in the saleyards overnight. Somehow he escaped and found his way some 56 kilometres to the punt which crosses the River Murray at Narrung. Alick's uncle was operating the punt, so he took the old fellow across and turned him free. Doctor arrived at the house gate and waited patiently to be let in.

How could you offer a horse like that for sale again?

Faith and trust
Stafford Pederick

It was always essential that a horse and its owner trusted and had faith in each other. I remember one incident in which these qualities played a very important part.

In 1945, from January until June 9th there had been no rain at all. When 10 inches (250 millilitres) fell between the 9th and the end of the month, it was necessary for seeding to be done straight away.

Nine horses needed to be abreast on the combine, and all went well until at a very wet and boggy spot, disaster struck. Of the nine horses, only two were left standing. The other seven heavy farm horses were down to their bellies in the bog, and had to be released quickly. It did not take long to remove the chains buried in the mud, to free the harness and bring the two standing horses to firm ground—but what to do with the others?

One by one, six horses floundered out as best they could, leaving one named Freddy still stuck fast in the middle. By now the bog had become a quagmire, which could not stand the weight of a horse. Our long association with Freddy, and his trust in us, were about to pay off. We looked at the situation and could see only one way to bring him to safety.

'Freddy,' my father said to him. 'We will have to dig a hole on either side to see your legs, then roll you over three times through the mud until you reach firm ground and can stand up.'

We started to dig, and Freddy stayed quite calm. There was no panic, even though he was imprisoned in the bog. When at last we had him free enough to start rolling him, he trusted us enough not to kick or struggle in any way.

Value of a champion
Carolyn McConnel

Value was a brown stock horse mare bred by my husband's family from a mare off the famous Glenhaughton Station at Taroom, Queensland. By the time we were married and I got to know her, she was already a brood mare, as she had fallen at a campdraft and broken her fetlock some years before. Instead of putting her down, she had been sent to the Vet School in Brisbane. They had somehow saved her, although her fetlock was stiff and swollen and her knee had a decided sideways bend, but she was in good nick and got along at a pretty good pace when she wanted to.

She was never a friendly horse and stayed well away from people, although once she was caught, you could do anything with her. We bred a couple of good foals from her—and then she had her last foal, a replica of herself, a pretty brown filly by our own quarter horse stallion.

The foal was only about a week old when my husband, John, had to leave for Brisbane early and I was on my own. I was washing up when I noticed Value and the foal were outside the garden fence. This was most unlike her, and she was neighing a lot. I went out, and was sickened to find her offside leg snapped at the bent knee. It was just swinging, and I knew the only thing we could do was put her out of her pain. First I had to catch her foal somehow, because I was frightened that if I shot her, the foal would take off and go through a fence. I needed help for this, but none of the neighbours was home and there was no vet in the area.

When I did get through to John, he said he would be at least two hours getting home and that I would just have to stay with her. She was damp with sweat, but calm in her resigned way. She would lay her head on my shoulder and sigh, and would nudge me whenever the foal came bouncing up. It would take a suck and prance off again before I could get a halter anywhere near it. If I went to move away, Value would nicker to me and I realised she needed my support to cope with the pain—and I needed a box of tissues for the pain I was feeling seeing her go through this.

Finally John arrived and we decided to catch the foal first, as by then it was getting sick of all the inactivity and was going for long runs down the paddock, which worried Value, who was still standing where I had found her that morning. We got the kids' old pony to help us, and finally, with Value's co-operation, managed to get a rope on the foal. I had had to walk under the mare's belly and around her heels trying to get the foal to walk into the loop of rope, as we didn't want to scare either of them by swinging a rope around—and the foal had no intention of coming up to anyone.

As I led the protesting foal and the old pony away, Value nickered just the once and suddenly lay down. Her job was done, the foal was in good hands and she was finally able to give in to the agony she must have been in. John shot her and shed a few tears, too, and we agreed she had been the gamest horse we had known, and the most intelligent. We found later where she had fallen a good mile from the homestead, and followed the marks where she had dragged her broken leg to get to us for help.

I am sure she knew she was beyond help herself, as all her attention had been on the foal, but she knew that the foal needed us and so she had made that gallant effort to get it up to us. The foal was poddied and is one of our best working horses today—never an easy ride, but she can go anywhere and never hesitates, no matter what you ask of her. She is almost as game as her mother.

Just fooling
Gordon Faithfull

Back in the 1930s, when we lived on the farm, wood was a very vital commodity for heating, cooking and washing. Much time and energy had to be devoted to the getting of wood. My responsibility, with the assistance of Blossom, a draught mare, was to fetch a supply of branches from the paddocks; these would then be cut by axe into suitable lengths for the stove, copper and fireplaces.

Blossom was a huge, powerful horse, standing some 16 hands high. I would set to work cutting those branches and then hitch them to the drag chain. Blossom—who had been around for many a summer—would then put her head down, lean forward and pretend she was cruelly overloaded. Sometimes, one or even two branches would be jettisoned in order to enable Blossom to move, and eventually we would make it home with the diminished load.

Dad happened to meet me at the woodpile one time and asked why I had not dragged in a decent supply of wood. My indignant reply was that Blossom couldn't pull any more. Said Dad: 'I think we'll go up and try for another load.'

Dad secured some twenty branches with the drag chain then spoke sternly to Blossom. You know, that cunning old horse arched her neck, leant into the collar and walked on without a hint of effort.

Home from the ball
Elsie Dunn

My brother, sister and I once went 17 miles to a St Patrick's Day sports day and a ball, after which we drove 17 miles home again. Silver, a tall, iron-grey trotter, was the horse we had in the sulky on that occasion. Since we were very tired after the big day and all the dancing that night, my brother let the reins rest on the mudguard at the front of the sulky, leaving Silver to trot home while we slept. This always worked well. However, this time, Silver must have veered off the road to let some other trap pass because when I awoke at 5 am we were stationary—and very lopsided. I woke the other two, and we discovered that one wheel of the sulky had fallen into a ditch.

Silver, sensible horse that he was, was just standing quietly waiting. We all got out and my brother and I lifted the wheel out of the hole and Silver dragged the sulky back onto the road so we could complete the trip home.

Night driving and horse sense
Zita Ward

My father was returning home from droving a mob of sheep to the saleyards, about 32 miles away. He was driving a horse and sulky, and by the time he got to our end of the valley, it was pitch dark, and a heavy fog had come down. The road was only a dirt track, and although it was very familiar to him, he became quite disorientated and was having some difficulty in forcing the horse along.

Twice the horse stopped and would not move. When Dad got out to investigate the second time round, he found the horse up against a fence, because he had steered him off the track. Totally perplexed by this time, Dad decided to let the horse have a free rein instead of trying to guide him. Soon they were trotting along comfortably, ending up at the boundary gate to our farm with no further problems.

It is a wise man who gives over to the instincts of his horse on a dark and foggy night.

Driverless Punch in the scrub
Hurtle Baldock

One of our most intelligent farm horses, Punch, was very handy when logging scrub. The scrub was pulled down by a boomerang-shaped log—six to eight metres long. It was built from seven pieces of mallee, and if shaped correctly, would climb the trees until enough leverage was obtained to break them off or they would come out by the roots. The log was pulled by a team of horses or bullocks on either end. The outside team was driven along the edge of the standing scrub, while the inside team of horses, in single file, pushed its way through the scrub at the right width. Punch seemed to know exactly how wide that log was, as he always led his single file team without interference from a driver.

Thirty miles through the scrub
Max Verco

In 1935 when I came to this district, there was nothing but scrub. We tackled this country with axe, grubber, crowbar and draught horses, as well as stock horses for mustering the 40,000 acres. There weren't any roads, so all sheep had to be brought in by droving them from the nearest rail-head, which was Bordertown, 30 miles away. The reverse applied when I had sheep for sale, but on those trips, I had a bit more time for socialising once the sheep were loaded onto the train.

After droving all day it was pretty good adjourning to the pub for a few drinks. At about ten o'clock, when I had caught up on news from around the district, I would put old Ginger back in the cart and start off home.

Once I got away from the town, I would curl up in the bottom of the cart and go to sleep. Ginger, like so many horses then, had a lot of brains and always looked after his boss magnificently—taking me 30 miles home through the scrub without any trouble.

Gently does it
Norm Giles

A neighbour's team was jibbing with an 80-bag load of wheat on a table-top trolley. The driver could not get his team even to try to pull the load. He was using many adjectives about the jibbing horses. After quite some time, my dad, who was a wonderful horseman, went up to the driver and asked if he could help him. All my dad did was to stroke every horse on its face and talk to it. Then he told the chap to give him the reins. Dad just said quietly to the horses, 'Right-oh, lads, get up', and away they walked with their load.

Horses are far from being silly. They know when they have their driver or rider bluffed.

Keeping things orderly
Hurtle Baldock

At one stage I was working a twelve-horse tandem team. When I put the winkers on the six leaders, I noticed that they always lined up at the harness room door in their correct positions. Whether it was intelligence or force of habit, I don't know.

A naked Captain
Lloyd Collins

I grew up in the Victorian Mallee and in the 1930s, when I was 14, I began driving a team of ten draught horses. One particular horse stands out through all those years of ploughing, sowing and chaff-cutting because of his odd behaviour each morning. His name was Captain.

While all the other horses would be dressed in their harness in the stable and then driven out to the work site in the paddock, Captain preferred to go naked. He absolutely refused to have his headstall, collar and hames put on him until he reached the paddock. Instead, he walked out behind all the other horses, which were coupled together and ready to be hitched to whatever implement we would be using that day. He would stand nearby and watch while they had their trace chains attached. Then I would say, 'Captain, take your place.' Once everything was ready, he would happily walk into his position in the team, and stand quite still while I dressed him for work.

Kicking embargo
Hilda Cherry

We were droving a mob of cattle from Inverell to Forbes and, as always, people offered horses to take along. The usual story:

'He's not a bad horse, has no vices, just needs work.' One of these such horses was a beautiful bay which, after his owner, we named Moffat. While attempting to shoe this animal, we discovered he loved to kick. He kicked at anything and everything, in all directions. His intention clearly was to hurt whatever he connected with. After some weeks on the road, it was decided he was quiet enough for me to ride. (I was rather inexperienced in those days.)

We had reached Barraba, and had to cross the cattle over the railway line, through some narrow gates. When we arrived, railway fettlers were working on the line nearby. My job was to block the cattle from walking down the line toward the workers.

Everything was fine until a big, horny cow decided to make a run for it. I pushed Moffat to block the cow. However, as I had been riding since early morning, I hadn't been off to tighten my girth. As he surged forward, my saddle rolled round—and I found myself on the ground between his legs. I covered my head and waited for those legs to lash out as usual—but nothing happened. He just stood there quite calm.

I stood up to jeering and laughter from those rotten railway fettlers, who had been so busy making fun of me they hadn't bothered to block the cow. I remounted Moffat and retrieved the cow, and no harm was done, except a little hurt pride.

Why Moffat decided not to kick that one time is beyond me. He was still kicking at anything and everything all over the place when we returned him to his owner some months later.

Remarkable sagacity
Doug Harkin

I left school when I was 14 and spent 30 years working draught horses. During this time, I never ceased to be amazed at their remarkable sagacity.

One night a flood swept away some fences bordering the highway alongside our farm. In the morning, after searching nearby roads and forest, and not finding even a hoof mark, we decided they must have trudged along the highway. As a last resort, we went to our old farm, which was about 20 miles away and the other side of a town of some 8500 people. And there they were—six of them, standing looking over the gate. It was about twenty years since we had left that farm. Only one or two horses in that team had been alive when we moved away, but for some extraordinary reason, they had led the others home, even though it had meant traversing the town.

Bonnie, the blocker
Allan Brewer

I had a chestnut mare called Bonnie that I bought at the Jindabyne horse sale. It was back in 1977 and I was droving for the meat wholesaler, J R Meats. We used to pick the cattle up from the old Wodonga saleyards and the trucking yards and walk them to the meatworks. This entailed crossing the Hume Highway and following the stock route under the railway line.

As there was always a lot of traffic when we were putting the cattle through the gates, I would leave Bonnie facing the traffic whilst I counted them in. This became an almost daily event and Bonnie would stand blocking the traffic until I called her. In that one year we walked 27,400 head up that road. In the end, Bonnie could almost do the job by herself.

Queenie to the rescue
Garth Dutfield

About 1946 or so there was a bad drought, and my father was lopping box trees to keep his sheep alive. He had two chestnut mares, Queenie and Duchess. The former was quiet and as reliable as daylight itself. Duchess, however, was a bit skittish.

The tree lopping took father out early in the morning and brought him home after dark each day for the months that the dry period lasted. Each trip was aboard either one of the two mares, and he carried lunch, water, an axe and a tomahawk. This particular day, as luck would have it, he was mounted on Queenie, the quiet one.

He headed for the high kurrajongs of the back paddock. After tying up the horse, he climbed up and started the lopping. Some time into the work, the axe either snagged or glanced off green bark and ended up deep in father's knee. After wrapping his shirt around the blood-soaked knee, my father found he could not mount the mare normally, but had to climb up on a stump to get on.

Queenie seemed to know something had happened, either by the scent of the blood-soaked clothing or the urgent nature of her master's voice. Not a foot went wrong, no stumbles, no frantic homing rush—as most horses seem to adopt on the homeward leg of the journey—just an even, gentle pace. At each gate, she manoeuvred into position automatically so the stricken rider could loose the latch chain.

On the last leg, when her rider was starting to lapse into unconsciousness, Queenie started walking faster. She rounded the sheepyards, passed the horse paddock and the other horses, and came to a motionless halt at the back gate, where a startled wife, niece and two small daughters hurriedly tended to a very pale rider. After father was taken care of, my younger sister asked Mum, 'Is Daddy going to die? He really looked bad.'

On recovery, Dad freely admitted that if it had not been for Queenie, he would have most likely bled to death in the paddock.

On remote control
Joy Nunan

For years Old Darkie had been the best horse in the team, the marker horse that had trodden the straight line. When he became too old to do heavy work, he became the tip-dray horse, hauling the super and seed to the paddock at seeding time.

All day he would stand in the dray munching at his leisure on his ration of chaff and oats in his nosebag. His master just had to give him a call and he would move up to the combine so the boxes could be refilled. At the end of the day, Darkie would be told to 'Gee up' home, which he would do at a steady pace across the ploughed ground, through the gate into the next paddock, on into the race and then into the yard, without knocking any gate posts or taking a wrong turn.

FIVE
Team work

Little exemplifies the concept of team work more than the sight of heavy horses hauling huge wagons laden with

wool and bags of wheat. The 19th century painting by George Lambert, *Across the Black Soil Plains*, shows a bogged wagon and about a dozen horses plunging and straining in knee-deep mud while their precious load of wool bales from inland Queensland lists perilously. Lambert captures the sort of team work that was vital, of selfless, unstinting effort by all, and not a slacker among them.

Team work is a highly prized attribute in the human herd too, judging by the numerous workshops for team building and leadership conducted by businesses, large and small, around the nation. Even sporting teams these days no longer rely on their common goal of winning. Members are psychoanalysed and have their strengths and weaknesses assessed so all can give their best.

All this human training probably doesn't achieve in terms of unity what a well-matched horse team had. Linked physically by leather and chains, they also seemed to have their minds wired like telephones. One bright idea to change direction, bolt or stop would be instantly shared, as would the joint decision to obey as one the voice commands of their handler. We'll not see their like again, not the big working teams where more than 10 tons of horse flesh could be controlled with a word. All that remains are the re-created horse teams where individuals are brought together for a few days to commemorate historic events and give those of us who have never witnessed such raw strength first-hand a taste of the past.

At Ballarat's Sovereign Hill, the working horse era has been carefully reproduced as it was on the goldfields with authentic vehicles, costumes, harness and breeds of horses, with one exception. No longer can horses bred for work be allowed to get a sweat up. We're all too squeamish now according to those with whom I spent a day travelling on a Cobb & Co coach and a delivery lorry.

Politically corrected horse days

Step through the gate of Ballarat's Sovereign Hill and you're part of the goldfields of 1856. A Cobb & Co coach clatters past pulled by four matched bay horses. A Clydesdale walks in circles operating a bucket-lifting machine worked by a series of pulleys. Nearby another pulls a rake around a watery channel to break up clay. The sounds of creaking harness, groaning wooden beams, clanking chains and hooves grinding over hard ground are authentically part of the era. Walk through the streets, dodging horse manure and watching out for the next coach load of passengers, and through a doorway you'll see a blacksmith banging on a shoe, or horses resting in the hotel's livery stables. Behind the post office, a horse hangs its head over the door, presumably having returned from its mail run. Outside the freight office, a trolley driver rests in the morning sun, the reins slack in his hand, while his heavy horses flick their tails lazily and toss their heads. People go about their business in and out of shops, replicating the normal hustle and bustle of a busy goldfields town. Actors, authentically dressed, act out the dramas of the day and visitors find themselves swept along in their role as extras in the scene.

Grant Daniell, the trolley driver, tilts back his hat and gives a cheery grin. He is one of twelve full-time and casual horse handlers at Sovereign Hill, working in a glorious equestrian time warp. 'Most of us here have a passion for horses,' Grant says. He's been on the job for about three years, breeds and trains horses at home in his spare time, and has probably spent more time in stables than houses. Knowing horses as well as he does, Grant says it's a pity the authenticity of Sovereign Hill can't be extended faithfully to the town's working horses. Because the general public now has so little to do with horses, Grant says the handlers are all under instructions not to let any of the horses actually 'work'. How far apart city and country, past and present now are. The poetry of true horsepower, the honesty of toil has been subverted in the name of so-called animal welfare. Here were horses each capable of pulling a ton of weight for hours on end, being pampered like household poodles. To satisfy the concerns of an ignorant public, the horses are harnessed for just two hours at a time and have to be kept fat to cover even the last rib that normally shows in a fit working horse. 'We have to make sure we take 85 per cent of the carriage weight by using the foot brake going down a hill,' said Grant with a smile. 'The horses aren't allowed to lie back into the breeching. If they did, people would call the RSPCA. People don't understand that if horses are holding a carriage down a hill it is correct for them to come down in the hindquarters with their hocks down low near the ground. They think if the pole horses are straining, it's cruel, especially if the lead horses are walking normally, which is what they are meant to do. They even call the RSPCA if the horses stand in a puddle or in the rain.'

Having got that off his chest, Grant hopped down from his seat and started unhitching his team to swap them over with fresh horses from the stable yard up the hill. He said Sovereign Hill now had 43 working horses, all selected for their quiet temperament so they could be happily patted by a curious public. All are brought in at about four, trained for their various tasks, then retired at around fourteen. Numbers some years ago were cut back to about twelve when tourism went through a quiet patch. The feed bill is enormous—each horse eats through $4500 of feed a year. 'They like to have the horses fat here because they are easier to manage, and people are alarmed if any horse isn't round.'

Grant said one of the highlights of the job was having the old horsemen come up for a chat. 'Often they'll tell us the horses are not harnessed properly, that the straps are too loose, that you can't get a horse working properly like that. So we have to tell them why it's not authentic, that we can't let them get a sweat up.'

Grant says resident harness makers, wheelwrights and the carriage shop keep all the gear in authentic working order. But one of the difficulties often faced is in getting second-hand sets of harness at clearing sales. 'We're usually outbid by Melbourne women paying big dollars for collars and winkers as decorations,' he laughs.

Up on his perch above the four bays, stage-coach driver Rick Bredin manoeuvres the Cobb & Co through crowds, around sharp bends and down a steep hill—just as his great-grandfather had done for fifteen years from 1862 over the nine hours of stages between Melbourne and Ballarat. 'They tell me the drivers didn't live to a very great age,' Rick says over the crunch of steel-shod hooves and tyres on hard ground. 'In summer people were always buying them a drink, so they died of alcoholism. In winter, they died of pneumonia because they were always so cold and wet.' For 24 years Rick has been at the reins of the Concorde Jack coach, so called because of its jack seat on the back. With six people up the back, three on the roof, one beside the driver and eight inside, and luggage, the coaches took a fair bit of handling, as no doubt did the passengers too. Rick said he'd had his share of incidents even inside the pretend world of Sovereign Hill. A child once tied his baby brother's pram to the back of the coach in the main street when he got sick of looking after it. Rick took off for a bush drive, which started with fording a deep stream,

with the pram in tow. Disaster was only averted when he heard a lot of yelling to stop.

With that, we rounded a bend and, just ahead, was an elderly group of tourists in the middle of the road. One was in a wheelchair. The horses were trotting and pulling hard up the hill. The distance between the lead horses and the group of people was closing fast. 'Move over, please,' Rick called out, just as his grandfather would have done. But the group, while acknowledging the coach's presence, stood its ground as though what they were seeing was not quite real, as if it was an image on television. Rick hauled on the reins. The leaders came back to a walk and the coach wheels missed the group's feet by centimetres. 'People don't understand these things anymore,' Rick lamented in what had now become a familiar refrain.

Away from the action and noise, just over a small rise and on the side of a hill overlooking Ballarat, a huge airy modern stable houses the horses. Spotless, with rubber floors in the wooden loose boxes that are trimmed with red mesh and iron railings, it was as far removed from the flamboyant theatre of the goldfields re-created beyond the hill as its horses are from doing a solid day's work. In the peace of the day yards, beautiful big horses rested under trees, their distinctive Clydesdale faces shining ghost- like. Tended by people with a passion for the working horse era, they are a valuable and, for most people, a last link to the horses which helped grow food, delivered goods to the door and provided transport and power. It's a pity that few these days will ever again see that power fully expressed. We seem to have lost the plot somewhere by thinking it necessary to protect modern sensitivities from the sight of raw, sweating, straining muscle power. Is hard physical work really so frightening?

W H Ogilvie
'The Horse Teams' [excerpt]

But who can forget the beauty
Of that long and patient yoke,
All collared and chained for duty
An hour ere the magpies woke—
The proud heads bent in endeavour,
The shoulders taking the strain
With never a baulk and never
The shame of an idle chain?

By the letter of the law
Denis Adams

The teamsters who operated the big rigs never bothered with reins. It was handier and more comfortable riding beside their teams on a pony. That way they could jog ahead to check out a creek crossing, or drop back for a few words with anyone they met, while the iron-shod wagon wheels rolled ever onward, burnished as silver as the shoes on the horses' great hooves.

The teamster could check the load as he rode by. Yes, pony was the only way to go. Few directions were necessary. A horse team was not silly enough to leave the track, once set in motion. No reins were necessary. All it took was a click of the tongue to start them, a 'Gee over', or 'Way' perhaps, to keep them on course. And stopping a team of tired horses was never a problem. My own old neddy when tired would walk more and more slowly, ears pricked, deliberately misconstruing any sound I made as an order to stop.

Dad told me a story about his Uncle Steve, who never used reins on his team hauling supplies from Adelaide to Maryvale Station near Alice Springs. What trips they must have been. The men driving their wagons and teams all camping together and smoking their pipes and yarning around the campfire. It was about a three-week trip.

Dad said that, one time, as Steve's outfit came lumbering into the northern outskirts of Adelaide, a policeman stopped him. Steve was riding his pony, with the team following.

'Don't you know the law says the driver must be seated on the wagon?' the policeman demanded. 'Aren't you aware that a team of horses must be guided by reins, held by that driver?'

'My horses have never had reins,' Steve protested. 'They'd go mad if I tried to put bits in their mouths. As for sitting on the trolley ...'

'That's the law,' the policeman told him imperiously. Then he tempered justice with mercy. 'I don't believe it says anything about bits.'

After some thought, Steve tied the pony to the back of the trolley and dug out a roll of binder twine. Tying an end to each of the leaders' winkers, he ran the lengths of twine back to the front of the trolley, clambered up, and winding the loose twine up in his hands, called to the policeman: 'Now am I legal?'

The policeman nodded and waved him on regally.

Steve clicked his tongue, and the team moved off, with him standing on the front of the trolley like a driver for Cobb & Co, holding his utterly useless string reins all the way into Adelaide—and back out again—calling all the necessary commands as he flourished the 'reins'. The letter of the law had been complied with. Honour on both sides was satisfied.

Like a troop of soldiers
Allan Schiller

It seems difficult to imagine a big team of twelve, fourteen and up to twenty horses being controlled by the voice and personality of the driver, entirely without reins. I never managed to achieve this, although I found the horses did respond quite willingly on most occasions to my command of 'Whoa!'

My father explained that the attainment of effective control and good response from a team resulted largely from the horses having a feeling of confidence in their driver, and the ability of the driver to project his control over them by voice and personality. He said, too, that the placement of horses of differing dispositions as leaders, shafters and body horses in the team was important. He said he once saw one of the teamsters of our pioneering era, Peter Ward, controlling his team as perfectly as an officer might a troop of soldiers. They were pulling a heavily laden wheat wagon and went down the main street of Pinnaroo, turned short through a gateway, went along a narrow lane and around a tight turn before stopping precisely at the unloading point—all solely under control of the driver's voice. How I wish I could have seen such a wonderful sight!

The power of a horse
Dick Mills

I wasn't fond of every individual horse that we had on our place, Millbrae, but when they worked as a team, I really admired them. When I went out to take over the reins at midday, as I sometimes did, I often couldn't see where the team was, because the paddock was hilly. But suddenly I would feel and hear the thudding vibration of 24 big, shaggy feet on the damp ground. Then into view would come two rows of twelve upright legs, pumping up and down like pistons. Sometimes they'd be strutting out to the off or the near to correct direction in response to the slightest pull of the driver's rein.

There was no better evidence of the united power of the team than when I walked behind the stump-jump plough. The earth would be flung upside down by each of the four mouldboards and the green sward immediately changed to a rich red-brown.

The servility of a team as they worked was remarkable; it was almost as if there was nothing they enjoyed more than to do as we bid. There were limits to such hard labour as ploughing, however, for in heavy soil it would only take perhaps three hours for the team to tire. They would get slower and slower, and turning at headlands became an agony for anybody as geared for progress as I was.

When there was any undue slacking, the worst offender got a clod tossed onto his rump to hurry him on. When they were obviously tired, though, the only real alternative was to get around to where the heap of nosebags was and stop for lunch, even if it wasn't yet twelve o'clock.

Sometimes the horses told the driver plainly that they had had enough, for on coming to a sudden rise, they would stop unexpectedly. I knew then it was no use forcing them, for it is the nature of a good team to work if they possibly can.

Another amazing thing about a team was its united sensitivity. If they stopped, they all stopped together, as if they had consulted each other like a band of union men striking together about some grievance! Well, in that case, just as with a team of men, I had to be sensitive too—sensitive enough to see if there was justice in their cause. I don't think I was a hard boss, but I confess to getting a bit cross at times, chiefly because I knew I would be asked why I hadn't got the paddock finished or would be reprimanded for coming home early. Sometimes the team tired so badly that by lunchtime it was necessary to return home for another team or, if that was not available, to continue on with a block placed under one plough, lifting it in the air so that the load would be 25 per cent lighter.

At ploughing time a weakness that often stopped work was sore shoulders. When removing the harness from the horses' steaming necks, I would check for sores where the collars fitted.

Sometimes the problem could be overcome by special treatment to either the collar or the horse, but more often that was ineffective. To be without a certain horse, such as Prince, our biggest Clydesdale, was sometimes impossible and ploughing would have to stop. Prince was inclined to be sluggish, but he was indispensable as the furrow horse. As the team turned at a headland, they would swing across the last ploughed strip. Prince's hooves would stop at the furrow and there they would stay and all the others would have to keep their proper place in relation to him. Prince made it easy for the ploughman because of that trained habit. He would only deviate slightly when made to by the driver to cope with a sideways movement or a bend in the course.

A team of Clydesdales is really switched on when it is in harness. All horses are equipped with remarkable swivelling ears that constantly rotate from forward to back through 180 degrees. The team, however, is so interconnected with the driver and each other that I only had to trigger the thought that precedes a command and their ears would all turn back together in a row, just as if I pressed a button on my computer and a row of figures all came up together. It was always quite fascinating to watch those ears flicking back and forth.

Some farmers used to breed teams looking like brothers and sisters, but when it came to individuals' behavioural characteristics, there was little likeness at all. Every horse had a unique personality of its own, and you needed to be very smart to handle some of them.

For instance, there was Bounce, who was always reluctant to start, then when she did, it would be with a plunge forward that would start a chain reaction in the team. Very likely they would all have to be stopped while the driver made another attempt to start them. My father, a great horseman, had the answer to this. He purchased a set of roller chains. In this system the horses are one row behind another, with the trace chains from the leaders passing the rear horse in each case, then around rollers hitched to each end of the swing and forward again to the hames hooks of the rear horse. Dad then put Bounce in the rear. She very soon started properly, because if she didn't, her back legs would strike the swingle-tree and cause her pain when the leading horse of the pair started normally.

Bounce and the team matriarch, Joan, were often paired up to pull the trolley, but were they temperamental! I remember once the trolley—the equivalent of today's light truck—was standing with a heavy load of open bags of grain aboard. When the two were hitched to the load, they found it a little hard to move. Bounce reacted by bouncing and Joan by alternately throwing herself on the ground or throwing herself into the air! Before you knew what was happening, they had jack-knifed the trolley and it was upside down with the wheels in the air. It took the rest of the day to shovel up the mess. Oh, the joys of farming!

But then there was Punch—who was always popular. If it wasn't for Punch, then I think I too would have given up. This grand horse was the favourite for single harness, particularly the dray, which was subject to being overloaded or getting into difficult spots where it was hard to move. Punch could always be relied on to have a second try. You could reason with him and appeal to his sense of courage by well-chosen commands tempered with the tone of voice. He would never panic or sulk and invariably would prove himself as good as two other horses. He wasn't over-large, but he was a mass of muscle. You can imagine the general consternation when one day on the farm a vertical creek bank gave way when Punch was mowing. He received a terrible gash in the rump when the blade fell onto him. So determined were we to save Punch that we spent three months laboriously treating the wound and getting him back to strength. It was very difficult working the place without him.

Running from the stink
Joe Dickson

In the twenties, I remember going with Dad to Bowen Downs sheep station for a load of wool. A kangaroo shooter happened to be there and he asked us if we would take a bundle of roo skins the 42 miles to Aramac for him. Dad said that would be fine and to bring them the next day.

When he arrived, we had all the horses gathered around the wagon getting harnessed up. Half had their winkers on and I was on my pony. As soon as the horses got a whiff of the roo skins, they were off like a flash, just like a cattle rush. They took me and my pony with them to the first fence 100 yards away, which stopped them all right, but they stretched the wires in the process.

Anyway, we got them back after a bit of trouble, but from then on they were very touchy. We got the load on the move with much snorting and foot-stamping going on, as they let us know they weren't happy about the foul-smelling skins. They finally settled and we were travelling along the road when a fellow came along in a Chev truck, with a load of pigs on board. He pulled off the road to go around us, but the ground on the side was rough, so the pigs started to squeal. Our 24 horses—with 12 tons of wool and the stinking roo skins on board—bolted. I raced alongside on my pony and grabbed the leader, steering them out onto the heavy going, and eventually made them pull up.

Next day, further along the road, we passed through a gate in some scrubby country. A bale which was overhanging slightly caught the branch of a tree and brought it down with a terrible crash. So off went the team again. Once again, I raced alongside and caught the leader, but this time I had to keep them on the road, as there was heavy gidgie scrub all round and not much room to spare.

We finally got to Aramac without any more trouble and unloaded the wool and skins at the railway station. There they really let us know about their stinking payload by throwing their heads, stamping their feet, snorting and trying to shy away from the smell. We had a lot of trouble getting them to get in close to the goods-shed platform where there were other roo skins waiting to be taken away by the train. All they wanted to do was bolt.

After a few days we were on our way out again. On the second day, a solid tyre truck came along from behind. It was carrying some empty petrol tins on its tray, and when it went to go around us on the rough ground, the tins were jumping up and down and making a dreadful row. The wagon was empty, so we only had ten horses yoked up, but to make things worse, we had two young horses behind the leader. I raced up and caught hold of the leader, but the young horses were lunging around, trying to get past me. They pushed me and my horse off the road into the path of a big dead stump. I managed to get around it, but one string of horses went each side of it. It was a forked stump, about four feet high. I thought this would be the end of the shafter, a black mare, but when she came to it, she jumped in the air. Because of the pace we were travelling, she was carried clean over it. The wagon knocked the stump out of the ground.

Dad was on his saddle horse and it took two miles of hard riding before he managed to get in close enough to the wagon to climb aboard and screw the brake on. When we finally stopped them, they settled down and we had no more trouble with them. They'd never been like that until the roo skins and I'm sure that's what stirred them up.

Just one man and his team
Patricia Caffery

My father, Jack Burns, loved his horses, and with them on his property, Benloch, he managed through the Depression, floods and droughts. Unlike modern tractors, they always did their best and never broke down at vital times. Although he was a farmer all his life, my father never owned a tractor, nor did he live to see the modern monsters complete with air-conditioned cabs, luxurious seating, radios and cassette players.

A farmer can take pride in owning such machines, but nothing compares with the relationship shared by farmers of my father's generation with their wonderful draught horses—a man and his horses worked together as a team. A tractor is something maintained and used when required. The draught horses were individually cared for every day of the year.

The working day started very early, regardless of season. After a cup of tea, my father left for the stables, a large enclosed building with a raised platform down the centre and built-up, continuous troughing at each side. At the far end of the platform was the door into the chaff house. The side doors were opened, and then the paddock gate. The horses always went into the same position, where the collar, hames and winkers to fit each individual horse hung from pegs on posts beside them. As they began to feed, the collars and hames were put on each horse that was to work that day and each horse was tied by a neck rope attached to the feeder.

After the cow was milked and breakfast eaten, my father returned to the stable. The horses not required to work would be put back in the paddock. The others would have their winkers put on and then they would be put into their required formation— two threes for a six-horse team or two fours for an eight-horse team—and joined by a coupling. The reins would be attached and the team driven to the paddock being worked.

Each horse knew its own position, so the final yoking up was quick, and work began. The horses knew their own names and responded to my father's instructions. There were no luxurious padded seats, just the hard old metal plough seats, now so fashionable as garden seats. A real luxury was a hessian bag containing a little straw as a cushion.

At noon the team was unyoked, and as the horses reached the stable paddock gate, each horse had its bit taken out of its mouth and was let go to the creek for a drink. By the time they finished drinking and returned to the stable, the chaff was in the troughs for a light feed. After an hour, they returned to work until nearly sundown. When they returned to the stable, for a big feed, their collars, hames and winkers were removed. After his tea, my father returned to the stable with a lantern. Each horse was thoroughly groomed to remove all traces of dried sweat and then the collars were brushed, and finally the chaff was put in the troughs, ready for the next morning.

The horses did all the work on the farm. The only engine was the one which drove the chaff-cutter. In autumn they did the ploughing, harrowing, and sowing of the crops. The first part of the harvesting was cutting the headlands round each paddock with the reaper and binder. A few weeks later, when the stooked sheaves had dried out, the hay was carted in on the wagon, using two horses. Two stacks were built beside the chute into the chaff house and two were built in a stack yard in the horse paddock, to be fed out to the horses. The headlands from which the hay had been cut were then ploughed to give each crop a wide firebreak.

As summer warmed up, it was time to start stripping the grain. The header bin was emptied into bags, which were stood in rows at each end of the paddock. The horses enjoyed a breather while this was done. It was often very hot, so the horses were glad to finish work a couple of hours before sundown so that my father could return to sew the bags until dark.

Next was wheat carting. Two horses pulled the wagon to the paddock and stopped beside the bags of wheat. One special mare, Jess, was then yoked to the kicker. This was attached to the side of the wagon and each bag individually loaded onto it. Working only by word, Jess moved forward and the kicker lifted the bag onto the wagon. She would then back, lowering the kicker for the next bag. It was slow, because my father worked alone. After each eight or ten bags, he had to get up and position them on the wagon. When the wagon was loaded, eight horses, two abreast, were used to pull it to the railway siding, where the bagged grain was stacked in rail trucks and covered with a tarpaulin. Each trip took a full day, so eight nosebags containing chaff were taken for the horses.

The final part of the harvest was cutting the straw with the reaper and binder. This was carted in and used to thatch the haystacks.

Before the autumn rains, dams needed cleaning out, generally using three horses abreast pulling a wide scoop. As the big horses turned on the dam bank, the weight of twelve big feet consolidated the banks more evenly than modern bulldozers can.

There were many jobs that required only one horse: carting firewood in the dray, carting water in the furphy from the creek for the garden, and carting out hay and grain in the spring cart to the sheep. When the creek was in flood and the current too strong for a pony, a draught horse was used in the long-shafted sulky so my mother could visit neighbours.

My father bred his own draught horses and always had a good stallion. At harvest time some mares worked in the team leaving four-month-old foals behind in the stable. Despite their great size, by the age of three, they were always broken in very easily and took their places in the team without any fuss. Work seemed just a normal instinct to these horses.

Nowadays, with all the highly sophisticated machinery, very few farms are operated by one person. My father worked quite alone with his much-loved draught horses all his life. Admittedly, things were slower and men worked harder, but father always gave credit for his yields to his horses and was highly respected for the condition and quality of his team.

Team sports
Joe Dickson

For a bit of light entertainment, the teamsters used to have scratch pulling contests. They would bet as much as 50 pounds that their best horse would pull anyone else's backwards. Well, Dad's horse Mick was never beaten. The two competing horses were put back-to-back and their chains hooked together. Someone would call out 'Go!', and the horse that was pulled over the line was the loser. Mick's quickness at starting to pull was the secret.

Bogged in the creek
Joe Dickson

When I was 17 I was helping Dad, my brother Les and a friend of ours, Jack, cart wool from Bowen Downs. It was 1927. The three teams each had about 20 horses. We camped at a place called Cattle Hill, 10 miles from Aramac. Overnight a big storm came up from the west, so we were up early, mustered the horses and just had them yoked up when it started to rain. We had a quick bite of breakfast and started on our way. By this time the rain was fairly pouring down. We travelled all day and didn't even stop for lunch.

When we came to Belltopper Creek, it was running fairly high. Jack went across, then Les and then Dad, who had 11 tons of wool, the heaviest load of the three. He didn't get very far. The wagon bogged down badly on one side and the wheels on the other side were well off the muddy river bed—we could spin them around in the water.

Les unhitched a string of horses from his wagon and hooked them onto the side of Dad's wagon that was up in the air. When Dad told the six horses in that string to pull, I couldn't bear to look. I thought the wool would definitely finish up in the water. But after a lot of heaving, the wagon did right itself and we managed to get it through the river. While all this was going on, the rain kept pouring down. It took all the next day to cover 9 miles and we finally stopped the horses on a ridge one mile out of Aramac, where we let them go. The wagons had to be left there a week, because they were bogged down to the axles.

The Cockaleechie horse dip
Sylvia Laube

In the early 1930s a mysterious itch developed on horses in the Cockaleechie district on South Australia's Eyre Peninsula. They were so irritated that they would continuously rub on any post or rail available. The poor animals rubbed off their hair, became frustrated and timid—and looked terrible. What's more, a ton of horseflesh using the side of a shed or a fence for rubbing could cause a fair bit of damage.

Indeed, the situation was so serious that something had to be done. Mr Perc Vanstone, an early settler in the district, thought up the idea of dipping them. A meeting was called among the farmers and it was decided to build a large concrete dip, similar to a sheep dip. So the men clubbed together and dug the dip with pick and shovel. It was sunk down over 7 feet, then concreted, all the cement having been mixed by hand.

Strong stockyards had to be erected, so big posts were cut out of nearby gumtrees and the long bolts were made by blacksmith Charlie Laube in Cummins. The entrance to the dip was made narrow so horses couldn't turn around. To prevent the horses from rearing up, big steel hoops were bolted on to high posts. These came from wagon and sulky tyres that had been cut in half.

People were notified when a dipping day was arranged. Farmers with their teams, and most had an average of twenty horses each, would come from miles around. Some even sent their horses by train. While they waited their turn, teams would be tethered beneath trees in the surrounding scrub and given their nosebags. Horse dipping was also turned to good use as a great social get-together, with billies boiled and yarns swapped.

But then the real fun began. Some horses went in peacefully, but most played up and had to be forced in. It wasn't all that easy pushing and pulling a huge, reluctant draught horse into a hole full of water. They reared up, snorted, neighed, trembled and encouraged all their mates to do the same. The old ones that had been in before gave the most trouble. Many of them had to be forced in by putting a strong band behind their rumps and being pulled forward into the dip by a horse either side. Horses would go in with an almighty splash and workers had to stand back. A man was stationed to pour a bucket of dip water over their heads. The solution used in the dip was white, and may have been sheep dip.

All who took horses for dipping have tales to tell. Jack Pedler tells of his mate Charlie Hewitt: 'It was a stubborn old mare and even men with ropes pulling behind couldn't shift her. So Charlie hopped on her back. The old mare leaped in the air and into the dip—with Charlie still on her back. Charlie was well and truly dipped too.'

Gordon Fuss can remember on dipping days leaving home at 4 am with the tip-dray full of nosebags, driving four horses in front of the horse in the dray. His father, John, would be in front driving the rest of the team. They had to travel about 12 miles each way. Everyone brought along their cut dinners and a change of clothes—'Because when the day was over, we were like a mob of drowned rats and very tired.'

The remains of the horse dip at Cockaleechie still stand today, in a remarkable state of preservation, as a lasting memorial to the days of the itching draught horse.

An archaic interlude
Neil Macpherson

It was early 1942 and the war was affecting us all. My father, who had 1700 acres of good country at Currabubula near Tamworth, decided that he should grow some wheat for himself in an effort to get some extra cash to feed his seven kids. Up till then a sharefarmer had grown the crop, but my father only got one-third of the proceeds.

Since we had no machinery, tractors were unprocurable and fuel the same, my father, who had worked horses in Victoria, decided to get himself a team. He and I went to a horse sale in Tamworth, and out of the ring he bought nine draught horses. He scrounged around and acquired nine or ten collars and hames, a similar number of winkers and a set of equaliser or roller chains. All this was new to me, so he explained the theory of the roller chains: four horses were on the front row and four behind them, and each horse on the front was connected by chains to their collars through a pulley on the swingle bar and back to the collar of the rear horse. Hence, each horse had to pull the same weight and at the same speed, or else one was pulled backwards or forwards as the case may be.

The team was duly named, and I suspect he had known others of those names before. There was Captain, with his near eye missing, to be leader of the offside. Mae, a huge mare with her offside eye missing, was leader of the near side. There was also Queenie, Silver and Prince, and one just called The Chinese Horse. She got her name when she trod on my father's foot while he was trying to shoe her. After he stopped swearing and hopping around, he declared that she was just a so-and-so Chinese horse that had never been shod before, and as far as he was concerned she could go without shoes.

When we started working the team, Prince, being a young unbroken horse, was left out, but he galloped up and down all day alongside his mates. Eventually, we caught him, took out the Chinese Horse and shoved Prince into her place. We hooked him to the roller chains and tied his head to the horses on either side of him. Prince tried all sorts of tricks to get away, but he was pulled along mercilessly. He had to work or be pulled backwards onto the swingle bar. He soon woke up to this and by nightfall was broken in—and turned out to be one of our best workers.

I really loved driving that eight-horse team, and with the help of a few well-directed clods of dirt and a few strong words, they responded and worked very well.

I was dreaming along on the plough one day when I noticed the leading horses split and move aside. The four behind soon followed and it was only then that I saw a dirty great tree stump fair in the middle of the horses. I should have gone around it, but forgot it was there. So I whoa-ed the horses while I studied the situation. To my 16-year-old mind, uncoupling the horses and pulling the plough backwards seemed a waste of time, so I decided to gee up the team and drive the plough right over the top.

It took three days to fix the plough—and quite a bit longer to heal my pride.

We eventually did sow some acres with wheat and oats, about 60 acres all up. The method was archaic to say the least. After ploughing the hard ground, we broadcast seed over it and, before the birds ate all of it, covered it with a set of harrows. In August it rained and rained and the crop looked magnificent. But about that time, Dad died. I think I may have lost interest in the farm, and the horses, just then and I don't know if the grain was ever harvested. The horses were turned out, became fat and lazy, and then went back to the sale ring at Tamworth.

'Ellenvale'
'Yoking Up the Teams',
First published in *The Bulletin*, 1931

'Ere the first faint flush of morning streaks the star bespangled
    dome,
They are cleaning up the horses with the brush and curry comb;
They are sorting out the collars, they are cursing frozen hands,
In the semi-darkness struggling with the twisted leather bands,
And while someone's making outcry over couplings that are gone,
'Nancy' grabs a final mouthful 'ere they slip the winkers on,
Then a scuffle through the gateway and with leading chains
    a-sway,
They are bringing out the workers at the breaking of the day.
I can even hear the jangle of the hame hooks as they pass,
While the unshod hooves are slipping on the frost encrusted
    grass.
Down the slope towards the fallow, four by four and eight
    abreast,
With the heavy collars tapping on each broad and willing chest,
And the coupling ropes are tested when a filly reefs and squeals
As she stops a playful wallop from a leading horse's heels,
And as Sol explores the plainlands with his first enquiring beams
Around Charlton and Dimboola, they are yoking up the teams.

Six
Life's great lessons

Having to cope with getting to school by horse taught generations of children the great lessons of life. As well as the games on horseback and jinker races, children had to care for their horses and gear, and cope with unexpected thrills and spills.

In the stories recounted about the high jinx of their schooldays, the writers display ebullient self-confidence and fearless independence. How much of this came from having to work in partnership with their horses, without which they'd be stranded? Indeed, does having a working relationship with an animal make a human being a better person?

These questions occupy the thinking of two Queensland horse people, who just happen to like working with dogs, cattle and humans as well. Geoff and Vicky Toomby believe that many young people have missed out on learning basic life skills. The way they help these young people is to use their horses as teachers.

They have seen how a horse can restore confidence and encourage resourcefulness. They show young people, particularly those in crisis, that kindness and gentleness are essential ingredients in a partnership, whether human or equine.

Horse whisperers on a mission for lost souls

The type of work done by the horses of Geoff and Vicky Toomby is best described as unorthodox, esoteric even. The Queensland cattle station duo, with a lifetime of outback experience, use horses to help repair fractured souls. They say the gentleness of a horse helps the young, angry and confused to experience love, sometimes for the first time. The needs of a horse give their lives a sense of purpose. Geoff and Vicky live 40 kilometres west of Townsville on 3000 acres of beauty called Wonderland Station, so called because the Alice River runs through it—as in Alice in Wonderland!

Both expert horse people, they have been saddened in recent years by the plight of the young people they see drifting rudderless in many big rural towns. So they decided to do something about it. Using their knowledge of horses and dogs, they reach out to young people in an accessible way, demonstrating with a highly trained horse and wild, unbroken horses a philosophy of communication that readily translates to humans. Geoff and Vicky are regularly invited to appear at large agricultural shows as far away as Kununurra, Darwin, Mount Isa and Alice Springs, and they also host young people at schools on their property to learn first-hand how kindness and consistency in animal treatment triumph over intimidation and bullying. It is the approach pioneered by a great Australian horseman, Maurice Wright: the Jeffery method of horse training, mentioned in earlier stories.

With Vicky's buckskin quarter horse mare, Yellow Lady, they reveal the close partnership achievable when full trust is established between two creatures. Vicky spins the mare, backs, rides without bridle and saddle and gets her to lie down and get up with Vicky on board. She finishes the act by leading Lady out of the ring backwards, by the tail. Then with an untrained, unhandled colt, Geoff and Vicky show how a frightened animal that lashes out seeking escape can, through kindness and patience, become a willing ally, able to be ridden and even to lie down on command—in one day. The wild colt is a metaphor for troubled youth, the training analogous to the way young people should be treated and learn to treat others.

'We are trying to show people where they are going wrong,' says Geoff. 'Using animals, especially horses, they see how we should treat each other. Some of these kids are so mixed up, but all they need is a start. They are like a young wild horse that just needs understanding and to learn what people expect of them. Some have come from tough homes but some are just resentful that they are not getting enough time and love.'

Many are Aboriginal, plenty are not. 'The young Aboriginal people are very confused. They are caught between two cultures. But that doesn't make any difference once they understand the basics of teamwork and mutual caring.'

Geoff demonstrates his recipe for life with quiet movements, a soft voice and gentle persistence, winning the horse's trust. He backs off immediately if it becomes frightened or loses its confidence. 'Fifty per cent will watch the demonstration to see me get thrown, but that doesn't happen. What they do get is a better understanding that kindness and rewards are the way to go. That spills over into their understanding of other people. If I frighten that horse, he'll put up his defences and he'll find a way to defend himself. It's the same with these kids. It's no different.'

It is a compelling philosophy. A wild, angry young person is taught by watching a man turn a horse from a frightened beast to one that can carry a person and strive to please, even by lying down on command. If he is demonstrating his skills at a show, he'll even ride the horse in the grand parade. 'There are no tricks,' Geoff insists. He just shows the horse where its comfort zone is, right next to him. 'You just need a basic understanding of the horse, how it thinks. It's knowing when to stop, not when to keep going.' He keeps drawing those parallels between untamed horse and angry human.

Geoff and Vicky are retained by Kerry Packer's Consolidated Pastoral Company, which has seventeen stations in Queensland and the Top End, to train its young employees in horsemanship and to ride. Each Packer school attracts about 50 young people, drawn by the romance of the outback to work there, but most lack basic training in bush skills. 'It's all about getting back to basics,' Geoff says. 'They can all ride motorbikes, drive Toyotas and smoke dope, yet they can't ride a horse. They have to learn how a horse operates, how to care for him, and how, when mustering, to be part of a team and to rely on your mate.'

Geoff, 53, was a rodeo rider for some years and Vicky, 45, competes successfully at barrel racing on Yellow Lady. Vicky's parents, Dally Holden and Nora Vickers, were outback legends, both Australian champion saddle bronc riders. Travelling big distances is second nature so Geoff and Vicky don't mind where they take their truck and animals, so long as people roll up and take away a message about the interdependence of people and animals. Geoff's performers include ten dogs working heifers, sheep and ducks.

'People call me the horse whisperer and they can if they want to,' he says. 'But I am just a silly old ringer who knows a few shortcuts.' Geoff says the young of today haven't been given the right values. In some rural areas he knows he puts the figures for young people being in crisis, mixed up, unsure of where they are headed as high as three quarters. Peer pressure in schools is so intense, they make wrong decisions and choices. He says he and Vicky offer a refuge on their place to these kids, giving them time out, away from bad influences, and a chance to do simple things like collecting eggs from under a chook, patting a dog and mustering on horseback. 'The foundation of being human is being able to understand animals,' says Geoff. 'You can't be a caring and effective human being unless you do. By learning how to depend on animals, they learn emotions like affection and trust.'

So respected is their training approach that the Toombys will be presenting their programme at the Katherine Training College on a regular basis. As well as dog training schools and horse breaking, they also run Sahiwal cattle at Wonderland. In association with the Mount Isa Show Society, they have also established the Hippy Wilson Foundation to provide short-term camps for children in crisis. Hippy Wilson was the first indigenous station manager in Queensland. 'He was an exceptional person with the biggest smile you have ever seen,' says Geoff. 'He had a tremendous approach to people and animals, indigenous and whites alike. He was a great humanitarian.' Hippy Wilson died at 47 in October 2000 after an operation for appendicitis.

Geoff and Vicky at present do all their work at Wonderland with lost souls voluntarily. In the past four years, they have had 28 young people live with them for varying lengths of time and learn outback skills that have enabled nearly all to find work and lead productive lives. One of the most recent 'graduates' from Wonderland was Roy Storch, 15, who had got in with some bad influences in Mount Isa. His parents had heard of Geoff and Vicky's success with rebellious kids. Roy found himself doing everyday station chores like mustering and checking a mob of 1000 cattle, and after a couple of months was given a new start at Kerry Packer's Newcastle Waters in the Northern Territory. He now works at a race horse stud, has a zest for life and hunger for success. 'We just straightened him out by working him in the right direction,' Geoff said. 'We made him realise the only way to get ahead in life was by being honest. We did that through putting him in close touch with animals.'

Henry Lawson
'The Old Bark School'

Then we rode to school and back
by the rugged gully track,
On the old grey horse that carried three or four;
And he looked so very wise
that he lit the Master's eyes
Every time he put his head in at the door.

A pony for the teacher
Moyrah Robertson

Today is my 70th birthday, and a time for reminiscing!

During the World War II, I was a student teacher in Victoria. Since so many young men were away fighting, young girls who were finishing their training found themselves appointed as head teachers (temporary) in little one-teacher schools in country areas. I was sent away out to remote Morkalla, at the end of the rail line in far north-western Victoria, in sparsely settled saltbush country. I boarded with a farming family who lived about five miles from the school. As this placement came during the biggest drought in history, the roads were mainly sand drifts. Toby, a solid 12 hand pony who looked like a cross between a Clydesdale and a Shetland, came into my life about then.

Owned by a grazier south of Broken Hill, this shaggy rogue seemed to have suddenly got a hankering for the river country. He had wandered off and had eventually turned up at my father's property, Kalcurna Station, many miles south and on the northern banks of the River Murray, close to the South Australian border. The pony had negotiated many wire fences and gates on the way. We were told by his owner to keep him—'because he opens all the gates and lets sheep out'.

Dad decided to bring him through bluebush and mallee and completely uninhabited country 25 miles south of the Murray to where I was living. So for two years, Toby and I were a couple. He was happy each day to be tied up under a she-oak with a box of chaff and a bucket of water while I attended to my teaching duties. But at the weekend, he was the means of opening up a completely new life for me. I made many new friends on the surrounding farms, and as dances were held frequently, Toby and I would travel several miles to attend them. He would be tied up till home time—any time after midnight—and that was when his cat-like ability to see in the dark and find his way over dirt tracks was most appreciated.

When school holidays came round, he and I would take to the bush and go north, back to my parents' station. We had to cross a creek on a hand-pulled punt and then take a big swim across the Murray.

In my second year of teaching, I was sent to the school at Yarrara, which was about 50 miles from Kalcurna, but still in the same general area as my previous school. Our trip between home and school became a long day's journey, broken on the way for a bit of a camp, and a feed and drink for us both.

At one time, two friends and I decided to take the trip by jinker and made great preparations for the day on the track. Toby, being something of a glutton, must have had his own ideas about preparing for the trip, because he broke into the oaten hay stack and gorged himself. Our trip took eight hours, with the three of us helping to push Toby and jinker through sand drifts and up hills accompanied by his very odorous and noisy eliminations because of so much hay.

During my time in the Millewa district, Toby was the envy of all. He was more reliable than a bike, didn't need petrol, which was at that time rationed, and could negotiate the sandiest roads without getting stuck. Although he continued to open gates overnight to get at green feed, he was no trouble to catch, thank goodness, and seemed to know that he had a day's work ahead of him to take me to and from school.

Eventually he and I parted company when I left the bush to marry. Toby went blind from eating paddy melons, but for the remainder of his life, he was a privileged horse on my father's property and was allowed the run of the roads, to help him find his way to feed and water. Although he had no breeding and a slightly doubtful reputation, he was the best mate anyone could have. He lived to about 14 years of age and was sadly missed by all who had had to dodge him as they drove along the bush tracks.

The horses that took us to school
Joyce Shiner

Horses were a most important factor in our education in those days, as they were responsible for getting us safely to and from school each day. One horse we drove actually died in harness. Her name in the trotting world had been Queenie-Tracey, and when she was retired from racing, Dad bought her for the mail cart. She was one of his best horses for six or seven years, but when he took up land, he turned her out to grass because she was too light for farm work.

When school began at Pingrup, Queenie was the only horse he owned that was quiet enough to be driven by children. Queenie was a 'goer', but one morning, as we neared the school, she lay down in the shafts, and by the time we had loosed her from the sulky and harness, she was dead.

The storekeeper took a message to where Dad was sinking a dam and he brought two horses and towed her away. Sometimes we girls would wander off at lunchtime to put handfuls of wildflowers on the bones where she had been 'cremated'.

A replacement horse we drove was a beggar to shy. One day Georgina stood up in the sulky to take off her overcoat, which made the horse swerve. This caused Georgie to over-balance and fall sideways in front of the wheel. When we picked her up, she was none too pleased to find the brim of her new 'patent leather' waterproof hat was floppy and cracked where the wheel had passed over it—while it was still on her head!

The Deacon family drove a stocky black mare named Nancy. She brought them six miles each way daily without being urged, and they were never late. Nancy was always in good condition, with well-kept harness and well-greased vehicle ... and leather reins, a luxury most had long given up for rope.

A big, strong bay mare named Katy brought the Hulls six miles each morning, but Katy if tethered like any other horse—

by her neck—hung back, pulled the tree down and took it home with her. Therefore Katy was always to be tied by the front foot.

In summer when the thermometer moved above the century, school was dismissed to allow the children to get home early. One hot day our teacher, Edie, noticed her pupils seemed to be hanging around the horses and making no move towards going home. More than once, somebody was sent in to ask her if it was yet time to harness her horse, Baldy.

At last the teacher gave permission to have the horse harnessed. She then packed up and went out, wondering why they were all standing around. She says she sensed mystery afoot, but climbed into the buggy, flapped the reins and said, 'Get up, Baldy'. Baldy went, but the buggy didn't.

Suddenly the shafts dropped to the ground, with the horse way out in front. 'You young rascals,' laughed Edie, then everybody laughed. She said she had not noticed the traces still dangling in figures-of-eight from the hames. After that experience, she made a point of checking.

Jammed tight on the rein
Gloria Godlonton

As small children, my brother, sister and I travelled five miles to Gundaroo, our one-teacher school. We drove a dog-cart, which was slightly larger than a sulky and had rubber tyres. We had a wonderful taffy pony named Mike who jogged along quite happily most of the time. However, he had one fear. He would not tolerate the leather rein getting caught under his tail. We always had to be on the alert should he lift his tail, as he always kinked it to one side.

On a couple of occasions when we were not watching, he did manage to get the rein caught—with, for us, very frightening consequences. The first time was on a cold winter's morning when we were quietly trotting along at a good pace. I was holding the reins, as I was the only one with gloves. I was about seven years old at the time. Mike lifted his tail and tossed it over one of the reins. I tried my hardest to flick it out, but Mike jammed his tail down hard and was off like a rocket, at full gallop.

We were terrified. We hung onto the cart like grim death, with my brother leaning forward trying to free the rein. We could not pull the loose rein or Mike would have veered off the road and, anyway, a bolting horse does not heed the hands of a nine-year-old boy. Mike slowed down only when he was totally exhausted and in a lather of sweat. Only then were we able to free the rein.

It was on another of these occasions that a neighbour passed by as we came down to a walk. He reported to our father that we had been galloping our pony at a frightening pace and that Mike was dreadfully sweaty. We never could explain to our father just what happened and were severely reprimanded. I guess my father could be forgiven for not believing us, because on one occasion we did race Mike against a school mate on his bike, and were caught in the act.

The miseries of the school cart
Geoffrey Blight

The strange thing about going part-way to school by horse and cart is that, 50 years on, I remember far more about the process of getting to school than what I was supposed to have learnt when I got there. The main memory that flashes back so often is of us running late to catch the bus, and I would be 'busting'. I would hand the reins over to my sister and stand at the back of the bumping cart and relieve myself over the tailboard. That's where I learnt what 'getting your own back' meant.

True torture, however, was when the horse moulted in spring each year and large amounts of hair would float around. Should you get this on your face during rain, you get an incredible itch that has you trying to wash it off no matter what the circumstances. Sitting in a cart behind a moulting horse led my sisters and I to resort to 'bagging our heads' to avoid the irritation.

A flat tyre on the cart was also terribly frustrating, which led us to prefer the sulky with its non-inflated spoke wheels that were so good at showering us continually with fine sand when trotting across the wind. That, and the cold, is why we had a blanket over us. On frosty mornings our fingers were so numb that we had terrible difficulty unharnessing once we got to the bus stop. I can remember holding frozen fingers to the warm, sweating, hairy horse to try to get the circulation moving. The blanket was also very useful because of the habit all horses had of passing wind as they wound up, often accompanied by a staining dribble that would bubble out and sometimes float on the wind and land on our school clothes.

Another side effect of going by horse and cart was that after our early starts to cover the three and a half miles to the school bus by 7.40 am, and then being home very late each afternoon, I would nod off after tea and not do my homework. I can remember utterly failed attempts to complete homework in the cart while my sister drove, or on the school bus. Either vehicle always had the effect of making me violently carsick.

And what about those few times we alighted from the school bus to find the horse gone. Usually this happened in bad weather or after a storm. The horse would have pulled back, breaking his rope, or a hastily tied rope would have untied. The horse always went straight home, and on one occasion, we were lucky enough to have Dad bring it back. The other times, my two sisters and I walked home. Then I would have to ride back to the bus stop to get the cart, our school cases and the bread that used to be delivered by the school bus.

Despite all that, if I had the choice, I would love to be able to return to that unforgettable but wonderful part of my life.

Hitching a ride on Fridays
M J Mitchell

I am now 82 years old, but when I was 13 or 14 we had to go about five miles to a small, one-teacher school. I used to drive a horse and cart. In those days, the Education Department made a small payment of so much per child, which went towards the cost of running a horse. I used to pick up several children along the way, which more than paid for Paddy's chaff.

On Fridays Mum needed the horse and cart to go shopping in town, so we walked. There was another kid, called Donald, who also drove a horse and cart out our way. So on our long walk home, we used to chase him and hang on to the back of his cart. This, of course, made the shafts lift up and nearly pulled the poor horse off the ground. Donald would wave his whip around us to make us let go. Then we would run and catch up and do it all over again.

A struggling heap
Helen Best

The first school in our district—in the 1930s—was in the wool room of a woolshed, where the bales were stored at shearing time. One wall was a tarpaulin covered with pictures cut from the *Sydney Mail*. To this school, three families came. The Irwin children walked three miles from their farm, our family— the McNeills—walked one mile, but the lucky ones were the four Faulkner children. They came four miles on Paddy, a big, broad-backed, quiet old horse. There was plenty of room for Edna, Norman, Pat and Gordon, but one afternoon, my brother Maurice decided he would hitch a ride instead of walking home.

All went well until a child jumped out from behind a tree, waving her arms. Poor old Paddy got a terrible fright, shied and all five riders slipped off over his tail, landing in a struggling heap. My brother broke his arm, but it was the only mishap that occurred in the time Paddy was responsible for getting children to and from school.

An after-school lesson
Lorna Schwarz

During the 1930s the Schwarz family lived on a farm seven and a half kilometres from their country school. The children travelled to school in a cart pulled by Bill, a quiet, elderly horse. Bill could not be tied up—he would hang back on the rope. Instead, he was quite content to wait under the shade of a tree for the school lessons to finish.

The Schwarz children had always been warned by their parents to get in the cart and come home as soon as school was over, with the usual reminder: 'No playing around.'

One day the children decided they would go bird nesting in the nearby trees. They put their school bags and lunch tins in the cart, and off they went. Bill, having heard the bags and tins thrown aboard, thought he had the signal to start the homeward trip. So off he went. The children saw him take off—and what a chase there was. Bill evidently was enjoying himself and kept going at his usual pace until he reached home. The children had no hope of catching him, so had to run and walk the whole way home at the end of a long, tiring day. They didn't go bird nesting again.

Dolly
Lyn Chambers

As we lived on a farm five miles from the nearest school, my father looked for a reliable pony that I could ride. Dolly was recommended as a safe, quiet children's pony, and so she proved to be.

One very hot afternoon on my way home from school, I became drowsy and lay back with my head on her rump. After some time I awoke, and when I sat up, I realised Dolly was walking with her head down pushing a long line of cows that she had herded onto a narrow dirt track alongside the road. I recognised the cows as those of a farmer several miles back—so I dug my heels in and left them standing staring after us in wonderment. Dolly had been reared on a dairy farm and bringing in the milking cows had been one of her daily chores.

Like father, like son
Ian Burkinshaw

In 1934, I rode a pony to school that my father had ridden to school in 1907. This pony lived until he was 38 years old!

Hungry and wet
John Vallance

We put our old pony, Paddy, into the buggy when the three of us were attending the school about five miles away from our farm at Berrimal. Up till then, my sister and I used to ride double-dink on a special saddle. He was a cunning old horse, that Paddy, and left us with many colourful memories.

Our school lunches always used to be carried in a case, which we put under the buggy seat. Once we reached school, they were transferred to a safe in the porch. When ants started invading our lunches, we had to leave our food in our gigs and buggies. This was all right until the day came when old Paddy prised the case from under the seat, opened the lid and ate everything in it. He did this on a couple of occasions, devouring meat, cheese and jam sandwiches, and even our pieces of cake. Eventually we put a stop to it by tying a strap around the case with a keeper buckle on it, so we no longer had to go hungry.

If it rained during our homeward trip, Paddy would pull over and park himself under a tree until the rain had passed. The only trouble was that we three would be left sitting in the buggy out in the rain. We would belt him with a green stick we used to carry with us, but this never had any effect.

After he had done this on a couple of occasions, and we had got soaked through, Mum came down the road on rainy days to meet us wearing Dad's big oilskin coat. The first time she did this, she got into the buggy and, with the whip that she brought with her, gave Paddy the works on his rump for the next half mile, which he covered at full gallop.

The next time he tried leaving us in the rain, the mere sight of Mum in her raincoat in the distance was enough to change his mind. He pricked his ears and set off again at full trot. It only took a few more appearances by Mum on the road and he never tried that trick again. He had not been bargaining on that sort of treatment.

A small black goddess
Stuart Clements

Venus, a small, black Shetland pony, came into our possession in about 1939. I was about seven years old, and Venus was a few years older. She had been used by the neighbour's daughter in an attempt to get to school, but Venus had other ideas. She would go about halfway, buck the rider off and then go home. So she was given to me and my brother as our school pony. I'm not sure why she didn't buck with us; perhaps it was because she had two of us on her back for the 10-kilometre trip to school. However, she had other tricks, and was probably the most cunning horse I know. Her favourite entertainment was to run under low trees and wipe you off her back as quick as a flash.

When we got too big for her, Dad made a small rubber-tyred jinker and she pulled us in that for a few more years. After we left school, Venus was turned out into the paddock, to spend the rest of her life in peace, but that didn't last long. A friend of Dad's had two small boys starting school, so Venus was given to them. The friend picked her up in the back of an old Dodge buckboard and she was taken the 30 or so kilometres to her new home. The new owners rode her to school for a few years until the school closed and a bus took them to an area school. Venus was again turned out to retire.

Some years after that, we arose one morning and there, standing quietly by the old horseyard, was Venus. She had walked the 30 kilometres, and she stood around the yard for about a week. We made quite a fuss of her, but then her owner came and took her home again.

Venus died the next day. She was about 25 years old, and we think she must have known she was about to die and perhaps came back to where her memories were fondest.

Driving Trixie to school
Joyce Shiner

Last night I dreamt of old Trixie,
the diminutive Timor mare
that hauled us to school in a buggy
in weather foul or fair.

The buggy was far too heavy,
and the harness had room to spare;

but Dad did his best for her comfort,
while we kids had never a care.

She was bought 'unseen' from Koojedda,
and said to be nine years old;
and when she arrived, Dad could tell she was aged;
but school nags were scarcer than gold.

How I loved the feel of her shaggy coat
in winter so soft and warm.
To bury my face, and tell her my woes,
she seemed to understand.

She had a sense of humour,
and knew when fair was fair;
she had more sense than some humans,
that scruffy pony-mare.

When big boys tried to ride her
in the dinner-hour at school
she'd toss them off in fine style,
making them look right fools.

At times we forgot to take her chaff
in the morning rush to school,
and Dad would holler to Heaven
when we broke that golden rule.

One night Dad went to the stables
and was mystified to see
the old mare's stall was empty,
and she hadn't eaten her tea.

He went to the stables at daybreak,
and stumbling up the track
was her donkey-like form in the morning mist
with the hired-hand on her back.

He said he'd been to a party
at a place some miles away,
admitting it wasn't the first time.
He lost his job that day.

The years rolled on, we girls left school,
Georgina, Pansy and I.
The little old mare was pensioned off.
The boys had their ponies to ride.

Mother and Dad left early for
a trip to town one day,
leaving me in charge of the family
and the animals, while away.

Dad's last words were, as he cranked the Ford,
'See the old mare is fed,
and make sure she goes to the dam for a drink.'
But she wouldn't leave the shed.

Then I saw the boys, like two old men,
but I didn't interfere,
the older, shouldering the shot-gun,
the younger leading the mare.

How often, they heard their father say
'That poor old mare should be put away.'

*Next day we missed the little old dog,
and a brother rode away
to a lake-edge in the salt-bush
where the old mare's body lay.*

*He found the dog beside it,
keeping the crows at bay.
He brought her home on the saddle;
but he said: 'She wanted to stay.'*

*In less than a week, the old dog was dead.
They found her in Trixie's stall,
and buried her with her old mate,
in the salt-bush, collar and all.*

*May the Good Lord forgive us our Trixies.
We're learning better ways
to care for His gift, the noble horse
in these enlightened days.*

Seven
Horsing around

There's nothing like a good horse laugh to lighten the load. And the inevitable stories about things going wrong usually get the biggest laughs. Sometimes the 'disasters' were self-inflicted, or they were due to a practical joke. Often a horse was just doing what came naturally. They were stories that went into the family history to be repeated over and again around the kitchen table, usually starting 'Do you remember the time when ...' And everyone would put their heads back and swing on their chairs with mirth. The stress of the day would dissipate.

Another way of washing away the worries of the world is to hitch a wagon with all the essential comforts of life on board and plod along quiet country lanes behind a Clydesdale. Rod Dovey offers gypsy wagon holidays that are perfect for unravelling knots in bellies.

More than a mere wagon-hirer, Rod is a great raconteur and lover of the poems of Ogilvie, Paterson and Lawson; and he understands the benefits of a good laugh.

A wagon hauls away the pressures

Forget glitzy resorts, the mesmerising clop of a Clydesdale is the perfect antidote to whirling city pressures according to Rod Dovey, sharp-eyed observer of stressed-out people. Quoting Banjo Paterson and telling yarns about his collection of nine Clydesdales, white-whiskered Rod started letting his mainly city clientele loose with a horse and gypsy wagon to roam the beautiful country of Victoria's central goldfields. In 1977, he was the first in Australia to offer horse-drawn holidays and reckons you can see the tension peel away from grey and anxious faces as soon as they pick up the reins. The solitude of country tracks, the peace of transport without pollution and engines, and the romance of returning to the era of the working horse, Rod reckons, has saved the sanity of plenty of lawyers, politicians, doctors, CEOs and others subject to the industrial treadmill. He calls his business The Colonial Way to emphasise that most links with contemporary life are severed.

Looking the epitome of the laid-back rural, Rod scratches the chin of his similarly whiskered 25-year-old favourite, Ferdi, and you'd think Rod would have grown up with heavy horses. But when he had a flash of brilliance in the middle of the night to start a horse and wagon business in May 1977, Rod knew nothing about horses, nor was he particularly rural. A chemical engineer working with his own veterinary pharmaceutical business based in Bendigo, Rod craved a change of pace and lifestyle. By August, he had built the first of his six wagons and put it on display at a caravan show. He answered an advertisement in the *Weekly Times* for an ex-milk delivery horse called Goblin, a Clydesdale of uncertain age which he later discovered to be thirty. Not being a horseman, Rod was exploited mercilessly by horse dealers far and wide until he learnt what questions to ask. He says he went through 26 horses before he settled on his team of nine. 'In the early days I would be lucky to get one good horse out of three,' he laughs.

From timber loggers he bought horses that had been trained to step back then, somewhat alarmingly for amateur wagon drivers, jerk on the chains to get moving forward. Horses from railway shunting yards were the best. They had learnt to lean their full weight into their collar to get the heavy rail trucks moving. Rod said one ex-shunting horse he bought had been wonderful in the shafts, gentle and slow, ideal for novice reinsmen, but he later found out this horse also was around thirty. Nevertheless, he worked on until he was thirty-six. Rod said it had never occurred to him to ask what age a horse was. If it was around $400, quiet, a good worker and easy to float and shoe, he'd take it. He now pays between $1500 and $2000 for not-so-elderly horses.

Being a non-horseman turned out to be fortunate when catering for tourists who mostly are also new to horses. Rod knows the mistakes his clients can make, having made plenty himself. He teaches people to harness and care for their horse and sets up foolproof systems so a horse can't spring surprises on guests, like escaping at night and leaving his gypsies with a lack of horsepower. He uses high wires slung between trees in the campsites so the horses can move around without getting caught in ropes and breaking gear. He tries to anticipate the unforeseen but doesn't always succeed. Some years ago, a group of students celebrating the end of Year 12 spent a week touring the back roads and forests around Rod's base at Bridgewater on the Loddon River. Very early one morning the postmaster of Newbridge looked up from letter sorting to see a Clydesdale trotting down the main street. He rang Rod to warn him and then quickly followed with another phone call to say a group of young girls in nighties and PJs were in hot pursuit. Rod's blue eyes still twinkle with delight at the memory of all these distressed, scantily clad young women arriving to retrieve their horse.

Most trips are uneventful, says Rod, even though the art of horse driving challenges the odd gate post and produces the odd slightly bingled wagon. Rod laughs these off and prefers to talk about his nightly rounds delivering horse feed and supplies to the campers, mapping out their next day's route and taking away rubbish. Naturally everyone wants to yarn, and Rod finds himself falling into Banjo Paterson mode over a few red wines around the campfire, and his two-hour round might take five.

In the mornings he checks new campers out from their sites, ensuring they've dressed their horses correctly. With mapped itineraries designed to suit each wagonload, Rod's travellers can clop through Reg Ansett's picturesque birthplace, Inglewood, or visit a winery at Kingower, where huge nuggets were once found and the local population was 70,000—now it is about 30. They camp on Crown land, by streams, ruins or gold-diggings. 'They are free to let their imaginations roam as early settlers, drovers, travelling hawkers, Chinese market gardeners, whatever takes their fancy,' says Rod, who has won plenty of state and regional tourism awards.

Rod designed his wagons with a front axle that prevents jack-knifing and roll-overs, and car-type steering where the wheels turn, not the axle. He installed a big, flat water tank under the floor to keep the centre of gravity low. Each wood and fibreglass wagon cost between $8000 and $10,000, but with more than 3800 hirings, the wagons have paid themselves off handsomely.

Rod says 'gypsies' are often high-flying businessmen and the occasional politician. 'They come to spend 24-hour stretches with their children,' said Rod. 'One company director said as soon as he starts brushing the horse, all thoughts of work disappear, as though a switch has been flicked.' With no telephone and no television, and no mobile coverage, there's no choice about whether to relax or not.

Rod says being reliant on a horse to get around links people from high-pressure lifestyles with the basics of survival. He insists his horses be walked only. He maintains that being forced to travel at three kilometres an hour often changes these stressed- out, fidgety types forever, and plenty of them return for another dose of horse therapy.

People fall in love with their horses, often to the extent of spending hours combing manes and fetlocks until they are fluffed and floaty, and coats are polished like new coins. Rod recounts with glee the tale of a couple on a romantic interlude. When he called on them with supplies, he found the woman drumming her fingers on the door of the van, furious at the amount of attention being lavished by her mate on the wretched horse.

This life of petting and gentle travel doesn't suit active horses. Rajah was one horse that found this sort of life boring, so he took to rearing and breaking harness. He was sold to become a film horse. Josh, however, is one of the most requested horses. A handsome bay, he once worked for an asparagus grower, had been badly treated and finds life now very pleasant. Indeed, what horse wouldn't like a meal-break every hour? It's not that the horses are particularly hungry that they are plied with constant feed, it's simply another instance of horse handlers not wanting to offend urban sensibilities. Rod keeps his team fat on plenty of lucerne and oaten chaff and pellets of vitamins and minerals. It is also Rod's way of ensuring his horses keep healthy and don't get flattened by overwork. People also worry about the weight of the wagon loaded up with people and supplies. 'But it is only a 100 pound pull. Horses are capable of a 2000 pound drawbar pull. But if we worked the horses the way they did in the old days, people would be outraged.'

Under this regime of good food and easy work, the horses rarely need a vet and the wagons can easily handle year-round occupancy rates of 60 per cent. Rod got up to 75 per cent for a while, but it was such a frenzy of cleaning and maintaining wagons, keeping harness in good shape and horses spelled, that he was at risk of becoming as frazzled as his stressed-out clients.

At the end of a balmy day, by a dam among ironbark trees not far from the Thong Tree, a local landmark decorated by hundreds of pairs of Australia's famous footwear, two families were pulling in for the night. The horses were unhitched, harness put on the ground and horses let go to have a drink and wander in the bush nearby. A team of children roared around burning off excess energy. The horses were unconcerned by balls whizzing past their ears, and submitted to family life and being led by children who were not much higher than their mighty chests.

I commented that one of the horses seemed particularly hot and sweaty. After a few giggles from the driver I was told she had enjoyed the sport of holding it back behind the lead wagon, then geeing the massive animal into a canter to catch up. I silently mused that Rod, so particular and proud of his horses and the training he puts into the humans, would not be pleased. He was due to visit the camp within the hour. The driver said the horse would soon dry off. Besides, it was good fun going faster. As I came upon their wheel marks on the dirt track to their camp, I wondered what Rod would make of the unmistakable hoof prints of a cantering Clydesdale. I could imagine him slipping into these calming words in praise of the Clydesdale by one of his favourite poets, Will Ogilvie:

To each the favourite of his heart,
To each his chosen breed,
In gig and saddle, plough and cart,
To serve his separate need.

Blue blood for him that races,
Clean limbs for him who rides,
But for me, the giant graces,
And the white and honest faces,
The power upon the traces,
Of the Clydes!

Red hot ride
Wendy Muffet

Reginald Faithfull Muffet was an upstanding man of meticulous habits. He was also an excellent horseman and was still breaking horses in to work on his farm at Wirrinya well into his fifties. His son, Bob, a reluctant rider, used to tell with some glee of the occasion when he was conscripted to saddle his pony and ride with his father to keep a newly broken mare company. Rex, as was his habit, lit up his pipe before mounting, and all went well until about half a mile down the track, when the mare started to fidget.

'Get in close,' the old fellow barked. 'I think she's going to drop her head.' He quickly tapped his pipe out on the pommel of his saddle and stuffed it down the front of his bib and brace overalls.

Drop her head she did—and she could buck too! But the fireworks she put on were nothing compared to the old fellow's reaction when the red hot ash that he'd failed to tap out of the bowl of his pipe burnt through his overalls, through his flannels, and into the raw flesh beneath. Apparently the ride home was tense, with Bob keeping his grins to himself. The mare, sensing the mood of her rider, chose to behave beautifully. All the same, she was never to be one of his favourites—painful memories perhaps!

No dawdling, please!
Jill Dobbs

One of our favourite stock horses of the 1960s was a prettily marked skewbald mare, chunky but fast, who could turn on the proverbial sixpence. Skewy was an impatient lady, though, and if relegated to the tail of the mob of sheep or cattle we were driving, was apt to lay back her ears and bite any dawdlers, to hurry them along. As the person always posted to the tail of the mob in those days, I could sympathise with her misbehaviour.

One day I was promoted from my safe old moke to ride Skewy for a day's mustering with my husband, John, and the rest of the men. It was a dream run. Skewy and I did everything right, no thanks to me, and basked in general approval.

Then with all the cattle together, we settled down to drive them to the yards, 10 miles away, with me on the tail as usual. Everything was going well, so I had no qualms about popping into the acacias and squatting down, reins in hand, for a pee. In Skewy's eyes, this must have constituted dawdling—because she bit me, ferociously it felt, on the bottom. There is no such thing as a sisters-under-the-skin rapport between mare and female rider, whatever they say.

Muddled mounts
Charles Fenton

Clunes is a small country town of about 1000 residents 20 miles north of Ballarat. It is the place where, in 1851, gold was first discovered in Victoria, and its population in 1870 was seven thousand. Its profitable mines had seen the need for 43 licensed hotels to be in operation at the one time.

After the gold ran out, the population dwindled and the town became dependent on the surrounding farming and grazing areas. Hotel numbers had also dwindled, but those that were left were well used on Saturday nights when the farmers came into town to celebrate the end of the week's work. In the early 1930s, some of the farmers rode their horses in and tethered them to the hitching rails. Others drove a horse and gig, some rode bicycles and others walked, if the distance was not too far. The more affluent drove their early model cars.

Most of the moderate drinkers retired from the hotels at, or soon after, the early closing time, but the hardened drinkers seemed to find ways of overcoming that small difficulty and continued on well into the night. By this time their navigational skills had declined to the point where they had some difficulty in finding their way home on a dark night.

The cyclists had the greatest problems, because they couldn't balance too well and had to push their bikes home. However, the horsemen were more fortunate. The horses were quite sober and knew the way home as well as their masters. Having overcome the tricky business of mounting the horses, it was then just a matter of sitting there until the horse got them home. There was just one pitfall. Two of this hardened group had white horses and they came from opposite sides of Clunes. On one occasion they mounted the wrong horses and were taken home to the wrong farms—not the sort of problem to be sorted out in five minutes, and I guess it would have been well into the next day before the problem was resolved to the satisfaction of all concerned.

One of these white horse owners also had a bike, which he occasionally rode into Clunes for his hotel visits. One night he rode home on the bike, and the next morning he discovered he had two bikes—but no horse.

When the whistle blows
Geoffrey Blight

When the city of Fremantle took on the job of building the harbour groynes, it decided to change from horses and drays to mechanised trucks. The groynes were built using huge rocks, often weighing between seven and ten tons, far too heavy for the drays. So the horses and drays based at the council's quarry were sold off. A local chap who bought one of the council horses had an orchard only a mile and a half from the Fremantle depot. His idea was to use the horse in a single-furrow plough.

What he hadn't counted on was what would happen when the horse, which had been working well all morning, heard the quarry's lunch-break whistle. Catching his new owner by complete surprise, the horse immediately left the orchard—with the single-furrow plough dragging along behind him through the streets—to return to the Fremantle Depot for its lunch.

An intelligent horse
Ralph Dawson

Some 60 years or so ago, Mr Salter of Angaston decided he needed to purchase another draught horse for vineyard work. Accordingly, he rode over to Kapunda to attend the horse sale there. He was able to buy a good type of gelding that he thought would do the job he required it for, and so he rode home, leading his new horse and feeling quite pleased with himself for his day's outing.

On his arrival home, he turned the horse loose in the stable yard, whereupon the new arrival walked straight to the water trough and enjoyed a good long drink after his long journey. Then he turned and walked straight to one of the stalls and immediately began to eat from the manger.

Mr Salter said to his workman, 'See what an intelligent horse that is. You'd think he had lived here all his life, wouldn't you!'

'And so you should!' came the reply. 'That's the horse you sold last year!'

Serving his purpose
Ralph Dawson

My teenage years were spent living on a small farm near Saddleworth in the 1930s. Tractors had not come into common usage at that time, and many farmers reared the odd foal or two for their own use later on. So it was a common sight in the breeding season, in spring, to see the owner of a Clydesdale stallion traversing the roads, going from farm to farm, where a farmer required the services of his sire.

Usually the man conducting this escort service rode a pony gelding and led the stallion, but on one occasion he suffered a lapse of judgement and rode a pony mare instead. He was riding along the road, not thinking of anything in particular, when suddenly he was knocked off his mount from behind by something very big and very solid. Picking himself up from the ground, he saw that his place had been taken by the Clydesdale stallion. He had to smile at his own stupidity as he realised that the horse was only doing what nature had intended him to do. The man always rode a gelding after that experience.

Divided they stood
Margare T Shine

After a heavy week of breaking in horses on our place, Bon went off to the local town in the jinker with his pair of horses, Patricia and The Painter. He had a good day at the local pub and when the doors closed, headed for home. When he woke up on Sunday morning, he found himself still in the jinker. The two horses had come to a halt—one each side of a young redgum sapling. No gear had been broken—he was just a bit cold.

Hungry for action
Garth Fragar

Pegasus was a 14 hand bay gelding owned by one of our neighbours, a big lad in his mid-teens. After saddling Pegasus, the lad would always lead him behind the shed. We suspected this was to allow him to get the horse used to the tight girth and also to save his mates laughing if he was pelted off.

A chap came to inspect cattle and on being asked if he could ride a horse, said, 'Once I get on a horse, nothing but hunger and thirst will bring me off.'

The lad saddled Pegasus, led him to the chap and told him to check the girth. The chap tightened the girth, mounted Pegasus, and was promptly thrown. An onlooker said he had never seen anyone get hungry and thirsty so quickly!

Just out of reach
Alison Turnbull

In the early part of the 20th century when large areas of eastern Eyre Peninsula were still being opened up by settlers, the first police officer stationed at Cleve was Mounted Constable J J O'Loughlin. In those days a policeman's only mode of transport was by horseback.

One day, in the course of his duty, MC O'Loughlin rode from Cleve to Verran, a distance of about 20 miles. When the policeman dismounted at his destination, the horse got away from him and he was unable to catch it. It walked all the way back to Cleve, annoyingly just ahead of the constable, making its way along the long, hot, dusty track through thick scrub.

No matter what he did to try to catch his horse, it kept just that little way in front of him. He was quoted as saying, 'I would have shot the horse, but the rifle was still on the saddle!'

More in common with Ben Hur
Denis Adams

Grandma's obsession with church-going made Sundays a misery for Grandpa and the boys. Grandpa hated having his Sabbaths ruined by religion. He enjoyed things like a nip of whisky, fox hunting, organising buckjumping competitions and boxing matches for the young fellows, and Sunday was the only chance they got. The only bright spot about going to church was that it gave him a chance to show off his buggy horses that he bred for sale.

Dad used to say it was a hazardous enterprise untying the horses after church. Grandpa would take his seat, bracing his feet against the dashboard, and twining the reins around and around his arms. Then as soon as the rest of the family was on board, he'd cry 'Right!' and, risking life and limb, dodging the flashing hooves, Dad would untie the horses. The buggy would do a rapid circuit of the church, the iron tyres fairly screeching on the stone. Having seen all the other horses heading for home getting a head start on them, the frenzied horses practically did wheelies. Grandpa always gave his neighbours a good start—to make it more exciting!

As the buggy swept by, Dad would make a leap for it, dodging the wheels as they shaved past his bare knees. There was no stopping the horses now! The parson would purse his lips, thinking, no doubt, that Herb Adams had more in common with Ben Hur than John Wesley.

Maximum confusion
Wendy Treloar

New Year's Eve, according to my mother, was a popular time for young people to unharness horses while celebrations were in full swing and then put them back into the carts facing the wrong way. Another favourite trick was to put the cart one side of a fence, poke its shafts through the wire and hitch the horse up on the other side of the fence. Both pranks were designed to cause maximum confusion to under-the-weather revellers.

Ginger's escape
Joyce Shiner

I was about nine when we acquired Ginger, an insignificant-looking, rather bad-tempered little animal. As my sisters showed not the slightest interest in horses and my brothers were too young, I began to think of Ginger as my very own. He took us to school in the sulky and I rode him bareback on numerous errands for Mum to the neighbours delivering bread, collecting butter, that sort of thing.

On train day, Mum walked to the siding to get mail and stores, and would then go home with us in the sulky after school. It was Christmas week, and after school we harnessed up and drove down to the store to pick up Mum and all her Christmas shopping. I gave Mum the reins, then untied Ginger and jumped in. Ginger must have been feeling fresh after standing all day tied to a tree near the school, for as soon as we turned the corner towards home, he put his head down and galloped. With Mum and I both pulling on the reins and imploring him to go steady, he galloped almost a mile, until the Willcox's overtook us in their big Hupmobile, and helped to stop him. They then took Mum back to collect all the parcels that had bounced out of the sulky and took Mum and the little boys home, leaving us girls to get home with Ginger and the sulky.

When Jack Hunt, a young Pommy lad who worked for us, nominated his family for immigration to Australia, Dad fitted him up with sulky and harness, and Ginger in the shafts. I protested loud and long, until at length Dad convinced me the Hunts needed a conveyance more than we did—especially since we no longer needed him to get us to school. It was not until Dad confessed that he had provided Hunts with a turnout not so much as a gift, but in lieu of some wages owing to Jack, that I ceased my railings.

Poor little Ginger! Mrs Hunt was a huge woman, and with three heavy teenagers on board she drove him to the siding every Thursday. Not knowing anything about balancing a two-wheeler, they all sat back in the seat, almost lifting Ginger's feet off the ground. One day Dad noticed Ginger was looking poor. Realising that they would have no fodder for him, Dad told Mrs Hunt to call in whenever she passed, and take as much chaff or hay as they had room for. After that Ginger always galloped up the laneway to our place, whether there was room for chaff or not. One day he galloped so fast, and Mrs Hunt pulled so hard on the reins, that her feet went through the floorboards. Dad loved to recount the tale of this fat lady sitting in the sulky with her feet running on the ground.

Ginger must have had a very big heart for the size of him, but not big enough. One day, on the way home, he lay down in the shafts and died. I cried when I was told, because even though he was such a naughty little horse, he didn't deserve such treatment. I actually felt glad he died.

In their time of peril
Denis Adams

A neighbour who had served in an army transport unit in South Australia with horses and mules used to relate a humorous incident. A very bad electrical storm came up while they were on the move, and remembering all the stories of horses attracting lightning, they dropped their lead ropes and reins, hoping the animals would stay huddled together, while they fled uphill to a safer spot.

Seeing them go, the animals clearly decided they needed to be near humans in their time of peril. As one, they all raced in pursuit. What a sight it was, Cliff used to say, laughing. Men, horses, mules, all running around in wild confusion—the men yelling at their charges to go away and the animals crying out pathetically, as if to say, 'Don't leave me.'

Boots that made him walk
Bruce Mills

Boots was our part-Clydesdale-bred stock horse. With large square head, big feet and heavy bones, he was no good-looker, but what he lost on beauty he made up on temperament. He had such a quiet nature, we didn't even have to break him in.

In 1940 petrol rationing came into force because of the war, so Boots was harnessed to the buggy for commuting between the farm and our town. Over the years our once placid horse had developed a severe shying habit and took to bolting. Once, after heading off into the scrub, both harness and buggy were broken, but the next time it happened, the outcome was more amusing.

Dad was heading over to the railway siding and as he was passing the last two houses, he noticed his friend Tom walking down the road. He stopped Boots and said, 'Hop in, Tom. I'll give you a lift to the siding.'

Tom climbed aboard and they chatted on until Boots spied a large cardboard carton on the track that had been thrown off a truck at the drain crossing. Boots decided it was a terrifying object, and took to the bush, nearly throwing the buggy occupants out as they crossed the drain in a rough spot. Dad steered him back onto the road, feeling very smug that he had done so, but Boots then grabbed the bit and away they went, missing the turn to the siding and bolting straight over the railway line and way down the road to the next town. As it was downhill, they went a fair way before Dad was able to bring Boots to a walk, at which stage Tom jumped out.

'Hang on, Tom,' Dad said. 'I'll drive you back.'

'Not on your bloody life,' replied Tom, who set off on foot back in the direction they had come. He finished up walking further than if he hadn't accepted the ride.

Revenge of the nightcart man
Denis Adams

Septic tanks have destroyed a cherished part of our history. For centuries the nightcart man, with his horse and tipper-dray, filled a vital role in towns and cities. Not only that, he provided the raw material for numerous pranks and jokes. What local hoon could resist pulling the pin on an unattended nightcart, so that the unsuspecting nightcart man and his night's 'takings' were strewn along the road? Needless to say, the nightcart man did not have a very high position in society, so it was quite safe to bait him.

Dan, the nightcart man I knew in my youth, was a big, gruff old bloke with a hip injury, a souvenir of World War I, I believe. I'd often seen Dan sitting with his characteristic hunch on the front of his light, rubber-tyred trolley, his feet on the hinged part of the shafts, the tails of his two light, frisky horses brushing his cheeks. Dan obviously loved his horses. They were always well- fed and immaculately groomed, for as he used to say, you can judge a man by his horses.

Dad liked and respected Dan, and one day introduced me to him, as though presenting me to royalty. Later Dad told me (with many chuckles) how Dan had once turned the tables on one of his most abrasive critics.

The town postmaster was the complete opposite to Dan. A nit- picking, officious, little man who always dressed in a black suit and ruled his domain with a rod of iron. Both staff and customers copped the rough side of his tongue. Most of the townsfolk joked about Dan, but it was not meant unkindly. With the postmaster, it was different. He was disliked intensely.

Once when Dan was laid up with his bad hip, he missed a pickup or two. When he finally arrived to empty the Post Office dunny, it was overflowing.

As Dan came staggering out with the malodorous can on his shoulder, the postmaster waylaid him. Dan grunted an explanation for the delay, but the postmaster felt a good tongue-lashing might smarten Dan up a bit. He followed at Dan's heels, snapping and snarling like an aggressive terrier, right up to the cart. Only a foolish man would stand beneath an elderly man with a bad hip as he hoisted his can of doings up onto his cart. So who can blame Dan for upending the lot over the postmaster?

'You could say the postmaster had got his own back—literally!' quipped Dad.

No Christmas spirit
Kathryn Edwards

My great-grandfather owned a horse-drawn cab business in the town of Hay in New South Wales. My grandmother used to tell us of the time, at Christmas, when her father had to dress up as Santa Claus and drive the cab. He had driven the horses all that day, and then fed, watered and stabled them for a rest. He went into the house, cleaned up and dressed in the Santa outfit.

When he returned to the stables to harness up the horses, they didn't recognise him and caused a great racket, despite much gentle talk, cursing and shouting. Great-grandfather had no other option but to return to the house and put on his smelly old clothes again. After he had re-harnessed the horses and put on their winkers, great-grandfather climbed back into his Santa Claus suit while grandmother and her mother held the team. When he came back out, great-grandfather had to sneak up on to the cab without the horses seeing him.

Moving the Light Horse remounts west down Greenhill Road, Adelaide, in about 1935. Prior to travelling in ordered lines secured by chains, remounts used to be driven loose in mobs of about a hundred. Traffic disruption, invasions of suburban vegetable patches and destruction of washing lines by wayward horses were not uncommon.

Making dams and drainage channels required huge teams of heavy horses. Straining on their chains, this nine-horse team drags dredging scoops up a dam wall in Mill Park, Victoria, 1955. COURTESY OF THE WEEKLY TIMES

A cold morning in Corryong, Victoria, in 1911.

At Kallista, Victoria, Jack Jones and Bess pull out posts from old bridges which were being replaced along Sassafrass Ferny Creek. The area was too boggy and tracks too narrow for tractors. COURTESY OF *THE WEEKLY TIMES*

Jock and Isaac, two of Coopers Brewery's Clydesdales which every Friday deliver barrels of beer to Adelaide restaurants and hotels, clop down King William Street unperturbed by exhaust fumes, sirens, honking traffic and inquisitive pedestrians.

Don Black of Branxholme, Victoria, with Prince in the tipper dray used for general duties around the farm. This dray once belonged to the Melbourne City Council and was used by street sweepers.

The story of Esdale Flash Prince saw him transformed from show horse to an underground pit pony, to almost being slaughtered for pet food, then becoming champion Clydesdale stallion at Sydney Royal Show in 1969 and 1971.

Horse breaker Martin Oakes of Mount Sanford Station leads Australian Stock Horse mares and foals to the yards for weaning.
COURTESY OF STEVE STRIKE, OUTBACK PHOTOGRAPHICS

Stockmen at Mount Sanford Station push Brahman cows and calves into the yards.
COURTESY OF HANS BOESSEM, TODD CAMERA STORE, ALICE SPRINGS

Bill Chandler and his team binding oaten hay at Barmah, 1999.
COURTESY OF EDNA CHANDLER

Creek crossings and bush tracks around Bridgewater-on-Loddon, Victoria, are part of the fun of holidays in a Colonial Way gypsy caravan. COURTESY OF FAY BUSHBY

Victor Harbor's horse-drawn tram runs a daily service across the causeway to Granite Island. It is used by almost 200,000 people each year.

Bill Willoughby, horsemaster to the stars, on the *McLeod's Daughters* set near Gawler, South Australia. COURTESY OF JAMES ELSBY AND *THE ADVERTISER*

Ken Hobday, aged 72, and Blue on their first Tom Quilty ride at Toodyay, Western Australia, in 1995. COURTESY OF CHRIS ROS

Victoria Mounted Police Officers in tight formation hold back protesters during the World Economic Forum demonstrations at Crown Casino, Melbourne, in September 2000.
COURTESY OF NEWS LIMITED

Neville Holz and fellow riders complete the 8000-kilometre southern route of the Spring Valley Round Australia Heritage Ride in Sydney, August 2000.
COURTESY OF AGENCEFRANCE-PRESSE

After crossing the continent from coast to coast on the Spring Valley Round Australia Heritage Ride, Joy Poole sprinkles sand from Broome, Western Australia, on a symbolic horseshoe made on the sand at the Gold Coast, Queensland.
COURTESY OF NEWS LIMITED

Wendy Schaeffer wins Olympic gold on her pony club horse Tommy—punching the air in triumph as they finish their showjump round and take top score in the teams event.
COURTESY OF WENDY SCHAEFFER

The mighty rear that began the 2000 Olympic opening ceremony in the Homebush Stadium, Sydney. Steve Jefferys trained 'Ammo' to rear on cue in just three weeks.
COURTESY OF NEWS LIMITED

Steve Jefferys, 'Ammo'—the horse that did the Olympic rear—and Jana, Steve's performing border collie. COURTESY OF NICOLE EMANUEL PHOTOGRAPHY

Stuart Tinney on Tex, negotiating the water during the four-star section of the 1999 Adelaide International Horse Trials. They finished the competition in fourth place.
COURTESY OF AGENDA PHOTOGRAPHY, CANBERRA

Olympic dressage team contender and former rodeo rider, Brett Parbery, in extended trot on Victory Salute. COURTESY OF ROZ NEAVE

Guy McLean, Equitana 2008, Melbourne, stands on his Quietway performance horses, Hope, Kenny and Spinabbey, cracking stock whips in each hand. Sequel is underneath. COURTESY OF BERNI SAUNDERS

Three brumbies at a training clinic near Ballarat. All were rescued in 2007. From left, VBA Buddy from Kosciuszko National Park with Julia David, VBA Amaranth from Victoria's Alpine National Park, ridden by Colleen O'Brien, and from the same park, VBA Anzac with Kristin Morris.

Richard and Lucy Barrack camping near Texas in Queensland with their three horses Firefly, Sapphire and Molly. To learn about rural life, Richard and Lucy took their pleasure horses on a round-Australia working holiday.

Anne Lindh drives a Quadrem of ponies during a dressage test. It is such a difficult feat that Anne knows of no other Quadrems that have competed and of only a few other drivers in the world who have attempted driving four in a line.
COURTESY OF ANDREW GRAHAM

Leanne Bruce-Clarke performing the Roman Ride at Sydney Royal Easter Show 2000 on Montana, a palomino quarter horse, and Jasper, a stock horse.
COURTESY OF PONY EXPRESS TRICK RIDERS

Leanne Bruce-Clarke practises the tail drag beside a country road past her home. She is one of very few trick riders who can perform this trick. COURTESY OF ROSS CLARKE

Deborah Brennan performs the Cossack drag with horse Sultan, a paint quarter horse Arabian cross, in front of the crowd at Royal Randwick racecourse as part of a display on Australia Day by the Pony Express Trick Riders. COURTESY OF PONY EXPRESS TRICK RIDERS

Deborah Brennan performs the One Foot Stand. COURTESY OF STEVE WHITE

Toby Gorringe with his favourite horse, Rocky. Toby is a lecturer in horsemanship at Charles Darwin University and is based at Mataranka Station, Northern Territory.

Students of Charles Darwin University's Horsemanship and Cattle-handling Course assemble before heading out to muster Brahman cattle at Mataranka Station. From left, Angus Curley, Davey Campbell, and Andrew and Cleon Kenny.

Eight
Street work

The crisp clip-clop of hoofs on the road at dawn jogged across my childhood dreams. Iron shoes on bitumen warned that
soon a clanging billy or clinking bottles would land on the front steps. The milkie's horse was a utilitarian creature, not flashy like the baker's horse, which came mid-morning, swinging around the corner with sparkling harness and brass buckles and badges. The baker's van was glossy red and rounded on top like the loaves arranged on paper-lined wooden trays inside. We would swarm like blowies around its back doors. The polished horse stood with a back leg resting, swishing at flies, while its ears rotated impatiently waiting for the tongue click that made it lean into the collar and break into a smart trot.

The delivery horses stopped in my mid-teens, erasing all those friendly sounds and smells from suburban streets. In these days of supermarkets with massive carparks, it is odd to remember that essentials like vegetables, meat, milk and bread once were delivered daily to the door. Families could do without a car, now plenty have two. Progress seems difficult to define at times.

The stirring sight of horses in city streets is now for novelty value only. Wedding carriages and tourist coaches ply their popular trade. Companies like Coopers Brewery in Adelaide which recognise the magnetic power of a horse and cart to promote their products stage regular delivery runs through city streets. At Victor Harbor, south of Adelaide, the enlightened council operates a profitable horse tram business.

Karen in horse-drawn paradise by the sea

Karen McDougall reckons she's got the dream job. She is in charge of the world's last remaining horse-drawn tram to operate 365 days a year. It plies a historic rail track over water between Victor Harbor and Granite Island. Formerly a Gold Coast girl, Karen's got the sea beside her and plenty of horses. It was for horses that, at 18, she enraged her parents by tossing in a promising career in a five-star hotel to join the circus—the sort of thing many rebellious teenagers might contemplate, but few actually do. Her job was to look after eighteen performing horses and ponies with Sole Brothers Circus. She fed, plaited and put on their costumes and, for a while, thought she was in heaven. The routine of tents and trucks, and moving on every three days inevitably palled. After trying hotel work again, and breeding rats and mice for a veterinary laboratory, horses dragged her into the South Australian Mounted Police as a stable hand, and for five years she fed and exercised the greys.

When she was with the circus, Karen said she had admired her horse troupe for their ability to cope with perpetual change, being tethered to graze and performing their routines in plumes. Then she was bowled over by the police horses, their calm dispositions and high standard of training. 'But nothing beats these Clydesdales,' Karen, 33, enthuses during a day off before again resuming her 76-hour, seven-day roster which gives her every alternate week off. She runs the horse and staff side of the highly profitable local-government-run business that transports almost 200,000 passengers a year. 'Out of all the workhorses I have met, the tram horses are the most trustworthy, calm and willing to work. They are so accepting and put up with an awful lot. I don't think they have a mean bone in their bodies.'

It's highly appropriate that the days of horsepower should continue so emphatically at historic Victor Harbor, a hugely popular beach holiday destination an hour south of Adelaide. In the 1860s it was South Australia's main coastal port, linked to Goolwa at the mouth of the River Murray by a horse-powered railway. Goods bound for the river's paddle-steamer trade were hauled by heavy horses on the rail line across the sandhills and along coastal flats of the wildly beautiful southern coast. Although the railway is now operated by steam engines pulling heritage carriages full of holidaying tourists, heavy horses are pulling their weight over the causeway to the tiny island, where penguins and restaurants are the popular attractions. The green and gold two- storey trams first rumbled over the tracks in 1894 but stopped in 1954. In 1986, local horseman and historian Doug Bunker pressed the council to allow him to revive the trams and for tracks to be relaid. Having proved the venture was potentially a good earner for the town, he transferred it to the council which now aims to treble its horse-generated income within five years by selling naming rights to each Clydesdale to local businesses. One horse has already been snapped up by a winery which can use it for promotional purposes. Even so, Peter Bond, the council's manager of the horse tram enterprise, says money is secondary to the spin-off benefits from the link to a romantic era still remembered by many, as well as reminding people about Victor Harbor's role in the state's early trading history. 'Many a grandmother enjoys a return to the public transport system of her childhood,' he said.

Since 1986, more than a million people have enjoyed the nostalgia of the tram. Modelled on the original tram's design, the current trams have modern gadgetry like tapered roller bearings, which need a pull of only about 50 kilograms to get a full load of 50 people moving. Because she is constantly asked about the welfare of the horses by concerned tourists, Karen has produced a brochure to answer their questions and allay their fears about the horses being overworked or treated cruelly.

Yet, the very day I was there the RSPCA had been summoned by an indignant observer because the duty horse was having to work against a crosswind on the causeway. 'But that's OK,' says Karen who's completely unruffled by what some might see as an affront to her horsemanship. 'They know us well and that we'd never do anything to harm the horses.' In fact, the horses have a cushy life: during peak summer holiday periods they work about three hours a day, three days in a row, then have a day off in a 100-acre grassy paddock. They also get to trot along the white sandy beaches in the early morning on their way into work, one being ridden and two or three others being led.

Although she has her own quarter horse, thoroughbred and Arab stallion, and has showjumped and evented, the plodding, hairy-footed Clydesdales have quite seduced her. It's their temperament that she loves. She sees them being patted by a curious and unfamiliar public incessantly. They are poked, prodded and hemmed in by admirers, but never has she seen any of them bite or even lay their ears back. They might get bored and nod off, but to help them be charming ambassadors for tourism a bit of unashamed bribery comes into play. Karen hands out bags of carrots every day, getting her customers to feed the horses with something healthy rather than their discarded ice creams and bread. 'It helps keep them interested in people,' says Karen, who uses about 60 kilograms of carrots a week. With several carrots usually poking out of her back pocket, Karen always expects to be asked what they are for as she goes about her business checking horses and organising staff. 'Oh, they are spare spark plugs,' she'll quip. 'We need them in case the horse's battery goes flat.' It's semi-vaudeville, part of the theatre of the tram. People and entertainment skills, interestingly, rate more highly than horse skills in this job, according to Peter Bond. Someone who likes people can always be taught about horses. It doesn't always work the other way.

Majestic passage through city streets

The sense of importance was almost overwhelming. We were clopping down a main Adelaide city street, looking down on cars, and turning heads, with wind in the hair and rocking gently with the rhythm of the trot. Timber, iron, leather and flesh—just the basics; yet combining to convey us majestically.

I had joined irrepressible Coopers Brewery teamster Mike Keogh on his Friday delivery run to city restaurants and hotels behind Clydesdales Jock and Isaac. Besides the lure of possibly having a good time, the task was to check out the assertions of old-time horsemen like Eric Lawrence that the day of the working horse was over.

We met at the company's Norwood depot, where Mike had the horses ready for hitching up to the company delivery lorry built around 1900. They were wearing a fine set of harness made in Adelaide in 1920 by Ben Braendler, a successful old- time exhibitor of Clydesdales. The harness, laden with nickel and featuring unusual high-peaked Scotch collars, is owned by the National Trust and was restored by Mike.

With five barrels of beer loaded on the lorry, we set off. Because we were in Adelaide, the trot into the city took only about twenty minutes—probably ten minutes by car. There wasn't much traffic, and drivers were polite enough. No-one revved or tooted trying to scare the horses, and Mike said such behaviour would be rare. With the lorry and horses being so noticeable and relatively slow, they create their own bubble in the traffic. People give way readily.

Not for us the sealed, sound-proofed cabin of an air-conditioned computer-buttoned fancy-styled limo, so alienated from its power source. But we, riding high in grandeur, with the reins in our hands, have no illusions as to where our power is coming from. We watch it at work—hocks pushing, muscles bulging, heads bobbing, huge feet lifting. This raw, sweet-smelling horsepower is accompanied by the sounds of flapping leather, jingling harness bells and crunching, iron-rimmed wheels.

We delivered a couple of barrels to the renowned Red Ochre Grill, from a back lane jammed with untidily parked cars. The horses took a break while Mike dropped the barrels down with a clatter and rolled them in the back door. How he thought we were going to get out of that congested dog-leg lane, I had no idea. But off we went and, somehow, in the junction of the lane, with just whiskers to spare, a quick three-point turn was made and we trotted out into the traffic again. Since we were playing teamsters for real, Mike thought we had done enough to earn a break at a nearby pub. This horse-and-cart age was really growing on me.

The horses were hitched to a post by the verandah where we sat. We had sandwiches and ale and watched as curious people stopped and patted the horses. The most interesting reactions came from shy Asian people, wanting terribly to touch, but afraid of what might happen. Several had never seen horses before. With encouragement from Mike, one very timid woman made fleeting contact with Jock's satiny skin, and went away shaking her hand and giggling with delight.

A few more deliveries later, and we clopped down King William Street, in three lanes of cars and buses, pushy taxis and bicycle couriers. The horses didn't mind a fire engine screaming past, exhaust fumes up their noses, or being jammed on all sides by vehicles, and I suppose what's more important, their road speed in afternoon traffic was no different from anyone else's—except for the far swifter bicycles of couriers.

Coopers teams delivered beer from 1862 until motor vehicles took over in the 1920s, but in 1987 the tradition was revived, principally as a public relations exercise for the family-owned brewery. Nevertheless, the Friday deliveries are serious business. Many clients request delivery by horse and cart, judging that a bit of old-fashioned nostalgia from an era perceived to be more trustworthy, kind and gentle doesn't hurt their image.

To the musical beat of those iron-clad feet, Mike Keogh relates how the horse delivery business has him truly hooked. It's what he is happiest doing. At 43, though, he was coming in for a bit of flak from the old-timers who saw him as a bit of a rookie, even though he had been competing at shows in harness classes since 1978.

'I want to be the best possible driver and get to the top,' he says with a determination that shows in the set of his jaw. 'It's become an obsession with me.'

In pursuit of that aim, he spends time in libraries tracking down the great old show drivers and studying their style. He sees himself being like some of those old chaps and still winning well into his seventies. Receiving a recent invitation to compete at the prestigious Royal Windsor Horse Show gave his ambition a mighty boost, not that he could consider taking any of his five Clydesdales contracted to Coopers with him to England.

As we trot back to the depot, returning five empty kegs, Mike's enthusiasm for the business has him agreeing that the day of the delivery horse is far from over. In Adelaide especially, where distances are still manageable, and the traffic civilised, yet suburbs are as isolated as any, horse-drawn deliveries would still be feasible—so long as the horses are very quiet, and the driver very competent. Certainly, the cost of purchasing a horse, harness and trolley (somewhere around $5000), and their upkeep, wins over a motorised van hands down.

Bakery horses sparkled in Ron's hands

When I was 14, I envied more than anyone in the world a small neat man with slicked down hair called Ron. To horse-mad me, he had the perfect existence. It was 1962, and Ron was in charge of Parker Bros Bakery's 50 delivery horses. Sheer heaven was to stand at the doorway of the stables every night after school and gaze for hours at all those blissful animals tied up in their stalls while Ron bustled about checking harness, clipping legs, pulling manes and blacking hooves.

It took a year before I ever had the courage to step inside that wide doorway to be enveloped in the smell of phenol that Ron washed the stalls out with, and to get close to the black, oiled harness flashing with chrome and red leather, and ringing with bells. Eventually I was invited to groom some of the quiet horses; and one day, Ron told me to climb aboard Mitzi. In ecstasy I rode this rotund, grey mare around the asphalt yard several times.

That night I flew home on my old purple bike, nearly bursting with excitement. Unfortunately no-one else seemed to think riding a bakery horse was anything terribly special. Even when one weekend I came trotting up the front drive of our house on the startled Mitzi—who was used only to stopping outside houses, not entering their gates—no-one was very thrilled. Old Mitzi was to become a regular Sunday afternoon visitor over the years, enjoying a munch of green grass on the lawns.

Thus passed my innocent teenage years, and such were those trusting times—bread and milk money would be left in tins on the verandah, the delivery man would chat like a friend, and a horse could trot the streets without being threatened by hoons—a young girl was quite safe in the company of strangers.

Thirty-two years on, with the smell of freshly cooked bread in big wicker baskets and images of horses walking from house to house still alive in my memory, I decided to track Ron down, for he was surely one of the last of the old-time delivery-horse stablemen. I found him, now aged 72, living where he had all his life, within a block of the ABC building in Adelaide. Out the back of the house he shares with his sister were the stables where he used to keep his own family harness horses, but now they are home only to his memories. Photographs of all his favourites hang on the walls with old bridles, bits and a stiff, cobwebbed saddle.

Ron Cloy, still neat, with the same slicked-down hair,

smilingly remembered that gawky girl in glasses on the purple bike who stood and stared each night. 'The stables were a mecca for all the children in the area who liked horses,' he said. And for the next few hours, in a sitting-room crammed with horse ornaments on every shelf, he shared his own passion for the horse with another who also never outgrew it.

Coming from a long line of great horsemen, Ron started at Parker Bros at Maylands in 1945 as a relieving driver, covering twelve different delivery rounds a year while the regular drivers were on holiday. His horse was named Federation, and Ron reckons he was the best and most intelligent horse of all those he worked in a lifetime with horses. Every month he would be on a different round, but 'Fed' knew every round from one twelve-month cycle to the next.

'Some rounds interlapped, and he knew which he was on,' Ron said. 'He did not stop at any customers served by the driver doing the adjoining round. In some streets I would go in one gate of the house and out through the back gate to the street behind. Fed would walk around to wait for me, that is, if people didn't stop him—not knowing that he was purposefully going about his business.'

Between 1948 and 1950 drop-centre vehicles were introduced to replace the two-wheeled high carts drivers had previously used. Ron remembers the new vans as a great advance. 'The driver could walk in and out either side and they provided him with shelter. If the horse was well-trained, you could average one customer per minute,' Ron recalled. Each cart carried between 450 and 500 loaves and most of the 39 rounds had an average of 350 customers per day.

At the age of 30, Ron took charge of the Maylands stable. His day started before dawn, then he went home at 10 am, and returned in the afternoon to greet the horses back from their six or seven hour shifts. It was a seven day a week routine of grooming, feeding, clipping and keeping the stalls clean.

'It was hours and hours of work a week. I never ever worried about how many hours I worked. I always thought the horses came first. On hot nights I'd even go back at midnight and let them off for a drink at the trough, and on weekends, I used to often clip half a dozen so they were smart for work on Monday.

'We used to turn them out as if they were going into the show ring. Eight or ten vehicle turnouts on any given day could have gone into any show ring. We always bought good horses and had good harness. We were very conscious that every time they went out in the bread carts, it was a public relations exercise.'

In 1965 Ron was warned of impending bad news. 'The horses are going,' he was told, and from then on he started looking for homes for them. Some ended up on fruit blocks in the Riverland, pulling trolleys which fruit pickers stood on. I was offered Mitzi, but for some reason my parents didn't fancy having a bakery horse in the back garden. Average price was 35 pounds, about what had been paid for them. The harness however, made by Harry Hailstone, top class and well-maintained, went for between five and ten pounds a set, having originally cost 120 pounds. The famous drop-centre bread carts with their rounded roof shape and red glossy paintwork brought just 10 pounds each.

Gone were the days for Ron of taking four or five horses a day tied to the breaking cart, pulled by Colonel, the bakery's show horse, up to old Bill Arthur, the farrier at St Morris. Gone were the all-night efforts of preparing several dozen quiet horses in plumes and ribbons so they could pull floats in the John Martin's Christmas pageant through the streets of Adelaide. Gone were all the intrigues about which drivers had girlfriends they visited on their rounds, leaving their horses to sleep for an hour or two outside in the street. Gone also were the days when horses would jack-knife the carts as they turned their backs into driving rain, or of bolters rushing back to the stable at the completion of their round; and gone too was the copious supply of straw and manure for the market gardeners of Piccadilly in the Adelaide Hills.

The vans never really replaced the horses. They weren't as quick at home deliveries, taking up to an hour longer on some runs, especially in narrow streets where horses could manoeuvre more easily in tight spaces. They won, however, on long trips to distant suburbs; and gradually, as expensive technology tends to do, the vans redefined the job to suit themselves. Home deliveries were abandoned, and vans just took their loads direct to supermarkets and small shops, with an efficiency the horse could never achieve.

Ron was assigned to the bread room of the bakery, and retired early because of illness. Of the 150 horses that went through the stables in his time, he still remembers nearly all their names and stall numbers.

Meanwhile, out in the suburbs today, hordes of lonely old people are stuck in their homes without daily company; young mothers are trapped, unable to shop in peace without a gaggle of difficult toddlers, pushers and safety-capsules. A clopping horse and a friendly driver running from house to house with a wicker basket trailing the scent of freshly baked bread would no doubt be most welcome.

Patient servants
Margaret Hancock

As a city-born girl, my memories of horses are those of the city working horse—patient horses who moved slowly from place to place. I recall on a number of occasions as I waited for a tram, watching the council draught horse harnessed to a dray, while the elderly (well he seemed elderly to me) council worker shovelled and swept up the dirt in the gutters. The horse would wait, head dropped, until given the word to move on just a few paces. He needed no-one to hold his reins. His job was well-defined and well-rehearsed—just plod a few steps forward on command, and nibble in his nosebag to reduce the boredom while waiting for the dray to fill. He only seemed to wake up when he was driven off to some dumping area to empty the load. I felt sorry for him. His life seemed dull, yet he never moved unless he was asked and seemed contented with his lot.

The milkman's horse was heard, but seldom seen. His arrival in the street at about 6.30 am, with the accompanying clank of milk cans and billies, heralded time to wake up. The open, chariot-type vehicle he pulled got lighter as he walked the route that he knew so well morning after morning, seven days a week. He was aware of every stopping point and every street, working solo except for an occasional whistle from the milkman, the cue to move on to the next house.

The baker's horse was a more familiar sight, pulling the van of bread around the suburb. The baker usually knew each household's daily requirements, and the van would pull up at the gate, quite often driverless—the delivery man would walk from one house to the next, going to the back of the van to replenish his basket, and would leave a delicious trail of fresh bread smells behind him. Each order was placed in a tin on the verandah or some other prearranged, easy to find place. A word or a whistle would be all that was needed to tell the horse to move on to his next regular stopping spot ... And how many fresh loaves of bread had crusts removed or soft middles pulled out before the family loaf was rescued? Sometimes these horses left their 'calling card', and keen gardeners would rush out eagerly to collect it for the garden.

Just occasionally we saw another draught horse, with the hair above its hooves flapping with each step as he pulled a dray at a steady jog around the area. Perched high on the seat, and holding the reins loosely, was an old fellow in grubby overcoat, a hat of sorts perched on his head and gloves with the finger tips cut off. His constant cry of 'Bottle-o, any old rags, bottle-o, old bones, bottle-o' had a certain repetitive musical sound, despite the rasping voice which called the tune. The horse would stop, almost unbidden, as the householders brought out their empties and bones and would then resume his steady plod, plod, plodding when the deal had been completed.

Down the road a few yards from the school was the blacksmith's shop. It must have been the only operational farrier for the south side of Adelaide. It was a bit naughty to go and watch him through the big, wide open shed doorway because it was the opposite direction from home. The fascination was the dirt, soot, heat and horses—and that anybody should want to work in a place like that! Horses of all sorts and colours waited their turn— big and little, with stamping feet and swishing tails. The blacksmith with his leather apron stood with his back bent to the horse's head, taking off the old shoe and cleaning and filing the hoof ready for the new shoe. Here, too, one was aware of the patience of the horse.

The banging and the hammering and the human effort as the hot shoe was shaped and the nail holes punched fascinated me. And then the hiss as the shoe was plunged into the cold water, to be reheated once more before being applied hot to the horse's hoof. It was easy to while away half an hour watching, but at the back of my mind there was always Mum's reprimand to be reckoned with for being late home from school.

They all seemed friendlier then
Denis Adams

For a while during the war, as a boy in Kadina, I would often go with the milkman, entranced by the way his horse knew exactly when and where to move—and was only a tad disobedient when he diverted a step to snatch a bite of grass. Why they changed to trucks I never knew, for the milky's cart had no gears to change, no idling engine wasting fuel. No truck ever moved itself along a house or two, without even a word of command.

Our baker also had a horse and cart. Like all the men I saw around me then, he always seemed cheery, always courteous. And like all the tradesmen then, he never made mistakes. Bread was never wrapped or sliced, and the baker carried it jauntily in his basket from his cart to our back door. Once, for a treat, I was given the money for an iced finger bun. 'Come with me, young feller,' the baker invited. 'I'm going back to the bakery now. I'll get you a fresh one.'

The ice man used a wagonette, behind two horses. The kids all trailed him, looking hot and hopeful—and it generally worked, too.

A centenarian remembers
Linda Chinner

In April 1994 I celebrated my 100th birthday. Understandably, some events from the past are blurred, while others are clear.

As a young girl, I lived in one of the two houses built in the new Adelaide suburb of Millswood. It was a great joy to ride my pony, in the company of friends, across the surrounding paddocks. The pony's name was Prince, and he was somewhat pampered. On occasions when he was required to pull the governess cart, he would stand patiently in the breakfast room while he was harnessed. Once the job was finished, Prince knew he would be rewarded with a slice of bread.

Once he was in the shafts of the little cart, Prince often became unpredictable and would make the trip quite difficult for my mother, who was at the reins. However, a visit to our cousins, who lived at Peach Grove mansion, was assured of success. With visions of the succulent feast of melons awaiting him, Prince positively flew down the road.

Coming home was a very different matter. Prince would indulge in all kinds of tricky manoeuvres—his favourite being to scrape the governess cart against every brick wall he could spot. In spite of his cranky nature, we loved him dearly.

We did not use Prince for trips to the city. Instead, we would walk to the nearest horse-tram stop, which was located opposite the site of the Goodwood Orphanage. The placid old horses pulled a two-decker along Goodwood Road towards South Terrace in the city. As the horses ambled along their route, the driver would be busy collecting fares. Now and again, if he did not return to the reins in time, the horses would fail to make the right-hand turn into South Terrace. The driver would then leap from the tram, run to the horses and grab the bridle in order to turn them back in the direction of the foothills. It added a little spice to the journey.

The slow movement of the tram produced a travel sickness that I could never overcome. It made no difference whether I sat up on top or down below, the result was always the same on alighting! My mother did not enjoy taking me to town very much.

Our family's livelihood came from working horses. My grandfather had established a flourishing business in 1863 as shipping agents and carriers—J R Cocking & Co. My father and his brother worked for my grandfather in Topham Street in the developing city of Adelaide. The draught horses were kept on a property at Read Street, Glenelg, and a farrier named Worrell was employed to look after them.

Heavy draught horses were used on the longer runs to Port Adelaide, hauling merchandise from the sailing ships, and later steam ships, back to the city. The lighter horses would then deliver to Adelaide's well-to-do families in the nearby suburbs, frequently carrying bottles of claret and port, shipped in from distant foreign lands and carefully packed in straw.

The horse teams were also made use of for sporting events, conveying spectators and players to and from their destinations. A football team required to play a match in the hills would set off (in plenty of time!) in a drag, in which people sat facing each other on long seats. The powerful horses pulled with a will, but at the bottom of German Town Hill, everyone was expected to get out and walk, to reduce the strain on them.

The Easter races at Oakbank were always a favourite, especially for my mother, a keen race-goer and student of form. The horse teams would leave the city early for the race meeting, the drags filled with people wearing their best. Many of them would spend the night at Bridgewater and return the next day. No doubt, at the steeper inclines they were all expected to relieve the horses' load and walk too.

The drags were very popular and we had some wonderful picnics at Brown Hill Creek with my parents and their friends. The horses would quietly graze nearby until it was time to return. The women looked very elegant in their long cream coats and wearing shady hats with veils, tied beneath their chins.

As the years passed, my father felt it was wise to keep abreast in a changing world and gradually changed from horses to motor lorries, importing his first lorry in 1905. He was, in fact, the first in the carrying business to start making the switch. The days of the working horses were numbered, but the memories of them are still with me.

Summer memories of a milky
Des Dent

My first milk-delivery horse was a pony mare named Clippy. She was used on the milk round in Port Elliot, South Australia, in the 1950s. Since Port Elliot was a popular beach holiday spot, there would be a lot of extra visitors in summer. They would put their billy cans on the front gates or fences of wherever they were staying if they wanted milk. Clippy became used to this signal and many a time came from a brisk trot to an instant stop of her own accord, throwing me in among the milk cans. Between us, we never missed a customer.

Holiday time, while enjoyable because of the extra business, did confuse some horses. They would get used to doing the milk round the same way every morning. During holidays, we would run out of milk and have to go to the dairy to pick up more. On the way back, I would try to do the deliveries in reverse order, but one horse would turn around at each stop. He thought we were going the wrong way.

Clippy, however, particularly enjoyed holiday time, mainly because of the holiday makers at the Port Elliot camping ground. Children always rushed over with their cans so they could pat her and give her something to eat, but some of the older customers did not like to walk too far from their tents or vans. They would simply hold a few pieces of bread in their hands while they sat at their campsite and Clippy would never go past them.

The mare certainly regarded the camping ground as a source of good pickings. Because the local baker also made deliveries there, many customers would put their fresh bread and buns under one arm while collecting their milk and counting out their change. Clippy became quite good at delicately removing buns from under customers' arms, almost without their knowing.

When the camping ground was being lengthened and the sand hills levelled to make more campsites, the road down the centre became very rough. Children played in its sand and had dug a hole just to one side. I used to drive right through the camp and start serving customers on the way back. One morning I hit the hole. The float bounced up in the air, dislodging a 10-gallon can full of milk—and of course the lid just had to come off. The can came back and hit me in the chest and knocked me out the back of the float. Milk went all over me. My money bag opened and all the money scattered in the sand. For several days after this, children would come out each morning to the float with pennies and money they had sieved out of the sand.

My fondest memories of my milk round are of the friendly, honest customers at the Port Elliot camping ground.

Doing the rounds with Mick
Des Dent

Mick, a black horse we got, developed into a very good delivery horse. I had bought a drop-centre milk float from Webster's dairy. This had a roof, and I felt quite spoilt after all the years in the open float. I could whistle Mick on, only getting in the float to fill my orders.

One stormy morning, whilst I was delivering to Mr Cliff Plush, I heard Mick quicken his pace into a trot. I chased the float, but because it had to be entered from the side, I had to run past the float to get in. I did this and grabbed the handle to jump inside. My foot slipped on the gravel road. I hung onto the handle and was dragged until the rear wheel ran over my foot and ankle. About then, I lost interest in the horse and float and let go of the handle. By the time I realised my leg was not broken, the horse and float were nowhere in sight.

I hobbled to the police station, which was nearby, and woke up the local police officer. I was bleeding a bit and he said he would get me to a doctor, but I said I had to find the horse first. I thought he would probably do the round, so we followed the route and found him standing in the middle of the road between the Royal Family Hotel and Barton's Garage. I took the horse home and finished the round with the van. The horse, harness and float were undamaged, but I spent a week in hospital and three weeks on crutches. This was my only injury in twenty years of using a horse and float, most of which was done in the dark.

Storms were always a bit of a worry when using a horse in the early hours of the morning in areas with no street lights. If a horse is going to be cranky, a storm will bring it on. On a very wet and thundery morning, I was delivering in Barbara Street. Mick was walking down the middle of the road, and I had just delivered to a bungalow and was serving Mr Guy, when the horse fell over in the middle of the road. As I ran out he got up, but was quite upset. He had broken both shafts and the float was in the middle of the road with the trace chains still connected.

I was about to undo the traces when I noticed an electric wire sparking across the road. The float had a steel bar running around the top and the wire was touching this. Mick, who was very jumpy, swung back and touched the steel rail. I didn't have to undo the traces—he broke the chains himself. For a few weeks after this, Mick would not walk past Mr Guy's house on his own. I had to get in and drive him.

As I said, Mick was black, but he had a white blaze. He was quite co-operative about being caught in the early hours of the morning, but occasionally he would decide to take the day off. I would go to catch him in his paddock, but because he kept turning his head away from the torchlight, I would not be able to find him.

Mick was a good horse and got to know the round backwards. He would move on to the whistle, but I was not allowed to stop and talk. Mick would give me sufficient time to dish the milk out, but then he would move on to the next customer. If I was delayed, I had to run to the end of the street and bring him back.

A trail of damage
Des Dent

In the early 1950s we bought a new delivery horse which had not done a milk round before, but had been used by a bottle-o at Bowden in Adelaide. Dad and I went together on the round for a week or two to see if he would be all right. He seemed to be going well, so Dad started using him on his own. One windy morning, Dad came running back to me because the horse had cleared off. We got the ute out to try to find him.

We followed a trail of cans, lids and deliveries until we could see the lights of the float on the side of Waterport Road, by Langham's dairy, one of the dairies from which we used to pick up milk. He had turned between the fences and the power pole, and was stuck there. Two broken shafts, broken traces, no milk and, as we used to put excess pennies in a tin in the cream box, no pennies. He had left a trail of them on the road after hitting a corner post. Apparently he did not like flapping canvas, and the Alaska Ice Cream canvas blind on Rosser's shop had set him going.

Let fly with the rocks
Des Dent

A friend of mine, Theo Schofield, told me about one of his customers in Adelaide who was complaining about short measure with her daily pint of milk. Theo thought he knew what the problem was, so took his brother with him on the round one morning. The customer used to put out her china jug, and it was obvious that cats were sneaking in and lowering the level of her milk.

The Schofields left the usual quantity of milk in her jug, took the horse to the end of the street, then returned, armed with a couple of rocks. Sure enough, two cats were at the milk jug. The boys let fly with the rocks. One went through the window. The other smashed the jug of milk, and the cats got a hell of a fright. The lads whipped the horse up and got out of there quick smart.

Trotting out of step
Les O'Brien

My mum reminisced about how her grandfather persisted in relying on his horse and sulky to get around Sydney during the 1930s. This was at a time when trams, trains and auto- mobiles were beginning to clog the thoroughfares. Horses and wagons were being relegated to local deliveries and were being used less and less as commuter transport.

The old man had run a produce business for many years and argued that as horses had provided the basis for his livelihood, it was only fair that he should put faith in their abilities to continue to get him around. He had a knowledge of the alleyways, byways and short cuts that would make any modern-day cabbie green with envy.

The story goes that the family had planned a Sunday afternoon visit to cousins in Bronte, some 10 or so miles away. All, except the old man, were going by public transport; there was no way he was going to lower himself to such slow ways of getting around. 'Anyway,' he said, and we could sense a conjured excuse coming up, 'I've got a couple of things to drop off on the way. It'll save me doing it tomorrow.'

When the rest of the family set off, the old bloke was still pottering about with harness and loading up. 'Off you go, you lot,' he called out. 'You need all the head start you can get, and I'll still be there before you.'

Sure enough, by the time they had gone halfway, he was spotted trotting along a nearby street with his load aboard. Further on, they caught a quick glimpse of him disappearing up a laneway, still with a bag of chaff on the seat beside him. On a hill, they were slowed to a crawl when he caught up and passed, with the old mare merrily kicking up her heels, obviously enjoying the jaunt.

By the time the entourage arrived, hot and bothered from the final walk down the hill, there was the old mare tethered under an old fig tree, quietly whisking the occasional fly with her tail. The old bloke was sitting on the back verandah tapping out his second pipe and was recalled as saying: 'I don't know why you bother coming on them electric wagons. By the time you get here, it's time to be getting back.'

When I was last in Sydney, regularly queuing up at the traffic lights, I pondered the passing of horses in suburbia. I had visions of a horse and sulky tripping by on the quiet, shady streets, with an old man lightly flicking the reins and his pipe leaving the distinctive aroma of Dr Pat Special Irish Blend in their wake.

Nine
The job comes first

In the working horse days, slackers were not tolerated. Work was there to be done and a horse had to submit and take orders. If he wouldn't work, he wasn't worth feeding. Animal rights had not been invented.

The stories that follow give a salutary lesson in how things were done. There wasn't time for psychoanalysis of a horse's problems. It either got on with the job, or it was dead.

The humans involved with horses fared little better, but at least they didn't get shot!

'Those times were tough on horses,' says Eric

When Eric Lawrence looks at you with a characteristic sideways twist of his neck and says, 'The horses of 60 years ago were a bloody sight tougher than they are today,' you get the feeling he thinks much the same about humans today. Having started driving teams at 10, taking on a man's job at 13 working for a fruiterer, and breaking in horses at 16 on weekends off from a dairy job, he knows what tough means.

The dairy horses he drove in the 1930s pulled their milk floats up to 35 miles each night, then got tied up in stalls open to the weather in their off-duty hours. He can't remember them being any the worse for wear. In later years, when the roads were asphalt, three horses per round had to be rotated each week, because of leg soreness from the 27 miles trotted nightly. During the war, the horses on delivery rounds were so hard worked that he saw them fall down in the shafts with fatigue— and then be whipped to keep them going. 'Those times were tough on horses,' he says with a shake of the head and a distant look in his eyes.

By the same token, this wiry little man with the glint of the devil in his eye doesn't like what he sees these days. 'Horses today are not getting the work that the horses of my day got'— and by these horses, he means the harness horses that, at 75 years of age, he continues to break-in in the backyard of his suburban Footscray home, just as he has for the past 50 years since he moved there.

While Eric Lawrence might have the stature of a jockey, and a broken and twisted neck, as well as a few broken ribs from horse falls, he can still lord it over even the most statuesque of heavy horses. It's an authority that comes from growing up with them on his parents' small farm near Dandenong, and building his own life around them. He has shown horses for 26 years, was ringmaster for 47 years at the Dandenong horse sales, and has been a horse-dealer for 65 years. At the age of 10 he made his first 10-shilling purchase of an old steeplechaser and its saddle and bridle which, a few days later, he sold for 22 shillings and sixpence—plus he got to keep the saddle.

People continue to come to him to have their show horses broken to harness, as they have long done. His mastery is widely recognised, his knowledge rivalled by few. As his wife, Gwen, points out, Eric is one of only a handful of original old horsemen left who have experienced the genuine working horse era. As a consequence, Eric Lawrence is a frequent royal show judge, especially of historic turnout classes, where he is a fearsome and meticulous examiner of everything on harness and vehicles, right down to the type of matches in the lamps, the bolts in the floorboards and ferrules on whips, as well, of course, as the horse.

He's noted the resurgence of interest in heavy harness horses for tourist and business ventures and commercial public relations exercises. He proudly points to a picture of the Carlton United Brewery draught team as graduates of his training regime, which involves horses boarding for several weeks in his backyard stables and learning to drag heavy tyres up and down the cobbled lanes running behind the backyards of his neighbours.

But too often the story is the same, says Eric. 'People are no longer experienced at handling horses on roads. The car traffic is terrible and car drivers don't understand, so often the horse gets nervy, and the driver loses enthusiasm.'

The horse-dealer in him says there is plenty of demand for quiet, heavy horses by people like the asparagus growers at Kooweerup who need to plough between their narrow rows. 'But there are no more quiet horses,' says Eric. 'Horses don't get the steady, consistent work they need anymore, so they never become really quiet.'

Good, old-fashioned horse sense has also disappeared, he says. The general public no longer knows how to treat a horse standing harnessed to a cart in the street. They don't know that because the horse is wearing blinkers, it can't see behind it and that a sudden noise or touch on its flank or neck will set in motion the horse's flight reflex—that is, it will jump sideways, kick or bolt.

'People haven't seen horses working for 30 or 40 years, so they don't understand that you have to speak quietly to a horse before touching them, to warn them you are there,' Eric says.

So as far as Eric Lawrence is concerned, the day of the working horse in the suburbs and city is over, except for the wedding coach business, some tourist ventures and the occasional promotional exercise. He did break in a horse recently for a young Melbourne plumber, Michael O'Donnell, who uses the horse and cart to advertise his business while he gives hay rides to people. However, Eric says any tradesman who used a horse for work would probably find the general public protesting about perceived cruelties, such as leaving a horse standing between its shafts for up to four hours at a time, or having nothing to eat or drink while out on the job.

'They no longer understand how to treat working horses—and what they are capable of,' he says.

A battle of wills
Jim Kelly

My father often got himself into awkward situations that required some fast footwork to be able to survive. One such instance occurred during the 1930s Depression when he purchased a stallion and hired a groom to travel the farms of the district. Mares were mated to foal in spring or late summer so that they could still help do the team work over the busy harvest period. The service fee we charged was supposed to cover all costs and help bring in some much-needed cash.

Behind Father's chair in the breakfast room hung a large photograph of his pride and joy, Waldon's Radiant, champion Clydesdale stallion of the Royal Adelaide Show. He was a rich bay with black mane and tail, four white feet and a white blaze down his nose, a magnificent specimen, tall and proud. Holding the horse with obvious pride was Father in his best suit and one of those funny Homberg hats. I suspect he was worrying like blazes how he was going to get 380 guineas worth from his new purchase.

I vaguely remember the rotund little Irish groom with the broad rural accent who joined us when the scheme got underway. Trouble soon followed. The mares kept returning into season and Paddy and the stallion had to make repeat visits. The wall-mounted, party-line telephone would ring with an irate client. Then Dad would shut the phone-room door and shout at that stupid box on the wall—no doubt a common reaction from people who had spent their lives without the newfangled machine.

The job comes first

Waldon's Radiant left only three foals before he was retired and his name changed to Wally. Poor old Wally. We all felt sorry for him. He had been such a tall poppy and to come down to be a dray horse, and a gelding as well, was a most tremendous fall. He could not even hold his place in the team. It wasn't that he was lazy. A more flashy free-mover would be hard to find. He just would not pull. With his good looks and smart pedigree, he had got to maturity without ever having to pull, and it seemed that he wasn't going to start now. Father was a superlative horseman and knew from a long tradition of farming and years of experience that he was being backed into a corner by this useless, very expensive horse.

I remember the following story with such clarity that I sometimes wonder if I was there by design ... that I was being shown what happens to things that won't work. It was a salutary lesson for Wally. Perhaps it explains my own workaholic lifetime, too.

We had a silage pit, half full of sheaved barley. Wally was made to back the two-wheeled tip-dray down the slope to the working face, where, with pitchforks, we loaded perhaps a ton of silage into the dray. Father then released the reins and ordered Wally to 'Gee up'. The horse felt the weight in his collar but refused to move. Dad collected a four metre length of wire from the nearby rubbish dump, straightened it out, bent it double and twisted it. He ordered the big horse to 'Gee up' again. Nothing happened. Wally received a solid lash across the rump. The dray was positioned so that it could not go back because of the wall of silage. The pit was too narrow for Wally to turn sideways, as the earth wall on each side was two metres high. In front was the slope Wally had backed down half an hour before. I was sitting on the mound of earth formed when the pit had been dug. The 'Gee up' lash went on a long time, landing each time where it could not damage bone or cartilage.

Wally was soon in a sweat and marking time with all four feet. He refused even to try. It was a classic fight. A man's will versus the champion stallion's will. If the horse would not try to pull the load out of the pit, as Father knew he could, it was the end of the line. In a sense it was a fight to the death, as Wally would have finished up feeding the carnivores at the zoo.

Modern readers may have difficulty accepting this story of 60 years ago. There was no bad temper or unnecessary cruelty. Wally learnt an unforgettable lesson and spent the next 15 years working with great strength and reliability. But he carried the mark of that fight for the rest of his days. A white band of hair 8 centimetres wide and half a metre long, right across his lovely bay rump.

Grinned for a month
Garth Dutfield

There were times when horses could really try a man's patience. My father told of one particular rogue called Fairy, a quarter-draught bay mare, vindictively named by my sister because of her large feet (for a saddle horse), which at some stage of saddling seemed always to end up on your toe. If the feet didn't get you, she would swing round and try a quick bite, just as you tightened the girth. As a lad just out of school, Fairy was on occasion my mount when I went out after rabbits with the dog pack. On one of these occasions, while trying to shoot a rabbit with my single- shot rifle from her back, she had wiped me out with a low tree limb, and I was just aching to get my own back.

The rellies were up from Sydney—sister and brother-in-law were always a welcome sight. Brother-in-law liked to walk around, and on one meandering made the most startling discovery. Fairy had fallen into the 5-foot-deep well adjoining the shower sheep dip. There she stood with her head protruding out of the in-flow duct of the well, happily gazing around as though she had not a care in the world.

'You beaut,' I thought. 'We'll have to cut her up into little bits to get her out of there.'

My moment of joy was short lived, however, when father simply said, 'Go and get about ten bales of hay.'

I was a bit worried he was going to feed the flaming thing, but father simply chucked the hay in under the damned horse to raise her up so she could walk out. She was about two feet from the top when she decided to lie down. The old man turned a little red in the face, kicked her, twisted her ears, then finally, much to my glee, picked up a three-pronged pitchfork and drove its points firmly and deliberately into the stubborn creature's rump. Fairy rose up out of the well with an agility that would have put a hurdler to shame.

Brother-in-law wanted to put band-aids on the horse, but I didn't stop grinning for a month.

The one-man horse
Bill Clissold

I spent my young life out west of Cunnamulla and Bourke, droving, ringing on stations, and even snigging timber with a team of horses. In the 1960s I was breaking in horses at Singleton, New South Wales. A grazier rang me one day to take a thoroughbred gelding. The horse had never had a hand on him, except for when he was gelded.

Now, I'd often heard about those so-called one-man horses, but quite honestly, I had always viewed those stories with more than a little scepticism. With the grazier's thoroughbred I was about to have my mind changed.

A mate of mine, Brian, and I rode out some miles to the property to lead the horse back to my stables. When we arrived, he was already in the yard—a big, leggy brown, typical of his breed. He was by a horse called Steel Dust. After catching him and getting a head collar on him, I soon had him leading. He was quick to learn and very sensible. We were soon on our way back to town, leading him beside our own horses.

The next day I started handling and mouthing him. Three days later I was driving him in the long reins and saddle. Every time I approached him, I was greeted by a soft whinny. On the fourth day, I climbed aboard him. He stood for a moment, and then with a little urging, he moved away like an old horse. He progressed very quickly over the next few days, always acting the perfect gentleman and doing anything asked of him.

After a further week of riding him in the bush and traffic, I took him back to the owner. Upon arrival, I suggested one of the chaps there ride him, but they declined, saying they would ride him later.

It was a couple of days later that I received another phone call from the grazier, asking if I could take the horse back again, as he had thrown everyone that had tried to ride him. This seemed ridiculous, but I rode out to the property once again. I caught and saddled the so-called buckjumper. I mounted him, and he walked away like an old stock horse.

Still, the owner wanted me to take him and give him some more work, so away we went to town again. There I got my young mate to ride him; he used to follow the rodeos and could ride pretty well. The horse behaved as well as could be. Between us we gave that gelding a lot of work during the next week, and not once did he put a foot wrong.

Then the owner rang and asked if I would deliver the horse to a dairy farmer and his son at Camberwell, who would use him to bring in the cows each day. By the time we arrived there, the horse was pretty tired, as I had trotted and cantered most of the way. The father said he would ride the horse while he was tired, but as soon as he hit the saddle, the horse pelted him as high as a kite. Honestly, there was no-one more surprised than I was at this.

The son, a big burly bloke, said, 'Give me the mongrel. I'll show him who's boss'—or something to that effect.

No sooner had he put his foot in the iron and left the ground, than the horse dropped its head, and the way he bucked would have done old Mandrake, Rocky Ned or Widow Maker proud. The big bloke was thrown higher than a group of young oak saplings that grew close by. They virtually accused me of not riding him all the way, but having led him instead.

I caught the horse and went to mount him. I felt him tighten and snarled at him: 'Get up, you old fool.' He relaxed and I climbed into the saddle and rode off around the yard and out into the paddock, turning and twisting through the oak trees.

The dairy farmer refused to keep him, saying they lived too far from town if anything should happen to either one of them. So I went back to town and reported my difficulties to the owner. I offered to buy the horse, but he refused to sell him, saying they would finally end up riding him.

Some time later, my mate Brian told me he had seen the horse sold in the dogger's yard at the local horse sales. When I rang the owner, he said the horse had thrown every man and boy that had tried to ride him, so they had sold him as a dogger because they considered him so dangerous. A pity really, as to me, he was a really gentle hack—and the only true one-man horse I ever knew.

The brumby team
Jim Kelly

Few today would remember that Caterpillar tractors once used petrol. We had one in the early thirties, when cash to pay for any sort of fuel was hard to find. One of Dad's more successful schemes was to replace the nearly new tractor with a team of horses and leave the hungry monster in the shed.

The first move was to travel by car to Hawker, in the Flinders Ranges, to attend a large horse sale. The breeding of horses as remounts for the Indian army had been quite an industry in the more remote parts of South Australia, but with mechanisation, the trade had diminished and left sizeable numbers of brumbies roaming the gibber deserts and stony hills of the Flinders and beyond. He purchased for a few pounds a head twenty of the heavier types and arranged for them to be put on rail trucks and consigned to Saddleworth, some 22 kilometres from our farm.

Father reached home in time to saddle up his best hack and arrived at Saddleworth railway yards on a clear, moonlit night. He unloaded the horses, mounted his flash chestnut mare and trotted out of the yard and all the way home with the strange, nervous nucleus of a team sniffing the ground right behind him. At 2 am he had them in the stable yard and was just able to nip round behind them and shut the big, iron gate.

Little was known of the background of the mob, but a pretty mixed bag they were. A few had been broken in for packhorse duty on the cattle camps of the far north, but most were wild, untouched mares and geldings of any age.

I suspect it was July or August, the best time of the year to break in a team, because then we would be ploughing for that year's fallow. The ground then is soft and slippery, so some of the pupils' energy in the ensuing struggles would be dampened down.

The system to get a new horse into a team was, by today's standards, somewhat brutal. It was also unbelievably quick. Each horse was lassooed in a small yard and pulled up to a rail, where every effort was made to loosen the rope if the horse stood still. Within a few minutes, the quivering, sweating horse would stand, so then a handkerchief on the end of a broom handle was playfully rubbed over the back, rump, flanks, shoulders and legs.

The next step was to put on blinkers and collar. Then we brought in two heavy, quiet old Clydesdales, put one on each side of the trainee and tied him with shortish ropes to the collar of each old stager. Then double reins were thrown over the three horses, and after a round of a small paddock, they would be hitched to a heavy log. Sometimes, as a boy of seven or eight, I might be allowed to drive the small team round a 10-acre paddock while the men started on the next brumby. By that time, the horse had a name—Darkie, Roany, Star, The Kicker, The Paw, or a girl or boy's name that in some way reminded Dad which new recruit in his team was which.

I expect he mixed the new chums with some of the regular working team for a day or two, but soon, despite being kicked and bitten, he had sixteen of the brumbies working together and was very proud of his lightweight team.

Harvest time came and twelve brumbies in tandem (six in the front row, six behind), pulled the whirring, screaming header, while eight Clydesdales pulled the other machine. There were some spectacular tangles of chains and gear that required a pipeful of tobacco and a great deal of patience to sort out. But they were the times when the need not to spend cash on anything was a priority. The fact that it took three months' work a year to feed the horses instead of the few minutes it took to write the fuel cheques seems to have been easily overlooked.

Learning to live with the enemy
Charles Fenton

I was never a great horse-lover. This attitude probably dates back to 1920. We were then living on a grazing property at Mt Mercer, south of Ballarat. It was around the time that my father was teaching me to ride on a small pony, and the occasion that is firmly implanted in my mind was a few days before Christmas 1920. Father had walked nearly half a mile to the mailbox and taken me alongside on the pony to collect the mail. With the mail that day came the Christmas goose, enclosed in a hessian bag, with its head projecting through a hole cut in the end of the bag. On my arrival at the mailbox ahead of my father, the goose gave a loud squawk and bounced about within the bag. The pony took fright and immediately tossed me off and landed me on my head. I was not only put off horses, but geese as well.

My father sold the Mt Mercer property and, in 1924, purchased a farming property at Glendaruel, which is about six miles south-west of Clunes. I came home from boarding school to work on the farm at the end of the Great Depression, and prior to the introduction of tractors, farm utes and ag bikes—so I had to face up to the proposition of learning to live and work with a horse.

My first workhorse was a black gelding named Nigger. He was a saddle horse and also a good light cart horse, but he had two bad failings. Firstly, he was hard to catch, even in the small horse paddock and almost impossible without assistance in a 100-acre paddock. Secondly, he was a bad stumbler when being ridden.

The first occasion that Nigger stumbled and went down on his knees, I naturally went straight over his head, lost the reins and spread myself full length on the ground. Before I could get to my feet, Nigger had galloped off, and I probably spent the rest of the day catching him again. It became embedded in my subconscious mind that no matter what happens I should keep hold of the reins. The next two falls were a bit messy, but I kept a good grip of the reins and was able to remount immediately. The fourth occasion I managed to land on my feet, with the reins held firmly, and from that point onwards, I never landed other than standing on my feet, reins in one hand, and if I was carrying anything (spade or mattock, etc.), that would be in my other hand. I had converted a potentially dangerous fall into a state-of-the-art rapid dismounting procedure. I must have performed this act without fault another seven or eight times before getting a change of horse.

Of course you will say: 'Why didn't the silly bugger get another horse to ride?' The reason was simple. It was Depression time and a few spills from a horse was not sufficient reason to persuade my father to spend 20 pounds or more to buy another horse.

Up like bedposts
Joyce Shiner

In 1939 when petrol rationing became a reality, our neighbours' 'tin Lizzie' was put on blocks in the shed and Dolly the horse was brought back into use. Every fortnight the spring cart would go down the road, with the three men sitting on a plank across the cart, their weight pushing poor old Dolly downhill faster than her legs wanted to go. The main road was reasonably level and the run into town and back wasn't too bad, but coming up the incline to the farm was sometimes too much for her.

After one of those Thursday jaunts, Fred came across to ask Bly to have a look at the horse. He had found Dolly lying flat on the ground. When Fred asked Bly's opinion, he replied, 'I think she's dying.'

Fred was shocked. 'Why!' he cried. 'She can't be more than thirty.'

But die, she did. As twelve to fifteen years was reckoned to be a reasonable age for a working horse, we wondered how long Fred had expected Dolly to last.

When Fred came next day to ask what he should do with the body, my husband, Bly, answered, 'Pile some sticks and logs on it and set it alight where it is.' But Fred was so horrified at the idea of burning Dolly that Bly suggested, 'Well then, dig a hole as near to the body as you can, then roll it in.'

Unfortunately the ground was hard and dry, and before the hole was half deep enough, they levered the body in. Because the legs had stiffened overnight, they stuck up above the ground.

Again, Fred came to ask what he should do.

'Get the axe and chop them off,' was Bly's advice, but as that didn't appeal to Fred's sense of loyalty, he carried dirt in the wheelbarrow, reverently making a mound over the body, and leaving the legs still poking upwards like bedposts.

Solutions to getting on with the job
Hurtle Baldock

At one stage we had a mare that would kick the eye out of a needle, so when all else failed, we tied a chain securely to her tail for a day or so. After learning to live in harmony with that, chains didn't worry her and she lived a happy working life.

One horse insisted on rearing while being ridden, so I weakened a bottle so that it would break, filled it with warm water and when the horse reared, tapped it on the top of its head, releasing the warm water, which I presume he thought was his own blood, as he never reared again.

One chap, while carting bags of wheat, had a team of horses who had never seen sand. All was going well until about halfway to the siding, when they had to go through a large patch of sand. It wasn't long before the horses decided the going was too heavy, so they stopped and only tried very half-heartedly to start again, before refusing altogether. The driver knew what to do. He put the brake on, tied the reins back and climbed down off the wagon. He unhitched one of the team and rode it home.

When he returned next morning, the horses, not surprisingly, had changed their mind about standing still and were very keen to move. They settled into the job very quickly and pulled together magnificently. Their load of wheat was delivered with no further delays.

Stand still or swim
Brian Cooper

There was this bloody mongrel draught that would *not* stand still to be shod. An old farrier sauntered up one day and said: 'I'll show you how to shoe your horse.

'I'll be here at 4 pm. Have a big, strong post put in on the bank of the dam, about eight feet from the water's edge. Work him hard, then take him to the dam. Give him a drink, then tie him up to the post.'

The owner of the horse did as he was asked and was ready when the farrier arrived. The farrier then flapped his big leather apron in front of the horse. The horse reared and hung back on the rope. The farrier cut the rope and the horse fell straight backwards into the dam water.

The horse came out, shook himself all over and then stood quietly while the new 'boss' shod him.

Curing the jibber
Elsie Dunn

We had on our farm, among the Clydesdales, what my brother and I called a jibber. Whatever we had him harnessed to, whether it was logs or the slide with a tank of water on it, this horse, called Toby, would always take a few steps backwards before going forward—that is, he jibbed, and often stood on the trace chains, too. We would then have to unhook the chains to get them straight again. We got to the stage where we had had enough, so we decided we would cure him of his bad habit.

We harnessed up another horse from the team, Trooper, who was an excellent puller. Then we went out to the back paddock with the two of them hitched to long chains. We put the horses on either side of a small dry creek about four or five feet deep, and hooked their chains together. One of us stood at the head of each horse. At the signal, each of us said, 'Pull, Trooper' or 'Pull, Toby', which was the way we always started the team.

Trooper went forward into his collar and continued to pull. Toby, meanwhile, took his usual few steps back and consequently was pulled backwards by Trooper, right over the bank. My brother and I were both frightened, but unhooked the two horses and took them back to the stables.

However, Toby was certainly cured. When in future we'd say, 'Pull, Toby', he went straight forward with all his strength. We never told Dad of our cure, but he did say some time later: 'Good thing Toby has grown out of his bad habit.'

Priorities
Nancy Horsnell

After leaving primary school, my husband worked on the family market gardening property in the Adelaide Hills. Horses played an important part in his life, as they were used to work the land and take the produce to the Adelaide Market. From time to time older horses had to be replaced. It so happened that a new horse was needed in the spring of 1952, about the time we were to be married.

The wedding was on a Saturday evening and after a family tea at my parents' home, we were driven to the new house that had been built for us on the market garden property in the Hills. We had decided not to go away for a honeymoon.

Next morning, at 7.50 am, there was a knock at the door. My

father-in-law had arrived to see if my husband would go with him to inspect a likely horse.

Too tired after Nevertire
Mavis Appleyard

Paddy was a bow-backed, easygoing sort of horse that was used for anything from pulling the sulky to chasing wild pigs. Since it was wartime, there was no petrol for cars, so Paddy was in constant use transporting the men to work on properties far distant from their farm at Warren.

Dad and the boys worked as station and shed hands, shearers and fencers, so Paddy was often used for snigging fence posts, hauling wire and rounding up sheep. He was an invaluable work- horse, but he also had a role to play in their leisure time.

One Saturday night, one of the sons harnessed Paddy in the sulky and picked up a girl to attend a dance 13 miles away at Nevertire. It was either a send off or welcome home for a serviceman, the usual excuse then for a dance. Either way, it was a rollicking evening; the son lost his girl, so at 2.30 in the morning, he rather unsteadily hitched Paddy to the sulky and climbed aboard. No drink driving laws applied then, and Paddy knew the way home, so the driver clicked Paddy into motion, left the reins loose, and went to sleep.

He woke up to the sound of Paddy still clip-clopping along and the sun shining down on him. It took the driver some time to work out where he was. His befuddled mind gradually realised he was halfway to Nyngan, in the opposite direction to Warren. When he returned to the farm many hours later that Sunday, with an utterly worn-out horse, the reception he got from his father was not all that festive. At daybreak on Monday, Dad was to travel 15 miles to his job for the week. Try as he did to urge Paddy along, Dad still got docked some pay for being late for work.

Ten
Talented performers

The hidden talents of many horses can be discovered through skilled handling and training. This section deals with
ordinary horses with interesting foibles, extraordinary horsemen and the horses that entertain others for a living. Sometimes these 'talents' appear at awkward and inconvenient times. For others, the journey to stardom is perilous, as it was for Esdale Flash Prince who started life in humble circumstances, was saved from the knackery, then rose to glory as a workhorse show champion.

The great horse trainers of past and present get into the mind of a horse. Steve Jefferys starred at the opening of the 2000 Olympics on a horse he taught to rear in three weeks. His performing stallion Jamieson hilariously upstages snooty dressage horses!

Horse wrangling—the supply and training of horses for film and television roles—is one of the glamour jobs of the horse world. Bill Willoughby and veteran wrangler Evanne between them have been involved in most of Australia's major productions that have involved horses.

A day with the whip-cracker of the Olympic opening ceremony

As I showered in the gloom of a chilly Sydney dawn, I slowly became conscious of being watched. I had spent the night with Steve—he of the famous rearing stallion at the Olympic opening ceremony—and Sandy Jefferys. Just down the hallway from where I stood, two big eyes were staring at me. They were set in a black, intelligent head hanging over a stable door. The horse caught my gaze, then turned away yawning uninterestedly.

Steve and Sandy have a particularly close relationship with their horses—they all live under the same roof in a newly built two-storey house within sight of the city and the sea. Because the human part of the house is not quite finished, the shower is temporarily in the horses' wash-down area. Four timber-panelled, spacious stables are at one end of the ground floor and the Jefferys' kitchen and bathroom are at the other end. Human bedrooms are above the horses' quarters and the horses spend their days eavesdropping on conversations and staring at strangers when they have nothing better to do.

The stallion staring at me that morning was not Ammo, the stallion on which Steve charged into the Olympic 2000 stadium cracking his stockwhip and who gave two huge testosterone-charged rears, but Jamieson, a stallion who seems almost to be able to talk. He and Steve also performed at the Olympics, entertaining spectators during intervals at the dressage finals. Riding without bridle and saddle, Steve made hilarious mockery of the efforts of international riders by executing complex dressage movements such as pirouettes and collected trots with just a piece of string around Jamieson's neck. He further humiliates would-be experts by installing a dummy steering wheel on Jamieson's wither and 'driving' him like a push-button car through perfectly executed corners with correct flexion and perfect square halts. 'Coming down the centre line,' he asks, taunting his audience, 'have you ever saluted the judge only to have your hat fly out of your hand?' With that he throws his hat on the ground. Jamieson, having come to a perfect halt, then leans down, picks it up and passes it up to Steve. Jamieson and Steve perform regularly with their lovely assistant, Jana, a border collie who does her best to upstage everyone.

'I was always good with horses,' says Steve. 'Even though I had no training, I could always get them to do things. My dogs were always doing tricks too. It is a gift. I just seem to be good at winning their confidence.'

Steve rejects the horse-whisperer notion of having mystical spiritual bonds. His training skills come just from having a great love for horses and an enjoyment of working with them. 'I am a very stubborn person and a perfectionist,' he says. 'But you have to leave the lesson when you have the upper hand. A lot of people don't recognise when that is.' Steve says training is to do with asserting leadership over the horse which, as a herd animal, respects and likes authority.

While he found worldwide fame on the back of a rearing stallion, Steve said his performances with Jamieson were the most professionally satisfying. The knowledgeable equestrian audiences at Horsley Park who watched their routines appreciated the work that had gone on behind the scenes to train a horse to such a high level. They could understand the complexity of conducting a witty running commentary, which Steve does using a head mike, at the same time as transmitting meticulous signals through buttocks, thighs, knees, calves, feet and weight shifts. 'Some people said they had worked for a lifetime to achieve such collection and flexion, but I had made a mockery of it with no bridle or saddle, no whip or spurs,' Steve says with a smile.

Growing up in the outer suburb of Elanora Heights, not far from Ingleside where he and Sandy now live, Steve spent a lot of time hanging around Smokey Dawson's ranch, which ran a riding school. While he was still at school, he started breaking in horses for Smokey and met people like Heath Harris, the well-known film horse wrangler. Tony Jablonski, who organised the Man from Snowy River tableau for the Olympic opening ceremony, was another who helped out at Smokey's, so it seemed natural that Steve eventually should gravitate towards entertainment.

It is now ten to seven on a blustery Wednesday and Steve is on his way to the first appointment of the day. His bread and butter business is exercising other people's horses in and around Sydney's hilly, semi-rural suburb of Terrey Hills. Apart from being home to the excessively wealthy, this suburb is believed to be the most heavily horse-populated in Australia. Dressage arenas are as common as a second car, although not all bear signs of use. Horses are jammed into almost every available patch of land, in railed yards, stables and temporary electric-taped yards. Full-time grooms feed, rug and supervise their pampered charges. Stable blocks range from elderly weatherboard to architect-designed complexes with weather vanes and grooms' quarters above. This is indeed a horse-lover's paradise, albeit with a board and stabling tag of at least $160 a week. Riding trails, public exercise arenas set among natural scrub, lots of people to give riding lessons—and all this is available less than an hour from the city.

This is Steve's stamping ground. He works the area with skill and charm and is one of the district's most sought after horse experts. With that Olympic aura, he is also one of the most glamorous. The trim body, high-cheekboned, boyish good looks and steady, quiet gaze don't go astray either.

First client that day was a three-year-old brown stock horse gelding that Steve was trying out for a family wanting something quiet and sensible. He had picked it up for a reasonable price the week before because it had at one stage been caught in a rope and had broken its jaw, although few signs of the injury were obvious. Through persistent gentleness, Steve had been able to win the nervous horse's trust, and that morning it had its first set of shoes fitted without drama. He then gave it an hour's workout, put it over a few jumps and said if it continued to improve, he would put an $8000 tag on it, the going price in the area for a reliable mount with good conformation.

Steve charges $60 an hour for his teaching, training and exercising duties. He says some parents willingly pay around $300 a week for each of their children's horses to be exercised by Steve because they see horseriding as a way of keeping their children off the streets and away from trouble. Most of his clients live in Sydney but belong to the nearby Forest Hills pony club where Steve regularly instructs the 120 members.

We travel to the next estate in dense bush where an over-fat mare is being prepared for a show. The horse is sparky from lack of work. Steve, light in the saddle and light on the reins, gently works the mare through her silliness until she eventually canters evenly, although she puffs like a heavy smoker. Horses populate tiny yards all along the walkways to the dressage arena. Well-fed, but otherwise neglected, they appear to be kept like exhibits in a zoo. Steve says it is common to find horses cooped up like this. I am appalled that few get exercise and most never leave their yards. The mare is unsaddled while Jana, who accompanies Steve wherever he goes, holds the halter rope. Smiling and modestly flapping her eyelids at her brilliance, she braces herself as she sits on the back flap of the 4WD to tug the horse back into line as it moves to one side. The horse wears layers of rugs and hoods which, along with night lights, keep coats short and shiny for appearance's sake.

Steve packs his gear away and tells how at 19 he spent two years breaking in horses for famous trainer Tommy Smith. For two years before that he had worked at a large complex learning the art under head breaker, John Drennan. At 21, he went to America to spend three years on a Texas ranch training cutting horses and being taught equine artificial insemination. A call from Rupert Murdoch and Ken Cowley brought him back to work at Murdoch's Cavan Station at Yass, where he was in charge of the quarter horse stud. 'I was giving Lachlan pony rides in those days,' says Steve, who at 44 looks about ten years younger.

Talented performers

The track to the next appointment took us past Ammo's paddock. We stopped to look at a docile horse quietly grazing. He bore no resemblance to the horse with flashing hoofs which had threatened on opening night at Homebush to knock Steve unconscious by rearing with excitement in the low-roofed waiting room. The atmosphere generated by 130,000 people in the stadium and television cameras beaming to millions worldwide had ignited the horse. Steve, however, says he was not nervous. He had a slight fear though that Ammo might not stop, as they galloped in to execute the two scheduled rears. After all, the horse had been taught the trick in just three weeks after another horse failed to meet SOCOG's approval because it was too wimpy-looking. Until he met the spotlights of the stadium, Ammo had never stepped out in public, not even to a gymkhana.

Next stop for Steve was another agistment centre with day paddocks and comfortable timber stables. A full-time groom cares for sixteen horses, two of which Steve rides five times a week. He puts a part-Arab chestnut through shoulder-in and half pass routines to lighten him up and make him safe for his child rider. Thunder and lightning have started crashing around the skies but Steve and the horse work on unperturbed. The groom, meanwhile, rushes from paddock to stables putting precious charges away to prevent them rushing in fright through fences. After the second horse has been ridden, the fourth for the morning, Steve gets home by 11.30 am to help an owner deal with a horse that is heavy in the hand. Even Steve's skills can't compensate for a neck set too low. Nor will they correct gross obesity through overfeeding. This horse, like so many others he sees, is podgy and unfit. By the time the one hour session has finished, the horse is a steaming, sweating mess. Steve delicately and tactfully suggests yet again that perhaps the owner could cut back the feed. He says he has very little success getting people, most of them novice horse owners, to stop pushing huge quantities of high octane tucker down their horses' throats.

'They treat them like pets,' says Steve, meaning they like to buy expensive mixes and the latest fad foods for their 'babies'. Chaff and meadow hay apparently don't have enough sex appeal.

Steve and Sandy have between them about 100 riding students. Sandy is a former Sydney Mounted Police officer and competes in dressage at Prix St Georges level. She, naturally enough, was one of the 120 riders who appeared in the Man from Snowy River segment of the Olympic opening. Steve was given the task by his old friend Tony Jablonski of selecting the horses and riders, as well as organising logistics of training, transporting and warming up the participants on the big night. People and horses had to have the right temperament to cope with such a big group exercise as well as the ability to handle flags and noise. Some horses had to wear ear plugs, so loud was the stadium sound system. Riders had to keep their involvement secret even though they had to attend a 10-day training camp, trials and rehearsals at the Homebush stadium between 10 pm and 2 am. 'The biggest problem was keeping up morale,' Steve said. 'People were getting sick, and very tired because of the long days of practice.'

The horses, however, triumphed. They showed the world how important they had been to our nation's history and brought tears to many an eye. Steve, Tony Jablonski and Ignatious Jones, the designer of the Snowy River segment, hope to honour the horse at an annual Snowy River Muster each Easter. They want it to be as famous as Edinburgh's Tattoo.

Bill takes the stars in his stride

Bill Willoughy is a crusty sort of bloke. He talks straight, the no nonsense talk of a bloke from the bush, a bloke who does calf roping at rodeos for relaxation and who's been named champion a few times. He lives at the small settlement of Booleroo Centre in the mid-north of South Australia—and when he is not breaking in and training young horses, he is mixing with film stars. Bill might, in his understated way, call himself a 'specialist livestock contractor' on his CV. He could equally as well big-note himself by saying he has supplied horses to every major Australian feature film since *Breaker Morant*, a string of telemovies and mini-series, as well as the hugely popular series *McLeod's Daughters* which was shot near Gawler, South Australia. He could also throw in for good measure that he was the winner of the first Man from Snowy River competition in 1995, riding Sir Galahad.

Bill, 48, is part of the well-known Willoughby clan who are all tied up with horses in one way or another. He and brothers Greg, a showjumper, and Jim, horse breaker and trainer, and sister Julie, a campdrafter, are more than adequately keeping alive the spirit of their father, Tom, who in 1950 was named 'Australia's greatest all round horseman'. This honour came after he had won at Brisbane Show three diverse sections— the saddle bronc title, the gentleman rider class and the showjumping. In his lifetime he won eleven Australian rodeo titles. Now Jim's daughter Megan, 20, and Bill's twins, Jane and Lachlan, 15, are continuing the rodeo tradition. Jane recently won the national junior barrel racing championship and junior roping championship and Lachlan is the Australian calf-roping champion, the youngest person ever to win a national rodeo championship. Megan recently spent a year at Georgia University in the United States on a rodeo scholarship for barrel racing.

Bill has 30 well-trained film horses on his 600-acre cropping block. Twelve of these are seasoned performers that appear in almost every film with an equine cast. Ben, a little chestnut quarter horse, has been in every major picture since *Breaker Morant* in 1978. He was a handy campdraft horse in his private life. Film work, says Bill, brings many more challenges.

'It's a demanding job that needs super quiet horses that almost any idiot can ride. They need to do a variety of things and put up with an unbelievable amount of bullshit. They have to cope with horrid situations with the most unbelievable man-made scary things that flap around their ears and sometimes go off with a bang. And they have to work among about $1 million of electrical cords and equipment, with cables swinging over their heads, and not put a foot wrong. And the people who have the cheque book also want them to look good too.'

Bill says when an actor's double, a competent horserider, does all the fast and complex riding sequences, that same horse has to immediately switch off and become patient and docile for the close-ups and cut-aways of the actor in the saddle.

One of Bill's current 'stars' is his big white horse, Beau. *McLeod's Daughters* viewers will remember him as Oscar, the horse ridden by the character Tess. A 14-year-old veteran of film and television, Beau seems to have worked out what a camera is for. He sometimes gives a horsey sort of smile and he radiates presence, that indefinable quality that directors constantly seek. 'He's kind of a lovable sort of horse,' says Bill. 'He never does anything wrong.' Which, at $400,000 an episode, is fortunate. No director would want some fool of a horse blowing out the budget by misbehaving, whatever that might mean to those involved. Indeed, this is the tricky part of Bill's business. 'The days of people being in touch with animals have long gone,' he says. 'Every time I start on a new film, I have to train a new crew to understand how animals operate. Even so, they still write things into the script which make my job even more challenging.' One story line required a palomino mare to give foal, just like that, out of season and with only about nine months' notice to Bill, when gestation is eleven months. That's why a rash of advertisements suddenly appeared in every newspaper and horse magazine right around Australia seeking a mare due to foal sometime in March. Two suitable mares, one in Queensland and one in Sydney, were found and Bill had them transported to the farm which forms the film set for the series. A crew was put on round-the-clock standby to capture the births.

'They pay me a lot of money to be patient,' Bill says, laughing about another almost-impossible demand for sheep to drop lambs in mid-summer. Again, he's worked the grapevine and come up with some out-of-season ewes, but he's probably wondering what the writing department will come up with next.

Bill has a big team of people to help with the horses, as well as family stalwarts. Jane and Lachlan do a lot of on-film riding. Jim takes on the job of second-in-command on big jobs. Having the right people and a good team, Bill says, is what keeps him getting contracts. Unlike some other suppliers of livestock, Bill says he'll travel anywhere. 'We go anywhere there's a cheque,' he says. The pay might be good for his workers, but many locations are testing. 'We may be trucking horses out at 4 am, putting in a big day on the set, then getting back to the camp at 11 pm, and doing the same thing day in, day out, and handling rough bush conditions.' Between jobs, Bill trains dressage, polo, campdraft and show horses for other people. He also runs horsemanship clinics. 'Contracting is like farming,' he says. 'There are big cheques, then a long time of nothing.'

Bill's got a shed holding about $300,000 worth of harness, saddlery and vehicles to cater for whatever era or circumstances a film is depicting. He says there have been some years when none of it has left the shed, but things have been busy in the past few years with *The Drover's Boy* (1999), *Chuck Finn* (2000), *Trackers* and *Rabbit-Proof Fence* (2001), and *McLeod's Daughters*, which finished its eighth and final season in January 2009.

All for a piece of carrot

Behind the scenes of some of Australia's most famous film celebrations of bush culture, heroism and horses was someone who herself became something of a legend. Evanne, horsemaster to the industry for 25 years, provided and trained the equine stars of *The Man from Snowy River*, *The Silver Brumby*, *The Light Horsemen*, *Pharlap*, *Breaker Morant* and *Burke and Wills*.

Surrounded by the most extraordinary menagerie of performing animals at her farm just outside Melbourne, I found her taking a breather after directing animal action for *On Our Selection*, Steele Rudd's wonderful Dad and Dave stories that were shot at Braidwood, New South Wales. As well as the 60 horses on the farm, there were camels being trained for *Tracks*, a feature film re-creating Robyn Davidson's lone trek across Australia, an assortment of dogs used in films, and rabbits, as well as a fantastic assortment of carriages, wagons, sulkies and buggies and a mountain of harness.

Evanne ('I don't use a surname'), now 53, learnt her skills from the late Jim Wilton, a man she speaks of with great reverence as the best trick horse trainer and breaker that Australia's ever seen. 'If he'd gone to America with all his tricks, he could have been rich and famous,' she says. This man whom, she says, 'thought like a horse' and therefore could train them to do the most extraordinary range of things, was 'as cranky as anything to the human race', but was basically kind. It wasn't easy being his student.

With her total complement of 130 film horses (70 live on her farm on the northern tablelands of New South Wales), Evanne scoffed at suggestions they were not really working animals. 'Every one of them has to earn its living,' she said. 'They have to be as fit as race horses to do tricks asked of them such as rearing. During film shooting, they may have to rear as many as ten times for a single take.'

Evanne grew up at Avalon Beach, Sydney, and as a horse-mad teenager started collecting horses until she ended up with five of them housed in the Brand family's suburban backyard.

'One day I touched a horse in a particular spot and he reared,' she said. 'This fascinated me, but unfortunately I didn't know how to make him stop.'

So she set about learning and hasn't stopped training animals since. When she married at 21, she started doing film-horse work in what was then a fledgling industry. The Marlboro man commercials with the palomino horse and Ben Hall were first efforts and other famous credits since include *We of the Never Never*, *Archer*, *Picture Show Man*, *Evil Angels*, *The New Adventures of Black Beauty* and *Lightning Jack*.

These days her son, Cody Harris, helps train and handle the film horses. It was probably inevitable he would enter the business, especially after those early pony club days when he discovered the delicious pleasure of playing tricks on his instructors with a pony that would lie down on command. Everyone present would become very concerned when the animal kept collapsing, fearing it was about to die. These days, Cody, among other things, trains horses to fall at speed onto a soft pad of straw, which in films is disguised under sawdust and dirt to make it look as though they've been shot.

In this tightly controlled industry where cruelty is illegal, slow, gentle training is the essence. Infamous practices like 'toe-tapping', which involves a cable anchored back to a solid object and attached to the front of the foot are absolutely banned. This 'trick' made galloping horses cartwheel and fall heavily, often sustaining hideous internal injuries. Usually these horses were destined for the knackery, anyway, which was how the practice was justified—at least, in some people's minds. According to Evanne, however, such barbarism is quite unnecessary. A stunning range of extraordinary feats and effects can be achieved, so long as there is plenty of training time.

'You can teach them anything if you get the script early enough. It's what you put in beforehand that counts,' she said.

When the highly rated *The Man from Snowy River* television series was being filmed, or in fact, any of the many other epics in which she and her teams of horse handlers and grooms have worked, the life on set is not far removed from the 'real' working horse days. For *Snowy River*, Evanne supervised up to 76 horses living on site for nine months of shooting. She and her staff were up and feeding at 5.30 am. They exercised and groomed about twenty stabled horses that filled the leading roles. Filming was five days a week, starting at 7 am. Harness horses spent eight to ten hours between the shafts, either endlessly repeating action to get the right shot, or waiting around with nosebags on.

It's a hectic schedule that sees Evanne also giving riding and harness driving lessons to actors before they take over suitably quiet horses that fit the roles to be played. She winces as she recalls good horses roughly treated by unknowing novice riders during film action, but shrugs those painful memories off as being an unfortunate side effect of the film-horse business.

Evanne has her own portable set of steel horseyards transported to the film site. She takes several shipping container loads of horse gear on the back of semi-trailers, arranges feed deliveries and for harness to be cleaned and oiled. In addition, the 'star' horses have to be kept up to the mark with their 'tricks'. These may involve learning to push an actor into a waterhole, picking up ropes and carrying them, rearing, lying dead or running free along a pre-determined course. Stand-in horses for the stars will also have to be taught the same tricks, and horses may have to be painted or coloured for particular scenes.

About a dozen of Evanne's workers are multi-skilled. Trained to do stock work, side-saddle, dressage and jumping, they can also pull stage-coaches and sulkies, do tricks and liberty work, and also win royal show ribbons. In 1993, as a tribute to her skills, Evanne received a coveted Australian Film Industry award, the Byron Kennedy award, which is judged by the industry itself for a colleague who has excelled in any previously unrecognised category.

Film-animal work is often high pressure, but because of its obvious glamour it attracts scores of contenders chasing the perceived riches. But while the contracts can be lucrative, the costs of running a film 'zoo' on call for whatever animal tricks advertising or film makers may want are also considerable.

Training horses to trot past cameras and ignore lights and funny sights and noises is not difficult, but orchestrating stallion fights on cue and other violent action would be daunting to most.

The secret, according to Evanne, is to train slowly and gently, with plenty of 'bribery' in the form of carrots, and the perseverance to 'irritate and annoy' the performers to put their legs and bodies into whatever position is required. To create those stirring scenes of galloping brumbies, Evanne uses lead horses trained to come to her call, and then all the other horses follow. Simple.

Blondie, the palomino star of Elyne Mitchell's *The Silver Brumby*, and definitely the prima donna of Evanne's team of twelve trick-horse actors, showed how terrifyingly vicious she could pretend to be on a simple cue. The whip placed in certain positions had the horse laying back its ears, lashing out sideways, rearing and striking—which is what she had to do in her fights as the brumby stallion, Thowra. Move the whip again and the part-Arab mare was back to her pretty-faced, gentle self. Then, on command, she would pick up a coil of rope and carry it to Evanne, walk backwards, paw the ground and bow. After each trick she got a piece of carrot.

Following the release of *The Silver Brumby* in 1993, Blondie performed nightly at Sydney Royal Show, showing off tricks from the film to huge audiences in the main arena. Without bridle, halter or leadrope, she cantered free, in marvellous flowing counterpoint to the disciplined show hacks, which need reins, bits, riders and spurs to give their best. It took a year of solid training to produce those results, but in preparation for any new task in a film, Evanne will work each horse three times a day for ten minutes at a time, or until the trick has been performed correctly, for months. Being away in its paddock or yard for a rest is the horse's reward—after, of course, those treats of carrot.

Next into the roundyard came the stunningly dappled grey mare, Lindy. Lindy doubled as The Brolga in *The Silver Brumby*, has been seen in many films under saddle and in harness pulling stylish carriages, and was in the TV series *Blue Heelers* once as a 'dead' horse. She is also a winner of show ribbons as a harness horse. Harness horses and showing them are Evanne's main love, and her extensive collection of carriages features a $25,000 superbly restored landau and a beautiful black and silver-adorned hearse. The show harness she uses was all made by Evanne, a skill, rare these days, which she picked up from many talented old-time craftsmen, in particular a master-saddler who had worked at the Royal Mews.

Meanwhile, the beautiful Lindy is cantering around and warming up in the portable roundyard. She rears on almost imperceptible cue and shows off outrageously, then headbutts Evanne forward, and 'dies'—all for a piece of carrot.

On with the show

For sheer exuberant tackiness and gaudy showmanship, there's nothing that quite beats a circus. It is pure, transitory theatre, turning bare paddock to flamboyant fantasy with tent, flags, lights, trumpets and flashing sequins. This world of constant change is the working environment for troupes of arched-necked horses, glittering under spotlights as they rock through their routines around the sawdust ring.

Compared to the working farm horses of centuries past, circus horses lead a pampered, almost slothful life. Six or so performances a week lasting about ten minutes each is hardly a big strain. Sure, they practise new tricks, get worked to keep fit and spend a bit of time each week travelling between sites, but in return they get good feed and plenty of relaxation. The keeping of animals in circuses is loudly criticised by animal liberation groups; but the use of performing horses surely has to be one of the great non-issues. Far worse off are those horses kept as pets which are not worked and allowed to founder. Inactivity and too much feed is the greatest ruination of good horses in these so-called civilised times.

Carlos Gasser, 32, acrobat and horse handler with Circus Royale, has a circus pedigree that stretches back to the great European performers. His three acts include Sahib, an 18-year-old Anglo-Arab stallion, bought for $150 as a young colt. In five months the horse had learnt to rear on command, lie down, bow and sit like a dog. Even after all these years, when the fanfare for his act sounds, old Sahib still prances with anticipation. Because circus animals are so much under the scrutiny of public gaze, Sahib will soon retire, so there can be no criticism that the horse is too old to work. Carlos's pride in his animals' achievements is clear, but so too is nervousness about misguided perceptions of ill-treatment. That aside, he laughs about the drawbacks of having all stallions (which are used for their showiness) in his troupe, especially when spring fever pulses through their loins.

Just before the evening performance in a Queensland town some years ago, Sahib, all dressed up in red plumes and shiny yellow bridle, side-reins and girth, stood waiting to enter the ring. When he was unclipped by the handler, instead of cantering through the curtains into the spotlight as he always had done, he spun around and galloped off into the night. He had picked up the scent of cycling mares, and he wasn't hanging around to go through his routine for anyone—not while there were mares needing his help.

Since the circus was leaving town early next morning and the tent would be pulled down after the show, a plea to the audience had to be made: 'If on your way home, you should see a chestnut horse wearing plumes on its head, please call us urgently.' Sahib was found five kilometres away, still in plumes and shiny yellow harness, drooling with lust outside a paddock of mares. He'd galloped across a busy highway to get there, which must have given a few motorists something to think about.

Leading an attack against the animal liberation lobby, which wants to see all circus animals banned, is Lorraine Grant, president of the Circus Federation of Australia, director of Ashton's circus and great-granddaughter of its founder.

Performing horses have always played a very important part in the Ashton's program. Favourites are the steady, broad, resin-backed horses which canter smoothly around the arena while acrobats swing and jump on and over them, high school Andalusian dressage horses, and the diminutive 25-year-old miniature pony Chico—who his handler, Jan, thinks must have Alzheimer's disease. Chico has recently begun to do only whatever tricks he feels like doing during his nightly performances.

'The trouble is,' says Jan, 'I never know from one performance to the next which tricks he has decided to do, and which he has dropped!' Nevertheless, having been upstaged by the little black rascal once again, when he insisted on making numerous bows instead of putting his front legs on the boxes edging the ring, Jan gave him his customary post-performance carrot. 'If I don't, he'll think I'm cross with him,' she said.

'There is no cruelty in the transportation or training of circus animals,' says Lorraine Grant. 'We train with patience and consistency, repetition and reward, building on the animals' natural ability.'

According to Lorraine, the remoteness of most people today from animals that work for a living has resulted in widespread ignorance about their behaviour, needs and abilities.

'They think it is demeaning for an animal to do tricks, but for the animal it is just another job.'

Esdale Flash Prince
Research: Bruce Macarthur and Tim Peel

The story of Esdale Flash Prince is the very stuff of legends. Indeed if it wasn't a true story, few would believe it. The horse's extraordinary life took him from the Melbourne Royal Show ring to the coal mines of Muswellbrook, then to a knacker's yard. From there he was rescued from becoming pet food only to be judged, eight months later, at the age of 16, Champion Clydesdale Stallion at the Sydney Royal Show, a feat he repeated at the age of 18. Tim Peel, well known these days as a Clydesdale breeder, first saw Prince when he was a pit pony underground in the coal mines at Muswellbrook in 1967.

The Peel family had used horses on milk runs in Sydney from 1909. In the 1960s, however, their stables and paddocks in the prestigious Vaucluse area no longer fitted the harbourside council's development plans. So they sold most of their 14 half-draught horses, motorised the milk run and kept only a few of the better-bred mares. These were taken back to their farm at Kellyville. One was a registered Clydesdale whose line the Peels decided to keep going, so they looked around for a stallion.

When several horsemen told Tim that there was a good-looking, registered stallion working at the Muswellbrook mine, he checked him over, then took his mare to him. For four years, the quiet-tempered stallion had been dragging coal skips back and forth from the coalface, moving a total of 120 tons of coal each day. Prince had been bought for the mine at the dispersal of breeding stock at a nearby stud, and got his first taste of work at the age of twelve. But according to his mine handler, Joe Maloney, the horse 'never made a fuss about it—he was always the perfect gentleman'.

In 1969 when the mines dispensed with horses, the stallion was sold through the Maitland saleyards. For $162, he had been bought by a Rooty Hill knackery to be turned into pet food.

'I got a phone call from the knackery owner, who knew I was breeding horses,' says Tim Peel. 'He told me that a pretty good stallion was going to be killed the next day and he thought I might like to rescue him.'

Tim immediately recognised the markings and noble carriage as those of the mine stallion that had served his mare. He bought him and took him home to the farm. The Peels were still using horses to feed out hay to their 400 milking cows and to pull the four-wheeler for fencing and odd jobs. So Prince was back in harness.

'Not long after we got Prince, a friend called Dave Rees urged me to support the Clydesdale section at the 1969 Sydney Royal Show—because for the first time in years, there had been no representatives of the breed at the 1968 show.

'I told him we would be starters, so eight months after we got Prince he entered the showgrounds and beat the rest of the stallions for the broad ribbon.'

Shopping pioneer style
Chris Stoney

Up in the high plains of Victoria, a feisty group of pioneers ran cattle on leases in the rugged, inaccessible terrain that these days is explored by thousands of bushwalkers, fishermen, campers and horseriders. One of these cattle families was the Hoskins, who took up 1000 acres along Mitchell's Creek in 1881.

Being isolated and a long way from the nearest town, the Hoskins came up with a novel way of doing their shopping. A packhorse would have the packs put on it and a shopping list inserted in one of the bags. After being led down along the Jamieson side of the sliprail fence, the horse would be slapped on the backside and sent downstream. A day or so later their old grey horse would wander into the Jamieson store, where the storekeeper fed and stabled him for the night. The next day, loaded up with the Hoskins' supplies of sugar, tea and flour, the horse would be sent on his way back up to Mitchell's.

Shake a leg, Glen
Shirley Low

Why is it that the devil itself seems to enter into a horse on a windy day? Our horse Glen was a wonderful stock horse, but wicked on a windy day. He also had a trick of lifting his right leg, asked or unasked, to shake hands.

On windy days, when the horses were needed for a day's mustering, all attempts to catch Glen were in vain. He would whirl away from the yard at the last moment, mane and tail flying, tummy rattling with excitement, and doing everything but laugh, it would seem.

It was then we would have the humiliating task of catching a neighbour's horse in order to catch our own. Finally, having got him safely in the yard, we had to put up with him wanting to shake hands! This wasn't usually what we had in mind for the wretch of a horse.

Stop start Jack
Peter Richardson

When one spends up to nine months of the year in the saddle out droving, one has to acquire a great respect and admiration for the horse. They're loyal, and every horse has its own personality. They also seem to have boundless energy; even at the end of a long and tiring day, a good horse will always find some hidden source of energy if needed. At times they knew what had to be done, and how to do it, better than I did.

I recall one amusing thing that happened on a droving trip. We lost one of our horses that pulled the cart, so we were pleased to be able to purchase one from a station along the track. We could not get much information about this horse except that his name was Jack, he was broken to harness and was extremely quiet. So we took him on, not that we had any other option, anyway. We had to harness him to the cart next day, as two horses were not really enough for the load we had. I thought it would be better to try him in the shafts with the other two abreast in front.

All was in readiness, so off we went. But we travelled only about 25 yards, because Jack decided to stop dead in his tracks and tried to go backwards. He just sat on the breeching and was dragged along, so I stopped for a while, got out and had a look to see what could be bothering him, but there was nothing. So we started off again—and got another 25 yards or so, and the same thing happened again. So we continued like this, making very slow progress. After many hours and quite a few cuts with the whip, we eventually got fully mobile.

When we returned to the station where we had bought Jack, we told them about this strange behaviour. It so happened the station hand who had owned him was there and he told us about Jack's previous life.

He had spent quite a few of his early years drawing water from the well. All he knew was to go forward, stop, then go back to lower the bucket again. His previous owner was surprised the horse still remembered this routine, as it had been many years since he had done that job. Jack continued on with us until his retirement and became a great mate and faithful servant.

Flying Bob
Alex Haley

Dad fancied himself as a bit of a horse trader, buying horses that needed sorting out—which he got my brothers and me to do—and then selling them for a profit. Dad was very pleased by this and often bragged how many pounds he made—but he seldom offered anything to compensate for the bruises that we inevitably received.

There was only one horse we ever had trouble with—a little pony called Bob, bought by Dad for the younger boys to learn on. My brother Tom couldn't tame him, so he was turned out as unrideable. He was probably a halfbred Shetland-stock horse from the mountains, and very smart. You could pat him, catch him anywhere, and he would eat sugar from your hand or a slice of bread, but as you walked away, he would take a firm grip on your behind with his teeth. A pat in the paddock always resulted in a bite on the behind; it couldn't be avoided. When he was ridden, he wouldn't buck or go wild, he would just canter along as good as gold, and then—for no reason and with no warning—he would stop dead in his tracks, placing his head between his front legs at the same time. Over the top the rider went with an awful thud, and we all agreed that Bob landed you much harder than any other horse.

One school holiday period, boredom overtook us as Dad had taken time off to take Mum shopping. The three of us, Harry, Geoff and I, decided we should teach Bob to go into harness.

Bob was brought into the horseyard and a bridle was put on. A collar was found to go close to fitting, as nothing was small enough. Eventually we had it all sorted out, so we hooked him up to the sledge, which was made from a fork cut from a tree with a chain attached to the front and with boards nailed across the V. This was used to teach horses to go in harness and pull loads. Geoff was nominated to lead Bob. Harry and I stood on the sledge to make the load. Bob went forward, but didn't like the weight on his shoulders too much. After a few paces, he threw his head back, pulled free from Geoff, opened his mouth and dived at him. Geoff ran, and Bob followed. Geoff dodged one way and then the other, still Bob followed. Geoff ran into the sheepyards, with Bob and the sled close behind. Only when Geoff ran up the drafting race, which caused the sled to become jammed, did Bob stop.

After a week or two of hard work, we reckoned Bob was ready to go in the cart. Dad had asked us to bring up some hay from the bottom stack, so we decided this was it. We would show Dad what we had achieved.

Bob was harnessed and hooked up into the spring cart, so called because it had no springs. It had two gig wheels, a small tray and two shafts. It was suitable for bringing hay to various parts of the farm. Bob was small and the spring cart looked too big for him—and of course it was. He pulled the cart to the haystack and we loaded up with sheaf hay. Harry figured that if we put a big load on, Bob would have to behave, because the load would be too heavy. Well, it was loaded and poor Bob seemed to be only touching the ground with his toes.

He did very well until he passed the woolshed, where a post had been removed near the track, leaving a hole. Bob wasn't holding very steady as he passed the post hole and one wheel of the cart dropped into this hole. The cart and load tipped over backwards, lifting the shafts into the air. Bob was elevated too, and remained suspended two feet from the ground by the shafts pointing up in the air. We heard a car coming, so we popped inside the shed to discuss how to get Bob down. The car was Dad's and I can still hear his incredulous tone.

'How in the name of the Almighty did you get up there, you little rogue?' he questioned Bob.

The three of us had trouble sitting down for a couple of days due to the marks Dad's razor strop left on the place where Bob liked to bite.

Bob did, in time, become a reasonable cart horse and we drove him to school in the gig. From time to time we would ask someone to hold him while we got into the gig, pretending he was flighty; but we all knew what would happen when the helper turned him loose. Bob would give a parting nip, which was often accompanied by a piercing scream from the person who was helping us, for the first and last time.

When the farm was eventually sold and the plant and animals auctioned, we all shed a tear as the little cart horse brought the sum of 12 guineas.

Versatile Bessie—but watch out!
Doris Svenson

Bessie was a medium-sized horse—one of those versatile do-anything animals. She was my parents' pride and joy, and had in fact been given to them as a wedding present.

Bessie could take her place in a team if she was required to, and did the job well, however this was not often asked of her. She was mostly used as a commuter horse and was usually kept in a paddock handy to the house. Our house was about one and a half miles from my grandmother's place, from where all the work seemed to start and stop, so my father often rode Bessie to and from work. She was a good saddle horse.

Once we children started school, my father—when it suited—would harness up Bessie and put her in the trap, so we could ride with him as far as Grandmother's house before setting off on foot for the remaining mile to school. It was better than walking all the way. This was the role that Bessie was best suited to—a cart horse.

For all the good points that Bessie had, and for which my parents loved her, she had one fault for which I seem to remember her vividly. That was the poor control over her rear end. This was particularly evident if you happened to be the smallest child who, due to insufficient room, mostly sat on the floor at the other people's feet and very close to the horse's tail.

We were always equipped with a 'buggy rug', which was red tartan wool on one side and the other side had a waterproof finish. The purpose of this, of course, was to protect us from any sudden showers of rain. We all learned very quickly, especially the small children at the front of the trap, to hastily seek shelter under the rug at the first sign of Bessie's rising tail—to protect us from quite different sudden showers.

Sunday morning service
Helen Best

Trying to start our unreliable old Whippet car early on Sunday mornings was not always successful. We used to push it out of the shed and down a slight hill, hoping for a start. Quite often it didn't, so my uncle would bring the quietest of his team, Blossom, to help.

Amid much laughter, fussing, cursing and shouting, Blossom would tow the old car up the hill for another attempt, whilst we stood around in our Sunday clothes, waiting for the engine to kick over.

Eleven
Horses in uniform

No other country in the world can do pageantry and pomp on horseback like the British. Clattering down Pall Mall, with riders impeccably turned out in shining breastplates, plumes on their heads and lots of red serge, gold tassels and black leather, the realm's gleaming horses marching in formation are indeed a stirring sight.

In Australia, horse pageantry is light on. No longer are there big phalanxes of jogging horses with riders holding flags and sitting erect in ceremonial uniforms to add gravity or elan to special public occasions. But we had our own famous Light Horse regiments and these stories from the past re-create some of the splendour, sadness and fun of those times.

The mounted police are enjoying a resurgence in some states, especially Victoria. The value of horses in violent demonstrations and for crime patrols is being newly appreciated. In September 2000 during the S11 anti-globalisation rallies in Melbourne, the horses of Victoria Police's Mounted Branch stood firm but unruffled in the face of thousands of raucous, jostling protesters waving placards. They had been involved in a pioneering training programme for crowd and riot control. The television images of big, steady horses and gently persuasive riders have since led other mounted branches around Australia and overseas to examine what is going on behind the red brick walls of the police stable and training complex just off Melbourne's busy St Kilda Road. Some have introduced similar training programmes.

Big steady police horses deliver calm persuasion

It was Tuesday morning, and the weekly riding and drill session was underway in the branch's huge indoor arena. Through high, paned windows running along one side of the gable roofed, heritage listed building came the sound of ballet music from the adjoining College of the Arts campus. From the other side came traffic noise and the pounding of a building site. That aural mix of grace and machine power seemed to suit perfectly the disciplined schooling session on the tan bark. Five fit, well- muscled horses trotted looping circles; taut, lean, uniformed riders listened intently to Level 1 EFA instructor Senior Constable Jan Saunders, sixteen years with the Mounted Branch.

'Keep contact with your lower leg and push through opening hands,' she urged the riders, who regularly appear at football matches, as ceremonial escorts, at parades and the Grand Prix as well as on routine traffic duty, general crime patrols, searches, demonstrations and crowd control.

The wood-panelled arena was latticed with shafts of morning sun which ran across gleaming rumps and arching necks. For an hour solid they worked and no horse or rider raised a sweat. It was unusual to have time for a pure riding lesson, Jan said, but useful for correcting minor riding faults to help horses perform better.

It was the next hour under the supervision of Senior Sergeant Greg Williams that put the flatwork, which some happily admit they find a bit tedious, into context. One minute the horses are galloping full tilt into a fast and furious flag-and-barrel race, nostrils flaring, the next they return instantly to slack-reined relaxation and calm. There was much shrieking and laughter among the riders who were having as much fun as kids at pony club. There was no ruling about them settling down, as the horses did after getting their blood up.

'We are very selective on what we breed,' said Greg Williams, who is supervising a programme of crossing thoroughbreds and Warmbloods. 'The horses have to put up with unbelievable hassles, so it is critical they have very calm temperaments. That's why we are not accepting any more gift horses.' Since 1994 Senior Sergeant Williams has been in charge of all aspects of the branch: its horses, their feeding, breeding, training, the riders and budget. A dry-witted bloke, he's a team player who leads from the front. He saddles his own horse and, if hands are short, dungs out loose boxes and unloads fodder.

Gift horses have long been part of police culture, but gradually gifts have been phased out, except for a few exceptional offers such as the two-year-old purebred 17 hand Warmblood, possibly worth $20,000, which the owner had no time to work. The police certainly offer the sort of good home every horse seller dreams about. Apart from fabulous loose boxes of generous proportions in the historic light-filled stable block adjoining the indoor arena, the horses lead a disciplined life with meals delivered promptly and two days off a week in line with their riders' hours.

Slow race horses regarded as too good to turn into pet food often made their way to the police, and not always the slow ones. Robert Holmes à Court donated the 1984 Melbourne Cup winner, Black Knight, to the branch after he had earned prize money of $454,850. He apparently made a passably good police mount. 'Some years ago we had a good look at all our horses and found we were spending a lot of time training thoroughbreds, many of which didn't make it as police horses,' Greg said. Too often they would fizz up under pressure or not be able to handle the stress of life on the beat.

He now sources frozen semen from imported Warmblood stallions, which are renowned not only for their height and solid frames but for their steady temperament. They were traditionally a general-purpose breed from West Germany used for pulling carriages, farm work, cavalry and riding. He also bought a

Warmblood stallion after seeing him at a show, where he was tied up to a float with mares all round him and then calmly completed a showjumping round. One thoroughbred stallion, a grey, is also based out at Attwood, the police stud farm at West Meadows. The mares in the stud are selected from the best performers in the mounted branch.

While he was talking the arena was transformed into a playground for the kind of 'games' the horses might face on the street. Tall barriers of plastic drums were built, banners were hung up, plastic sheeting and streamers arranged on the ground. This is the forum for the crowd control training that the Victoria Police horses specialise in and for which they have received widespread praise from within the force and beyond.

A small crowd of non-riding officers is co-opted to assemble noisily in the arena and wave banners and umbrellas, shout slogans through megaphones, rattle metal containers and generally make a nuisance of themselves. In pairs, horses and riders walk slowly but authoritatively to the unruly rabble. With kind voices, the riders ask politely but firmly for the pretend protesters to 'move back, please'. They do it in such a way that, combined with the imposing size of the horse and lofty height of the rider, compliance generally follows in the real situation with little argument. Indeed, who can argue with half a ton of animal that quietly pushes through the densest crowd? Even if it's not the polite but persuasive tone of the mounted officer, the warlike dress of the horse is enough to inspire respect. Dressed in demo gear—Perspex face shields attached to bridles that have steel wire sandwiched in leather straps and reins that can't be cut, and wearing special shoes with steel undersoles to protect hooves from being bruised on stones or ball bearings— the horses are an awe-inspiring (dare I say it?) weapon. For a population with little daily contact with horses, the fear of being trodden on is alone enough to move people along. In practice sessions, rubber balls are thrown at the horses and they have to push through the wall of plastic drums, making it topple noisily, and then walk over the resulting 'debris'. They have to push past streamers and banners—and all this work is done at a very slow, even walk, unhurried and calm. Police horses over the years have helped at the Beatles tour, the anti-Vietnam War demonstrations and the (1971) Springboks Rugby Union tour. Their value as gentle crowd controllers has been more appreciated recently and the 34 horses and riders in the Mounted Branch are finding themselves being called on ever more frequently. 'We are teaching the horses to have a more passive approach and to take what is handed out to them,' Greg Williams said. They are taught to lift the level of pressure they apply to meet what is offered but the riders will always say 'please' when they ask crowds to co-operate.

Riders are protective of their equine workmates and say they get annoyed if they are ever hurt by protesters. The horses are not allowed to be aggressive, just authoritative. 'That's why we are breeding bigger and more imposing horses,' Greg Williams said.

That height is a useful tool, too, on street patrol in areas such as Footscray and St Kilda where crime and drugs are prevalent. Not only do horses have a large visible presence they give officers a good view over fences, into backyards. 'It's amazing what you learn,' says Greg. 'People come up and talk about what's going on because we move slowly and are accessible.'

During the S11 protests, the Branch had 32 horses on duty each day between 5 am and midnight. Greg led from the front. He says only about one hour involved 'push and shove', but at one stage when people were punching police, he pulled the horses back in a tactic designed to confuse and bluff protest organisers. When they asked what was happening, 'We said if they didn't stop punching police, we would push them out of the way.' The wall of plastic drums in the arena just then crashed to the ground again as a young horse walked through and was rewarded for its efforts with a pat.

The World Economic Forum protests further reinforced the value of police horses when a politician's car had been trapped by crowds for 45 minutes, despite the best efforts of foot police. Six horses forged a path through the crowd effortlessly. Greg Williams told the story not to boast that one segment of the police force was better than another, just to illustrate that each had its strengths.

Every twelve months, Greg Williams goes to Charleston, South Carolina in the United States, as a guest of the police chief there to train his mounted unit. The crowd control training techniques trialled and adopted in Melbourne have been successfully adopted there—but perhaps not as successfully, Greg says, because they use only gift horses and have difficulties with differing tempera- ments and training methods. Another member of the Branch, Sergeant Craig Matters, was at that time on a six-week scholarship to Amsterdam, Israel and London to examine their training and exchange ideas.

Using frozen semen, the force's best mares are impregnated and then the embryo is flushed and implanted in a lesser mare, leaving the breeder to cycle again. That way, the best mares produce a great number of foals, giving the Branch a good, even team of well-conformed horses. Foals are broken in as two year olds, start work at four or five and retire anywhere between 14 and 22, depending on how their bodies stand up to the demands of the job.

A resident saddler works at the Branch servicing the huge numbers of Keiffer Aachen and Stuben Wotan it uses and making the demo bridles specially designed at the Branch and now being sold to other mounted branches in Western Australia and New South Wales.

Greg Williams says the Mounted Branch is very cost effective. Compared with running a police car, he says a horse is extraordinarily cheap. Victoria's Branch has 34 members, New South Wales has 31, Western Australia 24, South Australia nineteen and Queensland has twelve. New Zealand is just starting horse patrols, as is the Australian Capital Territory.

The horses lead a beautifully disciplined life, woken at 5 am and moved across the wide alleyway to their day boxes for breakfast. The officers muck out the boxes and groom their horses in readiness for the day's work. At 2 pm the horses go back into their night boxes for afternoon tea and to rest on deep straw bedding before their evening meal. Rations are Coprice and good quality clover hay, a diet designed to keep horses 'cool' yet strong. The heritage stable wing is huge, airy and spotlessly clean with rows each side of cream and brown painted, wood-panelled stables separated by steel bars. The atmosphere is peaceful despite the sound of traffic zooming past. On the mezzanine walkway going around the walls above the stables, officers' lockers hold uniform, their horses' bridles and reflector boots for night patrol.

Greg has his own farm where he raises cattle. As a child he rode ponies, then later trained trotters. He joined the police force in 1971 because it offered a chance to work full time with horses.

One of the special highlights in his career came in 1998 when he, Senior Constable Jan Saunders and Senior Constable Kevin Knowles were invited to compete in Canada to celebrate the 125th anniversary of the Royal Canadian Mounted Police in Regina. On borrowed horses, untrained to police work and certainly not used to the competition skills of tent-pegging, sabre fighting and shooting, the trio beat all home teams. They had only a few days to train their very novice horses and Greg smiles with customary humility but unmistakeable pride. 'We showed them what Australian horsemen could do.'

The (unofficial) charges of the Light Horse
Addye Rockliff

I joined the 22nd Light Regiment as a very green 17-year-old boy on 22 January 1939. There had been some sabre rattling in Europe and the Commonwealth Government set out to raise the militia force from 30,000 to 70,000. I had to adjust my age by one year, as the minimum age limit was eighteen. I became a member of a regiment whose headquarters were at Ulverstone, a town on the mid-north-west coast of Tasmania.

There were two events of note during my eighteen months with the regiment. The first was being part of a Vice Regal Cavalry escort, which I believe was the only one ever conducted in Tasmania. I suppose it was part of the recruitment propaganda of the time. The governor was to open the local agricultural show, so with only one rehearsal, we had the horses formed in sections according to matching colours. We were armed with a lance that had a swallow-tailed red and white pennant just under the steel tip. The base fitted into a leather bucket on our right stirrup. We trotted in formation at 10 miles an hour before and after the governor's car, and at the showgrounds, formed a single line abreast to be inspected. It all went without hitch, was a wonderful sight, and I was glad to be part of it.

There was, however, a side to the escorting event of which the governor would have been quite unaware. During preparations, we were being drilled in a hall that was three blocks from where our horses were stabled over our lunch break. We were required to saddle up and return to the drill hall at the other end of the street for the afternoon session. The first group to be mounted had just ridden onto the street when someone called out, 'Let's have a race!' Since youthful exuberance was high, they were instantly all galloping down the street, with complete disregard for the three intersections.

A particular friend of mine happened to be riding bareback, as he had left his saddle at the drill hall. A small car entered one of the intersections and stopped halfway across, in the midst of the galloping horses. No doubt the driver was flustered at finding himself in the middle of a Light Horse charge. My bareback friend was so positioned that he had no alternative but to let his horse jump the car. In those days motor transport was not common and the rules for intersections had not been addressed.

The other event was a stampede. We were in camp on a property called Mona Vale, a few miles south of Ross in Tasmania's Midlands. Winter was approaching; there had been a lot of rain and heavy frosts, and a cold wind was blowing from the central highlands across the open plains. The horses were cold and needed more exercise than they were getting.

The horse lines were muddy and the neck ropes were wet and slippery. All 350 horses were taken out daily for water, with each man leading three horses. After half an hour the hands clutching the neck ropes become numb and the arms ache with the pulling of the horses.

Eventually, the inevitable happened. Two horses at the rear of the column broke away, and in two seconds, the whole lot were galloping in fear of each other. The noise was terrific—thundering hooves, the flapping rugs, and neck ropes cracking like whips. Men were knocked over and injured. One man trying to dodge the oncoming mob was caught by two horses that were tied together. Their rope got him just under the chin and he suffered concussion.

About 50 of the horses found their paths blocked by permanent buildings and fixtures, and these were swiftly caught, my own among them. They were saddled quickly and parties set out to bring the rest back to camp.

However, the frenzied mob of remounts, after leaving the camp, had struck the road leading to the main highway, which went through the town of Ross. Some of the fittest horses were stopped by police at Campbelltown, 15 kilometres away. Stragglers were found along all the roads between. These had been shouldered off bridges, unable to get through gateways, or had collided with a variety of fixed objects. Some of these were injured, and some seriously. Those with broken legs were destroyed where they were. By nightfall, I think all had been accounted for.

A hospital enclosure was built at the camp, using floorboards from the tents, to provide some shelter from the cold and wind. Every government vet working on the injured horses was kept very busy. Many quickly recovered and returned to duty, but by the end of camp, three weeks later, 35 were removed to a remount depot, where eventually most were destroyed. The cost in horses' lives must have been close to forty. There are always risks when a lot of animals of any kind are herded together, but it seemed a high price to pay.

I transferred to the Infantry in mid-1940, and ended up as a prisoner of the Japanese in Java. As prisoners we had some brief contact with a Japanese mounted unit which was equipped with Australian horses. We had a strange fellow feeling with those horses when we saw they were being treated as badly as we were.

Moving the remounts
Jack Cawley

A familiar sound in city streets during the 1930s was the loud clattering as strings of about 100 army remount horses were moved between depots. Remount was the name applied to all army horses, which at the end of World War II were completely phased out, as all mounted units were disbanded. The great majority of these units had been based in the metropolitan area, and the army maintained numbers of horses in each state to supply their requirements.

In South Australia a unit known as the 4th Military District Remount Section, with a principal depot at O'Halloran Hill, a secondary depot at Woodside and a large stables and yards complex at Keswick Barracks, was responsible for training and maintaining some 140 to 150 remounts. My father, Lieutenant-Colonel Frank Cawley MC, was officer-in-charge of the Remount section between 1922 and 1939 and I grew up as a child and teenager in this environment. Indeed, I was a cadet attached to it for a few years. Members of this elite unit were a group of very versatile horsemen, mostly diggers from World War I. Not only were they colt-breakers, farriers and saddlers, but also farmers, for they grew all their own fodder. These men performed all necessary mounted ceremonial duties as required by state occasions.

The horses were spelled in paddocks in the Adelaide Hills, which meant they had to travel through many closely settled suburbs to reach the barracks on the edge of the Adelaide city square mile.

Prior to travelling 'on the string'—a long line of horses tied four abreast and all connected to a central chain that was linked to a horse ridden out front—these mobs of horses were driven loose in mobs of around 100 head. The hindrance, even danger, they caused to other traffic does not need elaboration. The nuisance value to residents along their path may not be so obvious.

The most frequently travelled route was along the busy South Road. The good citizens who lived in well-populated areas must have heaved a collective sigh of relief when no more loose mobs came their way. Despite the vigilance of the outriders, it was not uncommon for cunning old remounts to divert smartly through an open front gate for a refreshing roll in a vegetable patch. Upon being chased out by an angry housewife, there was always the chance they would knock over the clothes-line props and make a mess of the washing. There was the ever-present hazard also of footpaths fouled in a most unmilitary manner, or of hedges having chunks bitten out of them.

Fortunately, in those days, people were not so prone to sue for damages over such incidents. Housewives were content to arm themselves with brooms to ensure their gardens were not invaded. People generally understood the ways of animals then; indeed many of them would have had a buggy horse down in the backyard, which no doubt occasionally caused them similar problems.

Another well-beaten track for the loose mobs ran between spelling paddocks in separate areas of the Hills. This was my favourite track and I made every effort to tag along when the mob headed that way. One of my tasks was to assist the junior man to hold the grazing horses together while the senior members visited certain licensed premises 'to confer on the next leg of the trip'. I did not mind this at all, as they would emerge after 30 or 40 minutes laughing and joking in high spirits, and sometimes we staged two-horse races on straight stretches.

By contrast, when the horses were on the strings, incidents were few, no doubt due to the fine horsemanship of their handlers. A photograph shows a double string in the foreground, followed immediately behind the wagon by the outrider, who in turn is followed by a single string of remounts—about 100 horses all told. It also shows that each lead rider, or pointsman, is leading a horse on either hand. These are the most valuable remounts— officers' chargers, special animals which required individual care. It can be seen that many of the remounts near the head of the string are half-draughts or 'gunners'. They were used in the six- horse teams which drew the artillery field-guns.

The essential trick in managing these strings was to keep the main chain from becoming slack. If this happened, and one or more of the horses got a leg over the chain, there was the possibility of a certain amount of chaos, including injuries, broken halters and loose horses—and eventually, a difficult explanation of the circumstances to an unreceptive father, who was wont to believe that men, not horses, were to blame for such occurrences.

Only the most honest of horses were used as point-horses; they were invariably those used as leaders in the gun teams. These were magnificent horses, including many fine mares, of great courage and intelligence, which would respond immediately to their rider's signals and never give up trying. They were leaders in every sense of the word. The men involved needed to be very alert, to prevent the string from wandering. Turning corners required great care, as the natural tendency for the string was to cut corners, and it could be very exciting for the centre pointsman trying to keep the horses off culvert posts and parked cars.

The strings usually moved at walking pace, but did trot when necessary, particularly for the first couple of miles when they were fresh from the paddock, or when time had to be made up. The tremendous clatter of 100 freshly shod remounts trotting through the Hills village of Summertown remains with me still.

Recollections of a chief superintendent
Jack Cawley, QPM

The Royal visit of 1954 was fast approaching and as Sergeant-in- Charge of the SA Mounted Police Cadre, I had spent eighteen months buying and training suitable horses and schooling riders for the ceremonial duties they would perform. By early March, we had been given the details of the various escorts we would be required to perform, including routes and timings, and I really worked the men and horses hard over that last period, sometimes traversing the routes late at night, or around daylight, so as to avoid traffic. We did that much road work that some horses were wearing out a set of shoes in a week.

Great care was taken in looking after the horses, for each man knew if his designated horse was injured, he could expect to be riding a very inexperienced mount as a replacement. I shared this concern, and it did nothing for my nerve when, early in March, Adelaide experienced its worst ever earthquake. I recall hearing a loud noise and being thrown out of bed in the early hours of the morning, then heading for the stables at top speed, leaving my wife and children groping around in the dark for candles. I found the horses standing as if petrified, with startled and puzzled expressions on their faces. Perhaps they thought that I had gone overboard with some new training device.

The night guard told me that the horses had been unusually quiet and immobile for several minutes prior to the 'quake. It was most unusual for the stables to be completely quiet—there was always the rattle of a manger chain as one of the 40 or so horses changed position—so it seems that the horses had some warning.

My wife has never completely forgiven me for my reaction to the 'quake, and maybe I did have my priorities a bit mixed up, but it would have been a very serious thing for me if any of the horses had been harmed.

There were some real characters among the greys, including Police Horse Frond. He was one of the fine, old station horses purchased in 1936 and lived to quite a ripe old age. Hundreds of dawn patrols around the East End Market and also the Central Market resulted in Frond becoming very partial to certain fruit and vegetables, and the odd berry or flower. At a time when ladies wore hats, often festooned with artificial fruit or flowers, he would grab a mouthful of these embellishments, unless his rider was very alert.

Police Horse Vincent was a likeable larrikin responsible for some mysterious goings-on in the main stable block. The constable on night shift reported that the stable lights were mysteriously coming on and going off at irregular intervals and that though he had carried out immediate, intensive searches of the area, he had been unable to locate the culprit. The mystery was cleared up the next night. Vincent had discovered that by rearing and making some minor contortions, he could reach the pull switch which operated the main bank of lights. He was caught red- handed pulling the switch cord with his teeth.

Normandy was another outstanding police horse, very intelligent and very brave. I cannot recall him ever being frightened by any of the usual things that scare horses. I rode him at many big fires in the city at night, and found that speeding fire engines, wailing sirens, flashing lights or fire itself caused him no worries at all, even at very close quarters. At one big fire, firemen were using grappling irons to pull sheets of hot iron and burning timbers down onto the roadway, where, astride Normandy, I was trying to keep members of the public out of harm's way. Normandy marched back and forth without even a passing glance.

Crowd control, especially at protests, was often a hazardous exercise. In 1971 demonstrations against the presence of the South African Springbok rugby team became at times very aggressive. At one time, an angry mob vented its political frustrations onto a mounted constable and his horse, Delta. Under siege from firecrackers, the rider was singed and deafened for a few days. It would have been great if there had been an organisation similar to Friends of the Dolphins to prevent ill-treatment of the horses. Apparently protesters saw harassment of animals differently 24 years ago.

We returned to barracks after midnight and I noticed nothing untoward when I checked over the horses. Next morning, however, Delta was showing signs of discomfort, which progressed to an attack of colic. I called a vet, but the horse showed little response and by the following morning he was in bad shape. Three vets attended, the horse was anaesthetised, rolled on his back, and propped up with bags of chaff while he underwent major abdominal surgery. The vets worked urgently for a considerable time before they located and untwisted his bowel. Our joy quickly turned to despair: he died just when we were expecting him to recover consciousness. The stress he suffered at the hands of the protesters, or the colic which it induced, undoubtedly caused Delta's death. They killed him as surely as if they had shot him.

Singing for their tucker
Dick Hobley

Feed time for the 150 or so squadron horses was always a cause for much celebration—by the horses. Even if our own farm mounts had been drafted into our regiment, the 10th Light Horse, based at Bunbury, they soon learnt the routine of military life, as well as what many of the commands meant, particularly those to do with food.

A typical day for a Light Horseman started with reveille at 6 am, followed shortly after by a second bugle call peculiar only to horsed units. This was called 'Stables', and was quite melodious in the early morning air. Someone even proposed words that went somehow as follows:

Oh come to the stables
All those who are able
And water your poor horses
And give them some c-o-r-n
Water your poor horses
And give 'em some corn.

So we marched to the horse lines, some 150 or so yards from the tent lines, where our horses—for which we were paid an extra 10 shillings a week if we supplied our own—were tied side by side in long rows to ropes stretching between posts. Another rope, parallel and on the ground, ran behind their back legs, to which each was fastened with a strap around their nearside fetlock—so they couldn't kick each other.

Our first job on reaching the horse lines each morning was to remove the canvas rug from each horse and groom it thoroughly with our standard-issue brushes and curry combs. Then the horses were untied and led to water, usually one man to two horses, while the remaining men were on wheelbarrow and shovel duty cleaning up the deposits of manure from behind each

horse. While the horses were at water, the nosebags containing their ration of feed were brought out and placed on the ground in front of each horse's position on the line. These were filled overnight with chaff and small measures of oats and bran by the night picket and left unmixed.

Once each horse had been returned to its place and tied up, anticipation ran high along the lines. The officer-in-charge would bellow the order, 'Stand to your Feed.' The men standing alongside each nosebag snapped to attention, and at the same time a ripple of excitement would spread through the line of horses. With nickers of expectation, heads would toss, and feet stamp. Then came the next order, 'Mix Feed', which would be followed by even more excitement along the line of waiting mounts—shuffling and more throaty calls of encouragement. Finally the order of 'Feed' rang out, greeted by a loud cheering chorus of whinnies from the recipients. The morning horse chores completed, the men were then marched back to the squadron parade ground to prepare for their own breakfast, leaving the horses to enjoy their feed in the care of the men who had been allotted the duty of 'day stables'.

The English horse
J L Gallagher

I am not the sort of bloke who makes a habit of stealing horses, but I did pinch one back in 1918—and it did not trouble my conscience a bit. I had inherited a fine horse from one of our troop sergeants who was evacuated with serious wounds. Black Prince was the horse's name. He was by Pistol, the son of Carbine, the Melbourne Cup winner, and was reckoned to be one of the best horses in the regiment. He carried me well and I was pleased to have him under me when we charged at Beersheba. Later we were sent into the Judean Hills as infantry and our horses were moved back to Ramleh. Unfortunately, German planes raided the horse lines and hundreds of horses were set loose in an effort to reduce casualties.

When the raid was over, Black Prince could not be found. He was discovered, eventually, on the horse-lines of a British artillery battery. Our blokes did the right thing and politely asked for his return, but the Brits knew they were onto a good one and refused. In fact, they claimed that he had always been with the battery.

Until such time as a remount could be sent up to me, I was allowed to pick a horse from captured Turkish animals. I chose a nice grey Arab stallion that had been an enemy officer's mount and liked him very much, but the arrangement was only a temporary one. Grey horses are too conspicuous, and as this one was also a stallion, he was not too popular on the horse lines, but he served me well in the meantime.

Because shipments of Australian horses stopped in 1917, due to the dangers of German submarines and a shortage of ships, few good types were available as remounts. I was given a heavy, roman-nosed Argentine that looked as though he should have been in a milk cart. He could not run out of sight on a dark night, and it was obvious that he would fold up quickly when worked hard. We all agreed that my new horse was a liability and started hatching wild plans to steal back Black Prince.

After a bit of discussion we decided we would let the Brits keep the black horse, but we would swipe an animal of similar quality from them. This meant that it had to be an officer's horse, as British lower ranks usually rode horses about as good as my Argentine remount. By contrast, the officers had blood horses that would make any horse-lover green with envy. However, many of these fine, energetic chargers had too much go in them for their riders, and this was the key to our plan.

A friend of one of our mates was in one of the remount squadrons and had been on loan to the Brits as a rough-rider. Most of his work consisted of exercising officers' chargers so that they did not get too energetic for the officers concerned. He was free to come and go as he pleased and had access to some of the best horses in the army. The rough-rider showed the correct degree of indignation when told of the loss of Black Prince and agreed that Australia's honour was at stake. He told us to leave everything to him and he would send word when a suitable horse became available. Somehow our squadron leader heard of the plot, and while professing to know nothing about it, mentioned where a set of Australian Army hoof brands could be found. He also mentioned several troopers who were expert in changing horses' appearances.

We had to move quickly, for it was rumoured that a big push was imminent and we were sure to be moving from our present camp, which was only a couple of miles from the British base where the rough-rider was working. He sent me word. I was to ride out at night and meet him at a spot midway between our respective camps.

So after alerting my mates, I saddled my useless remount and rode to the rendezvous. The rough-rider was there already, holding the reins of a beautiful bay horse. In seconds we had swapped saddles and bridles. The Argentine would be taken back and left on the British horse lines in the charger's place. Suspicion for the theft would fall on late visitors to the camp. The rough-rider was not worried about being seen leaving the base. It was dark and he assured me that British sentries did not have a bushman's eye for a horse. They were used to him coming and going and as long as he rode the same colour horse, nobody would notice that he had switched mounts.

I enjoyed my ride back to camp, and my mates were waiting for me when I rode in. A series of subtle changes, hoof brands, and even a fake brand plucked into the hair on his shoulder soon had my English horse looking like any other Australian troop horse. I was worried, though, because little could be done to alter the beautiful lines of the horse. To me, he stuck out like a sore toe. I would know him again if I found his bones in the stew.

The storm broke just as we were saddled and ready to march. A very valuable horse had been stolen from the Brits and our brigade's horses were to be inspected. I sweated blood for a while as a group of officers came along the ranks, but I need not have worried. Neither horse nor owner gave any sign of recognition as the inspectors passed.

Despite his obviously pampered upbringing, the horse settled well into his role as a trooper's mount. He was willing and as tough as goats' knees, lapping up the attention that I lavished upon him and responding well whenever I needed an extra effort. He carried me through that terrible retreat on the Second Es Salt Stunt and was without water for so long that the girth was too big for his shrunken belly. Together we participated in the most successful cavalry actions of modern times, and in many engagements I had reason to bless his strength and courage. Only once did I wish that he was not quite so good.

We were scouting the advance on the old Roman town of Tiberius and the intentions of the retreating Turks were unknown. They could have left the town, they could be waiting to surrender or they could be holding it in strength. There was only one way to find out. Four of us scouts were ordered to advance into the town or advance till we came under fire, whichever event happened first. If the Turks were going to make a fight of it we would be the first ones to find out.

We decided to go in at the gallop, in the hope that our speed would make us a bit harder to hit. Someone shouted, 'Go!' and the four of us spurred toward the town. My horse swept past the others and I crouched low on his neck, waiting for the first shots. They did not come, and at first I thought that the enemy were gone, but as we drew nearer, I glimpsed grey uniforms moving among the buildings. The Turks were still there. We were in easy rifle shot but there was no firing, so I did not alter course or slacken pace. I was gambling on the fact that the enemy troops were waiting to surrender as I let the horse stretch out. It was no use trying to turn around. If they wanted to shoot me they would get me anyway.

My mates were a long way behind as I raced past the first couple of buildings and started to steady my mount. There I was, the first Australian soldier into Tiberius. I tried to ignore large groups of fully armed Turks and hoped that none of them were nervous types. It was a strange sensation to be surrounded by so many of the enemy and I suddenly wished that I had not won the race to the town by such a long margin. Even when my three mates galloped up, the situation looked far from good. Fortunately, the Turks had decided to surrender.

The English horse survived the war and we won a few quid with him at inter-service race meetings, but then the order came that we were all dreading. The horses were to be handed in to the remount depots. A few would be kept for the army of occupation; unfit animals and those older than twelve years were to be shot and the rest sold locally. We were horrified at the thought of our loyal horses falling into the hands of the Arabs, for we had seen too many examples of their cruelty. The troops were disgusted that their horses should be treated in such a manner, but the orders had to be obeyed. Our officers let it be known that if a man said his horse was older than twelve, no-one would look at its teeth. It was a cruel choice, a bullet or years of suffering and misery worse than what they had already endured, but it was a choice that I did not have to make.

I went down with the Spanish 'flu and was seriously ill for some weeks. The British unit from which we had originally stolen the horse was in the district and my mates undertook to smuggle him back to them, in the hope that he would be saved for incoming British troops. They never told me if they were successful, and I did not have the heart to ask. I would like to think that he went back to a life of ease in England, even though such a fate would be highly unlikely.

Defending the shores
Dick Hobley

My time with the 10th Light Horse Regiment was from July 1941 until the unit, the last fully horsed unit in Australia, was disbanded in May 1944. During this time, at least some portion of the regiment was on continuous coast-watching duty on Western Australia's west coast.

Our regiment was given the task of patrolling a 60-mile stretch of coast just to the north of Perth. Each troop of 32 men was made responsible for a 15-mile stretch of beach and sandhills to watch for enemy submarines and foreign landings. These patrols were always done at night, in silence and regardless of weather conditions. Since we were not allowed to carry lighting of any kind, we had to develop acute observational skills in order to determine if anything unusual was occurring. It was thought that enemy forces could come ashore to probe

Horses in uniform

Australia's defences or to replenish fresh water supplies. Things we had to watch for were boats pulled into the beach, tracks, voices, and any objects which had appeared since our previous shift the night before.

We found, through long experience, that by far the best conditions were clear nights with no moon. Our eyes soon adjusted to the lack of light and the horses were quite relaxed. We often had trouble controlling our horses on bright, moonlit nights. The shadows of clouds scudding in off the sea made them particularly jumpy and nervous.

So each night, men and horses combed the beaches before returning to their posts at dawn. The horses were watered and fed and the riders tried to get some sleep before saddling up again next night. After a month of coast-watch duty, another squadron from our Wanneroo camp, 12 miles inland, would take over.

Although accidents and incidents were few on those night patrols, there was a certain amount of danger, and not always did this have anything to do with a foreign enemy.

On one occasion, when the regiment was based in Bunbury and we were out on a night manoeuvre nearby, a friend of mine, Bill, had a rather unpleasant experience. We were negotiating some very steep sand dunes when Bill's horse suddenly staggered and dropped dead from a coronary. It came to rest with its legs pointing uphill, but with Bill still astride, his head pointing downhill, and unable to move. The weight of the now-dead horse had him firmly pinned down and the steel arch of the pommel of his military saddle was jammed into his groin. Because the incident occurred at night, it was a little while before we were aware of his plight and able to lift enough of the weight of the dead horse to allow a much-relieved, but still intact, Bill to get free.

Storm over the seas
Chris Stoney

At Barclay's Flat on the Bluff Range in Victoria's high plain country, the evening air was oppressive as an approaching thunderstorm swept up the Howqua Valley towards the Great Divide. James Barclay, one of the first to run cattle on the high country beyond the Howqua Valley, was worried. His best mare was on the point of foaling and his concern increased as the most violent storm for years broke overhead. With the help of Jack Bullock, his partner on the cattle run, James quietly caught the mare and tied her under the lean-to verandah of the hut, out of the worst of the storm. As the elements raged, a brown filly was successfully born, and was named Storm on the spot by the two men.

Some years later, Jack Bullock, who in 1914 had flipped a coin with James Barclay to see who would fight for his country and who would look after their cattle, was in France as a member of the 4th Light Horse. He was sitting idly on a rail of the army horseyards watching a large shipment of new horses milling around. Something about a brown mare caught his eye. Was it the carriage of her head or was it her eye that made her look familiar? Jack's mates scoffed when he said that he knew the horse. He went into the yard and caught her. The brand J B on her shoulder increased his interest in her. However, initial inquiries showed the mare probably wasn't even born when he left Australia for the war.

Not satisfied, Jack Bullock went to the sergeant in charge and after a long search of the records, it was established beyond doubt that the mare had been purchased from his partner, James Barclay of Mansfield! The mare was indeed the foal, Storm, which Jack Bullock had watched being born in 1914—and had not seen since because of his almost immediate departure to join the Light Horse.

A B 'Banjo' Paterson
'The Last Parade'

With never a sound of trumpet,
With never a flag displayed,
The last of the old campaigners
Lined up for the last parade.

Weary they were and battered,
Shoeless, and knocked about;
From under their ragged forelocks
Their hungry eyes looked out.

And they watched as the old commander
Read out to the cheering men
The Nation's thanks, and the orders
To carry them home again.

And the last of the old campaigners,
Sinewy, lean, and spare—
He spoke for his hungry comrades;
'Have we not done our share?

'Starving and tired and thirsty
We limped on the blazing plain;
And after a long night's picket
You saddled us up again.

'We froze on the wind-swept kopjes
When the frost lay snowy-white,
Never a halt in the daytime,
Never a rest at night!

Great Australian Working Horse Stories

'We knew when the rifles rattled
From the hillside bare and brown,
And over our weary shoulders
We felt warm blood run down,

'As we turned for the stretching gallop,
Crushed to the earth with weight;
But we carried our riders through it—
Sometimes, perhaps, too late.

'Steel! We were steel to stand it—
We that have lasted through,
We that are old campaigners
Pitiful, poor, and few.

'Over the sea you brought us,
Over the leagues of foam:
Now we have served you fairly
Will you not take us home?

'Home to the Hunter River,
To the flats where the lucerne grows;
Home where the Murrumbidgee
Runs white with the melted snows.

'This is a small thing, surely!
Will not you give command
That the last of the old campaigners
Go back to their native land?'

They looked at the grim commander,
But never a sign he made.
'Dismiss!' and the old campaigners
Moved off from their last parade.

Twelve
Tales of misadventure

The stories in this section are all from the old days. They are of incidents that were so spectacularly terrible that you'd hope nothing like them could be repeated in modern times. Not only could horses bolt leaving a trail of damage, but heavy machinery brought its own inherent dangers. People were frequently killed and horses also died when things went wrong. Unfortunately, death and injury still occur on farms with tractors and motorised machinery, the successors to heavy horses.

Horseriding deaths also still occur regularly each year. After a series of tragedies during eventing competitions worldwide, jumps are being redesigned to prevent them acting as a fulcrum over which a horse and rider make a slow forward somersault, the most dangerous fall because of the likelihood of the horse crushing the rider. Administrators have introduced new rules and emphasise the need for high standards of horse and rider training. Even leisure riders are urged to attend riding clinics, use approved helmets and learn safe methods of handling horses.

Will Ogilvie
'Rider Less'

A broken bridle trailing,
A saddle scratched and scarred—
And Brown Bee at the railing
That rings the station yard;
No stockman sits astride her,
But, by those flanks a-foam,
Wild Terror was the rider
That lashed the good mare home.
His saddle and his bridle
We've softly laid aside,
We'll leave the rough gear idle
Till he comes back to ride ...

The last straw
Dick Hobley

It was January 1936, I was just 14, and harvest was in full swing. Having left school about halfway through the previous year, I was helping my father by sewing bags and being the general wood and water Joey. We were camped at the out-camp at the northern end of the property for convenience.

As one harvester had broken down it was decided to rotate the two teams on the one machine that was operational. We would work right through the day by changing teams at about 1 pm. This routine had been followed for some days quite uneventfully until the day that one team 'bolted'.

Being 1936, and some three years before bulk-handling was introduced at the local siding, the wheat was emptied from the harvester into three bushell bags and arranged in a dump in rows of three, probably twenty bags long, depending

Tales of misadventure

a bit on the size of the truck that was going to cart the grain to the siding. Wally, the teamster working for the farmer with whom we were share-cropping, was emptying the grain box of the harvester when Dad arrived with our team to change over. He left the fresh team standing behind the harvester while he began to unhook the chains on the team that had worked through the morning. Without warning, the front team took off, circling the dump of wheat, with Dad hanging grimly to the reins and Wally running along behind in an attempt to catch up.

From my vantage point at the hut on the other side of the fence about 50 yards from the action—where I was boiling the billy for lunch—it looked like some crazy comedy routine. I was awestruck at all this machinery running around out of control, and the sound of jangling chains, thudding hooves and clacking harvester.

There were these eight heavy horses—four in front and four behind—in chains, galloping along pulling the harvester. The other team of eight fresh horses started to follow along, also yoked up in tandem. As the speed of the front team increased, the machine, which was not designed to travel faster than about three miles an hour, started ejecting all sorts of belts and chains off its cogs and wheels.

The first time around the dump of wheat sacks, the 10-foot comb of the harvester, which is offset to the right of the team, ripped through some nearby standing bags of grain, skewering a whole row of sacks, and dragged them along like sausages on a stick. Surprisingly, this didn't seem to cause any slackening of pace. On the second revolution, the fresh team, normally quite reliable and docile, found itself overwhelmed by the chaos. The so-called tired team with all those, by now, empty bags impaled on the combs had caught up with the rather puzzled fresh horses on their circles around the bag dump. So there they were, the fresh team, two rows of them coupled four abreast, galloping for their lives just in front of the comb fearsomely laden with dragging wheat bags.

A cloud of dust rose over the scene, and Wally, who had almost given up the chase behind the machine, tripped and fell. Before he had time to scramble up, one of the fresh horses that had broken its coupling from its three companions and was blindly careering along in the dust, trod on him. Wally emerged out of the billowing clouds of dust, limping, with torn clothing and a grazed hip.

Dad, who in the meantime had been trying to get control of the reins, could not stop them circling left around the dump, because the offside rein to the leaders had become wedged into part of the forecarriage of the harvester. Eventually, he too was forced to abandon ship, and the horses—released of any restraint—headed out into the middle of the paddock into the unstripped crop. They did several large circles, similar to a bee leaving a waterhole, then they headed straight for the biggest tree in the shade patch in the corner of the paddock. This they hit fair and square in the middle of the comb, which brought their progress to a rather sudden halt.

The one horse that had not been involved in any of the preceding events was Dad's old saddle horse, Star, a lively bay gelding who also did duty as part-time sulky horse when need arose. I was instructed to return to the horseyards, yoke Star into the sulky and pick up as many of the belts and chains and tools and general bits and pieces of the harvester I could find that had been scattered around the paddock. The men would retrieve the loose team of fresh horses and unyoke the thoroughly discredited morning team from the shattered remains of the harvester.

Horses seem to have the ability to transmit their moods from one to another, so Star, who would have heard all the commotion in the wheat paddock, was rather jumpy by the time I got him into the shafts of the sulky and heading through the gateway to do my job.

Halfway through the gate, he suddenly veered to the left, just enough for the wheels of the sulky to hit the gatepost a glancing blow. Star sprang forward, and the leather traces broke. The shafts slipped out of the tugs on the sulky saddle and their points were dragged along the ground. The only things at this stage that were keeping the horse attached to the sulky were the reins, which I was holding onto desperately, and the breeching straps on the harness. All this was too much for Star. He started to buck to get rid of the weight of the sulky as it pressed down unfamiliarly on his rump where the breeching straps passed and tied onto the shafts. And since he was successful at severing this connection with the sulky, all that now remained were the reins.

At about this point, the two metal uprights at each side of the splashboard bent forward under the strain of my desperately braced feet. I was dragged out over the splashboard and the sulky came to rest. I now had two choices—hang onto the reins and be dragged across the paddock, or let go. I chose the latter. Star disappeared at full gallop towards the furthest corner of the paddock, with loose reins and broken harness flapping behind him.

I limped back to camp to report this second misadventure for the day to my father, who was still trying to untangle the team wrapped around the tree. To say that he was not amused would be an understatement. From the wheat paddock, he had been able to witness Star's performance, so there was little need to say much. He just stoically set about repairing the other harvester, and in a few days' time, continued reaping.

We decided that the morning team obviously had not been as tired as they should have been, and being Wally's horses, they had probably spooked when Dad started unhitching them. In future weeks we also decided that Star would no longer be any good as a sulky horse; after the accident, he spent his time in the shafts continually looking around behind him, as if he was checking that nothing was going wrong.

Took fright
Bruce Rodgers

There was always a danger using horse teams, because if they took fright and bolted while a man was in the middle of the team hooking their chains on, he did not have a chance, as the
implement would be hard to avoid. My father and his brother were partners and one morning they were attaching horses to a wagon that was used for carting water, 1000 gallons per load, but it was empty at the time. They had an eight-horse team and were putting a young horse they had bred, but which had been in the team only a few days before, in what is known as the body of the team. My uncle was in between the young horse and its teammate hooking up the chains, when something, or it seems nothing, startled them and they bolted. My uncle hung on to the hames for about 45 yards and then fell to the ground. He was killed instantly by the wheels of the wagon passing over him.

After a hard day's work
Joe Dickson

My father owned a team from 1908 to 1948 which he used to cart wool and other loads around the Longreach area. On one particular trip in 1948, Dad and my brother Les each had 12 tons of wool on their wagons, which they were hauling from Brookwood, 12 miles west of Muttaburra, to the railhead at Longreach. It had been a very hot day, so they camped the night at a very big waterhole on the Thomson River. After Dad had unyoked the 24 horses in his team and Les had unyoked his twenty, Les drove the horses down to the river for a drink.
The water was very deep and the banks were steep, so the moment the horses walked into the water, they had to swim. Suddenly Les realised that they were all swimming to the

other side of the river, so he cantered down to where the river narrowed and crossed there. By that time the team horses were coming out of the waterhole, so he pushed them back.

When they swam back to the middle of the waterhole, Major, the leader and best horse in the team, went under, came up again, and then went down for a second time. He didn't come up again. Next morning we found him floating on top of the water, smothered in turtles. Dad said the horse had got cramps after his hard day's work. He had been our best worker, always keeping his chains tight and the team straight. He was sadly missed.

Danger in fright
Rudi Fuss

I am now 90 years old, but in my early years on the farm, I had a close association with horses that lasted for 40 years. Looking back on the number of horse teams operating and the long hours we spent with them, it amazes me that there weren't more fatal accidents.

There was one occasion in our area, though, where a team under the control of one lad, began to fidget, then took fright, split and turned back towards the implement. They pulled it back on top of him, killing him instantly.

Then there was a riding horse I purchased to carry me to and from work, a distance of one mile. I used to carry a tin lunchbox, which I had on a string over one shoulder. On one particular occasion, the box must have hit the ground as I placed a foot in the stirrup. It made a loud noise, which frightened the horse. He took off, dragging me about 20 yards. I seemed to live a lifetime in those few seconds. Had my foot not come free, I would certainly have been dragged to death, as the horse seemed to go berserk and galloped around for quite a while. Although I rode him a few times later, I never enjoyed it.

'Doctor' treats the survivors
Roy Hentschke

During the 1914 drought, my father was able to maintain a twelve-horse team only through resorting to feeding them cereal straw from thatched shed roofs and shelter stacks. At the break of the drought, he was making plans for his cropping programme the following winter season, with only limited hay and chaff available for his team.

One morning a traveller called in with two light draught horses in a four-wheeled buggy, or trap, as they were known. After introducing himself as a specialist horse doctor, he advised the use of a special powder to remove blood worms and sand from the stomach of the horses, which of course would give the team a better chance of coping with the light rations they would be on. Father bought enough to drench the team and a few days later, carried out the drenching. All horses were treated except for a pair of two-year-old geldings in a back paddock.

Tragedy struck within hours when the horses showed evidence of sickness. Local vets were called in, as well as farmers who had a good knowledge of horses, but it was no use. All drenched horses died within a day. Small amounts of powder were analysed and it was found to be arsenic.

The horses' bodies were dragged to an area in the scrub and fired with timber. The burn marks of those fires are still visible on the sheet limestone today as a graphic reminder of a terrible disaster. The two young geldings named Nugget and Duke lived on, and in 1932, when I worked the horses as a lad, they were included in a team of eight pulling a four-furrow plough.

The traveller was never seen again.

The horse stayed
Denis Adams

In 1903, according to the late Oliver Mould of Milang, two men were loading rubble onto a tip-dray out east of the Wellington Ferry. When some of the rubble hit the horse, it bolted along the lane towards the Murray River. When it reached the bank, it tried to stop, but could not get a foothold on the punt flap, so horse and loaded dray went into the deep water. Oliver thought they retrieved the dray later on, but the horse stayed.

A kick in the mouth
B L Doyle

As a very green, but willing, city teenager, I was given the job of making charcoal for the station vehicles fitted with gas-producing units. This was up at Cloncurry, at 'Byrimine', in 1940. I had been equipped with pick, bar and shovel, a light draught mare that had only ever been used for pack work, an old dray, and a freshly oiled, but very old, harness that had hung in the shed for several years. The pack mare had never been driven in reins, so it was decided to lead her off another horse.

With no prior experience in the charcoal-burning game, I got stuck into the task, which involved collecting and burning timber in pits. A few weeks later I had some bags of good clean charcoal produced. But I must have been getting a little weary, because I made a mistake late one afternoon that the dray mare didn't appreciate.

I had stopped to dismount, to load some billets of dry, old bloodwood onto the dray. It's possible the mare in the dray had taken an extra step, but when I lifted my right leg to swing it over the back of my riding horse so I could drop to the ground, I inadvertently hit the dray horse in the mouth. She immediately pulled back, and as I was leading her with quite a short rope and was afraid of losing her, I held on to my end tightly. The old leather winkers couldn't hack the pressure and parted between her ears. I will never forget the look on that mare's face when she saw the dray behind her. I sat on my horse and watched in amazement as the packhorse, and her dray, took off in a frenzy.

She careered through the scattered dead timber, with her load becoming lighter as each billet of cut wood fell off. After a few hundred yards, when all the wood had fallen off, she lined up a couple of solid trees, just the same width apart as the dray wheels. Both wheels hit the trees simultaneously and the poorly maintained harness exploded. I can still see the hames flying high above the scene.

I caught the mare at the horse paddock gate, standing head down with the collar behind her ears.

Two times the loser
Wendy Treloar

A horse was all that old Carl owned. He was an identity in our district and, clearly, he loved that old horse. He talked to it constantly as he transported both himself and produce around the town. While he was delivering a load of posts one hot day, Carl took his draught horse up over a dam bank so the horse could have a drink. Unfortunately, the steepness of the bank caused the load to slip forward, pushing the harnessed horse and dray into the dam.

Poor Carl was sobbing by the time he reached my Dad and his brothers, having run miles to summon help. The men dived and fought the cold water, stiff harness and the unnerving sight of a drowned horse. Eventually they got the dray back up onto the bank, but not only had Carl lost his old friend, but any further chance of work.

In with the horses
Denis Adams

A wagon and its four-horse team went into the Murray at Wellington in the late 1800s, I think it was. The outfit had crossed on the ferry from the Tailem Bend side. As their owner, a Mr Burgess, led them up the bank, they jibbed. The wagon rolled backwards, taking the horses with it. Mr Burgess clung valiantly to his team and would have gone in too had not some bystanders grabbed him.

Mark of a chisel
Bruce Rodgers

It was spring and our horses were running out in the paddock. One morning I rode out to bring them back home, but two were missing. I looked around and noticed they were both lying down some distance away. On investigation, I found they were both dead, and lying on their left side next to each other.

We had had a thunderstorm during the night and both horses had been struck by lightning. They had a mark in the forehead as though a big wood chisel had been driven in. Their noses were scorched black.

Pulled down
Denis Adams

The town of Peake was once known as Polly's Well. The mare Polly had been drawing water from the well in a 50-gallon 'bucket' with hinged lids in the bottom. She jibbed, and as she shrank back from the hands urging her to do her duty, the weight of the full bucket pulled her down the well. She had to be cut into pieces to get her out.

Reverse action
G Hutchinson

Tom was the station cowboy. His main mission in life was to milk a few cows in the morning, cut a bit of wood for the cook, tend to the gardens, do a few odd jobs about the place, then get the milkers in and lock the calves up. Sometimes he would have to harness the big black Clydesdale horse and go in the dray for a load of firewood. If the old horse was in a nasty mood, and he thought the load was too heavy, he would sometimes jib. When he jibbed and refused to go forward, there was no point putting more pressure on him. He would simply run backwards. The more you belted him, the faster and further he ran backwards.

Tom's workload increased dramatically when the cook went away for a couple of weeks. In addition to his usual chores, he also had to cook for the manager, three ringers and himself. And in addition to that, the dam supplying the homestead with water had gone dry, so he had to cart water from a deep hole in the creek about a mile away.

The four men had gone away mustering early in the morning. Tom did his washing up, milking and so on, then went in the horse and dray with the old steel ship's tank on it to get a load of water. He backed the dray in close to the waterhole, then began the laborious job of filling the tank with a bucket.

When the chore was completed, he asked the old horse to move forward, but the horse was in one of its cranky moods and refused to budge. Tom gave him a good hard crack on the rump with one of the leather reins. The horse hit reverse gear and ran backwards until the whole show was in the waterhole.

When the musterers returned home that evening, there wasn't much activity at the homestead—no tea was cooked, the fire wasn't even alight. Then someone found a note under a tin of jam on the kitchen table. It read: 'The horse is in the crick drownded and I am gorne.'

Thirteen
Farewelling the big horses: the Clydesdales depart

The end of the heavy horse came relatively quickly, hastened by the drought of 1941, which made fodder very expensive.

The option of using a tractor that didn't need dressing and feeding at dawn and could work without fuss on a hot day suddenly became very attractive. It was a painful decision though, to send your best mates to slaughter, or pension them off in the back paddock where they frequently pined for company and daily routine and became dishevelled from lack of grooming, shoeing and health care. Expect a tear in your eye.

No other way
Geoffrey Blight

On a cold winter's morning in June 1957, I gathered up the old, disused dry harness, and picked out six sets of winkers and couplings from the eighteen sets I had at one time known. Then I walked half a mile to a spreading redgum, under which stood a 35-year chapter of my father's life.

Six very old Clydesdale horses stood motionless as I slipped on their headgear for the last time. Slowly manoeuvring the grass-foundered old veterans into a line, I began a very slow and painful 5-mile trek to the nearest siding, and its waiting rail wagon. Behind me, Charlie, Harry, Violet, Bloss, Carb and Rose shuffled and stumbled. Every step was difficult to the

Farewelling the big horses: the Clydesdales depart

legs that strode out at seven miles an hour in their younger days.

We passed a heap of ashes, witness to the painful death of Bonny, who had been down for some time before Dad found her. It was this that had brought about the decision that had me on my present errand. Although he had considered shooting the horses, Dad only owned a 410 shotgun—and this had proved hopeless in helping Bonny. Dad was forced to end her pain in a manner no man could be proud of.

We passed the dam where, three years earlier, Duchess, the jet black mare with her mother's white baldy face, had reared and panicked in the second line on the scoop. Dad had slashed the hame strap to get her out of the chains, then watched as the frightened old mare attempted to gallop, then stagger, a few yards before giving in to a heart that could beat no more.

Through the gate we stumbled, into the paddock from where we had dragged Dick's giant lifeless form twenty months earlier. I had found him lying dead—and it was on that day that muscle finally surrendered to metal—we had eight no longer. Harry was used to drag his lifetime offsider to a scrubby crematorium—while I led the seven ageing survivors to the paddock of plenty, to live out their remaining lives.

With Bonny's lingering death, a kindness had become a cruelty. Now we were walking down a road, the same road that 27 years earlier, a 15-year-old boy, six giant Clydesdales and a sprightly young half-thoroughbred called Carb had jogged and fidgeted. They had joined the road gang that all the family relied on to see them through the worst depression in our nation's history.

Men begged for a day's work for food in those dark days, but horses were scarce. The lad—who was to become my father—was working seven days a week, caring for and driving his charges. My grandfather was so proud of the five well-trained youngsters and one old mare that Dad had grown up with. This pride sits on my mantelpiece to this day in the form of a huge trophy, won repeatedly between 1937 and 1945.

Slowly we moved on at a shuffling pace that would surely take us five hours to cover five miles. We passed the stallion's paddock, empty of the proud giant that once pounded its double fence. As we drew level with the old homestead, I could see my grandmother milking the cows. Dad must have been around somewhere, but I couldn't see him.

The horses looked towards the old stable, with its rotting straw roof, she-oak pole walls and mallet stick gates. Dad and his father before him had spent much of their lives in that stable—time spent among the stalls and boxes; the chaff house at the end. A long row of pegs was laden with hairy massive collars and winkers, in line with the rump of each horse. What painstaking care they had taken when, after a day's work, the horses had been swum through the dam and then laboriously groomed in preparation for their annual pilgrimage to the local show—there to be presented to the community as the pride of a family, to be judged by all the keen eyes and glib mouths of the experts. They'd be released at the end of it all, unbeaten and decked in glory and full harness. Faithfully they would troop the 10 miles home unaccompanied, to stand in that stable and wait the arrival of the district's proudest teamsters.

As an 11-year-old boy, I had battled to reach and lift those massive collars onto the warm, smooth necks. The memories remain of standing to my full height in the feed trough and still failing to reach Charlie, who stood over 18 hands, and Violet, who always stepped backwards, no matter how much I coaxed her. How I prayed for the day when I could harness the whole team, throw open the jail-like stick doors and, on my own, walk down the road at the head of a double line—a 'real man'.

The day arrived when finally I did reach Charlie's wither, and desperately, I raced to harness the rest, building a pile of blocks next to Violet so I could reach. With feverish anticipation, hoping

Farewelling the big horses: the Clydesdales depart

my father wouldn't turn up too soon, I threw open the doors and danced around among the heels, ducking under their necks as the eight horses marched out and were clipped in a double line of four. Then I turned and ran at the front, and the waiting mouldboard. As I passed Dad, who was still feeding the calves, his hidden pride expressed itself with bemusement. 'What's the bloody hurry,' he said.

There had been the same wry smile eighteen months earlier when on having his lunch brought out to the paddock, he had invited his son to fulfil his dream of mounting the plough and having a drive. He watched as the youngster sat erect, reins sagging all the way to the ground, then shouted his first 'Giddup', 'Come back' and 'Gee off' as he made a perfect lap of the 5-acre piece. On his return, he had halted with a 'Whoa' and anxiously asked, 'How's that?' The smile said 'fine' as the boy got down, but then came the words: 'Let's see how the team fare on their own.'

Hanging the reins over the depth lever, he shouted, 'Giddup', and resumed his lunch while a disappointed boy watched the team do a further perfect lap—without a reinsman.

How angry and upset I had been when teased about it, telling my father he could come home for his own lunch if he was so clever. But, underneath, there was always an extraordinary respect for a team I knew was only a reflection of my father and grandfather's exceptional horsemanship.

Finally we passed our recently built house. The only remaining permanent monument to the 55 years of the family's life on the land was now behind us. The only other reminder in view was the cold blue metal of the Fordson kero tractor that had displaced these old brown has-beens. With total supremacy, it daily spat smoke and bragged loudly of its victory. But today it stood silent as the losers passed by for the last time, for its victory had not been one gained without a fight.

Dad only learnt to drive a horseless carriage at the same time as I did, but it was me who was given the job of trying out the new blue four-wheeled wonder. Dad was still so wary, while I was so ambitious and proud, so sure it was truly God's gift. I thought of how I would show my 'horse-proud' father what true power was, as the old and the new went to work together.

Being able to hitch up so much quicker, I didn't notice the challenge of the teamster's gait. Away I went, full throttle in top gear, five miles an hour, not once looking back at Dad hitching his team. When I hit the wet spots in the paddock, I had to drop a gear, tugging at the throttle to hold a grinding three miles an hour. Then I had cleared the wet and again hit top gear, relishing the new-fangled finger-tip workhorse.

Suddenly I became aware of a familiar noise, one I hadn't expected would ever be associated with this greasy, snorting machine. I swung round to see eight pairs of nostrils blowing fire and challenging the right to the job and the land. They stormed clean past me, no matter how hard I tugged or kicked the throttle. And there was that familiar bemused smile, and the pipe trailing whisps of smoke, as my father lolled idly on the seat as he passed me by.

That day the horses won completely. As I made my second run around the paddock, the new blue wonder dug herself a hole in the mud and sat down in defeat. She had to wait for 32 ageing legs to show pity and pull her out. But their victory was short-lived—Dick's death saw to that.

But now time was going fast, and we were going slowly. It tore at me to think that age and idleness, and unlimited feed, had reduced the high-stepping disciplined champions to the painful, limping casualties behind me. I was walking in front, then at the side, finally behind, as I forced the refugees from what had always been their home. God, how it hurt to strike them—to keep them moving on.

But no matter how time moved, still would I stop to rub and pat those familiar outstretched heads. Old Harry was battling. Once he had been the strongest of them all, the one on whom

Farewelling the big horses: the Clydesdales depart

my grandfather had daily staked his life. He was the hay-grab horse, who worked completely unmanned, hitched in the opposite direction to the wagon team, or at the stack. Forward and back, forward and back he would go as the steel grab was filled, then was swung high over my grandfather's head and opened—so many thousands of times. Any mistake, panic or break could have brought the steel grab crashing down on the man as he worked spreading and levelling the stalks below.

Old Bloss was also struggling. Her familiar white baldy face looked so sad. She was the team's hardest worker—never a loose chain held Bloss. Honest as the day is long, she was the horse to which the young, inexperienced horses were hitched. Between her and Rose, they would keep the youngsters in order, no matter how green.

Rose had her ears back—a silent message for me. She was the shaft horse, good on the britchen when brakes were needed. All day she would stand, untied in a two-wheel lorry, loaded with seed and Super, at the paddock's corner and move up to the drill when beckoned.

Violet was the nervous one, the most beautiful of all, but touchy—only ever a team horse, not like the others. She had her place, and God help the man who tried to shift or change her.

The sight of the old school-house suddenly pulled me from my dreams—we were nearly there. It was already noon. The rail truck sat silently at the loading ramp as we crawled into the sleeper-rail stockyards. I unclipped each horse and let them chew on the abundant wild oats of the rarely used pen—a 'last meal of the convicted', it seemed. I shuddered at the thought of the one-way journey that lay ahead.

I led each horse up the ramp and swung them around to make room for the next. When all were on, I didn't shut the door, but stood there looking, checking, rubbing and stroking the moulting outstretched nostrils. I gave into a wish to sit one last time astride Carb—the horse who had taught me to ride.

A sharp whistle brought me to. I slammed the door shut, and clipped the transit cards in place as an impatient train guard grumbled about having to break the train and shunt for one truck of 'broken down nags'. I climbed to the top of the loading ramp and watched as the hissing, choofing steam engine bumped the nervous horses into line.

With the shrill of the whistle and the slow shoo, shoo, shoo of hot steam, away rolled Harry, Charlie, Bloss, Rose, Violet and Carb. After 120 years in Australia, and countless generations before that, a family tradition was about to end—and I was to end it—our dependence on the working horse. How, at that moment, I wished there could have been another way.

Then the last carriage was gone.

Later, as I sat on the beautiful blue leather seats of our new car, and saw the tears in my father's eyes, I understood his absence—and would always remember those tears. From that day on, my world became that of unthinking, cold, shiny machines, machines that never sweated, never bled, never loved, never died. The cheque my father received for the horses' abundant bodies was donated to our local home for the aged—a reminder to him always of those magnificent creatures who, like us, grew old.

Clash of the cultures
Denis Adams

Grandfather's contempt fairly seared the paintwork on their first tractor—an insipid little Fordson. It could never start with him watching.

'Give that thing a pull, Harry,' he'd roar, and the poor, cowering little thing would go bounding and bucking along the drive behind a twenty-horse team, backfiring and blowing black smoke till it started—out of sheer terror, Mum used to say. It was always kept out of sight, like a leper, used only for menial tasks like cutting chaff.

When the first motorbikes appeared on the roads, a lot of young blades used to come quietly up behind a horse-drawn vehicle, then opening the throttle wide, they'd roar past right under the horses' noses. You can imagine the reaction. Lucky no-one was killed. Grandpa used to tie a noose in the end of his buggy whip and try to snare them as they came up behind him. After a few near misses, the local lads gave him a wide berth.

It was sad seeing the demise of the faithful workhorse, but there are still a few around. Who knows—perhaps there will be a place for some in the future. They are cost-efficient, non-polluting, quiet running, their waste is a valuable fertiliser, and they can be recycled too; during Napoleon's retreat from Moscow his men ate their horses, but Hitler's troops could not eat their tanks.

The tin horse nuzzles the old boys aside
Jill Dobbs

I only learnt to ride when I got married because it was plain that if I didn't, I would see almost nothing of my new husband, John. When he wasn't actually in the saddle doing water runs three times a week, in hot weather, or stock work, he was breaking in horses, or shoeing them, or instructing the succession of 16-year- old boys who passed through his hands how to treat the saddle sores and girth galls they had caused. John was as light as a feather in the saddle himself, upright and unmoving.

He liked being with horses. He was, as his father put it, the sort of horseman who would walk four miles to catch his horse, in order to ride three miles. Not that he was fond of walking. Twice, to my knowledge, when vehicles stranded him out on the run in pre-CB radio days, rather than walk home, he walked to the nearest watering point, waited for the horses to come in, caught one, and rode it home without saddle or bridle, and only a stick for a rudder.

John stopped breaking in horses for us and for the station several years ago when it became apparent that there was going to be no-one to ride them but us and the children, who weren't always going to be with us. The staff had dwindled in numbers and those we had were mechanically minded rather than horse oriented. John himself had found the convenience of riding a motorbike irresistible for some years before that.

The 1982 drought accounted for the older and weaker horses, and all we are left with now are the few that were young and strong and lucky, then. They have worked hard in their time, though, and now they are retirees, John continues to guard what he sees as their right to stay on here, even in these dry times.

As he goes about his business in the paddock on his 'tin horse', as he calls his Yamaha 350, he often comes across these old work mates, who stop eating and look up. Occasionally, he stops the bike. The horses don't run away, but they don't come closer any more, either. I don't think he even actually speaks to them, so if they reminisce together, all these old guys, it must be by mental telepathy. But I daresay that's how a lot of communication was between them in the old days anyway.

'Get a bloody horse'
Alex Haley

There were no tractors on our farm. We used draught horses to do everything. When the neighbours, the Barrs, bought a second- hand International tractor and invited Dad and my older brothers to go and watch it work, Dad said they were silly people, as with the war and all, it wouldn't be long before there wouldn't be fuel to run the damn thing. My brothers were impressed by its simplicity. All you had to do was turn on the fuel, pull the choke out, put the crank handle in place and pull up quickly. When the engine fired up, you hurriedly pushed in the choke, and after it ran for a few minutes, you turned off the petrol and switched over to kerosene, and you were ready to start work.

Compared to a 4 am rising from a warm bed and tipping ten buckets of chaff into ten feed boxes, brushing ten horses and putting their harness on, the brothers said to Dad a tractor might be a good idea. Dad said we would buy one as soon as they brought out one that runs on chaff. 'But you wait and see,' he said. 'In a year or two they will all be going back to horses.' Dad eventually got to drive a tractor for the first time on an orchard at Ardmona. The tractor was part of the walk-in/walk-out purchase deal. My eldest brother, Bill, told the story best of Dad's performance. Dad had planted two lemon trees in a space among the peaches where two had died. Dad was pleased with the lemon trees' progress, so when he drove the tractor for the

first time, he certainly didn't want to run over them.

The tractor was towing a delver for making channels, which Bill was operating. Bill yelled—'Turn right!' Dad looked back—'What?' but as he looked back, he turned the wheel left. Bill bellowed— 'Watch where you're going!' Dad, not used to noise, said— 'I can't hear you.' He looked to the front, to see a lemon tree disappearing under the front of the tractor. 'My bloody lemon tree ...'—and in his panic, he thought he was driving a horse and yelled—'Whoa back, you bastard.' The tractor continued on.

Bill shouted from the delver—'Put the clutch in.' 'What?' said Dad, looking back, but the tractor continued on into a peach tree, where it stalled. This happened at about four miles an hour. Dad jumped off the tractor and rushed to Bill, who was rolling around on the ground, apparently injured, but after a minute, Dad discovered that Bill was rolling on the ground from uncontrollable laughter. Dad stomped off to the house, calling back over his shoulder—'Get a bloody horse.'

The workers cost nought to run
John Pickering

One horse for the sulky, another for the dray,
Others strained on ploughs and drills—all dead and gone today.
One thing isn't dead and gone, the thoughts of yesteryear,
The sounds and smells of all those friends we held so near and
    dear.

Thirty working horses, plus the stallion in his stall,
We learned their personalities and came to love them all.
Some you wouldn't stand behind, others liked to bite,
Then there were the skittish ones that took off in a fright.

The long, hot days of summer, lunchtime in the shade,
Cold tea from a bottle that once held lemonade.
Horses with their nosebags were happy with their lot,
They did their job and did it well although the day was hot.

When diesel power replaced the horse it was a sorry day.
While the horse cost nought to run, for fuel you have to pay.
Mechanical contrivances wear out and cease to work,
Repairs are very costly but a horse will never shirk.
Horses just replace themselves, they breed, get old and die.
So give me horses every time and that's the reason why.

Team memories
Max Williams

Les and Joan Miles have been our friends and neighbours for over 40 years. We got talking the other night about the early days, around 1919, when Les's father first settled the land around the Parwan district in Victoria. Les was the only son of a family of five, so at the age of 10 he was expected to get the milk from their dairy to the station by 7.30 am to catch the train.

'You had to be quick,' said Les of the horse that pulled the milk cart. 'The second the last milk can went on, the horse took off. If you didn't jump on straight away, you'd be left behind.'

Like most animals that do a regular job, this horse knew the ropes, and once at the station, would back up between other carts at the ramp, just like an interstate truckie.

The journey home was considerably slower. 'You could hardly get him out of a walk,' said Les.

In 1935 the family acquired more land and turned mainly to cropping, which meant they had to build up their horse numbers to about twenty-four. Like any farm, especially where there is livestock, there were a few unexpected incidents. Les recalls the time his father, cutting hay with the binder, luckily dismounted just as a whirly-wind, sucking up dust and straw, spooked the team.

The whole outfit took off at a great speed, straight up a 100-acre paddock, the binder cutting all the way and throwing sheaves out 12 feet from the machine. Horses and binder finally came to a 4-foot high rock wall, which was topped by two rows of barbed wire. This is where the machine and horses parted company. The horses finally found their way back to the stables, with harness and pole dragging behind. The binder lay wrecked at the stone fence—and was still in the same spot over 50 years later.

Les told me of the horse they had called Amy Johnson, after the famous aviatrix who had flown over their property after her flight from England in 1930. Asked how the horse got her name, Les said, "Cause she was up in the air more often than she was on the ground!'

Thus were horses Les and his family's working companions, until the drought that began in 1941 and lasted three years. Feed became so scarce that the horses took to foraging in the straw and sand blown against the rock walls. Many horses became sick with colic and either died or had to be shot. The drought pretty well marked the end of farming with horses for Les. The tractor moved in—it didn't take the time, money and feed that horses had.

At first the tractor didn't do a great deal more in a day than horses could, but that soon changed as tractors got bigger. Old horse machinery wasn't in much demand, so it was parked and forgotten, to be keenly sought after at a clearing sale on the place 50 years later.

I asked Les to recall the best and worst things about his time with horses. The best, he said, were the bonds formed with the horses, and the pride in having a well-kept team. The worst was watching the suffering of the horses during the drought.

I came home that night in a thoughtful mood. I don't think I'd have liked farming with horses, because of the long hours and hard work—but there were some compensations. Farms were smaller, which meant more people in the district. More people meant more social life, most of it self-generated. Now we have our larger farms and, apart from the occasional wave over the fence, seldom get together with our neighbours.

Retribution
Wendy Treloar

My father-in-law, Colin Treloar, was not a horseman. In fact he didn't like them at all and was counting the days until he could get a tractor. According to one of his sons, Colin owned one particularly nasty character of a horse. Getting rid of it seemed catalyst enough to finally go mechanical. However, when Colin came to sell the horse, he discovered everyone else in his district was buying tractors and selling horses.

Despite all those years of willing service, the teams were worthless. Colin realised the only way he could get rid of the rogue horse was to shoot it. Collecting his gun, he rode the horse a long way through the scrub and down into the salt lakes. He was quite sure the horse knew what was in store for him and Colin said he felt a twinge of guilt. However, he lined up the gun, looked the horse in the eyes and shot it through the head. The horse dropped and Colin began the long walk home.

He'd not gone far before he heard horses' hooves stumbling along through the trees. With eyes popping and mouth agape, he watched the supposedly 'dead' horse trot past him. Colin spent the long walk home cursing wartime ammunition, which was obviously out of date—and a horse that didn't stop to pick him up!

In deference to the iron horse
Allan Schiller

My father bought his first tractor, a Fordson Major, in 1949. It arrived during preparations for seeding and we set it to work initially drawing a spring-tooth cultivator. Dad kept his horse team, so that year we had the horses driven by Dad, and the tractor by me, both working in the same paddock and pulling similar loads.

The Fordson was just a shade faster than the horses, so two or three times a day I would overtake them. When I was within a chain or so, Dad would turn out and come in behind me. The horses soon woke up to that; as soon as they heard the tractor behind them, even if it was twenty or more chains to the rear, they would want to pull out and turn. This became such a nuisance that I had to move to a different paddock, far enough away so the horses could not hear the motor of the tractor at work and anticipate what, in effect, was a gesture of deference to it.

Kicking into action
Paul Brown

I can remember my old man trying to adapt to tractors after a lifetime of draught horses. We had a female draught horse called Beauty who used to hang back in the traces which were linked to one of the pieces of primitive equipment they used then. The other five horses used to just get on with their job and pull, but Beauty was a prima donna, so Dad used to have to climb down off his seat and kick her in the side with his boots to get her attention.

He then took the extravagant step of buying a Farmould M tractor, which had to be started by a crank handle that had a nasty habit of kicking back and breaking wrists or arms if it hadn't turned the motor over. We four sons, ranging from small and lean to 20 and lean, were called in to assist in an atmosphere fraught with imminent peril and terror. The oldest son was ordered to the crank handle first—and then down to the youngest, which was me. Dad intervened himself after each boy tried to kick the engine over. Dad never got used to the fact that tractors were not, definitely not, draught horses.

So as the afternoon wore on—in real fear of the tractor—our old man, each time he wasn't trying to crank, used to further terrify us by kicking the tractor wheel as though it was that recalcitrant horse. In dulcet tones he would whisper, 'Come on, you little Beauty, come on.' It was the greatest threat in the world, and if tractors—like we boys—had had ears, it would have fled the shed.

The heavy horse memorial
Dick Mills

At the end of World War II, Dad purchased an old crawler tractor, but kept the horses just in case it didn't do the job. That proved to be the case, so the horses had a reprieve for a year or two. Sadly the day came when all except one young horse were sold. We didn't ever dare ask about their fate, but suspected that they became crayfish bait; we felt very sad.

Twenty years later, the contributions made by all the magnificent Clydesdales over 100 years or more were remembered by a band of South Australian horsemen. They erected a functional building at the Wayville Showgrounds as a heavy horse memorial, and it stands in use to this day to acknowledge our debt of gratitude.

These days, great tractors rated at 100 horsepower and more spin their wheels helplessly where two or three massive horses like our old Punch would sail away with the same load! But progress must happen, even if it is erroneously called 'horsepower'!

Glad to be rid of the bastards
Geoffrey Blight

Sam was a hard man, tough as nails, ready to fight with the best of them. Loud mouthed, he would argue all day long and was as Irish as the Blarney. He could be cruel; he worked hard and was merciless on those that didn't do the same.

Horses were his headache—how he hated the bastards. Though he rode and drove every day, he longed for the time when farms would be rid of the lazy, dumb rotters that drove him crazy. They were always going lame or getting stuck in a fence. His motley draught team were a scruffy lot of cast-offs. Being too tight to buy good horses, he ended up with all those that others threw out or gave away. They'd kick, they'd bolt, they'd jib—and he belted them for it. Scars told of their many misadventures.

Sam couldn't be bothered with a brush and no-one ever saw him pat a horse with anything but his boot—while calling them an array of names that made the gumtrees blush. But he fed them well, while moaning endlessly about putting up with them. Horses that no-one else could handle worked for Sam. Few teams had seen the acres and miles they covered.

Over a beer, you would always hear him bragging of the tractor and truck he was going to have—so he could get rid of his useless nags. Gradually, the mixed sweat of Sam and his horses made money, and after 25 years, his farm prospered.

Finally the day came: first a truck, then a shiny new tractor were seen heading for his place. As they passed the pub, the publican brought a laugh at how old Sam could now shoot his 'bloody mongrel' horses. It wouldn't be like Sam to waste tucker on them and no-one would buy that lot of notable rogues. When he turned up, bragging of his brand new tractor, everyone laughed when someone asked if he had shot his scrubber team yet. Sam joked, telling them the bastards had bolted when they saw the tractor and so far he couldn't catch the mongrels. The joke grew as, with time, someone realised the horses were still around.

For a while, Sam escaped on excuses—he'd run out of ammo, they'd bolted again, his yard wouldn't hold them—but he would do it 'tomorrow for bloody sure'. But 'tomorrow' was a long time coming, and so was the rain. Things turned bad, real bad.

Finally Sam's wife joined in quietly, telling Sam the horses had to go. There wasn't enough feed and water even for the precious sheep. Sam became angry and yelled at her, 'All right! All right, I'll do it now, if it pleases you. I'll do it right now. It'll be a pleasure!'—and he stormed off.

His wife knew how desperately Sam had tried to sell the horses, but no-one wanted horses now, even if they were free. She watched, worried, as Sam, with his rifle under his arm, kicked, swore and roared as he rounded up the ten horses and vanished over the hill to the scrub of their back block.

Farewelling the big horses: the Clydesdales depart

She didn't hear the shots, but a long black column of smoke told her he had done the job. For some reason, she wished that Sam could have done what many other farmers had done—got a pro to put them down. Surprised that he took so long, she went in search of him and finally found him sitting in the empty stable, a heap of old harness at his feet. Her request that he come and eat went unanswered, but she knew he had heard and knew not to argue. She had retreated only a few yards when she heard vomiting and called out, only to be told to 'Go to Hell' and that he wasn't hungry.

It was a fortnight later when Sam and his family drove the A Model to a local dance. He had a few beers in him when someone joked about the drought, how bad it was, and had Sam shot his horses yet? Sam laughed unconvincingly as he bragged that he had blown what little brains they had all over the back paddock. His wife quietly turned away and let it pass. After all, only she knew how her husband hadn't eaten and had wept for three days after that trip to the back paddock.

This story was told to me by Sam's widow, fifteen years after the teamster had 'rejoined his team'.

One last plea for the working horse
George Cox

We used horses for work until we had bought and paid for three 640-acre blocks of land. I always said that I would not pay for a tractor to work on somebody else's land. We grew a lot of wheat with the horses and, in fact, in 1944 when there was a big drought, we were the only ones out of the fifteen share-farmers working on the McClelland property, Windarra, that still used horses. We were also the only ones that Mr McClelland got his share of wheat from that year. No-one else stripped theirs.

A great change came over the country after World War II, as not only did the big teams disappear from the country, but everybody's farms were getting bigger and bigger, and they are still increasing. One farm after another changed over to tractors, and nobody was quite sure why, because a lot of the farms had built up outstanding teams of horses and had copybook farms. By 1950 nearly all the farms had changed over to tractors. Most farms did not have enough land for the machinery they had, so they had to increase the size of their farms or get out, so as the farms got bigger, the people got fewer. Schools were closed because there were not enough pupils; blacksmith shops, saddlers and so on were out of date; and consequently the small towns got even smaller. People went to the bigger towns to try to find work. The quality of the farming deteriorated, as there were not enough men around to dig channels, dig out rabbits, cut thistles or look after the fences. A lot of the land is now misused. It is overcropped and clay banks are ripped up.

It is hard to visualise the farms as they used to be, a family on every block of 640 acres with a team of horses and replacements, plus a pony or hack or two around the place, followed up with a couple of milking cows and a hundred chooks to keep the table going. There were always plenty of working men on the farms, and in fact, the football team used to have 60 footballers to pick a team from. Now, they can barely get half a team.

I suppose we call this progress, but I think this all boils down to the fact that we have got rid of all the horses and people out of the country. We send all the money for machinery and fuel out of the country (or most of it, anyway). We are taxed, and rightly so, to keep the families that cannot get work, because the tractors are doing it all. The people have gone to the city, and the horses have gone to the dogs.

Farewelling the big horses: the Clydesdales depart

Epitaph
Maureen Turner

There's a lonely patch of mallee at the back of Tandragee
Where a host of memories hover, and it almost seems to me
I can hear a trace chain clinking every time I pass,
I imagine I hear Clydesdales walking softly through the grass.
And so, I like to pause a while, just there, and sigh and dream
And conjure up a memory of a silent, plodding team.
The handsome nearside leader, his proud head bent in strain,
Pushes hard into his collar as he tightens up the chains.

Before the throbbing engines came to force him off the roads
To take away his glory, as they took away his loads,
He, and all his kinfolk, in the dust and in the mire,
Were toiling through the weary years, the Clydesdale and the Shire.
It was they who hauled the lurching loads and carted all the gear,
They, too, deserve the honour and the name of pioneer.
Every man who won the West, the greatest and the least,
Owes so much to all of them, each patient plodding beast.

At the back of Tandragee in that shady mallee glade
Strong white bones are bleaching as they lie there in the shade.
No monument of marble, no headstone carved and white,
Just the scent of eucalyptus wafting through the night.
The everlasting daisies were never planted there,
No-one trims or mows it, it is left to nature's care.
Yet if horses have a Heaven, it's there it must be found
For I can't dispel the feeling that I stand on hallowed ground.

Fourteen
The new golden era

Australia has a rich heritage of horsemanship. Its various strands weave together through our history. Our explorers and drovers, bushrangers and mailmen, teamsters and coach drivers all played their part. This nation's development depended on horses more than any other animal. Our Olympic equestrians are part of the continuum of fine horsemen and horsewomen who have hauled this nation to greatness.

The sport of eventing for which Australia won gold medals at consecutive Olympic Games—Barcelona, Atlanta and Sydney—is the ultimate test of equestrian skills. It is the grand opera of horse sports, with three individually demanding disciplines: dressage, cross country and showjumping. Success requires a long apprenticeship, methodical training and top-class coaching.

The stories of some of our gold-medal eventers tell of their struggles to reach the pinnacle of riding, and also examine what it is like to be full-time professional equestrians, something that did not exist until recent times.

Wayne Roycroft, Australian equestrian team coach for the past four Olympics, can take much of the credit for those three gold medal performances. He competed at three Olympic Games, winning bronze at Mexico in 1968 and Montreal in 1976. His father, the famous equestrian elder statesman Bill Roycroft, rode alongside him on both bronze medal teams and won gold in 1960 at the Rome Olympics. Wayne's wife, Vicki, is a four times Olympic showjumper.

Wayne grew up on a dairy farm at Camperdown, western Victoria, and rode a horse bareback to school from the age of four. 'When I left school I went off to be a ringer at Balbirini Station, south of Borroloola on the Gulf of Carpentaria. Looking back now, the skills of those bush riders, the amazing stockmen I worked with, are very much a part of what is seen as our distinctive Australian style, particularly in the cross country phase. Our riders attack the job, just as if they were running down a steer. They take everything in their stride, just like you have to when you are in a flat gallop trying to turn a mob. Perhaps we have inherited some sort of genetic bravery that's been passed down from the great old riders of the past.

'A legacy of discipline, hard work, commonsense and horsemanship, so essential in modern riding, was perfected in the heavy horse era by great old horsemen with huge teams to yoke up each morning before dawn, and who often coped with cranky, unwilling horses.

'Throw in a bit of the dashing soldier from the cavalry days, heaps of talent and, of course, a mighty good horse and you're almost unbeatable. Our Olympians are a blend of all this. By their successes, they pay tribute to the horsemen of the past.'

Winning takes more than belief in a dream

Sometimes success has the appearance of coming too easily, but by tossing off the achievement of winning an Olympic gold medal riding her pony club horse simply as the fulfilment of a childhood dream, Wendy Schaeffer underplays her amazing feat. While every horse-mad child may indeed fantasise that equestrian gold is there for the taking, the story behind Wendy's achievement is enough to put off any but the most pig-headedly determined, physically tough, obsessively disciplined person—and that's even before prodigious talent is taken into account.

Just 'believe in the dream', says Wendy Schaeffer, as if anyone could take a $600 pony club horse and make it the top eventing horse in the world. It was the day after her first horse died that she, as an ambitious 11 year old, obtained the little thoroughbred called Sunburst. Ten years later, with a gold medal around her neck and rosettes flowing from Sunburst's bridle, she was punching the air with jubilation in front of a television audience of millions. While we all like to believe dreams come true, this feat is unrepeatable. No-one in equestrian history had done anything like it before—and certainly not with a newly broken leg.

This is a story of a girl and a horse, of enormous mutual trust, of near disaster and extraordinary triumph. No amount of dreaming, nor even much luck, went into winning that gold medal, just passion and hard work. And a 15.3 hand horse, small by eventing standards, that proved he had the heart, toughness and durability to beat the best horses in the world in the heat and humidity of Atlanta.

Having watched her mother, Di, rise to international eventing ranks as a member of the 1986 Australian team competing in the World Championships at Gawler, Wendy sped through the junior eventing ranks, winning at age 13 a Grade 1 pony club event on Di's horse Sunhill Cloud, as well as competing with 'Tommy', as Sunburst was more generally known. Champing at the bit to be 16 and allowed to do a proper, grown-up Three Day Event, Wendy and Tommy burst onto the state scene and earned a spot in the 1990 National Young Rider Three Day Event team and then were part of the Australian team competing in New Zealand. Wendy and Tommy were also on both the senior eventing and showjumping state squads.

Two years later Tommy reached Advanced level, and then he and Wendy created history at the Gawler Three Day Event by being the youngest ever winner and winning by the biggest margin on record—some 35.8 points.

When the eventing team won gold medals in Barcelona in 1992, Wendy admitted she was jealous not to be standing on the rostrum too. She was just seventeen. Nevertheless, she already had been officially long-listed for the Olympic squad and written up as 'Australia's best rider'. She aimed to show how good she was by beating her friend and medallist, Gill Rolton, on home ground, which she did. In 1993, Tommy was named National One Day Event Champion, and they were in the national team.

Her life was hectic: competition every weekend, the usual tiredness on Monday at school while recovering, a one-hour bus trip morning and night, and constant anxiety to get home to work her horses. One can only marvel at her academic strength: in Year 12, despite simultaneously taking horses to the highest possible levels in the state, she also earned enough TER points to make it into physiotherapy, one of the tough courses to enter, following in her mother's footsteps.

When she finished at school, she went to England for three months as a working pupil, to check out the riding scene and establish contacts for the future.

Back in Australia, competing and riding full time, she passed first year physiotherapy and then took leave of absence from university for the next year. A frantic effort had raised $20,000 towards flying costs and living expenses for Tommy and her in England: she and Di had wangled a thoroughbred yearling to raffle, put on a fundraising party and Wendy had obtained a $4000 Institute of Sport Scholarship. With a bit of extra backing from her father, a physicist and quiet backroom supporter, she and Tommy moved to England in March 1994. For Tommy that was the last he saw of Australia until after the 1996 Olympics. Wendy was 19, and just three weeks after arriving came second in an Open Intermediate class with faultless cross country and showjumping rounds. Understandably, after beating some of the big riding names, she found England a little hostile, especially to foreigners doing well at their events.

She kept her focus on selection in the 1994 World Equestrian Games to be held at The Hague in July. Her emotions were in turmoil, and she was overtired. To pay for her horse's board in one establishment, she worked race horses from 7 am to midday five days a week and helped another rider with her horses. When she moved to another base she discovered the previous deal had been lenient. Not only did she feed, muck out and exercise another rider's event horses and do general grooming and tack cleaning in return for lessons and transport to events, she also paid 30 pounds a week for her board and 20 pounds for Tommy. This is what she writes in her account of the time: 'I felt tired and hassled by having to work so hard with Clayton's [Fredericks] horses but more so, I was worried that I might not have enough time or energy to spend on Tommy's preparation. My problem had become a psychological one. It was very hard for me to prepare for what was to be the biggest competition of my career when I wasn't in control of my own circumstances. I was reliant on Clayton and Lucinda [Murray] for transport and I couldn't really move as I had nowhere else to go that would provide me with better circumstances. It was also very hard to be working for people who you were trying to compete against.'

Her frustration increased as the final selection trial for the World Equestrian Games drew near, but with characteristic needle-sharp focus and determination she wrote: 'At this stage there were many rumours within Australian circles as to who was and wasn't going to be in the team. This speculation only further increased my obsession with getting to the WEG, my entire reason for being here.'

Lord Spencer's Althorp estate hosted the trial but so bound up was Wendy with competition that she was oblivious to her aristocratic surroundings. She managed to come sixth in the International class but, nerve-wrackingly, still had to convince selectors her horse was fit. 'You're in,' she finally heard, after trotting Tommy up under spotlights at 10.30 pm on a Sunday night for final vet inspection. After an intensive training camp, the team of six elite riders departed for Wendy's first foray into international equestrian competition.

'Finally trunks are packed, trucks loaded and we were away very early the next morning to Dover in order to catch the early ferry to Ostende in Belgium,' she writes. 'From here we travelled by road into Holland and down to The Hague. It was a sixteen-hour trip ... and I sure was glad to get there. It had been a long haul from Australia in early March to The Hague in late July, but we had survived and I was ready to embark on what was to be the biggest step in my eventing career, competing at the World Championships aged 19.' Wendy and Tommy finished sixteenth. A small technical error by Wendy had cost her third place, but they had come in under time, and Tommy had proved convincingly that he was up to four-star competition. 'It was an important milestone. Wayne [Roycroft] at last accepted Tommy had what it takes.'

In what must be seen as an appalling indictment of the Australian equestrian system at that time, those six riders representing their country, with little funded training, were then advised that they had to pay out of their own pockets to fly their horses home—at a cost of $20,000 each. Wendy had to leave her beloved horse to weather a torturously cold winter in England in the care of friends. 'Meanwhile back in Australia, I'm feeling tormented by the politics of the situation and the fact that my horse is across the other side of the world way beyond my control. I did consider selling Tommy,' she notes forlornly in her journal.

Wendy directed her attention and energy to her physiotherapy degree and managed to pass the first half of second year at the same time as competing with four horses. Back she went to England in July for another three months, to be reunited with Tommy and notch up some more eventing successes at important competitions. Back in Australia again in September she threw herself back into study, giving an extraordinary demonstration of her intelligence by bowling over two and a half physiotherapy subjects in just four remaining weeks of the second semester. Then more eventing, some coaching under Olympic coach Wayne Roycroft, a search for a horse for the Sydney Olympics, and creeping and unaccustomed self-doubt: 'I remember feeling at the time that I needed more encouragement and positive reinforcement. However, in hindsight this was probably a useful introduction into "toughing it out" in times of uncertainty which are unfortunately a large part of life as an elite equestrian competitor. This time though was a blow to my somewhat fragile psyche and it took me the first few months of 1996, the do or die year which I had hoped to begin with endless enthusiasm, to recover and rediscover my sense of purpose for what was to be the most eventful year of my life.'

She left Australia again in March for England and more success on the eventing circuit, but this is where her story of reaching the Olympics comes to its most tumultuous point and where a lesser creature might well have given up. Tommy was slightly lame just four weeks before the final selection trial at the toughest event of them all, Badminton. Part of his foot was cut away and for two and a half weeks he couldn't be ridden. Hardly an ideal preparation but, nevertheless, Sunburst and Wendy came eleventh. Heady with success, fired up with ambition and the impetuousness of youth, and with a spot on the Olympic team virtually assured, Wendy then made a reckless decision. Against the advice of her coaches, she decided to make a sentimental return to Australia for four weeks to ride three horses at the final Gawler Three Day Event. She would also ride a novice mare, Whimsical Sun, at the Naracoorte One Day Event. She thought it would help keep her competition-fit for Atlanta while Tommy continued toning and fitness work with expert grooms in England.

Wendy admits she likes 'living on the edge'. It makes her push herself to her limits, but with the big highs also come deep lows, the tragedies following the triumphs.

Wendy: 'Whim had been travelling a little greenly on the course and was in fact very "sticky" into the first water fence. I should have known better than to attempt the fast option at the next very difficult bank-to-bank combination. My natural aggressiveness and bravery wasn't tempered with caution as perhaps it should have been at this stage of the year, but rather it was artificially heightened by the post-Badminton high. I had walked the course feeling over-confident and a little too casual. My attitude seemed to be that if I can jump around Badminton, then I can do anything here at Naracoorte. Dangerous attitude.'

Whim didn't handle the bank and crushed Wendy's leg on a rigid sleeper wall at high speed. 'It was now 9.15 am on Saturday morning 18 May, exactly nine weeks from cross country day at Atlanta, and I was lying incapacitated with a definite broken leg.' The tibia had been shattered and would be difficult to heal quickly, plus the fibula had also been fractured.

'I probably spent half an hour feeling trapped by my own self-induced circumstances and very desperate. I didn't want to live if I couldn't go to Atlanta.

'Having struggled so hard in England for the last three seasons to be selected on the Australian squad for the Atlanta Olympics, I felt I had let everything go in the couple of seconds that it took to break my leg. Sure, I was young and there would be more Olympics but the fragile, volatile nature of our sport just makes it so difficult to even get anywhere near the Olympics ... I felt as though not only had I let down myself and my fantastic little horse but that I had disappointed my family, especially my mum, and my many close supporters who had all invested so much time, energy and emotion in getting us to this stage.'

With help from a medical relative, Wendy's leg was operated on that night by world-class surgeon and former international athlete Tony Pohl, who understood what was at stake. She was fitted with metal plates and removable plastic casts so she could exercise her leg and keep the muscles toned, and she used a

$4000 bone growth stimulator, borrowed from America, for ten hours a day while she moved around during the day. She was able to get back on a horse two and a half weeks after the accident, to be lunged and kept active. 'I developed a naïve but nevertheless dogmatic view that I was going to ride at Atlanta, broken leg and all.'

'Two days before I was due to fly back to Tommy ... I rode properly for the first time at four weeks post-op in front of a selection of the Adelaide media ... It did feel foreign to be riding again. Four weeks was the longest I had ever spent off a horse. Fortunately my leg felt strong and rising to the trot did not cause any undue discomfort.' She was given the OK by the Olympic Team Doctor, Dr Brian Sando, and returned to England, uncertain and worried. 'I felt I had to pretend that nothing had happened in Australia. Easier said than done though when I couldn't really walk properly and was struggling to ride effectively.'

Five weeks to the Olympics, the best Wendy could manage was fifteen minutes of riding on the flat. Keeping the full extent of the fracture secret from team selectors and ignoring the deep, dull ache in her leg, Wendy passed her final fitness test and got the nod for Atlanta and more rigorous training camps. Only some two weeks before the Olympics, and for the first time since Badminton in May, Wendy had her first jumping session. 'Of course, I had to portray confidence to those who were watching, but in truth I was concerned that my leg wouldn't handle the mechanical stresses.'

The rest is history. With Andrew Hoy, Matt Ryan and Philip Dutton, Wendy was named in the eventing team. Gill Rolton replaced Matt Ryan when his horse went lame and then broke ribs and a collarbone during the cross country phase. Wendy and her little pony club horse Tommy beat the best riders in the world with the best overall score. They would have won individual gold as well as team gold if the system had not been changed that year.

The new golden era

Wendy returned to Adelaide with Tommy to a whirlwind of tickertape parades and public appearances. She went back to university and that physiotherapy degree, but still had a steady programme of training and competing with a team of horses and the search for a horse for Sydney 2000 Olympics. She picked up a valuable sponsorship deal worth $80,000 for five years to help towards the annual $75,000 cost of running her team of horses. Things were going well.

In January 1997, a trip through New South Wales confirmed Wendy's gloomy philosophy that every triumph extracts a price, that the higher the achievement, the deeper the loss, and the higher the mountain, the deeper the valley.

With Sunburst and two other potential Olympic horses, Wendy was doing the World Cup showjumping circuit. She stayed with friends and the horses had good paddocks to relax in between work sessions. On Wednesday, 8th January, Sunburst did not come up for his morning feed, then came the frantic shout: 'Wendy, he's dead.'

'It was a soul-destroying sight. My fantastic little horse that had done so much for me and consequently meant so much to me was now reduced to a motionless body drained of life and spirit. I could no longer sense his latent energy, nor see the power in his body which he unleashed so instantaneously at the slightest fright and I could no longer feel that Tommy was there. What remained was a body with a hind leg that was badly broken just above the hock. The bone had come through the skin and had ruptured the femoral artery, one of the major blood vessels in the body.

'My emotions were strangling me. I couldn't think or feel anything. I had lost Tommy, my closest companion for over ten years. He had been the greatest part of my life, my ambition, my desire and my belief in that dream. Above all though, he was my best friend.'

In the biting cold of Hahndorf in mid-winter 2001, Wendy and Di are bandaging injured legs of horses after a disappointing weekend of competition in Melbourne. Mud and rain fit with Wendy's flat mood. Horse rugs need washing, stables have to be cleaned. Not having had quite the right horse for Sydney's Games, she feels she's still paying a price for winning gold at 21, having it easy compared to others who have tried repeatedly. Beating up on herself she seems to have forgotten that she fought overwhelming odds every step of the way. She even questions on that grey morning whether she should retire. This is the talk of someone who wanted to win at the weekend but had a silly fall and knocked a few rails. Winners don't like setbacks. She is wrestling with whether the battle is worth it. She has a promising four year old coming on, as well as Sun Glo of the sought-after Souvenir bloodlines, who wasn't far off making it to Sydney, as well as about twelve horses in various stages of education and experience: but what if she can't pull things together again? She regrets that the British system of horse grooms doesn't exist here. Where she had to pay for board and training in the United Kingdom, grooms in Australia get pay, free board for their horses as well as free lessons and lodgings. She rejoices, however, that Olympic squad selection now does entitle riders to immediate funding to transport horses overseas for competition.

Now a fully qualified physiotherapist, Wendy, 26, works two full days away from the farm. Her ambition and love of horses get her out of bed at 4.30 am to work up to six horses before she leaves for the clinic. She tells me she drops into the gym on the way home for a session of aerobic work to keep up her fitness. When we catch up again a few months later, it is clear that the true athlete's rigid discipline and determination have brought fruit. The self-doubt has gone, the scars over losing Tommy are healing, and she is confident she has at last found the horses that will do it for her all over again. Wendy and Riverside Othello, the young horse she calls Sniff, came third at the Adelaide International Three Day Event in November, earning a pay cheque of $13,000. At the Spray Farm International One Day Event near Melbourne, Koyuna Sun Glo, aka Buddy, blasted away the opposition with a winning margin of 10 points to earn $8000. She had signed new sponsorship deals worth $40,000 spread over two years. The gloom had lifted. She and Buddy have been named in the national squad for the World Games to be held at Jerez in Spain in September 2002, providing they go well at the final selection trial, the Sydney Three Day Event in May.

Learning the hard way

If anyone ever thought high level horseriding was only for the rich and pampered, Gill Rolton puts the lie to that. Her family lived in a tin shed when her father, a builder, went broke. She borrowed horses and floats, and the first few horses she owned were hardly ideal, one being an ex-pacer that couldn't canter and the other a pretty pony that bucked. Gill didn't even have the pedigree to become a twice-over Olympic gold medallist. Her family wasn't horsey, so everything she learnt was by watching, listening and soaking up the wisdom of Adelaide's Pat Hutchens, Keith Guster and Tom Roberts. When she did the show circuits in her holidays from studying physical education at teachers' college, she slept in the back of her car, needing to win prize money so she could buy horse feed and petrol. After working her way through horse jobs around the world, she bought a $200 weanling which became the champion Saville Row that blasted them both onto the three-day-eventing scene at their first appearance, leading the dressage phase by a mile against luminaries such as Captain Mark Phillips and Andrew Hoy—who had grooms and trucks while Gill went solo and slept in her car. No-one took her seriously, because after all, she was regarded as just a hack rider. When she was long-listed for the

Los Angeles Olympic Games, suddenly Gill England, as she was then, was noticed. She was 23 and hadn't started eventing till she was 21. Her first time over showjumps had been at 18. She turned down an offer of $24,000 for her horse.

'I don't think I am a very talented rider,' says Gill disarmingly frankly. 'I don't think I am a very talented jumper. I have just had a procession of very good horses.'

Thoroughly likeable, enthusiastic about anything to do with horses, generous with her time, Gill Rolton continues to foster talented horses and riders. She now has wound back her riding from the Olympic days of eight to ten hours a day. She is an equestrian television commentator, has recently written her autobiography, *Free Rein*, helps organise the Adelaide International Three Day Event and is one of the driving forces behind HorseSA which aims to unite the disparate horse interest groups, establish an Equestrian Academy for South Australia and develop a horseriding trail from the Barossa Valley, through Adelaide and down to McLaren Vale.

All through her horse history, Gill has taken the mongrel horses that others didn't want and made something of them, like Benton's Way which ended up at the World Championships in 1986 in Gawler. She even taught her husband, Greg, to ride and within a year he competed in Melbourne at a Three Day Event on a $200 horse. Then her good eye for talent landed upon her greatest triumph, Peppermint Grove, the stately grey with floating movement, a huge jump and wonderful heart. When she started eventing him in 1989, people weren't laughing at her any more.

She received offers of around half a million dollars for Fred, as she calls him. People never thought she was good enough for the horse, which she paid $15,000 to take to England to be in the running for the Barcelona Games. The deal in those days was that only horses selected for the Games had their trip home to Australia paid. People who couldn't afford the $20,000 return journey usually had to sell their horses. Fourteen riders were fighting for four places in the team. Women weren't regarded as tough enough, so the pressure on her to drop out was huge. After she came 7th in a top international event just prior to selection, she was shattered to be told to sell the horse. 'You're not a winner, you'll never make an Australian team, go off and have babies, that's all you're good for,' she was told. Motivated by boiling fury, she became even more determined. 'I wanted to make this team because I wanted to bring Fred home. I didn't want to lose my mate. The more they made it tough for me, the more I was just going to say, stuff you.' Business women talk of a glass ceiling. Gill said equestrian women at that time faced a manure ceiling.

Atlanta in 1996 was an easier campaign because by then the squad was selected in Australia and the tab for flying horses around the world was picked up by the organisers. But financial pain was to be replaced by emotional and physical pain. Gill couldn't repeat her brilliant runaway win at the Australian Championships in 1995 on a score of 45 penalties. 'That's what I wanted to do on the world stage at Atlanta,' she said. Instead, the world was left with the insulting and much-repeated television image of Gill and Peppermint Grove cartwheeling over the water jump, an image that perhaps revives for her the early scoffs and mocking that greeted her emergence on the eventing scene from the show ring. She describes 'tipping up' at Atlanta as 'unfinished business'. The fact that she rode with a broken collarbone, jumping huge obstacles successfully in excruciating pain before the spectacular crash and then went on to complete the course in a show of courage that rivals the legendary gold medal ride of Bill Roycroft in 1960 in Rome when he too had a broken collarbone, comforts her little. She felt she let down her horse. 'It wasn't fair to Freddy, because I believe I had the best horse in the world. People say it was a triumph, but for me personally, it wasn't a very nice time at all.'

Gill and husband, Greg, still live in the tin shed, now brick clad, sprawling and comfortable. The views over Adelaide from the hillside are magnificent and Fred grazes peacefully in a paddock near the house. There's a good horse called Aspire in her stable. She's bringing him on for his owners who bought him for $1500. He's winning well and is on the market for $50,000. She might have learnt her craft the hard way, but she's still got a golden touch.

It's all about persistence

Right alongside Cattai National Park where the whipbirds call, Olympian Stuart Tinney is warming up the top eventing gold medal horse in the world for the year 2000, the mighty Jeepster. The horse is newly back in work after a long spell and he's giving his gold medal rider a hard time. Throwing his head, resisting the bit, chucking-in the odd pig-root, he reverts to the dirty natured beast with fighting spirit that Stuart found on the showjumping circuit.

A year ago he was the best in the world from 250 of the best horses at the Olympics; on this day in the sun in Tinney's garden setting at Maraylya, quiet and undisturbed by loudspeakers, flags and crowds, he can't even get over a rail on the ground, baulking at it as if he was some newly broken colt. Karen Tinney hoots with laughter as only an equestrian wife can. Stuart, lean as a whippet, is silent and unmoved while he gently presents the horse again at the insultingly insignificant obstacle. Jeepster cat leaps the pole, then takes off, plunging and fighting as though he's escaped from a monster. Stuart calmly halts him, backs him up, asks the horse to trot and keeps persisting quietly, unemotionally until he gets some semblance of order out of the big bay thoroughbred. Again the horse is presented at a jump. The rails crash. Then comes an oxer, cross rails and single bars:

the sound of falling rails drowns out the birds in the dense native forest adjoining the hillside arena ringed by lavender and lawn. Karen scurries between jumps, replacing rails and trying to keep up with the horse's path of destruction. The best horse in the world is in a feral mood. A lesser rider might by now have said something, or shown impatience. Stuart Tinney sits neat, strong and still in the saddle, classic seat, perfect balance, soft giving hands. His perseverance was rewarded when the horse with the mind of its own found rhythm. Powerful and smooth like a well-oiled machine, he weaved through the jump course, giving flying changes on request and clearing everything effortlessly. He finished by jumping a single upright 44-gallon drum: end of lesson.

While Stuart, small and slim alongside the untidy great lump of a horse, squirted him down and dried him off, it didn't take a genius to see how fond he was of this errant hooligan. A horse with plenty of attitude, so long as it is also athletic and sane, is always Stuart's preference. Jeepster now is worth around $300,000 on the world market, but here there's no cotton-wool pampering. Stuart likes his horses to live like horses, out on grass day and night and only in the stables to dry off after work. 'I actually like them to be horses, not pets,' he says. 'What makes for good intelligence is learning to look after themselves.'

Bought for $7000, the tough-headed ex-showjumper is one of three Olympic standard horses that Stuart has brought up through the grades from the basics using his own techniques and philosophy. Central to his thinking is that he must be the dominant partner. 'I don't like them to tell me to get lost,' says Stuart, explaining that he calmly persists until a horse comes round to his way of thinking. 'Then they are easy to get along with because they don't challenge me. The ones that respect you go better for you.'

A working student, one of several from Britain helping out, takes Jeepster back to a bottom paddock. Stuart walks back to the arena for a private lesson with Corinne, a university student studying psychology and keen to do well at pre-novice level on her big dapple grey. By watching Stuart Tinney teach, you see the qualities that had him three times selected in the Australian Olympic squad on three different four-star qualified horses: Ava, Tex and Jeepster. He is patient, he is clear with his directions, gentle, interested, demanding and encouraging, a totally focused teacher, generous with his knowledge. After an hour of work to improve the horse's trot through leg yielding and shoulder in exercises, Corinne is delighted. Stuart enjoys having such an intelligent student who doesn't mind working hard. His methods of improving paces have developed from his own experience, which also included five years as a working student with the illustrious Roycrofts: Wayne and Vicki. He got free riding lessons and his keep, but no pay—just like Karen and Stuart's live-in students these days.

Karen, tall, fit, energetic and with traces of West Country accent, watches the lesson with me from the high bank at one end of the arena. 'Stuart was the only one in the whole world with three horses qualified for the 2000 Olympic Games,' she says with justifiable pride. Because they had always been short of cash, such is the life of equestrians working up the ladder, they could never buy seasoned horses. 'People suddenly ask huge money when they find out who you are,' and she goes on to tell the wonderful story of their life which improved dramatically with the winning of the gold medal. Sponsors came forward— Coprice, Bates and Vetsearch—and they have at last been able to build a new truck for eight horses and sleeping quarters for six. Daughters Jaymee, 3, and Gemma, 6, and two grooms usually accompany Stuart, 36, and Karen, 40, to competitions. The journey has been rugged though. The pair met thirteen years ago and set up as trainers of other people's horses as friendly but perfectly platonic business partners before realising what everyone else had apparently realised, that they were an ideal couple. 'We were so poor though, we had to bot rides in trucks to events,' she says. They bought the large hilly block at Maraylya, an hour or so from Sydney, and made advances like putting in the dressage arena and building the stables by selling a couple of good horses.

Bread and butter earnings come from teaching an average twenty hours a week. Stuart's first lesson might start at 6 am in Sydney but then he is back home to work his horses, whatever the weather, every day. So after Corinne's lesson, groom Amy has the next horse organised so all Stuart has to do is leap into the saddle. This time it's Toby, a grumpy Appaloosa that's put it over a couple of timid owners. 'This horse could go all the way to the top. But he has a big problem with resistance,' says Stuart. This is an understatement. Bought for meat value, the horse could fit nicely into a rodeo. He produces some majestic rears, stops sharply, tries to savage Stuart's right foot and only occasionally produces the sparkling paces that keep Stuart interested. Affable and relaxed throughout, Stuart is unfazed. 'I just pretty much do what I want to do, until he does it too,' he says, and eventually the lesson can end when the strong-boned fleck-rumped horse stops his nonsense and submits.

Stuart grew up in the town of Gladstone in Queensland. His father was a stock agent and had a few cattle. Horse-mad Stuart spent his childhood mustering, playing games at pony club, having lessons and eventually winning an Intermediate level Three Day Event. He worked in a bank and rode horses morning and night. All his earnings went into paying horse bills, but he even then was ambitious. He moved to Brisbane to be closer to coaches and got his big break when Wayne Roycroft was appointed state coach. Included in the squad, Stuart soaked up instruction on every aspect of the sport and, at 21, he decided to quit banking and become a serious, full-time rider. 'I wanted to compete internationally and very successfully,' he said explaining his decision to live with the Roycrofts. Although he could certainly ride, his knowledge, he says, was 'zero'.

To make it on the international circuit, he says you need to have an open mind and be willing to learn. 'You probably need to be a little arrogant at times too, but still be prepared to listen.' Stuart reckons only about one rider in 200 makes it, mainly because they fall down in things like stable management, discipline, riding skills, commitment and passion for the sport. As feeding of the eighteen horses on the place gets underway—a straightforward diet of Coprice, oats and lucerne hay, plus grass—we walk up through beautiful and sweet smelling gardens to the house, which overlooks the adjoining park and horse paddocks in the gully running between forested hills. Famous photos hang on almost every wall. The pictures of the 2000 Olympic team of Andrew Hoy, Phillip Dutton, Matt Ryan and Stuart receiving their medals, the great leaps over spectacular obstacles, the amazing leap by Tex into the crowd at Badminton in 1999 when Stuart lost his balance after the water jump. The beautiful Olympic gold medal is reverently brought out and given to me to hold. Stuart Tinney had waited a long time for that medal. Three times in the Olympic squad, three trips overseas to compete in Europe in an effort to win the attention of selectors, the expense and the disappointment before finally making it through with Jeepster to be best in the world, to the elation of Sydney in September 2000. It's all about persistence.

Fifteen
Horse people

They train, they travel and perform: horses are an essential ingredient in their lives.

A drover on a journey of life

Liz Murphy hitched a pair of chestnut horses to a cart and disappeared from civilisation for six months. We all make our various journeys through life but the nagging gypsy genes in Liz's veins demanded something more adventurous of her. Her journey was part of a search for her inner goddess, and to regain her self-esteem which understandably had got somewhat lost on the way. Liz, now 54, had married at 16, had three children, and put that marriage behind her at 33. She celebrated her independence by building a gypsy wagon. Liz had no experience at building things, but her plan was to hitch her wagon to a horse and travel with the children somewhere far away. The fact that she didn't know anything about horses did not deter her either. 'I didn't even know how to catch a horse,' the quietly spoken Liz told me with a smile.

Nevertheless, with the wagon completed—it was a covered gypsy-style conveyance—she began the search for a quiet, gentle horse. She advertised and before long met champion Clydesdale driver Mike Keogh. Being the forthright sort of chap he is (Mike's story is on pages 195–7), Mike vetoed the gypsy wagon as totally unsafe, persuaded her to sell it, and to team up with him, as his wife, instead.

Liz, dark haired and dressed in a colourful skirt, admits that, looking back, she was hardly ready then for any solo adventure. For the next 21 years, she and Mike established the famous Coopers Clydesdale team and restored three huge keg wagons for exhibition and promotion work. Mike taught her how horses think, how to handle them, about harness and vehicles, about safety and driving. Liz was the calm passenger up alongside Mike as he manoeuvred giant four-horse teams around agricultural royal show arenas. She plaited manes, cleaned harness, and threaded tails with ribbons. Liz was there as they clopped through city traffic on a trolley delivering barrels of beer to pubs. She watched Mike break-in and train horses at their Oakbank farm and met wagon-builders, harness- and collar-makers. Few would have known that the shy, self-effacing young woman alongside the ebullient and gregarious Mike harboured thoughts of one day managing her own team and again building a getaway wagon. The gypsy yearnings had never gone away. Liz found herself talking openly to Mike and her children about wanting to follow her long-held dream. 'Then I found I had to follow it through,' she says.

Out came pen and paper and she started drawing the type of wagon she wanted. It would have flaps in its sides to reach cavernous spaces for storage, comfortable beds, a place for washing and a well-sprung driving seat with a canopy to keep off the sun. She worked out the dimensions of her wagon with Tim Peel of Camden, New South Wales, a man widely respected for his deep knowledge of harness horses and vehicles. (Tim's story is also featured on pages 247–8.)

In the back of her mind was the memory of a hawker's wagon she and Mike had found near the Birdsville Track when they had spent some time droving on Peter Litchfield's Mundowdna Station. By then it was a wreck, but they were shown photographs of it when it had been painted with advertisements for Farmers Union Candied Honey, its original owner, Kevin

Bartsch, standing beside it. Peter had been repeatedly pestered to sell it but had rejected all offers. Even Mike had not been able to convince him that it would be faithfully rebuilt.

If she couldn't have the Birdsville Track wreck, she would create something like it. Wagon builder Clive King, who lived in the Blue Mountains, told her the cost would be $45,000. Work began and Liz made her first visit to Clive's workshop. Seeing the base laid out on the floor, Liz had an attack of the terrors. It was too big; the dimensions were all wrong. She rang Tim in a panic with tears streaming down her face. Calmly, he went through the dimensions, reassuring her that every measurement was just as it should be. It would not be too heavy or cumbersome for two horses. Wanting to believe, but frightened that she was wasting a small fortune on a disaster, Liz cried all the way back to Oakbank. As she arrived, she met Mike who had just returned from another trip to Birdsville. In his trailer, he had the wreckage of the original wagon. Since many years had passed since their first sighting of it, its woodwork had deteriorated to splinters. Only its hand-forged springs, hinges, axles, bolts, chains and hooks could be salvaged. But Liz sobbed, as they were no use now. She already had a wagon taking shape, albeit one that she feared was a clunking folly. This is where a touch of the gypsy magic comes in, where serendipity intervenes.

Slowly, Liz picked up each ancient iron piece, fondling it and marvelling at its patina and ability to survive the harsh climate of the outback. Out of curiosity, she started measuring them against the dimensions of her wagon under construction. One by one, she checked them. To her astonishment, to her utter amazement, she found every bracket, every hinge, and every hook, bolt and strut matched her design exactly. Not one piece needed reshaping. Even the springs were perfect. It was as if some extraordinary hand had guided hers as she designed her wagon. Her tears and uncertainty were replaced by new confidence in her project. She was en route to fulfilling something she had been destined to do. Not only that, $10,000 could be knocked off Clive's bill.

In June 2006, the wagon was ready for painting and fitting out back home in Oakbank. In August it was ferried with the two matched chestnut mares back to Tim Peel's farm at Adelong, from where the journey would begin. The stylish mares, Jesse and Belle, are quarter horse Clydesdale cross full sisters with white blazes and four white stockings. Mike had broken them in and they were quiet but, at three and five years of age, were inexperienced. A lone driver would not be able to take anything for granted.

Liz, now a grandmother, would be following the Murrumbidgee River from Adelong, through Wagga and Narrandera to Hay, then crossing the river and returning to Adelong, covering a total of around 1000 kilometres. She would camp wherever she wanted and whenever she felt tired. She had no finishing date, no timetable, no deadlines. She would travel as long or as little each day as she wanted.

In early October, she pulled out of Tim's front gate, with Mike beside her for the first week. On the first day, the swingle bar broke. She started out again, and soon fell into the rhythm she would follow for the next six months. At first the horses were fresh and fidgeted, and were easily startled. They had never seen much of the world beyond Oakbank. Once satisfied the horses had settled, Mike left.

On her own, Liz quickly found how physically demanding and time consuming even something as simple as opening a gate was—if she was to guarantee the horses didn't bolt, potentially tipping the wagon, and leaving her behind. She put knee hobbles on both horses to ensure they stood still, then opened the gate, removed the hobbles, led the horses through, reapplied the hobbles, closed the gate, removed the hobbles and climbed back on board. 'Hardly relaxing,' she laughs in retrospect.

But most days were. Liz took grassy tracks winding between trees along the banks of the Murrumbidgee River, stock droving routes used since the 1830s. She was on the move each morning by about eight, stopping at 12 for lunch and to let the horses graze. Then on the track again at two until four when she would make camp for the night. They would cover about 25 kilometres a day if they walked, about 50 if they trotted.

As the months went by, Liz says she never got bored or sick of her adventure. The river had always fascinated her—and then there were the people she met along the way, most of them envious of her journey and wanting to know more. Some travelled a few days with her, others a week. They all talked of the therapeutic experience of slowing life to a gentle pace, of living close to nature and stripping life back to its essentials.

The 1-ton wagon is an imposing creature, standing tall as it does, on its huge red-spoked wheels. 'I made the wheels myself,' says Liz and she says it so quietly without a hint of bluster that it seems almost rude to be shocked that a woman, this small, gentle woman, could be a wheelwright. Well, almost a wheelwright. She had found the wheels after advertising widely for the right sort and then with Tim's help, pulled them completely apart, turned new hickory spokes, forged new steel rims and then reassembled them by carefully fitting the cleaned and sanded spokes back into the bulky wooden hubs, and reapplying the wooden rims and metal tyres. Not made from scratch, but close to it—and damn heavy work.

The box-shaped body of the wagon is painted deep purple and has red and yellow line decorations. On the back door is a picture of Liz's pin-up girl, Morgan le Fay, the sexy sorceress of King Arthur's legends, who was also benevolent fairy, enchantress, healer, and lover of art and culture. Clearly, mystical and spiritual matters play a big part in this tale. Above the door hangs a sign saying 'Goddess Within', an intriguing, teasing, even playful, promise.

It is evident that this drover's wagon, even if it is inscribed on the sides with 'E.M. Murphy, Drover' is no ordinary conveyance.

Indeed Liz Murphy was doing much more than drive for 168 days along some thousand or so winding kilometres of riverbanks. She is making a grand statement of femininity, and showing that anything is possible. In the flowing skirts she wore on her journey, she cut an interesting swathe through riverine communities. Colourful silk fluttered from the front awning shading her driving seat. In a cage hanging under the wagon were two golden Wyandotte chooks which laid eggs each day. A red heeler, Buddy, trotted behind.

This vehicle for Liz's journey of self-discovery is a little more comfortable than the spartan quarters that housed past drovers and their families. But not by much. Comfortable bench seats by day, a big bed by night, shelves for books, a wash basin, a couple of baskets of clothes swinging from hooks on the roof, and screened windows allowing a cross-breeze make for a homely space. To the right of the back door stands what is probably Liz's most prized luxury: a miniscule Metters Chef pot belly stove, which once rattled along in railway guards' vans so men could warm their hands, boil a billy and cook a meal. It took Liz eight months of persistent searching and advertising to find one. She says just a bit of kindling will get a meal cooking and the wagon cosy. Ice boxes kept perishable food cold.

The only modern addition to the wagon is a small solar panel on the roof. Liz used it to charge her phone, to check for messages from time to time or to have in case of emergency. Not much did go wrong though—not the sort of thing you would need a phone for. Resourcefulness, initiative and patience solved most problems, such as the time she parked the wagon beside the river where the bank levelled out at the bottom of a slope. Next morning, she discovered exactly what the term 'cold shoulder' really means. This old-time horse term describes what happens when a harness horse is asked to pull a load before it has had a chance to warm up. Liz's mares refused to put their weight into their collars that morning to tackle the slope, preferring to back towards the river flowing close behind the wagon, away from discomfort. Scared, but with steely spirit, Liz turned the horses, warmed their shoulders by walking them and they took the slope when they were ready.

The equanimity of the 'Goddess Within' was certainly tested—especially the time the wagon got bogged in sand so badly that the two straining horses could not extract it. A local farmer had to extract it with a tractor.

The Goddess was nurtured though by nights under starry skies, by time and space for thinking, the companionship of a dog, by fresh eggs for meals, by natural horsepower, and a man back at home who could celebrate that the aspiring gypsy he met and married 21 years before was achieving a feat of horsemanship that few in this modern world will ever experience.

An odyssey with three horses

Lucy and Richard Barrack were restless. They were city people who had horses and a small farm from which they commuted to their Melbourne jobs. In their 30s, they decided it was time to see the real Australia, the outback, stations, red dirt and lots of cattle. And their horses would go too.

In March 2008 they loaded three chestnuts into a gooseneck trailer to set off for a year. They were sick of their jobs; Lucy was a contracts manager, and Richard was an accounts manager. They sent the rest of their horses off on agistment, put a tenant on their 70-acre farm at Metcalfe, near Kyneton, in central Victoria, and took the road north to the Kimberley to find work on a cattle station.

Neither Lucy nor Richard had ever worked on a station, had ever done stock work, nor had any of their three horses seen that many cattle. Who cares—they were going to sell themselves as contract musterers and farmhands!

As they lumbered out their gate with the Ford F250, the gooseneck with its comfortable living quarters, decent kitchen, composting toilet and shower, and their three quarter horse cross pleasure horses, to the Stuart Highway and Alice Springs, they admit to rising fear. They had committed themselves to a grand adventure that was now scary because of its uncertainty. These were two people who had been used to a comfortable and predictable existence, whose horse experience had been trail riding and horsemanship schools. Leaving their horses out of the odyssey was never considered. 'It seemed unthinkable to leave them behind,' says Lucy of Firefly, Sapphire and Molly. The pressure was now on to support themselves and the horses and to keep the Ford in fuel by doing foreign work in a foreign landscape.

On the three-and-a-half-week trip north, incredulous locals asked repeatedly just how these two city riders thought they could be station hands and musterers without a skerrick of experience. Lucy says they kept explaining that she and Richard were passionate about agriculture and that living in a rural area had stimulated their interest.

'We did not want to be hypocrites and sit in our armchairs having opinions about the cattle industry and how it works,' she tells me. 'We really wanted to understand how agriculture operated at the grassroots level and how people in the industry experienced it.'

They wanted the kind of Australian experience that few other city workers could ever get to know.

Travelling five hours a day, with breaks every two hours to give the horses a walk and a rest, they made camp near roadhouses and showgrounds, putting up yards if necessary. A memorable camp was at Uluru, where the resort owners were so surprised to have horses as guests, they allowed them to graze on the lawn. Before loading up, they rode with that imposing Rock in the distance. Then to Alice Springs, Katherine, Kununurra, south to Halls Creek, and then halfway to Fitzroy Crossing, they turned into Bulka Station. Before leaving home, they had registered with employment agencies and followed up leads but quickly realised large corporate stations were not for them: they generally had their own training and career structure for young staff.

Bulka, a family-owned station on the northern edge of the Great Sandy Desert, was happy to take them on and give them a chance. Owners Jim and Joy Motter always found it hard to get staff and mustering was upon them.

Joy laughs when I ask a year later what possessed them to take on two such inexperienced stockmen. 'It is not the first time we have had to take a chance,' she said. 'But for new chums, they were very good,' she said. 'We were fascinated that they would bring their three horses. They were so adventurous and wanted to give it a go. You've got to admire them.' Joy said stations usually have their own horses, but a shortage of experienced riders.

Full of enthusiasm at 7.30 on a Monday morning in a Kimberley landscape of red dirt, Spinifex, Mitchell, Buffel and Flinders grass, ant hills, flat top hills, spring-fed waterholes and cockatoos in the gums along Christmas Creek, Lucy and Richard found they were to join a team of eight experienced contract musterers for a solid three-and-a-half weeks of work, and no days off until the job was done.

It was then that they were faced with the reality of what they didn't know about cattle work. 'The thing I found hardest in the first two weeks was that feeling of uselessness,' says Lucy. It was not something she had experienced before in her working life. At 30, she had been used to being in control and on top of things.

She recalls how she had wanted to get involved with drafting cattle through the yards but had absolutely no idea what was going on. She spoke of the confusion of not knowing when to jump in and help. She and Richard had to learn to read cattle.

It was a few weeks before they even felt comfortable enough to ask questions. They were still very much the outsiders though, strangers in country where others were comfortable.

There was an incentive to succeed: if they could last for three months, if the Motters were happy to keep them on, their fuel costs for getting to Bulka would be reimbursed.

When the professional mustering team finished up, Lucy and Richard found they were to be Bulka's entire workforce for the next four months. 'Maybe we were just lucky that they were desperate for staff,' laughs Lucy. As well as all the stock work, they did general station work such as fencing and water runs—checking tanks, bores and troughs—and experienced life on standard farmhand wages instead of the big pay packets of corporate life.

Joy Motter said the locals were highly amused that Lucy and Richard chose to spend their rostered days off camping out by springs and waterholes among the paperbarks and wild fig trees on the station—instead of heading 140 kilometres to Fitzroy Crossing to live it up like everyone else.

But what about the horses who were as much city slickers as their owners? 'We are not sure at what point they became decent,' giggles Lucy, 'but they did start to pre-empt breakaways and read the minds of the cattle. Mind you, I don't know that any of them will be campdrafters. They are still basically pleasure horses.'

Happily, their horses are particularly sound-footed and don't need shoeing. If the ground is stony or particularly hard, they wear clip-on rubber boots, but they have needed them only four times. For injury or illness, Lucy and Richard put together a vet kit. Since Lucy's father is a surgeon, he trained them to perform simple procedures like stitching wounds. So far, only Richard has needed repairs—for a cut shin which Lucy fixed with five stitches.

After Bulka, they crawled slowly down the West Australian coast. They camped by beaches and on stations, rode in the waves, cantered on white sand and lived out a romantic dream. They carried enough water for the horses for three days of remote camping.

Their next contract was at Minilya Station, 150 kilometres north of Carnarvon, for a six-week mustering job of some 7500 cattle on flat coastal country with scrubby vegetation and sparse trees.

They lived out on stock camps, sorting and quietening cattle in teams of stockmen on both horses and motorbikes—while the manager supervised from above in a plane. 'Our horses might not be the greatest cattle horses around, but they get by,' says Lucy.

By November, they were helping out during shearing at Hamelin Pool Station near Shark Bay. They then headed south, staying at polocrosse and pony club grounds all around the south coast to Esperance. They would tap into the internet to track down facilities where horses could stay, ringing club presidents and being astonished at how welcoming everyone was. They spent New Year's Eve with one family near Serpentine, had polocrosse lessons at Margaret River and competed at campdrafting at Mount Barker, just generally joining in with the people they met along the way. Lucy said people seemed to be captivated by the stories of their travels and couldn't do enough to help them. 'I think the horse community likes to look after its own people,' Lucy said. 'Many of them travel huge distances for their sport, so they understand what it's like to travel with horses.'

Six weeks of holiday and it was time to get back to work— about as far away as you can get from Western Australia, to the other side of the continent, to Queensland. Across the Nullarbor, up to Broken Hill, Wilcannia, and on to a Bourke caravan park. 'There are plenty of horse-friendly places to camp,' says Lucy. 'And we were lucky enough to be taken in by people who'd say, "Why don't you just come to our place?" We have been astounded at people's generosity and openness.'

They were also amazed at how many caravan parks in the off-season were quite happy to take in horses. Fellow campers seemed to enjoy the novelty, especially their children. 'We are a bit of a circus act sometimes,' says Lucy.

They travelled from Moree Racecourse to the Goondiwindi Showgrounds where they used their computer to track down what jobs were available in feedlots nearby. Two days later they joined the staff as pen riders at the 40,000-head Whyalla Feedlot, near Texas, getting up each morning at 3.30 to start at 5 for ten days in a row followed by four days off. At present their job is to ride slowly through about 40 pens each day, checking the 250 cattle in each pen for any which are being bullied or are sick, remove them if necessary and care for them in the sick bay. It is a nice break from the tough pace of mustering and general station work.

But the Queensland mustering season is about to start. Before long, a couple of seasoned musterers from way down south with three chestnut horses, not champions, but handy enough, will be ringing around for work.

A year after pulling out of their front gate, and with Victoria's Black Saturday fires having just missed their farm, the world's financial system in a mess, businesses closing and jobs being lost, Lucy and Richard Barrack have no plans to return just yet.

The wisdom of safety first

In the peace of rural Hynam's polocrosse grounds, surrounded by tall red gums, the quiet voice and gentle demeanour of Steve Brady have the full attention of sixteen riders standing beside their horses. It is the October long weekend and Steve is giving a three-day school, one of around 50 he gives a year in every state of Australia, plus New Zealand. This is one very busy horseman. From his home on the coast north of Newcastle, Steve is almost constantly on the move and is booked up years ahead. He has been a full-time educator for sixteen years.

Steve is among the most respected of the many who teach modern horsemanship, but if you are looking for hype and hoopla, that's not his style. His is an almost studious approach to horse training. Wisdom gleaned from the great trainers of the past has been incorporated with his own methods with the aim of producing obedient, calm and respectful horses.

Forget just looking pretty in the saddle, Steve's principal goal is to train students to be safe. Pretty comes later.

Today's part-time pleasure riders have little in common with the working horsemen of years past: few have inherited skills. Underworked horses, unfit riders and a loss of basic horse sense can be a lethal mix. This market has been targeted by many trainers, often preaching like evangelists, who sell the benefits of 'natural horsemanship', a training system which is gently persuasive using an understanding of the psychology of the horse. The coercive methods of the past using force and intimidation are dismissed as old-fashioned.

Steve Brady tells me his students range from established competitors and professional riders to the returning riders, often nervous and needing to regain confidence. He was called in for a ten-year period to give five-day schools at many Northern Territory cattle stations, mainly from Janet Holmes à Court's Heytesbury Group. Occupational Health and Safety rules demand better horse-handling techniques. So everyone from the manager and head stockman down to the youngest jackaroo would be required to learn the kinder, more humane, safer and more effective methods of training horses. From the greenest colt to seasoned old plant horses, they would all be put through Steve's classes to learn obedience and respect in an effort to reduce horse and rider accidents.

Hooked to a head mike, Steve gives his introductory talk. There is substance behind his words. He has started more than 3500 horses under saddle in his 25 years in the horse-educating business. He has performed on highly educated horses in front of big crowds at Sydney Royal Easter Show and at Equitana.

He tells his students he is aiming for an obedient, calm horse, ready to go on with for whatever discipline. He would be getting riders and horses to try a large range of exercises to discover strengths and weaknesses. The number one priority is safety. He urges riders not to do things they are not ready for, or which the horse is not ready for. He is very calm and reassuring. He does not want any horse or rider to feel uncomfortable.

Steve explains he will be dealing with behavioural problems like invasion of space and not listening. He will be teaching the rider to be the decision maker in the relationship. He then gives his students a series of insights:

'Horses are smart—but sometimes, not very. They do foolish things like shying at a piece of plastic and then running into a barbed wire fence; shying at a parked car and then standing in traffic.'

'If we want to be safe both on the ground and in the saddle, we need to be the one making the decisions about when to move forwards, backwards and sideways.'

'We communicate and control our horse through a language of cues. Teach your horse lots of cues. The more you teach your horse, the safer you will be.'

'I would rather be on a horse in a panic situation that understands 40, 50 or 60 cues rather than on one that understands five.'

'Inside every quiet horse is a wild horse trying to get out.' 'Horse training is all about the release of pressure. The point where you release the cue is the point where the horse learns the behaviour that produces the release.'

'For us to be safe, we need the horse to be respectful of the human. Some, when they don't get enough leadership from the human, get arrogant, bossy and sometimes even aggressive.'

By morning tea break, ground work exercises have produced horses which calmly bend and flex, drop their heads, move their shoulders and hindquarters away and generally show more respect.

In the shade of a gum with a mug of tea, Steve tells how much the philosophy of horse training has absorbed him. He started out as a horse-mad boy coming from a non-horsey family in outer Sydney. He borrowed ponies and eventually saved up enough to buy one—and then did two paper rounds to fund its feed costs. His suburb of Willoughby had plenty of open space for paddocking. He used to ride two hours each way to pony club.

When he left school he became a farrier, and in his twenties he became a competition showjumper. It was then that he met the great J D Wilton, a legend in the history of liberty horse training, some say the greatest trainer in the world. J D took his troupe of performing horses around the country and Steve adopted him as his mentor, soaking up everything he could, and applying many of his ideas and methods.

J D was also famed for his methods for starting young horses under saddle. 'He had a great understanding of the horse's psychology from having started more than 7000 wild horses in outback Queensland between 1921 and 1939,' says Steve, who worked with J D Wilton for three years and remained good friends with him until his death at the age of 84.

One of Steve's great successes was Danielle, a horse he describes as his partner for starting young horses in the 1980s, and clearly a favourite. Steve had taught her to work without a bridle while doing highly advanced dressage movements such as piaffe, passage and tempi changes. She also did high school stock horse movements such as roll-backs, haunch turns and spins. He earnt himself a great reputation as a trainer through her brilliance and performed on her at royal shows and other big events.

'I was probably the first person in Australia to ride high school movements bridleless and saddleless,' Steve says. 'Danielle was being worked every day and was with me all day helping me lead and handle young horses. We had a very close relationship so I was able to train her to great heights over a long period.'

Smiling to himself at the memory from some twenty years before, he told me how his famous mare once usurped a performance—and made her own decision about which cues she would respond to.

Danielle had grown to anticipate and love the sound of applause when she bowed at the end of her performances—following a discreet signal from Steve. Her front end would go down with near-side leg extended and her head stretched to her knee, tail up high—the true artiste's universal show of humble gratitude. While they were doing a display at the Sydney Showjumping Championships, Danielle got a fright when a door banged loudly. She had been lying down, pretending to be asleep, but suddenly leapt up and trotted away. Steve called her back, but the audience, thinking this was part of the act, clapped. Danielle took that as the signal to give an elaborate bow—too bad about Steve and his special cues. This was her moment! Steve said he had no choice but to follow suit. 'I thought if she was bowing, I should take my hat off and make the bow too.'

Steve's clinics grew out of his awareness that people were treating their horses like pets, allowing them privileges, and turning them into big-headed and very dangerous creatures which had no respect. He also writes masses of articles explaining in detail how to overcome problems and puts them on the internet for free access (<www.stevebrady.com>).

Horses are herd animals and all herd animals need a leader, Steve explains. Humans these days, having lost contact with natural animal behaviour, often do not realise they need to take the leadership role. Modern society with its emphasis on equality and the anthropomorphism of animals has not been conducive to safe horse handling. Half a ton of horse flesh which does not respect the tiny, weak human alongside it is a recipe for accidents and injury.

Steve used to get frustrated with training horses for people. When the horses returned to their owners, Steve found they didn't know how to use the right cues to get their horses to respond. 'I found a huge need to teach people how to train and put cues on their own horses. It's harder to teach humans than it is to teach horses,' says the wise man of horse training with a smile.

These days too many horses are lucky to be ridden three times a week for only twenty minutes at a time. 'People comfort and feel sorry for their horses and humanise them,' says Steve.

After the break, more unmounted exercises in submission and getting horses to move away: 'Moving the hindquarters sideways takes the drive out of the engine,' says Steve. 'This is a valuable safety mechanism for slowing a horse's pace or to help pull it to a stop.'

Final day, and riders were doing one-rein stops, sidestepping, bending and turning horses with subtle cues, performing intricate riding patterns with nary a fizz or fidget.

'The horse's mind is its strongest halter so if I can control the horse's mind, then I can control the horse,' says Steve Brady. He does a good job too of harnessing riders' minds.

Confidence builder
Sandi Simons

When women give birth to children, they may also give birth to insecurity. When they are horseriders, they may never get back on a horse. They start worrying about what can go wrong, about how dangerous riding can be. Then there'll be comments like: 'Don't fall off. Who will look after the children if you end up in a wheelchair?' It's pretty hard to fling yourself into the saddle and canter off with the same insouciance you once had. Throw in the additional complication of your body being a different shape to what it was when you were lithe, young and fit, and you find yourself making excuses to avoid doing what you were once good at, and loved.

Even if the fathers of their children don't make concerned noises as they head off to ride with the local hunt club, there is still an inner voice that wheedles its way into the female brain saying: 'What if you break an arm? Who's going to do canteen duty next week, the washing, the cooking, gardening and the paid job?' The horse soon finds itself lounging around the paddock for extended periods. When it is brought in, fresher than it should be, the prophecy of injury is frequently a self-fulfilling one.

Sandi Simons, with five children, understands these problems for women. She endured them herself, finding endless excuses not to ride—although she and her horse-trainer husband, David, run a professional horse establishment at Drysdale, near Geelong, and hold training clinics all around Australia and New Zealand.

Riding is for many women almost a spiritual experience, Sandi says. 'Women have a special affinity with horses. They give women a chance to escape and enjoy something that no-one else is part of. When you ride, it is just you and the horse. It is a very special relationship. We use riding to soothe our souls and get in touch with our feelings.'

Sandi had been a successful dressage competitor, western pleasure rider, barrel racer and had shown hacks. She and David had travelled the rodeo circuit for 14 years all over Australia and lived for a while in Colorado and competed there. David had been a professional bronco rider and won the Victorian title four times and had been runner-up Australian Saddle Bronc Rider. He is now a competitive dressage rider. So in this world where every weekend there was another show or rodeo to attend, and in between, horses to train and break-in, Sandi found that with every new baby, she not only had proportionately less time to ride, but became increasingly scared.

She had a four-year break from riding—and couldn't get back into the saddle.

The turning point came when horseriding friends dobbed her in to present a 45-minute seminar at Equitana in 2000 on the topic of losing your confidence. Her friends had known that Sandi had been searching for a remedy by trying to find someone to help her. The quest was in vain. 'Trainers did not understand what I was talking about,' she said. 'They would tell me I was married to a great horse trainer. They weren't hearing what I was saying. So I had a bit of a meltdown, sitting on the floor in the kitchen, crying, saying I've got to give it up. I was sobbing my heart out. I couldn't keep doing it. It was too hard.'

Her friends knew all this and somehow understood what Sandi did not realise at the time: the solution lay with her. She had not had a fall, the horse was safe and quiet. 'But I blamed the horse,' Sandi says. 'I had done a great job training him, but I was fighting myself. I didn't have to come to the stables to have him do something wrong. I had the argument up at the house before I even arrived.'

So finding herself thrown before an audience of horse people at Equitana, Sandi faced her demons. 'I reckon it was the most profound moment in my life. I did a lot of deep breathing. I knew I couldn't back out of it. I just had to be honest and not care what anyone else thought.' With her 18 hand horse beside her, she took the microphone and started telling this audience of strangers her secrets. A direct and entertaining speaker, Sandi got their attention immediately. 'This is what I suffer from—I'm shitting myself every time I go to ride. I'm petrified. I've lost my nerve. I've had kids. I have lost my confidence.' She told her story and at the end of the session, found herself surrounded by women saying they understood, that they had the same fears. Many felt the same sense of failure. Some had had falls, some were put off by bad instructors, some no longer believed in themselves and some had badly trained horses. 'The greatest thing I ever did was admit it,' Sandi explains.

Women responded enthusiastically to her stories about being torn in different directions and losing her focus and confidence. Interruptions from children, the phone and meal preparations often led her to feel as though she hadn't achieved anything all day. 'But that's what we women create,' she says. 'It's because we give everything of who we are to these children and husbands, and life, whatever. And you agree to do that when you become a parent. But you get to a point where you just want something for yourself. I allowed my lack of confidence and lack of self-esteem to override my abilities. I had myself convinced I didn't have any ability.'

Sandi began working out how to bombproof her horse, to ensure it didn't move while she was mounting, wouldn't take off, shy, rear or buck. She developed a system of green and red light signals which indicated if the horse was relaxed or needed more groundwork. She used hip control of the horse to break the horse's strength. 'In a battle of strength, you will never win. You need to get back in charge—so with their head down, move it to one side, push the hip over. This disengages the hip, makes them crooked, so they lose momentum and stay calm. Horses are at their strongest when they are in alignment. Emotions can't be taken out of a horse,' she says, 'but you can teach them not to get emotional, and teach yourself to be in control of their emotions.'

'Even if a woman doesn't go near her horse for a month, she can use these cues to ensure it is safe. And if you are as busy as I am with lots of kids, lots of meals to cook, you also need it to be easy.'

Sandi's methods grew into a business and in 2005 she offered the first of her Confidence Camps, and now holds six a year. 'Most women will say how they would ride anything when they were young,' she said. 'They competed, jumped and galloped, so clearly they had plenty of ability. All that had happened is that they had lost their confidence.' Her oldest client was 91, a woman called Carol Cavenaugh who ran her own farm, had 13 horses and not enough time to work them. 'She had a beautiful white horse that was too wild to ride. David quietened it and she rode it. She was fitter than people half her age.'

Half of the women who come to the camps haven't been on their horses for two years. Sandi says her greatest joy has been seeing women, who had been in tears and had sweaty palms at the beginning of a camp, cantering along a beach and laughing on the final day. 'From being wound up in self-doubt and criticising themselves, I see excitement—and peace.'

Finding a better way

High in the grandstand, I am looking down on a vast indoor arena. The lights go down. The insistent thumping beat of Queen's 'We Will Rock You' blasts out. The ring announcer tells us we are about to meet a superstar, possibly the best horseman in the world, and a champion bush poet. Guy McLean canters into the spotlight on a small bay horse with a thin blaze. With no reins and no saddle, that little horse, in step with the blaring rock beat, did canter pirouettes and half passes, extended trots and levades at the four sides of the arena, then, astonishingly, cantered backwards, to finish with a deep bow—and all with scarcely detectable signals from the rider. It was an extravagant and extraordinary display of horsemanship.

When the music was doused, that rider held us in his hand just as if we were that horse. He would share with us his horse training philosophy and what he had learnt from a life spent full time with horses since he was three. He would tell us what he understood about a horse's way of thinking, how he had been able to achieve what we had just witnessed. 'I want to show you how I go about getting a horse to that level,' he said through his head-mike, said not as a boast, with no hint of cockiness. That 15.1 hand horse, Spinabbey, was so far his greatest achievement, the best he's ever bred. We in the audience were to be taken into his confidence. We indeed were to be part of something exceptional.

This was Equitana 2008, at Melbourne Showgrounds. Guy McLean has appeared at all six Equitanas held since 1999, but this was his first-ever solo performance. Three years before, he had astounded everyone during what was billed as a Horsemanship Challenge, a competition between three trainers to see who could first ride and control an unhandled horse. Guy was on the back of his in 28 minutes, not just sitting there, but standing up and cracking stockwhips and crawling under its belly.

So, before this huge crowd, under lights and with music and clapping, he would let us in on his secrets. He brought in a brown stock horse, clearly unbroken, yawing and straining against its rope and halter. Guy explained the colt had had 30 minutes of halter training only, just so it could be floated and brought to the arena. As Guy McLean started running the horse right and left at the end of the short rope by stepping towards its hindquarters, holding out a hand, then touching it lightly on the forehead as he let it stand still, he talked non-stop, confident but not cocky. 'Ninety per cent of horses I can stand on their back and crack a whip on their first ride,' he said. Few of us expected he could achieve that with this spirited colt during that evening, certainly not without even a round yard. He lunged the horse with a plastic bag tied to a stick, explaining he was concentrating on keeping the hind legs working separately so the horse couldn't rear or buck. When calm acceptance was achieved, the horse was rewarded by Guy moving out of its space and being allowed to stand still.

He doesn't pat the horse or fuss over it, only occasionally murmuring 'good' as encouragement. His eyes are almost constantly fixed on the ground, watching the colt's feet while keeping up a flow of words so we, the uninitiated, can learn. 'Movement is safe,' he says. 'You have got to get the hindquarters to move away. The best horses are reactive horses as, once they are trained, they become the most responsive. They step away when you put your leg on them.'

By being willing to stand still, drop its head and respect the cues he is being subtly and expertly given, the colt is rewarded by having two stock whips cracked near it. Already the horse has learnt that immobility is its reward. It hardly flinches, appreciating that rest is more appealing than running away. Then a crackling blue tarpaulin is wiped over the animal, its head is covered, and then the tarp tied to its tail. Again, it is lunged then the tarp is removed. The horse seems to have learnt to trust that nothing bad will happen. A bond has formed, and there are no signs of panic. Once again, touched on the forehead, its reward is to rest.

Without much ceremony, Guy then pats down each side, leans on the colt's back and springs on. The horse stands still. Guy encourages us to make as much noise as we can so we clap and cheer. The horse does nothing. After some more work with a rope around its girth and flank, showing a horse will get used to anything, and some more rapid-fire whip cracking, on goes a saddle blanket, and a saddle which is girthed up. A bit more lunging, a stop for reward, then Guy hops on again. He rides with the single halter rope at walk, trot and canter to the left and right. The horse finds the right lead. It stops and its reward is to have the whips cracking all around it. The horse does not move. We cheer, Guy stands on the horse's back, cracking the whips, and dismounts by doing a handstand and somersault. It has taken 90 minutes, a bit longer than he would have liked.

I needed to find out more about this man who harnesses the energy of horses with invisible cues, who loves a horse of spirit and fire, and gives them the gift of calm obedience. Four of his horses in the second part of the show had also worked at liberty moving with grace; one lay down and three others, with Guy on Spinabbey, side-stepped over it, while Guy's whips crackled like fireworks. This man was not only an equitation freak, he had also stilled the crowd with his original and deeply moving poems about the bush and hardship, poems he later tells me seem to write themselves, so quickly do they flow from his pen. He can write twenty verses in half an hour and recite them word perfect ever after.

Meeting me at Hervey Bay Airport under a big Queensland hat a few weeks later was this shy young man of good looks and quiet charm. Guy is modest and humble about his achievements and disarmingly open about his devotion to horses. Horses are so honest and straightforward, he tells me on our drive to his farm at Maryborough. He finds humans far more difficult to understand: he met many puzzling members of the species when, from the age of 15 until he was 24, he ran the horseriding side of his father's tourist ranch. As well as taking people riding, he performed inside the homestead on horseback, reciting the poems which have twice earned him the title of Australia's Best Bush Poet and won him a trip to America in 2000.

Guy tells me he is heading back to America before too long. Americans, he says, love equine entertainment and despite hard times they still flock to displays, rodeos and shows: 'It's escapism. People want to be uplifted.' Guy McLean loves entertaining people and showing them how to train horses using his quiet methods. When he was in America before, he noticed how top horsemen were revered and rewarded. He wants to be one of those. At 33, it is time to take the leap. He will take the four horses I saw at Equitana.

Guy says a fellow Australian, Clinton Anderson, has done very well in America, doing training clinics and shows. Guy wants to be part of that much bigger market. He would also enjoy seeing his existing series of DVDs of horse training and poetry readings reach a bigger audience, and maybe he could put on a television show and get enough recognition to be able to afford his dreams. He says at present he struggles to cover the costs each year to run his horses. 'I want to be able to make a difference,' he says. 'I would like to build a brumby sanctuary and be in a position to help charities. If I could be the Steve Irwin of the horse world, wouldn't that be wonderful.' He would also fight to reduce horse cruelty, especially in race training and the film industry.

This is the inherent problem of horse work. If you want to have great horses, you have to spend hours each day working them. To earn decent money, you have to spend time away from home which means the training goes on hold. Many horse trainers make videos so they can have an income while they continue working at home. The market here is small, though; the pay accordingly modest. So America is a dazzling lure where the dollars flow and horsemen are kings.

'It is wonderful to be told that I am one of the very best in Australia,' he says, 'but if I don't work every week, I can't keep this place going.' When he did the big royal shows around the nation with his liberty horses, whip cracking displays and rider training clinics, he spent almost the entire year away from his farm and 25 horses. On this gentle, semi-tropical day, among hills, trees and palms, where horses stand in every paddock and yard, this clearly is the place he loves to be, training valuable young Australian Stock Horses of noble pedigree in the huge sand-based arena.

Guy's horse training philosophy has grown out of years of observation, and trial and error. 'I have always been able to accomplish things very quickly with horses, even before I used the methods I use now. I always have a picture in my mind of what I am trying to achieve. Everything they can do naturally, I have the expectation they can do that for me. I don't put any limitations on their ability. My expectations are high so the result of that work is what you see with my fellows,' he says, referring to his four liberty horses.

'I like to start them in a one-rein halter because that gives so much more of the relationship back to the horse. I have to put a lot more control on a horse in one rein and have a lot more trust and respect for him than if I had a two-rein bridle in his mouth. With a lot of horsemen, it's all about control through pressure. 'I want to be able to have my horse want to stay underneath me. It is not about kissing and loving them. A lot of people think you should whisper in their ear and tell them how beautiful they are. Well, the horse that does that to them in the paddock is the one they least respect. A horse is looking for a leader. I try my very best to be that.'

From watching big mobs of horses running free, he has seen how the horse that is assertive is the one that is respected, the one the others will follow through a fire or a creek. 'You watch those dominant horses, they'll have to be tough on a young horse two or three times and then they'll never have to lay their teeth on it again.' Guy certainly doesn't bite or kick, or even lay a hand on them. Instead, it is through asking them to move and work, and rewarding them with rest that he wins them over. 'People love that I can just move my dressage whip and bring a horse sideways or lift him to canter. But in the beginning, you do have to tap them with it, but it's not an aggressive thing. I do this now so I can be soft for the rest of its life. A lot of people are soft all the way through the training, then when there's pressure on, just like the horse that pats and kisses the others, you will get kicked away. There's not that respect there. If I thought that loving them, and kissing them and cuddling them would make them better horses, then mine would be the best in the world. I just love them that much, but I know it doesn't work. I know I get a lot more accomplished by letting them stand still and think about what they've done than by ever patting them.'

The way Guy explains it, his horses choose to do what is asked of them because it is the easy way out. 'They think that if they are standing still with me on the middle of their back, that's the best thing they could do.' If they move when they should be standing, they'll be asked to move more than they want. If they stand, they don't have to do anything.

The logistics of getting a horse from semi-wild to safe are straightforward when Guy explains it. He emphasises how important it is to keep the hind legs moving separately all the time. Once on the horse, he tips its nose to the inside and keeps working on that hind foot. To avoid bucks and rears, he keeps those hind legs working separately by putting on only one leg at a time. 'You can understand why they run away, but if you can understand how they run away, you can stop the physical motion and that will stop the mental motion as well.'

'On Spinabbey, if I close two legs on him, he canters on the spot. If I rock my body back, he canters backwards ... he's special.' He loves that horse and his energy with a passion. 'It is the closest I've ever been to flying, riding him.'

Guy allows his horses to decide where they feel most comfortable. Sequel, for instance, doesn't like work so Guy capitalises on that by asking him to be the horse that lies down and has three other horses side-passing over him. Kenny, another of the liberty team, is a bit of a wag and likely to defy requests to lie down, only to submit later—much to the amusement of audiences.

His use of the crackling blue tarp is part of teaching horses to cope with anything and to trust the trainer. This approach is handy at country shows where fireworks are a feature. Guy will canter his horses around while crackers are exploding. 'They'll have more energy than normal but then I lie them down and we watch the fireworks together.' He notes that others' horses are frequently terrified and bouncing off stable walls. 'Mine know if they play up, I'll work them. They sleep while the fireworks are going off.'

At those country show outings, Guy used to ride around the arena bridleless and saddleless, thinking it wasn't anything unusual. After all, he was 15 when he first rode 'naked' a little brumby cross mare, Mystique, which he could slide, back and spin just with hand taps, shoulder movement and legs.

At one Queensland dressage championship, Guy rode a demonstration freestyle test doing flying changes every second stride, cantering backwards, making pirouettes and canter half passes—all without bridle and saddle.

'When you take the gear off, you are riding so much more with your mind,' he says. He rides always as if there was no gear. 'I connect every part of that horse's body to mine. I connect his shoulders to my shoulders. His feet to my feet, so the bridle becomes obsolete. It improves my collected work and campdrafting, cutting and reining.

'To ride them without a bridle and saddle is to know that they are doing it because they want to. You can't make things happen like that. It is because they respect you.'

Watching Guy ride, I struggle to see his cues. He is motionless. Indeed with Spinabbey, he says he only has to think which way he wants to go. Such is the level of training and closeness of the bond between man and horse. 'When I ride Spinabbey, I don't move my hands, I don't put my leg on him. I just look over there and he goes. He's just waiting for you to think there. The better ones will train you not to touch them.'

Saving the brumbies

Horses, outmoded on farms and unwanted by explorers and mustering camps, the cavalry or coach runs, were scattered like leaves in a wind across our landscape. Many were bred on classy bloodlines, with a dash of pony here, a touch of draught there, a bit of Caper blood from South Africa or an infusion of hardy Chilean breed—and usually crossed with speedy Thoroughbred and tough Arab.

In a wonderful demonstration of natural selection and survival of the species, the surviving horses were masters of their environment and flourished. The weak died out. Those which could adapt to stony ground, snow, or seasons where water and feed were scarce, were sturdy, tough, intelligent and sure-footed. Many were also blessed with excellent conformation.

Aerial surveys indicate that about 500,000 of these mixmaster horses roam the Kimberley, the Pilbara, the Northern Territory, northern South Australia, outback Queensland and the vast alpine national parks of New South Wales and Victoria, with pockets near Echuca and Coffin Bay. Most of these survivors of our pioneer past have thrived so successfully that they have earnt themselves feral pest status, to be targeted by state governments for destruction, often done brutally. They usually end up as pet food, or are shot from helicopters, and not always cleanly.

Gloriously, in June 2008 a first shipment of thirteen brumbies from the Kimberley flew out to Dubai. A sheik installed them in his plush stables to breed endurance horses for distances of between 120 and 160 kilometres. The horses are thoroughbred with a dash of Arab, tough and strong, descendents of elite cavalry or stock horses. They come from wild gorges, rainforests and grasslands of the Kimberley—their going rate for pet food in Australia is $20 a head.

These horses are the focus of the new Australian Brumby Alliance (ABA) which aims to get heritage status for brumbies in recognition of their link with our pioneer spirit. The Alliance is the initiative of Colleen O'Brien.

You could dismiss Colleen O'Brien as some dotty romantic in her quest to save brumbies from ending up as pet food or shot and left to rot. After all, she grew up on a diet of Elyne Mitchell's evocative 'Silver Brumby' stories. Colleen O'Brien, however, is no day-dreaming utopian. With a degree in Horse Management from Sydney University's Orange campus, and a level 1 EFA instructor's accreditation, she was for years a professional equestrian specialising in problem horses and teaching people to ride. Then she had her light bulb moment.

Flicking through *The Weekly Times* one morning at the farm near Creswick, Victoria, where she, husband David and two young children lived, Colleen noticed an advertisement which astonished her: 'Snowy Mountains brumbies—$120 each.' This was 2002; although a professional horse person, she had not realised that brumbies still existed, nor that you could buy them. She immediately telephoned and set off for Bairnsdale the next day with a float. Around 25 frightened horses were in a yard. In the driveway was the truck from the knackery. Colleen chose two pretty yearlings, but when another two scooted onto the float, the bloke said she might as well have them as the rest were going for pet food. 'Against my better judgement, I took all four,' she said. Most of the remaining brumbies were no older than three. 'He said he had advertised them for three weeks and this was the last day.'

Colleen O'Brien suddenly found herself on a mission which led her to form the Victorian Brumby Association (VBA). Those four brumbies revealed themselves as horses like no others that she had trained. Caught in the Victorian Alpine Park, they had a bit of Timor, and probably some British pony, Arab and Thoroughbred—genuine 'Man from Snowy River'-type ponies, sure-footed, smart and tough. They now enjoy being pony club and polocrosse mounts and one is even in harness.

Australia's wild horses bear the surname of the bloke who bushed his horses into the mountains around Sydney when he was transferred to Tasmania in 1804—Sergeant James Brumby. Or some say it's from the local Aboriginal word 'baroomby', meaning 'wild'.

Colleen found she could not break brumbies in like other horses. 'I realised then what the difference was between an unhandled horse and a wild animal. An unhandled horse has had human activity going on about it. These brumbies' only experience with people was being caught, which is not generally very pleasant.' One of the yearling mares kept trying to climb up and over the sides of the round yard, falling down and making another attempt. It took Colleen about six weeks of patience and gentleness to get their trust so they could be tied up, have their feet picked up, and be led.

Colleen sells unbroken but well-handled brumbies for around $500. She collects them after the alpine winter round-ups, making up to six trips in spring to the mountains with a ute and big stock trailer. Because she has to work around her childrens' needs, Colleen does each fourteen-hour trip in one day, leaving home at 3.30 am to return by dark.

That terrified yearling mare was eventually sold to a man in his late seventies living alone on a farm. 'He'd had his licence taken off him because of eyesight problems,' Colleen says. 'In his thirties, he had driven a horse in harness, delivering milk. He had never trained a horse to harness, never even owned a horse before, but she now trots him into the shop every day to get the paper and have a cup of tea with the owner.'

'We sell a lot of brumbies to people who have never had horses before, and they are really successful. I think the difference is that they will listen to their horse. The people who have the amazing results are nearly always first-time horse owners.'

Another unstarted brumby was sold to a 12-year-old boy, whose horse experience had been limited to being led around on a Shetland pony. 'He had his first trot and first canter ever on this horse as he started her under saddle.' Colleen explained that this horse had a lot of attitude, and was very reactive, but he trained her himself with supervision from Colleen at the clinics she ran. Avril, as she was named, had been a handful: tense, very frightened and very expressive of her fear, always trying to run away.

She then hands me the Association's 2009 calendar. There on the back page was Avril, captured from the Bogong region in the Victorian Alpine National Park only one year before, pictured with her owner, Liam, who was standing very tall and confidently right up on top her saddle while a very calm, relaxed and accepting Avril stands with reins dropped on her neck and no-one holding her. Liam told Colleen he mostly learnt by observing Avril and working out when she was ready for the next step in her training.

'Brumbies are almost dog-like,' Colleen says. 'They really look for leadership, and they look for a mate.' She says there are few lead brumbies in the wild, so they learn to watch their leader to survive.

'It seems to me these wild horses are very humble. The really beautiful relationships you see developing are with the people who go in and work with them kindly. They are looking for a leader and a friend and they are very sociable.'

One of Colleen's favourite brumbies is Anzac, captured in mid-2007, which she can now ride without a bridle, just a rope around his neck. Colleen had suffered post-baby nerves when riding her thoroughbred, but Anzac has never scared her. 'I feel safe on him.'

She says their calm nature has evolved because of the mountain environment. 'In the wild, if you are dramatic and fizzy and energetic, you get thin and die. The hot, fizzy horses have been taken out of the gene pool. You are left with these fairly stoic creatures.' Colleen said that compared with desert brumbies which needed to be able to run big distances to reach safety, alpine brumbies were adept at hiding. They will keep very still behind trees and be difficult to spot. 'They don't have a big flight response so they won't run 50 metres.'

The Association, which has a committee of six and 145 members, is primarily a rescue body but also promotes brumbies as sensible, intelligent, hardy riding horses. All brumbies are registered with the VBA prefix and given a name. The VBA accepts brumby numbers must be controlled but that this should be done as humanely as possible. It suggests that small populations of brumbies in national parks have a role to play in keeping vegetation down to reduce the heat of bushfires.

Alpine brumbies have worked their way so firmly into their lives that Colleen and David moved in 2009 to a much bigger farm, 160 acres at Beaufort near Ballarat. It is a sanctuary which they call Brumby's Run. It backs on to state forest, has rolling hills, old gums and plenty of water. They can handle many more brumbies for re-homing, run more clinics, take people for brumby rides and cater for tourists.

About 150 brumbies are removed from the Victorian Alps each winter, and while Colleen aims to save 50 each year from the knackery option, she has recently begun targeting brumbies from the Kosciuszko National Park, where there are about 2500. Colleen and her group prefer to support the more humane methods of the New South Wales alpine regions of catching brumbies. There, they are trapped in yards, lured by hay. In Victoria, they are run down and tied up—often for several days—then dragged onto trailers. Many are injured. The Association is pressing for brumby-running to be phased out.

About 35,000 specially bred remounts, Walers, came off stations in the alpine regions. After the war, and during the

Depression, many were set free. DNA testing, according to Colleen, shows that the brumbies of Guy Fawkes National Park in New South Wales are only 5 per cent inbred while modern thoroughbreds are 20 per cent inbred. The weaker, inbred animals tend to get culled naturally.

Colleen says the scale of our mismanagement of brumbies is highlighted by the fact that in America there are only 33,000 mustangs, horses which are famous and celebrated, and have their fertility and numbers carefully managed.

Meanwhile, 12,000 brumbies run free in Carnarvon National Park in Queensland, and half get aerial culled. With good seasons, those numbers climb rapidly again. There are brumbies near Echuca, descended from big horses used in teams a century ago, and ponies at Coffin Bay, whose ancestors were Timor and Welsh ponies introduced in the 1840s. The Coffin Bay ponies of 25 mares and a stallion are now Australia's only fully managed wild herd.

Colleen says in just the few years she has been promoting mountain brumbies as quiet ponies for children and adults, it's been exciting to find they have a ready made reputation as good sports. 'The Ballarat Polocrosse Association came up to me recently and said they used to get brumbies from the Alps, but the old man who supplied them doesn't catch them anymore. His brumbies were some of their best polocrosse horses, and they were keen to get more. It is good to know we have another outlet for our brumbies.'

For more information, please visit the Association's website at <www.victorianbrumbyassociation.org>.

Trick riders

Two women, blonde hair streaming, gallop flat out past me. As rousing, throbbing music plays, they are standing on top of their horses, straight and tall in shiny leotards with Australian flags held high, and smiling as though this was a perfectly normal way to ride a horse.

They come past again, their horses taking ruler-straight lines from one end of their run to the other. This time one girl hangs parallel to the ground by the horse's ribs; the other, energetically, athletically, frighteningly, vaults from one side of the galloping horse to the other, and does a somersault onto its neck. They're crazy, I say to myself. Then building to a finale, the Appaloosa horse comes flying past again, its rider with ankles held in leather loops is stretched out flat off its rump, over pumping hocks, hooves and floating tail, her arms held gracefully behind. These girls are fit, courageous, and obviously know what they are doing. They are the formidably talented team behind Pony Express Trick Riders (their website can be found at <www.ponyexpresstrickriders. com>). You might have seen them racing down the straight at Randwick, Rosehill or on Stakes Day in Canberra, at Equitana, a royal show or an equestrian championship.

Meet Deborah Brennan, a very tall and gracious former weapons training instructor for the New South Wales police force, former medic with the Australian Military One Commando Company, a champion pistol shooter, a gold medallist in martial arts, a film stunt woman and one of Australia's top horse trick riders. She has been trained by special forces military snipers and unarmed combat specialists, as well as some of the best equestrian trick riders in the world. Deborah was Nicole Kidman's stunt double in *Moulin Rouge*. She has also performed stunts in *The Man from Snowy River*, *Mission Impossible II*, *Water Rats* and *Superman Returns*. She is also mother to Tristan, 7, and wife and assistant to Gavin, who has his own film production company covering action sports. They live at South Tacoma, north of Sydney.

Meet Leanne Bruce-Clarke, petite, charming, a professional firefighter with the New South Wales fire brigade, an actress seen in *Water Rats*, *All Saints* and commercials, an actors' double seen in *Home and Away*, a Grade 1 stuntwoman who specialises in car slides, spins and motorbike stunts, a black belt and Australian champion in Tae Kwon Do and fourth in the world in her weight class, who does high diving to practise throwing her body out of control and saving herself. She is a former Residential Care Worker for people with disabilities, has worked with film people in big equine productions training movie horses, and currently teaches trick riding. Leanne is another of Australia's top horse trick riders. She is also mother to Hayley, 4, and Taihla, 19 months, and wife to Ross, a builder and former campdrafter and bull rider. They live at Aberdeen, in the Hunter Valley.

Neither of these girls is the slightest bit crazy. They just love trick riding, enjoy the exceptional bond they have with their horses and the thrill of performing in front of a crowd. They are happy to admit they are daredevils and enjoy the adrenalin rush that comes with doing their extreme sport. 'You have got to have courage,' says Deborah. 'A bit of anxiety is normal. It keeps you safe; it keeps you in check.'

Trick riding has fighting origins. Many of its manoeuvres are based on how the Cossacks avoided the arrows and swords of the Turks and Mongolians out on the Russian frontier. In 1891, American entrepreneurs brought out a team of Cossack riders for their popular Wild West Shows which featured characters like Buffalo Bill.

The Americans adopted trick riding as their own and have produced world champions such as Tad Griffiths, the famous film stuntman. It was from Tad Griffiths himself, and his legendary mother, Connie, that in 1996 Deborah Brennan learnt her craft as one of very few students they took on. She was then living in Las Vegas, studying acting and working in television. 'I had never seen anybody ride and perform equestrian gymnastics like it before on beautiful horses that tracked up and ran so well,' she said. 'I would help out on the ranch with their 20 head of performing horses.'

Sadly, Connie was killed whilst trick riding when her horse flipped over as she was performing Spin the Horn. 'I don't really have the words to do her justice, except to say she was the most inspirational woman I have ever met. I had a real bond with her and she helped me strive to be the best horsewoman and person I could be. She was revered by trick riders all over the world and was a truly wonderful human being.'

Tad was a tough instructor. By the second day of lessons Deborah had skin off her hands and that night dreadful blisters formed. 'My hands were a mess but I bandaged them and showed up for my lesson the next day. Tad asked to see them and then sent me home, telling me not to return until they healed. I had no doubt that, because I showed spirit and courage, he took me on. He respects strength of character.'

Another important mentor was John Brady, whom Deborah describes as one of the finest horse entertainers Australia has ever produced. He worked extensively in America as a trick rider, stunt man and stage performer.

Deborah returned to Australia when her one-year visa expired. She met Gavin, married, and found film and trick-riding work and performed in live shows including 'The Man from Snowy River' and 'Cavalcade Reins of Fire'. Her favourite trick is Splits to the Neck, which involves vaulting off her galloping horse, then on again by somersaulting backwards on to the horse's neck.

Another is Jump Over the Neck Backwards, several jumps and vaults from one side to the other—'a real gymnasts' trick,' she says. Both are more commonly performed by men.

Leanne was introduced to trick riding in 1998 by Deborah, whom she met through film and television work. She instantly loved it and started Australia's first all-girl trick riding team before going to America in 2001 to build on her skills. There, she rode with the Riata Ranch Cowboy Girls, a famous trick riding troupe.

Deborah and Leanne started Pony Express Trick Riders in 2002. Fate had brought them together: they were between jobs and living close by. Training their horses, Bandit, the Appaloosa, and Sultan, the paint quarter horse cross, to run those straight lines and cope with weights hanging off to one side and bodies leaping on and off takes about three months of initial training, then about a year to become fully trustworthy performers. Deborah and Leanne put them through movie horse training: bagging down, cracking whips, making noise, putting umbrellas up and down. 'We teach them to be brave,' Leanne says. They also teach them to hold the speed that is set when they turn to make their run, and to go straight, no matter what acrobatics are going on, through a lot of patterning and voice control.

After their appearance at Rosehill racetrack in 2003, Deborah and Leanne were approached by the Melbourne Cup king, the great Bart Cummings, impressed that the horses held their line even with riders jumping from side to side and hanging upside down. One of a trainer's greatest problems is racehorses lugging out and drifting wide to annoyingly cover more ground. Bart listened intently as the girls told of the hours of training they put in and how they growled fiercely if a horse strayed off its line.

Deborah and Leanne face the problem of many live performers—getting reasonable fees. Agricultural shows and rodeos want them for a few hundred dollars, when $2000 is more around the mark to cover insurance, travel and feed, and the hours of training they do each week. 'It's not that Deborah or I are spoiled, but if we were to do one of these dangerous tricks, like a tail drag or a shoulder stand, for a commercial or on a film set, we would be paid $5000 or $6000,' Leanne says. If only there were a few more film jobs ... but even at their normal performance rate, they have to settle for making just a few hundred dollars each after expenses. 'For live entertainers, that's what's discouraging. We don't want to make live horse shows extinct. They inspire people to do new and creative things with their horses. Sadly, great trainers often have to do menial work to survive. We look after our Olympic athletes, but everyone else battles.'

Leanne says she has become more conscious of the risks of her horse work since the birth of her second child. 'It's in the back of my mind that I may take a serious fall, which will not only affect me, but my family,' she says. 'My favourite trick is a shoulder stand which is head first, down the side of the horse. If the horse trips or it spooks, I could be very seriously hurt. At every show or every training day we are all well aware of the dangers.'

Leanne says she will keep performing so long as she keeps fit. She also loves training young trick riders and putting on shows with them. Already, some of the 26 students she has taught are working full-time—three of them at the Outback Spectacular on the Gold Coast. 'I get a lot of pride out of that,' she says.

She also gets great pleasure from working with angry and damaged young people as she did for a while in America. Girls were taught trick riding and by performing they often got themselves back on track, and inspired others to do the same. 'That's what I had wanted to do my whole life,' she says of the job that came to an end with America's changed mood and economy when the Twin Towers came down. 'That's why I got into trick riding. I wanted to do something with my life that would inspire others.'

What alarms these two professional and highly credentialled women is the number of young people they see who have been led into doing trick riding having had just a few weeks of lessons. Leanne says she ensures her students build up their strength slowly and learn technique in a disciplined manner. 'It's an extreme sport and it takes years to create accomplished, safe practitioners,' she says. She and Deborah often see young people putting themselves in dangerous situations before they have adequate skills and have often intervened to correct their techniques. 'Behind every trick are a whole lot of rules on what to do and what not to do,' says Leanne.

Four in a row

Tandem driving, being totally impractical, and supremely difficult to do, is reputed to appeal to the attention seekers of the world. The gay blades of Victorian England were chastised in the 1889 book called *Driving* by one crusty horseman: 'I always look upon a man who drives a tandem as a fool; he makes two horses do the work of one and most likely breaks his silly neck.'

One of Australia's premier tandem drivers, and one of few in the world to drive four horses in single file, can hardly be called a show off, or a fool. She is a quiet, careful, almost shy person, and her name is Anne Lindh. Living between Echunga and Mylor in the Adelaide Hills, Anne, 59, works as a social worker three days a week. Anne took up tandem driving mainly because she liked the look of it, but also because she loved the idea of the challenge. She knows of only four other tandem driving competitors in Australia. Unsurprisingly, she has swags of championship trophies, many Driver of the Year awards, and has been Australian Tandem Champion. She also drives Randem, three horses out front, and Quadrem, an almost impossible conga line of four horses which she has successfully put through a driven dressage event.

If there was any real need to have one or more horses arranged in a line out in front of the horse in the shafts doing the pulling work, few are sure what that need was exactly. Some say the horse out in front with slack traces because it was doing no work, and being still fresh, could be saddled up by a doctor to ride cross- country so he could reach a patient once the terrain was unsuitable for the vehicle. Similarly, a rider to hounds could get to the hunt by carriage and then ride the lead horse over fences.

Tandem seemed a novelty even in the days when horse transport was normal. In May 1890, *The New York Times* reported breathlessly on the tandem club's spring outing of eleven carriages in New York's Central Park which attracted a gallery of sightseers as well as photographers. Every cart was described in great detail, and all drivers were named, as was each lead horse and wheeler— just as if they were Formula One cars lined up for a grand prix. According to Paul Doliveux, a renowned international tandem driver from France and winner of major driving trophies around the world, a tandem is thought to be the most challenging combination to drive, and certainly the most difficult to drive well. The chances of things going wrong are very high.

Anne Lindh's carriage driving life had begun when her children grew out of their grey pony. A friend had offered to put it into harness and Anne began competing in Combined Driving Events (CDEs) soon after. CDEs require expertise over a dressage course, cross-country and then the negotiation of a set of cones against the clock in an arena. Anne started winning once she upgraded to a more athletic horse and acquired vehicles suitable for the sport. These days she has a historic-style sulky, viceroys, a scurry vehicle, specially made cross-country carts—a total of thirteen—as well as eight harness horses.

'When I had the two grey ponies, they were getting a bit boring,' Anne says. She was driving them singly then. At the Australian Driving Championships near Echunga in 1997, she saw a tandem combination for the first time. Something sparked in her head and she decided to put those ponies one behind the other. All she would need was a longer set of reins and some roger rings on the bridle of the pony between the shafts to carry the reins of the lead pony. She called on local driver David Searle to help her. In 1998, Anne Lindh emerged as a tandem driver at local shows and the Adelaide Royal.

She still occasionally drives a single pony, though—and won five gold medals at the 2009 Masters Games.

Tandem driving to an outsider looks a bit like herding cats—having as it does a leader which is virtually running free, restrained only by voice, and long reins. The leader does little or no work because, although it is usually required to be a forward- moving horse, its traces should ideally be slack. Being without shafts and out on its own, a disobedient or headstrong lead horse could cause chaos: it could turn backwards, turn too sharply or get too strong and go too fast. 'The main worry though is the flip. They can turn around and suddenly you've got the leader looking at you,' Anne says. Nor can tandem driving be done alone: an assistant is needed to hold the lead horse while the driver climbs into the carriage and gets settled, and again when dismounting.

Then, just for the fun of it, Anne decided to up the ante. In 2005, while looking through the international carriage driving magazine *Paard & Rijtuig*, written in Flemish, to which she subscribes, Anne saw a photograph of four spirited carriage horses arranged in a row, with a harassed-looking groom running alongside the leader and the reins in the hands of the driver, Egbert Emmink. She asked a Belgian friend to translate the story and decided to have a go at four in a row, the Quadrem. She had already successfully competed with a Randem combination for four years negotiating the FEI Advanced 3 dressage test and cones courses. Her lead pony, Nelson, was reliable, always going forward and straight, so she slipped in another wheeler to the Randem team. 'All I really needed was a longer set of reins threading through the roger rings,' she said. The four reins in one hand were heavy so she had them clamped. To her delight, they all went off happily in a straight line, then a circle, then a halt and a rein back. She entered the four grey ponies in a driven dressage competition, even negotiating a wooden bridge in the cones course which many with just one harness horse often baulk at. 'I was terrified that I would make a fool of myself, but they went beautifully. I didn't make any errors of course or knock a cone. I was thrilled to have done it,' she says. Anne knows of only a couple of other people in the world who have tried a Quadrem, but no others who have ever competed.

Anne's mentor is well-known horseman Rob Goldsworthy, 74, who has for twenty years come over twice a week to help her with driving, and act as her groom and coach.

'I am basically a bit nervous, especially with new horses. By nature I am a careful and conservative person, which is why I think I have survived,' she says. 'I have always had instruction. I have never presumed that I know it. Driving may not look hard, but it is knowing what to do when things go wrong. It's more anticipating what can go wrong. Because, once it happens, you are in deep shit.'

Anne goes on to tell how she recently saw a driver with four-in-hand lose control at the Australian National Carriage Driving Championships at Wandin. She heard a scream, turned around and saw four horses bolting through the car park with a cart rocking behind them. They crashed through a fence, tipped the cart and injured the driver and groom. 'A prang in carriage driving can be horrific. But these sorts of situations would have happened a lot in the old days.'

An extra pair of hands is a good excuse to take out the tandem, so on the warm spring day I was visiting, Anne brought in from the paddock a steady grey Australian pony, Penndower Protea, and a bay hackney pony, Beauwood Maxi. Quietly and with careful concentration, she dressed them while explaining she uses quick-release marine shackles in case of trouble. At the back of the vehicle there is a drop-section with handrails for the passenger, usually her sister Cathy, who acts in events as timekeeper and navigator, and does alarming sideways leans into corners. I was happy just being ballast and holding the horses while my driver took her place.

Both horses trot immediately on command up the road to a paddock where Anne practises turns, halts and backing. Turning signals have to be precise because this essentially is an exercise of follow-the-leader. She takes a loop of rein to bring the lead horse around and lets it out when he has—and the wheeler obediently follows. If the lead horse turns too sharply, the wagon would clip the corners. We trot between close-growing trees, making turn after tight turn—very impressive with just the two. The task of guiding a snaking line of four horses could never be a leisurely jog in the park—even if Anne Lindh makes it look that way.

Rough rider to dressage star

Dressage is the most formal and disciplined of horse sports: it is hard to believe its origins are so violent. Almost every manoeuvre carried out in the dressage arena relates historically to the equitation of warfare. French master teachers such as Salomon de la Broue (c1530–1610) and Antoine de Pluvinel (1552–1620) refined and documented the art of battle-horse training. Modern day dressage owes not only its French terminology to these great trainers, but also its methods and conventions.

There is a kind of historic symmetry in that one of the nation's best dressage riders, Brett Parbery, also comes from a battlefield of sorts—the rodeo arena. Only eight years ago, Brett was a rodeo bronc rider wearing chaps, spurs and big cowboy hats. He cuts a fine figure these days in top hat, tails and long boots doing Grand Prix tests on French Anglo-Arab cross Percheron gelding Victory Salute. Brett almost made the Beijing Olympic

Games in 2008: he missed out by just a couple of points. He is determined to make the Australian dressage team for the London Olympics in 2012.

Brett's fire for competing on bucking broncos had gone by 2000, but for most of his life until then he had been the consummate cowboy. Brett's father was a bronc rider, campdrafter and later went into cutting horses. As a boy, Brett and his sister had been trained in sound riding principles by their father and had competed regularly at shows and at pony club. Brett, however, idolised cowboys like Glenn Morgan, Steve Gibson, Bob Berg and Lindsay Clark.

'Bronc riding was what I considered to be the real cowboys' event,' he says. It was no surprise to anyone that he took up the sport professionally—despite being a long and lanky 6 foot 2 inches which made being really competitive on the circuit that much more difficult against chunkier, lower centre-of-gravity riders. It just made him more determined to train harder. 'Totally dedicated, that was me. I have never done anything in half measures.

'My weekends as a bronc rider were usually spent driving to rodeos. People think that we all stand around the bar and get drunk to ride, and then stay and party. I can tell you it is far from that lifestyle. If you take it seriously, which is what most of the good cowboys do, you spend your time keeping fit and fresh so that you can ride at your best. There is usually a pay cheque at stake and everyone wants it! Then we are usually off to the next rodeo.'

Wins and placings came and Brett qualified four times for the Australian Bushmen's Campdraft and Rodeo Association National Finals. He was the Australian Professional Rodeo Association Premier State Rookie Bronc Riding Champion in 1996. He also competed throughout America and Canada in their professional rodeo associations, even riding at the prestigious Calgary Stampede. 'I didn't set the world on fire as a bronc rider, but I was very competitive,' he says.

When Brett moved to the Hawkesbury area in New South Wales on five acres in 1998, he never intended to take up dressage. 'When word got around that there was a cowboy in the area, who had a nice position and could work his way through a rough horse, I started getting calls from dressage ladies in distress,' he says. 'After working with a few of these horses, I became more interested. One thing led to another and I found myself with an opportunity of a lifetime.' That opportunity was to ride a fully trained horse competing at Prix St George and Intermediate I level on the mare Leibling, owned by Vicky Brydon who had injured her back. 'Vicky trained me six nights a week for a year. I have never looked back since then and owe a lot of my success to Vicky.'

Brett made it on to the Australian Dressage Squad in 2005 and has notched up strings of state and national championships. He has spent about five of the past ten years in Europe training under German and Dutch riders—consistently the best in the world.

The appeal of dressage for this former cowboy is in the training and the connection built up between horse and rider. 'A true dressage horse for me should be athletic, responsive, elastic and obedient—just like the horse you would need to go to battle on, and come home alive.'

Victory Salute, who was with him in Europe while he was training and trying out for the Beijing team, is owned by Carolyn Lieutenant, herself a former successful equestrian. Brett says Sam, as he is called, is as honest as horses get. 'What he lacks in athletic ability, he makes up for in heart and desire to please. I love working with him and consider him to be one of those special horses of a lifetime.'

Brett was the national dressage coach of Singapore for two years and has coached other Southeast Asian nations. Four young Japanese riders are currently training at his and wife Mel's training stable in the Southern Highlands of New South

Wales. Mel is also a Grand Prix rider and between them they have fifteen horses in work in their indoor arena, Olympic-size outdoor dressage arena or jumping arena.

Like most professional riders, Brett trains, buys and sells horses, sources suitable horses for other riders and conducts clinics all around Australia, New Zealand and in Asia. Top world class dressage horses sell in Europe for millions of euros. In Australia, a really good horse could bring upwards of $150,000. Brett says he and Mel buy good young horses and train them up.

His favourite dressage movements are half passes—'because they feel good when they are right and they look really cool when they are done well,' he says. 'Pirouettes are one of the ultimate tests of collection so they are always a challenge.'

'I will say, however, that dressage is not for the faint-hearted. It is true that in that first year of dressage, I was bucked off more times than in my last year of rodeo!'

Reclaiming their place in the saddle

At Mataranka Station in the Northern Territory, history is reversing itself. A group of seven Aboriginal men is riding among ant hills and spear grass, mustering a mob of Brahman cattle. They are part of a course which will reclaim the place of Aboriginal stockmen in the saddle. For it was aboard horses in the swirling red dust of northern cattle stations that Aboriginal stockmen earned fame and respect for their skills with livestock.

Aboriginal stockmen almost completely disappeared from stations after the 1966 Wave Hill walk off for equal pay and the battle to reclaim ownership of their tribal lands led by Vincent Lingiari. White stockmen took over and the skills of the early Aboriginal stockmen languished; their descendents knew little of the world of station work. The old men saw their communities disintegrate and become dysfunctional. They had their own land at last, but not the skills or tools to work it. In their old Akubras, they reminisced about the days when they were kings on horseback, sad that they had lost their identity.

The first ever Indigenous certificate course of Horsemanship and Cattle-handling, is being run by Charles Darwin University for men from the Anangu Pitjantjatjara Yankunytjatjara (APY) lands, in the north-west corner of South Australia. The APY lands, which were handed back to their 3000 tribal owners in 1981, cover 102,000 square kilometres. The 30,000 cattle there at present are owned mainly by outsiders. The training and qualifications gained will enable them to work on an equal footing with white stockmen, to better manage their own cattle herds and to be mentors to younger men back home.

Toby Gorringe, Charles Darwin University's horsemanship lecturer, has witnessed repeatedly the benefits of putting Aboriginal people back in the saddle. A former Queensland ringer, he is a son of well-known drover Bill Gorringe, who drove Kidman cattle out of the Birdsville region to railheads at Quilpie and Bourke. He is also a master farrier who had his own business in Toowoomba for twelve years, shoeing horses for the great R M Williams and was the racecourse farrier. Toby Gorringe says the fact that he is Indigenous is also important: it ensures there are no barriers between him and his students.

Toby Gorringe teaches Aboriginal people from Northern Territory communities as far away as Borroloola how to ride and care for horses. His students' self-esteem is generally low but success with riding changes them. Once a month, the university also takes a horse to young offenders in a Darwin prison. 'You've no idea of the difference in them. You would see them walking around—they would keep their heads down. Now they are standing taller and making eye contact.' Toby Gorringe says a horse is the perfect vehicle to achieve such results—because it becomes a friend and teaches respect.

Thousands of brumbies run wild on the APY lands. Toby Gorringe said it made sense to teach as many people as possible how to trap and break in the best of them. The horsemanship course in 2008 ran for three weeks and attracted 30 students.

The brumbies were worked on simultaneously in seven round yards. Once caught with a head rope, they were hobbled and encouraged to smell Toby's hand to know he was a friend. They were then bagged down, a head collar was put on, they were lunged till they were tired, and the pressure was released when they faced up and came to him. By the second day, many of the men who had worked on their own horses were able to ride them without bucking.

'You don't break a horse's spirit,' Toby says. 'You don't have to choke them until they are nearly dead, like in the old days.' The sixteen students who graduated, he says, will go far. 'They are very gifted.' They had taken to riding and training very easily, had great balance and sensitivity, and picked up skills very quickly. Their heritage of hunting and tracking gave them a special affinity with animals.

At the end of the course, the students took their horses on a 20-kilometre cattle drive.

Davey Campbell, 34, one of those trainees, relaxes on the verandah on a warm Mataranka evening and talks about what the course has meant to him. Thousands of lorikeets squabble for roosts in nearby trees. Davey tells how he was taught to ride by his grandfather, a former stockman from Erldunda Station. 'The old man was old school, hard and rough,' he said. 'Toby,

he works with the animals. The old style was a bit cruel, but Toby showed us another style.' Davey has since broken in several horses using Toby's more gentle approach. 'It's good for me too. It educates me a bit more, so I can pass what I have learnt on to others a bit younger than me.'

He is hoping to get his own mob of 500 cattle soon and says he will need plenty of helpers for mustering and yard work. 'The younger generation from what I have seen is a bit lazy, all about mobile phones and games.' There are tentative plans for another course to be held at Alice Springs: 'This will be good for the younger generation. It keeps them out of strife,' he says.

Davey Campbell had been co-boss of that day's successful muster. 'Getting skills keeps your mind occupied and stops you putting yourself down. The horse is good for that because he becomes your best mate. You look after him and he looks after you. He gets you home.'

'You are all at one, you are all together, with the land, with the animals. It's like two brothers. I treat him like my son. I look after him probably better than myself. I talk to him a lot

when I am saddling him. I whistle him and he comes straight to me. And I like that. It makes me feel good when he comes straight away. And then I know I've got a good friend. There's a bond there.'

A few years ago at nearby Elsey Station, which is managed by Toby's brother Max, Toby and two assistants broke in 35 horses in two months. Toby invited the local school children aged between 10 and 15 years to help bag down the horses, and then ride them after two days if they were game—and most were. 'They did a lot of the work, had a go at the lot.' The children were only able to be involved in horseriding if they first attended school. This had lifted attendance to an unprecedented 100 per cent. Toby said the students, who went on to attend Darwin High School the following year, all completed their schooling, something which had never happened before. He can only guess that their horse-breaking and riding experience taught them something about commitment.

Glossary

bag down quieten a horse by rubbing or tapping its body with a hessian or plastic bag, sometimes attached to the end of a short pole
baldy a horse with a very large white blaze, often covering one or both eyes
body (of team) the middle section of a team
breeching strap that which goes around breech of horse and helps to brake the load when the horse sits back against it; often written and pronounced 'britchen'
campdrafting uniquely Australian sport developed from the cattle station skill of separating one animal from a mob. Competition horses are highly prized for their ability to 'read' cattle and deftly guide a single beast through a figure eight pattern in an arena. The Warwick Gold Cup is the premier event of the campdraft calendar
cantle high, rounded back part of saddle
Caper a breed of pony brought from the Cape of Good Hope, South Africa, by the First Fleet in 1788
clumper horse that is half heavy draught and half saddle breed
cocky-chaff husks of grain expelled by harvesters
collected what a horse is when its body is fully engaged; it is on the bit and 'in hand'
crupper strap looped under horse's tail to hold saddle or harness in place
cutting horse used to separate individual cattle from the mob. The best work without rein control and move athletically and rapidly from side to side
dee D-shaped fixture on a saddle, to which straps of saddle bags, bed rolls, etc. are attached
demobbed demobilised, released (from the armed forces)
dinner sometimes indicates midday meal out bush
'dog' (a horse) to send it to the knackery for dog meat
dogger a buyer of horses for pet meat or an animal to be used for dogmeat
Droughtmaster North Queensland breed of red cattle, derived from Brahman and Zebu bulls and mainly Shorthorn cows
Equitana a horse festival first held in Australia in 1999, then 2000, 2001, 2002, 2005 and 2008
extended trot where the horse's frame lengthens as it stretches its strides to the greatest degree possible
flying change a change of the leading leg at a canter without the horse slowing to a trot
founder a painful disease of the feet resulting in lameness, usually caused by too much or the wrong type of feed and not enough exercise (correct name: laminitis)

furphy water tanker, originally made by the Furphy family **galloway** horses standing 14.3 hands up to 15.2 hands in height **gnamma hole** Aboriginal waterhole

goose neck a large covered trailer with an extended neck to the towing vehicle. Often used for combined living and horse-floating quarters

graded Jap Ox achieving the top grade Japanese export beef category and bringing the best price

green (horse) untrained or inexperienced horse

half pass a sideways dressage movement

half-clumper horse that is quarter draught breed and three-quarters saddle horse

hames two curved pieces of iron or wood forming part of collar of draught horse, to which traces are attached

hand measurement of horse height, equivalent to 4 inches or 10 centimetres

haze to bully, to push hard

headlands ground left unploughed at end of strip

high school an advanced level of dressage training

hoof brands used by Australian Army to identify Light Horse remounts by burning their registered numbers into the wall of the hoof, using a small branding iron

irons stirrups

jib to refuse to go forward, to move backwards or sideways

jibber one who jibs

jinker a light, horse-drawn passenger cart, usually two-wheeled

knock up to cause a horse to be so worn out or broken down that it cannot be ridden

leaders horses at the front of the team

levade a low-hocked rear, a dressage manoeuvre

liberty horse a horse working without rider or gear, controlled by voice and body cues

lunge to move a horse at the end of a rope around in a circle

monkey the leather loop used as a handle on the front of a breaking saddle

mouth (a horse) to teach it to accept and respond to the bit

nearside the left side

night horse horse used to patrol livestock in a stock camp, steady, unflappable and usually with white markings so it is visible to cattle and does not startle them

offside the right side

one-sided in the mouth horse that is unresponsive to the turn signal on one side

over-reach when hind foot comes too far forward and cuts front leg or foot

party-line telephone line shared by two or more subscribers

passage a highly collected, cadenced, slow, exaggerated trot, a high school dressage movement

piaffe a stationary trotting movement of advanced dressage

Glossary

pig-root where a horse kicks both hind legs in the air as an expression of either joy or frustration

pirouette a turn where the hind legs stay in one spot and the front end changes direction

poddy (noun) a hand-reared animal; **(verb)** to rear by feeding with either teat or bucket

polocrosse a team sport developed in Australia, lacrosse on horseback, for teams of three players using long-handled racquets. Hugely popular in Australia and now played in many parts of the world. Top horses carry big price tags.

pommel raised front part of saddle

Queensland itch irritation caused by ticks

ringing to be working as a stockman or stationhand

roger rings attached to the sides of a harness horse bridle in teams, for the reins of the horse in front to pass through on the way to the driver

screw a worn-out horse

shafters horses between the shafts and nearest the load

shoulder in a dressage exercise where the horse bends its body so the front legs track to the inside of the hind legs

silage green feed conserved by sealing it in a pit or by other airtight means

snig to drag branches, posts, trees

splashboard upright or sloping rectangular piece of wood on front of horse-drawn vehicle to prevent passengers from being sprayed with mud or water

Super superphosphate, an artificial fertiliser

swingle-tree a crossbar on a cart, plough, etc.; it is pivoted in the middle, and traces are fastened to each end of it

taking the mickey (out of) to act disrespectfully or teasingly (towards)

'tick dodger' agricultural department inspectors employed to check tick in infested areas early in the 20th century—knowing that if they reported all outbreaks and eradicated all ticks they would be unemployed, they accordingly ignored some infestations—or 'dodged' them

tongue to pant

traces the long chains, leather straps or ropes by which a horse pulls an implement or vehicle

wagonette drover's or landholder's small wagon used to carry supplies

wheeler person responsible for moving horse-drawn coal skips in mines; the horse in a team which is between the shafts, therefore closest to the wheels

winkers another name for a set of blinkers, the solid jutting-out part of the bridle which prevents a horse seeing what is behind it. Almost always worn by harness horses

woolgathering day-dreaming or being absent-minded

List of contributors and characters

Adams, Denis, Apsley Vic., 'By the letter of the law', p. 149; 'Clash of the cultures', p. 336; 'In their time of peril', p. 199; 'In with the horses', p. 327; 'Keep it brief', p. 39; 'More in common with Ben Hur', p. 196; 'Pulled down', p. 327; 'Revenge of the nightcart man', p. 201; 'Stabbed in action', p. 34; 'The horse stayed', p. 325; 'They all seemed friendlier then', p. 239; 'Vignettes of the past', p. 25

Appleyard, Mavis, Warren NSW, 'Too tired after Nevertire', p. 265

Baldock, Hurtle, Buckleboo SA, 'Keeping things orderly', p. 138; 'Brumby reinforcements', p. 104; 'Driverless Punch in the scrub', p. 137; 'In an awful bind', p 39; 'Solutions to getting on with the job', p. 262

Barrack, Lucy and Richard, Metcalfe Vic., 'An odyssey with three horses', p. 375

Batchelor, Bob, Claremont WA, 'Pizz-Whizz', p. 76

Best, Helen, Barraba NSW, 'A struggling heap', p. 177; 'Sunday morning service', p. 290

Black, Don, Branxholme Vic., 'Staying with tradition', p. 19

Blight, Geoffrey, Narrogin WA, 'Glad to be rid of the bastards', p. 345; ' No other way', p. 330; 'The miseries of the school cart', p. 175; 'When the whistle blows', p. 193

Brady, Steve, Dyers Crossing NSW, 'The wisdom of safety first', p. 380

Brennan, Deborah, South Tecoma NSW, 'Trick riders', p. 402

Brewer, Allan, Koetong Vic., 'Bonnie, the blocker', p. 141

Brown, Paul, Mackay Qld, 'Kicking into action', p. 344

Bruce-Clarke, Leanne, Aberdeen NSW, 'Trick riders', p. 402

Burkinshaw, Ian, Benalla Vic., 'Like father, like son', p. 179

Caffery, Patricia, Numurkah Vic., 'Just one man and his team', p. 156

Cahill, Patty, Moora WA, 'Bush justice', p. 61; 'Solid worker', p. 77

Carberry, Bill, Apsley Vic., 'A great life for horse-lovers', p. 21

Cawley, Jack, Strathalbyn SA, 'Moving the remounts', p. 300; 'Recollections of a chief superintendent', p. 303

Cay, Hod, Coonabarabran NSW, 'Beauty and the beast', p. 58; 'Riding the outlaw', p. 71

Chambers, Lyn, Wonthaggi Vic., 'Dolly', p. 178

Chandler, Bill and Edna, Barmah Vic., 'Bill's Clydesdales stop the traffic', p. 13

Cherry, Hilda, Armidale NSW, 'Biscuit saviour', p. 128; 'Kicking embargo', p. 139

Chinner, Linda, Malvern SA, 'A centenarian remembers', p. 240

Clements, Stuart, Kimba SA, 'A small black goddess', p. 180

List of contributors and characters

Clissold, Bill, Maryborough Qld, 'The breaking of a stock horse', p. 69; 'The one-man horse', p. 255
Collins, Lloyd, Nyngan NSW, 'A naked Captain', p. 138
Condon, Frank, West Ryde NSW, 'By horse, of course', p. 35
Coombes, Des, Coffs Harbour NSW, 'Dave's explosion', p. 78
Cooper, Brian, Cummins SA, 'Stand still or swim', p. 263
Cox, George, Berriwillock Vic., 'One last plea for the working horse', p. 347
Daniell, Grant, Ballarat Vic., 'Politically corrected horse days', p. 145
Dawson, Ralph, Birdwood SA, 'An intelligent horse', p. 194; 'Serving his purpose', p. 194
Dent, Des, Victor Harbor SA, 'A trail of damage', p. 246; 'Doing the rounds with Mick', p. 244; 'Let fly with the rocks', p. 246; 'Summer memories of a milky', p. 242
Dickson, Joe, Aramac Qld, 'After a hard day's work', p. 322; 'Bogged in the creek', p. 160; 'Running from the stink', p. 155; 'Team sports', p. 160
Dobbs, Jill, Port Augusta SA, 'No dawdling, please!', p. 191; 'The tin horse nuzzles the old boys aside', p. 337
Dovey, Rod, Bridgewater Vic., 'A wagon hauls away the pressures', p. 185
Doyle, B L, Tenterfield NSW, 'A kick in the mouth', p. 325
Dunn, Elsie, Macgregor ACT, 'Curing the jibber', p. 263; 'Home from the ball', p. 135; 'Loading the wagon', p. 31; 'Protecting the crops', p. 38; 'Stitching hair from the spell', p. 40
Dutfield, Garth, Wellington NSW, 'Grinned for a month', p. 254; 'Queenie to the rescue', p. 141
Edwards, Kathryn, Kuranda Qld, 'No Christmas spirit', p. 202
Evanne, Vic., 'All for a piece of carrot', p. 275
Faithfull, Gordon, Omeo Vic., 'Just fooling', p. 135
Fatchen, Max, Smithfield SA, 'Mates', p. 12
Fenton, Charles, Clunes Vic., 'Learning to live with the enemy', p. 259; 'Muddled mounts', p. 192
Fragar, Garth, Little Hartley NSW, 'Hungry for action', p. 195
Fuss, Rudi, Cummins SA, 'Danger in fright', p. 323
Gallagher, J L, Torrens ACT, 'The English horse', p. 308
Gasser, Carlos, Qld, 'On with the show', p. 280
Giles, Hayden, Kooweerup Vic., 'Now there's only one', p. 16
Giles, Norm, Kersbrook SA, 'Gently does it', p. 138
Glendenning, Margaret, Everton Upper Vic., 'Horsepower', p. 36; 'Intelligence almost human', p. 130
Godlonton, Gloria, Bellingen NSW, 'Jammed tight on the rein', p. 174; 'Morning routine', p. 27
Gorringe, Toby, Mataranka Station NT, 'Reclaiming their place in the saddle', p. 415
Haley, Alex, Berrigan NSW, 'Flying Bob', p. 287; 'Get a bloody horse', p. 338
Hall, Thomas Rush, Heathcote Vic., 'Cutting a living from the bush', p. 99
Hamilton, Geoff, Legume NSW, '190 miles and still keen to travel', p. 107
Hancock, Margaret, Bute SA, 'Patient servants', p. 237

Harkin, Doug, Maryborough Vic., 'Remarkable sagacity', p. 140; 'Skipping the drinks', p. 128
Hentschke, Roy, Blyth SA, 'Doctor treats the survivors', p. 324
Hobley, Dick, Bremer Bay WA, 'Defending the shores', p. 312; 'Singing for their tucker', p. 306; 'The last straw', p. 318
Horsnell, Nancy, Birdwood SA, 'Priorities', p. 264
Hutchinson, G, Alpha Qld, 'Reverse action', p. 328
Hyde, Nancy, Green Patch SA, 'Shining eggsample', p. 129
Jefferys, Steve and Sandy, Ingleside NSW, 'A day with the whip-cracker of the Olympic opening ceremony', p. 266
Jones, Alan, Wayville SA, 'Don't spare the horses—the mail must go through', p. 114
Kelly, Jim, Naracoorte SA, 'A battle of wills', p. 252; 'By the light of the silvery moon', p. 30; 'The brumby team', p. 257
Keogh, Mike, Oakbank SA, 'Majestic passage through city streets', p. 231
Kerr, Ron, Borroloola NT, 'Unconvinced by the mechanical age', p. 74; 'A wagon on the track', p. 56
Laube, Sylvia, Cummins SA, 'The Cockaleechie horse dip', p. 161
Lawrence, Eric, Footscray Vic., '"Those times were tough on horses," says Eric', p. 249
Lindh, Anne, Echunga SA, 'Four in a row', p. 408
Low, Shirley, Port Lincoln SA, 'Shake a leg, Glen', p. 285; 'Working hard to have some fun', p. 98
McConnel, Carolyn, Esk Qld, 'Value of a champion', p. 133; 'Where the stock horse is still king', p. 51
McDougall, Karen, Victor Harbor SA, 'Karen in horse-drawn paradise by the sea', p. 228
McLean, Guy, Maryborough Qld, 'Finding a better way', p. 389
MacPherson, Neil, Tamworth NSW, 'An archaic interlude', p. 163
Marriot, Alan, East Brighton Vic., 'All so different then', p. 28
Martin, Eva, Dalby Qld, 'A bit of restraint', p. 105
Mengler, Vyvian, Tenterden WA, '125 kilometres to the rescue', p. 108
Mills, Bruce, Tumby Bay SA, 'Boots that made him walk', p. 200
Mills, Dick, Kanmantoo SA, 'The heavy horse memorial', p. 344; 'The power of a horse', p. 151
Mitchell, Gregory, Torrens ACT, 'Whopper', p. 64
Mitchell, M J, Manjimup WA, 'Hitching a ride on Fridays', p. 177
Muffet, Wendy, Wirrinya NSW, 'Red hot ride', p. 190
Murphy, Liz, Oakbank SA, 'A drover on a journey of life', p. 369
Nunan, Joy, Port Pirie SA, 'On remote control', p. 142
O'Brien, Colleen, Ballarat Vic., 'Saving the brumbies', p. 397
O'Brien, Les, Alice Springs NT, 'Trotting out of step', p. 247
Padman, Leta, Murray Bridge SA, 'Doctor returns', p. 131
Parbery, Brett, Penrose NSW, 'Rough rider to dressage star', p. 412
Pederick, Stafford, Kojonup WA, 'Faith and trust', p. 132
Peel, Tim, Camden NSW, 'Esdale flash prince', p. 283

List of contributors and characters

Phillips, Gordon, Heath Hill Vic., 'Consummate horseman, yet never seen a horse', p. 125

Pickering, John, Port Noarlunga SA, 'The workers cost nought to run', p. 340

Poole, Joy, Hunter Valley NSW, 'Joy Poole keeps the legends alive', p. 88

Richardson, Peter, Toodyay WA, 'Stop start Jack', p. 285

Robertson, Moyrah, Tranmere SA, 'A pony for the teacher', p. 171

Rockcliff, Addye, Riverside Tas., 'The (unofficial) charges of the Light Horse', p. 298

Rodgers, Bruce, Yeelanna SA, 'Farm horses—another view', p. 32; 'Logging the scrub', p. 100; 'Mark of a chisel', p. 327; 'Took fright', p. 322

Rolton, Gill, Happy Valley SA, 'Learning the hard way', p. 361

Schaeffer, Wendy, Hahndorf SA, 'Winning takes more than belief in a dream', p. 351

Schiller, Allan, Pinnaroo SA, 'In deference to the iron horse', p. 343; 'Like a troop of soldiers', p. 150

Schwarz, Lorna, Ceduna SA, 'An after-school lesson', p. 178

Shine, Margaret, Pigeon Ponds Vic., 'Divided they stood', p. 195

Shiner, Joyce, Albany WA, 'Driving Trixie to school', p. 181; 'Ginger's escape', p. 198; 'Ride-and-tie', p. 31; 'The horses that took us to school', p. 173; 'Up like bedposts', p. 261

Simons, Sandi and David, Drysdale Vic., 'Confidence builder', p. 386

Stone, Paul and Jane, Mount Sanford NT, 'Revival: the stock horse returns to restore calm to the north', p. 43

Stoney, Chris, Mansfield Vic., 'Shopping pioneer style', p. 284; 'Storm over the seas', p. 314

Svenson, Doris, Port Pirie SA, 'Versatile Bessie—but watch out!', p. 289

Tinney, Stuart and Karen, Maraylya NSW, 'It's all about persistence', p. 364

Toomby, Geoff and Vicky, Townsville Qld, 'Horse whisperers on a mission for lost souls', p. 166

Treloar, Wendy, Cummins SA, 'Maximum confusion', p. 197; 'Memories from the wheat country', p. 37; 'Retribution', p. 342; 'Two times the loser', p. 326

Turnbull, Alison, Cleve SA, 'Just out of reach', p. 196

Turner, Maureen, Junee NSW, 'Epitaph', p. 349

Vallance, John, St Arnaud Vic., 'Hungry and wet', p. 179

Verco, Max, Naracoorte SA, 'Thirty miles through the scrub', p. 137

Wade, Colin, Naracoorte SA, 'Mollycoddled', p. 81

Ward, Zita, Singleton NSW, 'Night driving and horse sense', p. 136

White, Denis, 'One hundred miles in twelve hours', p. 80

Willcox, Don, Thvenard SA, 'A rare breed today', p. 101

Williams, Greg, Melbourne Vic., 'Big steady police horses deliver calm persuasion', p. 292

Williams, Max, Exford Vic., 'Team Memories', p. 340

Willoughby, Bill, Booleroo Centre SA, 'Bill takes the stars in his stride', p. 272

Young, Lindy, Cavendish Vic., 'Saintly Shrimp', p. 122

www.ingramcontent.com/pod-product-compliance
Lightning Source LLC
Chambersburg PA
CBHW031228290426
44109CB00012B/207